Elias A. Long

Ornamental Gardening for Americans

A treatise on beautifying homes, rural districts, towns, and cemeteries

Elias A. Long

Ornamental Gardening for Americans
A treatise on beautifying homes, rural districts, towns, and cemeteries

ISBN/EAN: 9783337082802

Printed in Europe, USA, Canada, Australia, Japan

Cover: Foto ©Andreas Hilbeck / pixelio.de

More available books at **www.hansebooks.com**

Ornamental Gardening

FOR

AMERICANS.

A TREATISE ON

BEAUTIFYING HOMES, RURAL DISTRICTS, TOWNS, AND CEMETERIES.

BY

ELIAS A. LONG,

LANDSCAPE ARCHITECT; AUTHOR OF "THE HOME FLORIST."

ILLUSTRATED.

NEW YORK:

ORANGE JUDD COMPANY,

52 & 54 LAFAYETTE PLACE.

1905

PREFACE.

This book was written with a view of furnishing a low-priced, comprehensive American work on Landscape, or more properly, Ornamental Gardening. A great degree of conciseness was aimed at, with the desire to bring a large amount of information on all departments of the subject into a small compass. And now the completed work goes forth in the hope that it will more fully meet the want for information of this kind than any work ever issued in this country, at even several times its price.

I acknowledge with great pleasure the help found—especially in preparing the lists and descriptions of trees, shrubs and plants, in the works of J. C. Loudon, W. Robinson, Josiah Hoopes, Frank J. Scott, and a few others, whose names appear in their proper places in the body of the book. Mention must also be made of the kindness of Messrs. Ellwanger & Barry, of Rochester, N. Y., in at all times throwing open their nursery and specimen grounds, to my inspection, as an aid in preparing the descriptions in this department.

To Dr. George Thurber, editor of the *American Agriculturist*, I am specially indebted for valuable aid and

(III)

suggestions received, and for his interest in the work from the first. I am also indebted to the kindness of the Publishers of the last named periodical for the use of engravings, that appear in the descriptions of trees and plants.

If my book shall be of service in increasing a love for Ornamental Gardening and kindred delights throughout America ; leading those who consult its pages in the way of genuine pleasure, healthfulness, and profit in these, my highest ambition shall have been satisfied.

ELIAS A. LONG.

BUFFALO, N. Y., November, 1884.

CONTENTS.

PART I.—INTRODUCTORY.

CHAPTER I.

INTRODUCTION.. 9

Glances at the Past, Present and Future.—The Requirements of American Ornamental Gardening.—Ornamental
Gardening Literature. — American Progress in Special
Branches.—American Architecture and Gardening.—Ornamental Gardening for Americans.

CHAPTER II.

Profits of Ornamental Gardening 16

CHAPTER III.

Time required to produce Good Effects..................... 20

PART II.—MATERIALS OF ORNAMENTAL GARDENING.

CHAPTER IV.

The Ground and the Grass..., 23

CHAPTER V.

Woody growths.. 25

CHAPTER VI.

Deciduous Trees and Shrubs....................................... 27

CHAPTER VII.

Evergreen Trees and Shrubs....................................... 99

CHAPTER VIII.

Climbers and Trailers.. 118

CHAPTER IX.

Hardy Herbaceous Plants.. 124

CHAPTER X.

Annual Plants.. 156

(V)

CHAPTER XI.

Tender Plants 158

CHAPTER XII.

Miscellaneous Natural Materials........... 160

PART III.—ARRANGEMENT OF ORNAMENTAL GARDENS.

CHAPTER XIII.

Principles and Aims... 161

> Nature as a Teacher.—Major and Minor Features of Embellishment. — Variety. — Order and Simplicity.—Unity and Harmony. — Character. — Expression. — Convenience.—Breadth and Extent.—Richness and Finish.

CHAPTER XIV.

The Home Buildings... 166

CHAPTER XV.

The Surface of the Garden...................................... 167

CHAPTER XVI.

Walks and Drives... 177

CHAPTER XVII.

Use and Combination of Grass, Trees, Shrubs, etc................ 183

CHAPTER XVIII.

Climbers and their uses........... 199

CHAPTER XIX.

Flowering and Ornamental Plants................................ 206

CHAPTER XX.

Rockwork... 221

CHAPTER XXI

Water Features in the Garden................................... 227

CHAPTER XXII.

Hedges and Clipped Trees....................................... 231

CHAPTER XXIII

Garden Structures.. 236

CHAPTER XXIV.

Plans of Private Residence Grounds............................. 247

CHAPTER XXV.

Portico, Window and Roof Gardening............................ 265

CHAPTER XXVI.

School, Church, Asylum, Hotel, and Railroad Gardening.......... 272

CHAPTER XXVII.

Public Parks and Pleasure Grounds............................. 279

Future and Present Wants to be Considered.—An Ideal System of Public Lawn Gardening.—"Beautiful Paris" as a Model.—Paris, Past, Present, and Future.—The Lesson for American Enterprise.—The Large Park System.—Garden Boulevards.—A glance at Central Park, N. Y.—Small Town Parks.—Town Squares.—Planting Public Highways.—Rural Improvement Associations.

CHAPTER XXVIII.

Garden Cemeteries... 301

PART IV.—CONSTRUCTING GARDENS.

CHAPTER XXIX.

Planning Garden Improvements.................................. 308

CHAPTER XXX.

Laying out the Grounds.. 310

CHAPTER XXXI.

The Work on the Grounds....................................... 312

CHAPTER XXXII.

Planting................................... 320

CHAPTER XXXIII.

Lawn Making... 324

CHAPTER XXXIV.

Walks and Drives.. 327

CHAPTER XXXV.

Preparation for Special Purposes.............................. 331

CHAPTER XXXVI.

Garden Architecture... 335

PART V.—Maintaining Gardens.

CHAPTER XXXVII.
January.. 337

CHAPTER XXXVIII.
February.. 339

CHAPTER XXXIX.
March.............................. 346

CHAPTER XL.
April.. 349

CHAPTER XLI.
May.. 353

CHAPTER XLII.
June.. 357

CHAPTER XLIII.
July, August... 361

CHAPTER XLIV.
September.. 364

CHAPTER XLV.
October... 365

CHAPTER XLVI.
November, December.. 368

Ornamental Gardening for Americans.

PART I.

INTRODUCTORY.

CHAPTER I.

INTRODUCTION.

GLANCES AT THE PAST, PRESENT, AND FUTURE.

The art of Ornamental Gardening is, undoubtedly, backward in America at the present time. Progress is more apparent in some other arts; for example, those of architecture and interior decoration. There is nothing strange in this, however; our nation is comparatively young, and whatever is closely related to the useful arts, has had opportunities to develop, which ornamental gardening, painting, and other arts have not enjoyed. House building has received great attention from the first, and it is natural that, as prosperity increases, a love for the beautiful should manifest itself in this sooner than in the more independent fine arts. Neither is it strange that gardening, and other arts of this class, in America should contrast unfavorably with the same in some European countries, for long before the birth of our nation these arts have had abroad a comparatively free field in which to advance.

(9)

If our backwardness in the fine arts is thus accounted for, the grounds upon which to base predictions of future progress, are no less clearly defined ; while in the pioneer century there was naturally a lack of means, to-day, wealth, rapidly developing taste, and in fact, everything needed for fostering the fine arts, abound with us. Nothing shows our real progress more strikingly than our decennial census returns. Ninety years ago there were less than four millions of people in the entire United States. Sixty years ago there were not yet ten millions ; at thirty years ago we had reached nearly twenty-three, and 1880 showed a population of about fifty millions. Wonderful as are these figures, our general prosperity has more than kept pace with them. To-day the large percentage of people owning homes ; the thousands of savings banks to care for the surplus money of the masses ; the multitude of possessors of moderate and of great wealth, all tell of a degree of prosperity unparalleled in any other country. This state of things is destined to have a marked effect upon the future of the fine arts in America. Great Britain, France, and other European nations, may surpass us in conservatories, gardens and parks to-day, but the time will come when we must excel in all of these, as we do in most of the useful arts and inventions.

THE REQUIREMENTS OF AMERICAN ORNAMENTAL GARDENING.

What is needed more than all else, is popular education with respect to the beauty, adaptability, and arrangements of the subjects of the vegetable kingdom for creating delightful garden and providing fine landscape effects. This is a matter in which the average American is far behind the Englishman, or the people of some other European countries. We are far from being a nation of garden lovers, or of people who take great delight in beautiful, well arranged, home-gardens, and in caring for them.

It should be better known, that there are fully one thousand different species and varieties of ornamental trees and shrubs, besides great numbers of hardy flowering plants, all possessing distinct features of beauty, that will thrive in the greater part of the United States. One who walks among our home gardens and grounds, and sees the same plants in each, might suppose that only a few scores of these were known. The same kinds, such as have always been planted, are repeated everywhere. The same fault is also conspicuous in many cemeteries and public parks. It is not too much to say that a degree of poverty generally prevails in our ornamentation of home grounds, that would not be tolerated in the interior furnishings, or in the appearance of the house itself. There are as good reasons for adhering to the fashions in houses of fifty years ago as to the selection and arrangement of trees that prevailed at that time. The reason why a knowledge of materials, their kinds, arrangement and needed care are essential to success in ornamental gardening, is because fine results depend largely upon continued attention to keeping up the garden. When the architect has planned and finished the house, the interest in architecture, so far as that house is concerned, is at an end. But when a garden is planned and planted it remains a perpetual charge. If it is slighted or neglected, the original work of construction is well nigh lost. It is an intimate acquaintance with trees and plants, first in doing or in directing garden work, and later the watching their growth and development, that give to the occupation its greatest charm.

THE LITERATURE OF ORNAMENTAL GARDENING.

A comparison of our garden literature with that of England, for example, indicates a general lack of interest in the subject. We support but one periodical—a monthly, devoted to general ornamental and useful gardening. In London alone, there are published no less than five periodicals devoted to the subject, and these are weeklies, of large size. I make no mention of agricultural and other papers with good gardening departments, nor of the monthlies and "guides" that are issued by seedsmen and florists, for advertising purposes, as these are found on both sides of the Atlantic. The interest in the subject in England is also indicated by the numerous books treating on gardening.

Such facts show that the English possess a much greater love for, and knowledge of, everything pertaining to gardening than do Americans. They also explain why many of our own native trees, shrubs, and flowers are better known and appreciated abroad than at home. These native trees, etc., are often introduced into cultivation abroad and are sometimes brought back into our own gardens through the enterprise of foreign nurserymen and gardeners.

AMERICAN PROGRESS IN SPECIAL BRANCHES.

To conclude that Americans are unable to appreciate beauty in the products of the gardener's art, would be a mistake. If we suffer by comparison with Europe, as regards general ornamental gardening, we may turn to the progress we have made in some special branches of the art, and from this take hope for the future. In the production and consumption of cut flowers, we see something like American spirit and enterprise. Millions of dollars are invested in the growing of flowers and plants, to meet a popular taste that hardly seemed to exist some fifteen years ago. From a small beginning this trade has developed year by year, until now we actually have reached a standing as producers and consumers of flowers, that is looked upon as another "American Wonder."

And why not, for there is nothing in all Europe to equal the American cut-flower trade. In London, for example, this trade is but a fraction, as compared with that of New York, though it has a population nearly three times as great. This state of affairs, though it may show developement in only a single direction, should be regarded with satisfaction, as its tendency must be to create a taste for general gardening. Certainly those who purchase flowers for the love of them are the better prepared to appreciate choice trees and shrubs and fine garden effects.

The improved large cemeteries of America, show on the part of our people an appreciation of the finer results of the gardening art. Years ago Boston, Philadelphia, and some other cities, conceived the idea of roomy garden or park-like cemeteries, and large areas were laid out as ornamental gardens of sepulture near these cities. Now nearly every large city has an improved cemetery, and altogether there are in America a number of such burial places that are the most beautiful the world affords. There can be no doubt as to the value of these in cultivating a love for general ornamental gardening.

Good progress has been made in America of late years, in the matter of public parks and gardens. These afford the room for planting fine collections of trees, shrubs, etc., and some now contain extensive plantations of these, affording opportunities to the people for becoming acquainted with kinds, and effective arrangements. In the Buffalo Parks and Boulevards, more than forty thousand trees, shrubs and vines, in over four hundred varieties, were planted within the past ten years, and are rapidly developing their beauty. It is noticeable that as this rather extensive arboretum develops, the appreciation of arboreal beauty increases among the people, inciting new interest in adorning homes with trees and shrubs. For several years associations for the

improvement of towns and villages have been in successful operation.   These, by planting trees and promoting
a love for gardening, have already produced excellent
results.   Such societies are full of promise, and their
existence shows a proper public spirit.

It is gratifying to note that instances in which persons
of means provide free pleasure gardens for the people are
becoming more numerous.   The work of rural improvement in the State of Connecticut is receiving inestimable
aid, from men like Mr. Henry C. Bowen—who at his
own expense, has laid out a public park of sixty acres
and given it to the people of Woodstock, and the Field
Brothers who have shown similar liberality at Haddam,
Conn., and some others have followed their examples.
In the West, Shaw of St. Louis, Wade of Cleveland, and
others, have by their noble liberality made entire communities happier, healthier, and better, and the works
stand as monuments more enduring than stone, keeping
fresh for all time the memory of the worthy donors.
Scarcely second in any sense to such benefactors, are
those who throw open their magnificent private gardens
to the public, to be freely enjoyed under reasonable
restrictions.   In time let us hope to see many followers
of these worthy examples among the thousands who are
favored with great wealth.

AMERICAN ARCHITECTURE AND GARDENING.

A taste for the beautiful developed in one field of art, is
also a help to others.   Land owners now-a-days, as they
look from the modern artistically designed house to the
garden, are with growing frequency, asking the questions,
"is not the garden as susceptible of improvement as
the house? Cannot as great changes for the better be
worked here, over the styles of a generation ago, as are
being effected in our architecture?" Extended observation shows that thousands of property owners throughout

our land are putting such questions. While it is often true that no direct means may be at hand for suggesting and carrying out fitting improvements, still the mere fact that conditions exist which suggest the questions, is sure to hasten the day when gardens, and garden adornments, in keeping with our improved architecture, will prevail throughout the country.

That various influences are at work in awakening the American public to its needs and opportunities in the line of improved ornamental grounds, there is little doubt. But there is great room for progress; the field is a wide one. The best efforts of all who take an interest in this subject, amateurs and professional gardeners; florists and nurserymen; editors and writers; are needed for developing correct taste and methods, so that, as the demand for improved pleasure grounds increases, there may be at command the best possible system of these for our climate, and for the tastes and means of our people—one that shall be essentially American.

"ORNAMENTAL GARDENING FOR AMERICANS."

In order to contribute a share towards meeting the public want in this line, the present work has been prepared. With excellent opportunities for knowing the needs of the people, the author aims to present, in simple style, plain instructions as to the materials, arrangement, construction, and keeping of private and public gardens. To make a book which should be suitable as a constant garden companion, convenient, reliable, comprehensive, and practical, has been a constant aim. It is believed that the subjects are presented in so clear a manner that any intelligent person can, by its help, not only successfully undertake the oversight of an ordinary garden, whether doing the work with his or her own hands or directing others, but may, by study, become so familiar with this subject in all its departments, as to be

proof against impositions by the ignorant who pretend to
be gardeners, and also the representations of dishonest
tree agents.

Throughout the book the common names of plants are
adhered too as much as possible, for the reason that the
botanical names often prove a barrier to an acquaintance
with them, while common ones invite it.   But as the
real need of botanical names is recognized—which being
in the Latin language are the same in all nations,
and serve to guard against the confusion that without
them would be inevitable, they are given in parenthesis.
In case no common name is in use, then the botanical
name often is printed as though it was the common one.

The same subject is often touched upon in different
parts of the book, thus, the materials of a Rockery are
referred to in the Second Part, the arrangement of the
Rockery in Part Three, Construction in Part Four, with
Notes on Management in Part Five.   A copious index at
the end will always lead to the desired topic.

CHAPTER II.

PROFITS OF ORNAMENTAL GARDENING.

"I wouldn't cut down that tree for a hundred dollars,"
is an expression one may often hear from property owners,
as they point to some favorite.   The valuation of the
tree is often placed two, three, or five times as high.
What did such a tree cost ? Perhaps one or two dollars
fifteen years or so ago for the tree, preparing the soil and
planting, and next to nothing in the years since.   From
the time the roots took hold of the soil, and a beautiful
show of foliage and branches appeared, increasing year
by year in size, soon giving a pleasant shade and perhaps

flowers, it has been a constant source of delight. Was
the setting of that tree profitable, considering the value
at which it is now appraised, and the pleasure it has afforded ? Profits like these are in the common order of
things in intelligent planting.

In my experience, I have assisted in so improving a
place of two acres in extent, by varying the grade, filling
in marshy parts, arranging walks, drives, trees, and
shrubs, that for an outlay of less than six hundred dollars, the improvement before the first season was past
was so marked, as to increase the owner's asking price
by twenty-five hundred dollars.

Instances could be multiplied to show that, for from
two to five per cent of the value of a place, spent on
garden improvements, returns of from ten to sixty per
cent in increased value have been realized in a short
time. Trees, shrubs, climbers, and plants in choice
kinds, well arranged, develop rapidly and greatly increase
the valuation of a place, through augmenting the beauty
of the architecture and the general effect. The presence
of these always makes a less expensive house look finer
than a costlier one, which presents nothing in the heat of
summer, or in the storms of winter, for the eye to rest
upon, but bare walls and harsh outlines, unbroken by
any trees or other vegetation.

Many a man with the means and disposition will pay
several thousand dollars to architect, builder, and fur-
nisher, for a house, with the view that the beauty and
comfort purchased will yield satisfaction proportionate to
the cost. To such a person it may be said, that one thousand dollars prudently invested in arranging and planting the home grounds, may be made to pay a much larger
percentage of pure pleasure and interest, than the same
amount put into the building. If one who is about investing five thousand dollars, or a smaller or larger
amount, in improving a home, should keep back five per

cent of the sum and invest it in improving the surroundings, it may be made to yield far better returns in the
years to come, than if nearly all had been spent on the
house, and a mere pittance allowed for the grounds.

Will it pay to plant trees on the average farm? A view,
such as may be sometimes had, of two farms, of the same
size and general situation, but presenting strong contrasts in the presence and absence of trees and shrubs
respectively, may throw light on the question. One of the
farms may have half a dozen large shade trees about the
yard, some climbers over the piazzas and buildings ;
dense clumps of evergreens, both for beauty and to serve
as wind-breaks. It may also have a number of broad
shade trees in the barn-yard, along the lanes, the boundaries, creeks, and in other places where nothing else can
be profitably grown, yielding grateful shade and shelter.
The other has not a sign of sylvan beauty, with every
part without shelter by trees from the summer's sun or
the winter's gales. The trees on the first farm may
have cost one hundred dollars for stock, setting, etc.,
while any disinterested person would estimate the value
they add to the place, at ten-fold greater than their cost.

No better method can be devised for rendering farming
a pleasant occupation to the young, than the judicious
use of trees and garden beauty about the grounds. Our
attachments to trees becomes almost as strong as to persons, and if there are fine ones growing about the home,
and with them some good shrubs, climbers, flowers, etc.,
they will add new strength to the chain which binds
the heart of youth to the hearthstone, and to the rural
pursuits among which they have been reared.

The view of this subject, which relates to gains far
above those that can be computed in dollars, is an important one. It has been said that " the hope of America
is the homes of America," whatever adorns one's home
—be that in the town or country—and ennobles his domes-

tic life, strengthens his love for country, and nurtures
the better elements of the nature, in those who are
thrown in contact with such improvements. To promote a love for trees, shrubs, vines, and flowers, by cultivating and studying them, develops in children a love
for the beautiful in nature, in art, and still more in character. Nothing is truer than that the love of nature
sharpens the senses, and quickens all the intellectual
faculties. Were parents to provide to the fullest practicable degree, the simple means for encouraging the love
of ornamental gardening, and of the study of Botany,
and other closely allied sciences at home, they early secure
for the young a source of high enjoyment, that is un-
known elsewhere, one which elevates the mind and fills it
with noble aspirations. Besides these things, the mere
spending of time on the part of all, and especially of
children and women, in the exercise and enjoyment that
comes from associating with, and caring for plants, is
highly conducive to health. It is largely because of their
rambles and exercise in the open air by the women of
England, that they generally present the bloom and vig-
or of youth until far advanced in life. It would be both
easy and inexpensive to provide the majority of American
homes with these opportunities for health-giving exercise.

It pays to do well whatever is done in ornamental
and landscape gardening. In starting such work, it is
too often undertaken without anything like a definite
plan. It would be quite as reasonable to work without
a well-considered plan in building our houses, yet we find
that large sums of money in the aggregate are paid to
architects for house-plans and superintendence of work,
while for the surroundings, little thought is given to calling in the services of the trained gardener. When the
day comes that the landscape gardener will be consulted
along with the house architect, in matters of home improvement, then a less sum of money will go farther to-

wards purchasing real beauty, pleasure, and comfort, than when the latter alone is employed.

A large part of the work of the landscape architect now consists in planning for the remodelling of places laid out years ago in bad taste and ignorance. In every instance of this kind, there is in some degree entailed the three-fold expense of first doing the work, then undoing it, and lastly doing it over again; had it been well conceived and executed at the first, the work would have answered for many years.

In speaking of the profitable advantages of planting shade trees in cities, Mr. Thomas Meehan lately wrote as follows:

"Passing through a street in Philadelphia, on which blocks of first-class houses had been erected on both sides, but evidently by two different owners, there appeared to be a wonderful difference in success by street trees alone. There was a pretty row of Carolina poplars on one side; on the other side no trees at all. This side had innumerable notices of houses 'to rent,' but on the tree-shaded side every house was occupied. Both blocks appeared to be houses of about equal age and value, and there was no apparent difference between the two. There seemed every reason to believe that the presence of trees alone had given the one side the great advantage."

CHAPTER III.

TIME REQUIRED FOR PRODUCING GOOD EFFECTS.

There are many who love trees and shrubs, but are kept from planting them by false notions respecting the time it will take to secure a good effect and shade. It is possible to so treat trees, that in ten years they will not grow the same number of inches; but on the other hand they may, by fair management, reach a hight of from twice to three times as many feet in ten years from planting. The difference lies in matters that ordinarily are in a large degree within our control. When trees remain almost at a standstill for a long time, it indicates either that they were of poor quality when planted; or, in rare cases, that the soil cannot be fitted to meet their wants, but very commonly that they are deprived of the food and moisture they would appropriate if they had a chance. Trees and plants are much like animals in this; that they may either be starved to death, or they may be liberally supplied with food and have proper care, to produce the most satisfactory results as to development and beauty. As a general thing, deep trenching or subsoiling, with liberal manuring, and then thorough culture if the trees and shrubs are growing in borders, or free watering if standing in the sod in seasons of drouth, are the things needful for producing the best returns. Because these points are not better heeded, three-fourths of all the trees and shrubs in private grounds are set out poorly, grow slowly, and hardly make a decent showing in a life-time.

To show what growth may be expected in trees and shrubs under fair treatment, I give some measurements made in Buffalo Park of trees and shrubs, which were planted seven and eight years before :

American Elm,	19 ft. high,	15 ft. broad.
Silver Maple,	22 " "	14 " "
Norway Maple,	17 " "	14 " "
Sugar Maple,	16 " "	10 " "
White Poplar,	30 " "	25 " "
Balsam Poplar,	35 " "	15 " "
Lombardy Poplar,	40 " "	
Norway Spruce,	16 " "	8 ft. broad.
Black and White Pines,	12 to 15 " "	10 to 12 " "
Strong-growing Shrubs,	5 " 12 " "	5 " 10 " "
Dwarf-growing Shrubs,	2 " 4 " "	3 " 5 " "

Let it be borne in mind, that these dimensions are for growths under what may be considered as ordinarily fair

treatment, as regards manuring, culture, and the important point of summer watering. In small collections,
instead of those containing many thousands, as in the
case here referred to, better results might be expected.
As an illustration, I also give measurements made on the
banks of a lake, where the roots could take up an abundance of moisture, and where the soil naturally abounded
in vegetable matter. It should be noticed, however, that
the measurements which follow, mostly apply to a class of
smaller growing trees than those named in the list above:

European Alder,	30 ft. high,	20 ft. broad.
Willow,	30 to 35 " "	25 to 30 " "
Cut-Leaved Birch,	28 " "	15 " "
Bird Cherry,	23 " "	20 " "
Strong-growing Shrubs,	8 to 15 " "	8 to 12 " "
Dwarf-growing Shrubs,	3 " 6 " "	5 " 10 " "

Downing tells of a Silver maple, twelve years planted,
that had a trunk one foot in diameter, and which made
shoots six feet long in one season. Hoopes describes a
Burr oak, twelve years from the acorn, that was seventeen
feet high. We may occasionally meet trees and shrubs
growing wild, that have made growths equal to any indicated by the figures here given.

It is well to know that, as a rule, shrubby growths develop signs of mature beauty sooner than do trees.
Planted in good soil, these take hold quickly, and in a
few years show beauty in habit, foliage, and flowers, that
is scarcely excelled in after years, though they may increase in size. On this and other accounts I usually recommend a free use of the flowering and other shrubs in
planting both large and small places.

Planting is often delayed from year to year, until sufficient time has passed to have allowed the trees to make
large growths, had they been set when first the idea was
entertained. Almost any shrub or tree, with good treatment, may be counted on to reach a very pleasing size
in from two to six years from planting. How soon such
a period slips away!

PART II.

MATERIALS OF ORNAMENTAL GARDENING.

There are now estimated to be in the vegetable kingdom about one hundred and twenty thousand different species of plants. Out of this vast number the arboriculturist and florist have selected a great many, which are classed as ornamental.

In the following pages such description is given of the natural materials which may enter into the work of ornamental gardening, as may serve to convey an idea of their uses.

CHAPTER IV.

THE GROUND AND THE GRASS.

The soil of the earth's surface has this paramount importance, that it is the home of the roots of all ordinary forms of vegetation. While there are many kinds of soil, such as sandy, clayey, loamy, and peaty, varying much in character, yet such is the adaptability of plants to soils, and so susceptible are these to improvement by the arts of culture, that some kinds of plants can always be found that will thrive readily in any properly improved soils. On the preparation of soils, see Part IV.

Almost as common as the ground itself, are the grasses which clothe it, and which constitute a distinct and extensive botanical order. That they are very important in ornamental gardening, every one knows; we could imagine nothing more desolate in appearance than the

(23)

barren aspect of our earth, were the carpet of the grasses lacking. The list of kinds used in lawn-making is not very large, these named below being the kinds found most desirable for this purpose, in our climate.

Rhode Island Bent Grass (*Agrostis vulgaris*, var.), a grass of fine quality in some sections, when sown by itself.

Creeping Bent Grass (*Agrostis alba*, var. *stolonifera*), thrives in partially shaded places; excellent for small yards.

Red Top Grass (*Agrostis vulgaris*), a valuable kind, doing well as a lawn grass in almost all soils.

Green, or June Grass (*Poa pratensis*), also widely known as "Kentucky Blue Grass," is one of the best species, thriving well in dry, and also in somewhat shaded places.

Perennial Rye-Grass (*Lolium perenne*), one of the best grasses south of Philadelphia, starting early in the spring, and of a good color.

Yellow Oat Grass (*Avena flavescens*) stands drouth well, but should be mixed with other kinds.

Dog Tail Grass (*Cynosurus cristatus*), suited to dry hard soils and hills.

Red Fescue Grass (*Festuca ovina*, var. *rubra*), adapted for gravelly banks; coarse.

Reed Canary Grass. (*Phalaris arundinacea*), a coarse grass, suitable for marshy and wet places.

Tall Fescue Grass (*Festuca elatior*), suitable for moist, strong clay soils; in shady places and along the sea coast; coarse.

Sweet Vernal Grass (*Anthoxanthum odoratum*). The newly mown grass of this species emits a pleasing fragrance, on which account it is considered desirable to add a small quantity of its seed to other kinds.

White Clover (*Trifolium repens*) is sometimes mixed with the grasses, but is not recommended for rich soils or for lawns that are kept watered.

CHAPTER V.

WOODY GROWTHS.—TREES AND SHRUBS.

In trees and shrubs we have some of the finest forms of natural beauty. These present a great variety of ornamental qualities, in habit, foliage, and flowers, and possess wide adaptability for beautifying purposes. In nature,

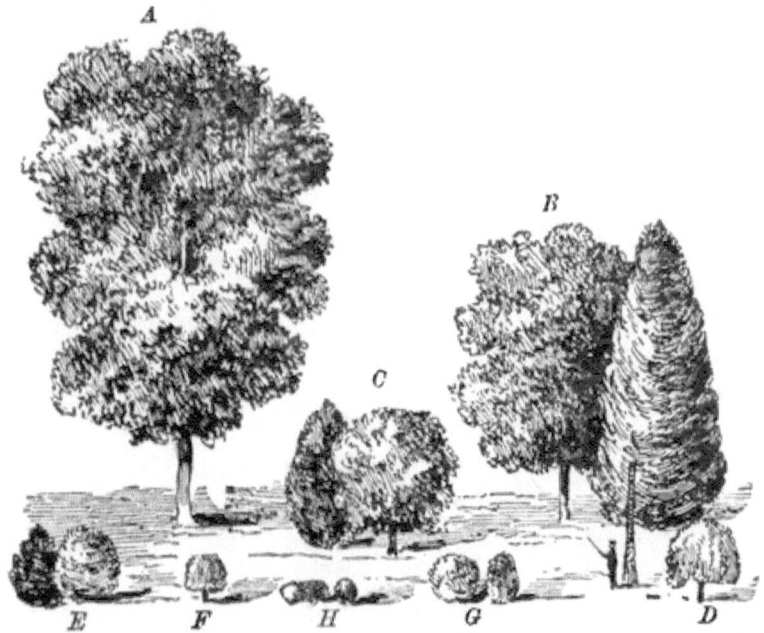

A, 60 feet and upwards; B, 30 to 60 feet; C, 15 to 30 feet; D, tree 9 to 15 feet; E, shrubs 9 to 15 feet; F, tree 5 to 9 feet; G, shrub 5 to 9 feet; H, 1 to 5 feet.

Fig. 1.—THE COMPARATIVE SIZES OF TREES AND SHRUBS.

mountains, plains and valleys all support kinds peculiar to these localities and that are perfectly at home in them. Planters who know only the comparatively few kinds of trees and shrubs that are commonly seen in American yards and pleasure grounds, can hardly be aware what they miss, in not employing larger assortments of trees.

2

The lack which generally prevails in this respect is inexcusable in the face of Nature's liberality in providing.

Those who are interested in the study of trees and shrubs, with a view to making up lists for planting, find that the size to which these attain at maturity, is an important consideration. Hence in the enumeration of the trees in these pages, care is taken to give the sizes to which the kinds attain. A classification as to size is introduced, the different and relative sizes being represented by letters, as shown by figure 1, and the appended explanation. In the descriptions throughout the work, the letters given answer as keys which, by the help of the engraving, lead to a correct idea of individual and relative sizes.

Let it be understood that in all cases the sizes indicated are only approximately correct, as difference of soil and other circumstances have much to do in causing deviations in the hight of the same species.

The general plan of arrangement in the following chapter is, to begin with descriptions of large-growing kinds, and end with the smaller species. No alphabetical classification is here attempted, but for convenience the different kinds are thus arranged in the index.

To save repetitions of botanical terms (which are usually in parenthesis), the generic name which appears in the head line, is represented by its initials throughout the descriptions of the species of each genus. When there is more than one variety of any species, the abbreviation var. (thus, var. *regalis*), precedes the variety name of all that follow the one first given.

CHAPTER VI.

DECIDUOUS TREES AND SHRUBS.

The term deciduous is applied to those trees and shrubs, the leaves of which fall in autumn, and is used in contra-distinction to evergreen, or persistent.

THE ELM. *Ulmus. A. C.*

The Elms in their different species afford much diversity, and as they grow readily in almost any soil and situation, they almost without exception give great satisfaction to planters.

THE AMERICAN WHITE OR WEEPING ELM (*Ulmus Americana*).—A well-known tree with spreading, curving, pendant branches, and of stately, picturesque appearance. Where space admits, it is one of the best street trees, because of its inclination to form a long trunk, *A.*

The ENGLISH ELM (*U. campestris*), with its numerous varieties, forms a valuable section. The normal form is tall and irregular in shape, its branches leaving the trunk almost horizontally. Leaves smaller and more regularly cut than those of the American, *A.* Berard's English Elm (var. *Berardi*) is a miniature tree, slender and pyramidal in habit, with distinctly cut leaves, *B.* Clemmer's English Elm (var. *Clemmeri*) differs but little from the type; of rapid growth, *A.* Webb's Curled-leaved English Elm (var. *crispa*) is dwarfish, with curled leaves; distinct, *B.*

Some of the varieties of the English Elm incline to a pendulous habit, such as the Weeping Small-leaved English Elm (var. *microphylla pendula*), a charming tree for small lawns, if grafted at six or eight feet high, *C.* The common Cork-barked English Elm (var. *suberosa*) is a desirable tree. Weeping Cork-barked English Elm (var. *suberosa pendula*), a picturesque grower, *B.* The Twiggy English Elm (var. *viminalis*), with small leaves and slender branches, is distinct and beautiful, *C.*

Some of this section have characteristic foliage, which renders them valuable, such as the Variegated-leaved English Elm (var. *variegata argentea*), with the leaves distinctly mottled with silvery white, *B.* Golden-leaved English Elm (var. *aurea*) has its leaves blotched with yellow. Purple-leaved English Elm (var. *purpurea*), a handsome tree, with the leaves purple-tinged early in the season; compact and upright in habit, *A.* Nettle-leaved English Elm (var. *utricæfolia*) has large serrated leaves, of peculiar appearance; fine habit, *A.* Curled-leaved English Elm (var. *cucullata*), with curled, hood-like leaves, sharply notched, *B.* Plume-like English Elm (var. *plumosa*), another curled-leaved variety, the branches and foliage of which have a plume-like appearance.

There are also belonging to the English Elms, a beautiful compact-growing variety, with dark foliage, called the Serrate-leaved English Elm (var. *serratifolia*), *B;* the Belgian Elm (var. *Belgica*), of rapid, spreading growth, much planted in European streets, *A;* Cornish Elm (var. *Cornubiensis*), of vigorous upright growth, *A;* and the Monumental Elm (var. *monumentalis*), of distinct columnar form, dense and slow-growing, *C*, besides some others that are less distinct.

The SCOTCH, or WYCH ELM (*U. montana*), and varieties possess great value for ornamental planting, usually having large leaves, broad forms and heavy verdure, and some are pendant in habit. The type is a fine spreading grower, *B.* The Weeping Camperdown Elm (var. *Camperdowni*) is of unsurpassed excellence, and when grafted eight feet high, forms, with its long, dark-green leaves and masses of luxuriant, hanging branches, a striking and picturesque object; with slight training the tree forms almost a perfect arbor, *C.* Of others, the common Weeping Scotch Elm (var. *pendula*) resembles the Camper-down, but is rather less valuable; it has peculiar freaks of growth, the branches sometimes leaving the tree obliquely, then again in a horizontal or perpendicular direction, *B*. The Rough-leaved Weeping Scotch Elm (var. *pendula rugosa*) is a valuable tree, with large, rough leaves, *B*. The Crisp-leaved Weeping Scotch Elm (var. *crispa*), has crisped leaves. Huntingdon's Elm (var. *Huntingdoni*), and Blandford's, or Superb Elm (var. *superba*) are Scotch Elms of value, the former very erect, *A;* the latter, a majestic tree, with smooth, grayish bark, the foliage attractive in color, and forming a fine specimen soon after planting, *A*. The Broad-leaved Elm (var. *latifolia*), a handsome grower, *B*, and Dampier's Pyramidal Elm (var. *pyramidalis Dampieri*), an elegant pyramidal grower, *B*, are desirable varieties. The White-margined Scotch Elm (var. *alba marginata*) is a delicate-growing variety, said to be superb if grown in partial shade. The Ash-colored Elm (*U. montana,* var. *cinerea*), with fine, rich-looking foliage, *A*, and Dove's Elm (*U. Dovæi*), of pyramidal shape, and vigorous, being valuable for street-planting, are worthy of mention as ornamental species.

The native RED, or SLIPPERY ELM (*U. fulva*) is a fine tree for large lawns or street planting, but the growth is somewhat straggling, *B*. There is also a weeping form of the last named (var. *pendula*), which is well spoken of.

THE OAK. *Quercus. A. C.*

An Oak that has had ample time and space for development, is almost the perfect type of all that is grand and expressive in a tree. The species are very numerous, varying much in habit, size, and general appearance, and deserve more attention in ornamental planting than they have yet received. While some grow slowly, others are scarcely excelled in their freedom of growth. The first ten described below are natives of the United States.

SCARLET OAK (*Q. coccinea*), a rapid grower of pyramidal form, with beautiful, light-green, deeply-cut leaves, which turn to an intense scarlet in autumn, *A*.

WHITE OAK (*Q. alba*). This typical oak is large, broad, and majestic; leaves with rounded lobes, pale-green above and glaucous beneath, *A*.

SWAMP WHITE OAK (*Q. bicolor*); handsome and tall; its large, sinuate-toothed leaves turning scarlet in autumn, *A*.

BURR or MOSSY CUP OAK (*Q. macrocarpa*), of spreading growth, with very large, deeply-lobed leaves, which show some variation in size and form; acorns large, cup mossed.

SOUTHERN OVER-CUP OAK (*Q. lyrata*), a Southern tree, hardy in the North; with large, obovate-oblong leaves, crowded together.

SHINGLE OAK (*Q. imbricaria*). Laurel-like, lanceolate-oblong leaves, turning to rich carmine in the autumn, *B*.

RED OAK (*Q. rubra*), a handsome, rapid-growing tree, fine as a single specimen; leaves large, sinuately-cut, assuming a deep red in the fall, *A*.

PIN OAK (*Q. palustris*), a rapid-growing, pyramidal tree, valuable for streets; branches slightly drooping, with bright, glossy foliage that is very ornamental.

CHESTNUT OAK (*Q. Prinus*). Leaves serrated, resembling those of the chestnut, a most beautiful species; will grow in very poor soil, *A*. Cut-leaved Chestnut Oak (var. *lacinata*) is a variety of the preceding, with cut leaves.

WILLOW OAK (*Q. Phellos*), remarkable for its narrow, willow-like leaves and slender shoots; distinct, *B*.

ENGLISH OAKS.—These are distinct, and embrace some very valuable sorts. The common English Royal Oak (*Q. Robur*) is a grandly beautiful tree of rather slow growth, leaves of an uniform color on both sides, *A*. The following are some of its leading varieties: Louett's Oak (var. *Louetti*), differing from the type in having larger leaves rather more lanceolate in form, *A;* Purple-leaved Oak (var. *atropurpurea*), a beautiful tree but a slow grower, with dark purple leaves that hold color all summer, very effective, *B;* Dark-leaved Oak (var. *nigricans*), said to be darker than the purple-leaved variety, *B;* Golden-leaved Oak (var. *concordia*), a most effective variety, the leaves with a rich, yellow tinge, and presenting a peculiar waxy appearance, *C;* Silver-leaved Oak (var. *argentea variegata*), leaves somewhat mottled with white at their edges, *B.* There are some sorts that have striking leaf-forms, namely: Contorted-leaved Oak (var. *contorta*), with peculiar twisted leaves, *B;* Curled Pyramidal Oak (var. *cucullata*), the leaves of which are curled on their edges; Cut-leaved Oak (var. *laciniata*), one of the best cut-leaved trees known, leaves nearly divided to the mid-rib, tree of elegant habit, *B;* Large-leaved Oak (var. *macrophylla*); var. *latifolia cucullata*, singular looking, with broad leaves slightly turned down at the edges. The Weeping Oak (var. *pendula*), with long, slender, willow-like branches, and the Pyramidal Oak (var. *fastigiata*), a remarkable tree, growing somewhat like the Upright Poplars, but more slender, *B*, all belong to the English or Royal Oak, and are desirable in ornamental planting.

Of other foreign kinds the Turkey Oak (*Q. Cerris*) is very desirable; of rapid growth, with tall symmetrical head; finely lobed, bright, shining leaves, which, after turning brown in the autumn, remain far into the winter on the tree, *A.*

Mongolian Oak (*Q. Mongolica*), a rare tree with long, deeply notched, green-glaucous leaves.

There are several desirable Japanese species, among them: *Q. Daimio*, with broad, glossy, dark-green leaves, of leathery texture, covered with brownish down when young; *Q. dentata*, with deeply-toothed leaves that give the tree a pleasing appearance.

THE HORSE-CHESTNUT AND BUCKEYE, (*Æsculus*). A–E.

The Horse-Chestnut, including the American Buck-eyes, are much esteemed as ornamental trees the world over, for their regular forms, heavy, deep-green foliage and their flowers, which latter give the tree a magnificent appearance for weeks in the spring.

The COMMON or EUROPEAN HORSE-CHESTNUT (*Æ. Hippocastanum*) is hardly excelled as a lawn or street tree; in time losing largely the sameness of form, which is conspicuous, and to some objectionable in the young trees, and taking on sufficient irregularity to produce a charming effect of light and shade. In old trees, some branches will almost droop to the ground. A slight objection to the tree is the litter it produces by dropping its buds and nuts in the fall, *A*. There are several fine varieties, namely: the Double White (var. *flore pleno*); the Double Red (var. *rubra flore pleno*), which possess the advantage of not producing fruit, hence litter on this account is avoided. The flowers of these are very attractive, and the form of growth may easily be kept shrub-like, *B*. Memminger's Horse-Chestnut (var. *Memmingeri*) is a variety, the leaves of which are sometimes slightly sprinkled with white, making the tree interesting, *A*. The Cut-leaved Horse-Chestnut (var. *laciniata*), has handsome leaves deeply and delicately cut, *B*. Van Houtte's Dwarf Horse-Chestnut (var. *nana Van Houttei*) is dwarfish, and very desirable for small places.

The RED-FLOWERING HORSE-CHESTNUT (*Æ. rubicunda*) is now regarded as a distinct species; it is of slow growth, with dark-green leaves, and producing brilliant red flowers in showy racemes, *B*. There is a Golden variegated variety (var. *foliis aureis*), and a Dwarf Red-flowering variety (var. *nana*), both of which are desirable, *C.*

The CHINESE HORSE-CHESTNUT (*Æ. Chinensis*), of comparatively recent introduction, is a rapid grower with large leaves.

The BUCKEYES, sometimes called the Smooth-fruited Horse-Chestnuts, were formerly placed in a separate ge-

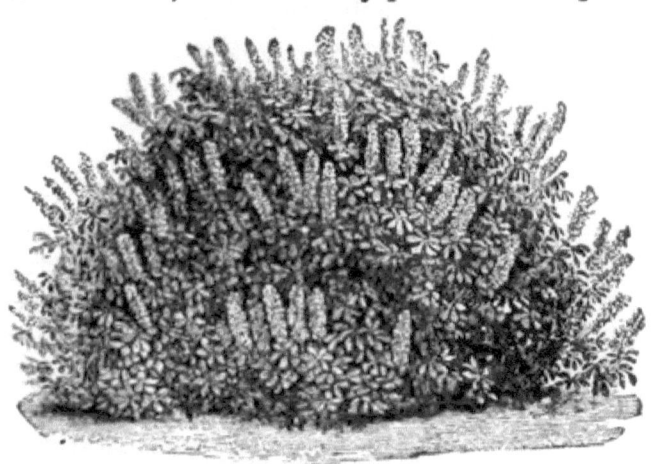

Fig. 2.—DWARF HORSE-CHESTNUT.

nus, *Pavia.* Botanists now group them as a section (*Pavia*), of *Æsculus.*

The OHIO BUCKEYE (*Æ. glabra*) has large, smooth leaves, and panicles of small, pale yellow flowers in early spring, *B.*

The YELLOW BUCKEYE (*Æ. flava*) is a beautiful low tree or shrub, with pale green, downy leaves and bright yellow flowers, *C.*

The RED BUCKEYE (*Æ. Pavia*) is a native of Virginia and southward, forming a small-sized tree, with brownish red flowers, *G.* From this has sprung a number of small Buckeyes, such as the Dark Red Buckeye (var. *atrosanguinea*), with dark flowers and smooth leaves; the Flesh-colored Buckeye (var. *carnea pubescens*), the Purple Buckeye (var. *purpurea*), with flowers of the colors indicated by the names: Whitley's Buckeye (var. *Whitleyi*), a fine variety, with brilliant flowers and handsome foliage.

Among other Buckeyes, there is one known as *Æ. carnea superba*, which is very distinct, with showy dark crimson flowers; and two very dwarf kinds, namely the Long Racemed or Small Buckeye (*Æ. parviflora*), figure 2, a valuable species of low spreading habit and attractive white flowers. The Dwarf-pendulous Buckeye (*Æ. pumila pendula*) has drooping branches. These dwarf Buckeyes (*C-D*), are well adapted to small grounds.

THE CHESTNUT. *Castanea, A-C.*

The AMERICAN CHESTNUT (*C. vesca*, var. *Americana*) is a beautiful, neat tree, with long-pointed leaves, that have scalloped edges; produces sweet fruit, *A*.

The SWEET or SPANISH CHESTNUT (*C. vesca*) is a fine lawn tree, yielding a superior quality of fruit; a little tender north of Washington, *B*. There is a variety with slightly white margined leaves, known as var. *argentea variegata*, but the growth is not very satisfactory, *C*.

The DWARF CHESTNUT or CHINQUAPIN (*C. pumila*), a native of Ohio and southward; is a neat grower, forming a globular head, with lance-oblong leaves, which are whitish underneath, *C*.

A recent introduction is the JAPAN CHESTNUT (*C. Japonica*), which promises well for hardiness, beauty, and fruit-bearing qualities.

While preferring light soils, the Chestnuts also do well in clayey loams.

THE POPLAR. *Populus. A-B.*

No other trees will, as a rule, attain to effective proportions sooner than the Poplars, and on this account they possess special value in ornamental gardening for creating effects quickly. Most of them are valuable as single specimens on the lawn. They are objected to by some, because sprouts come up from the roots. These are not difficult to keep down. The Poplars are desirable for back-grounds, shade for stock-yards, and to plant in out-of-the-way places.

The WHITE or SILVER POPLAR or ABELE (*P. alba*) is a fine tree with heart-shaped, dark-green, smooth leaves, silvery white beneath, *A.* The Gray Poplar resembles the preceding somewhat, but is more upright, and with leaves not so green above, or so white beneath.

ALBA NIVEA is a variety with larger leaves than the type, but resembling it in other respects. All of these, while valuable trees for ornament, are disposed to sprout from the root.

The LOMBARDY POPLAR (*P. dilatata*) is the well-known erect, spire-like species, growing rapidly, and possessing peculiar value on account of its manner of growth, *A.*

The NECKLACE POPLAR, or Cotton-wood (*P. monilifera*), is a vigorous tree, with the young branches angled; it has large leaves, and its catkins resemble a string of beads.

The CAROLINA POPLAR is a vigorous ornamental shade tree, *A.* A variety of this, named "Eugenie," is of pyramidal habit and rapid growth, with handsome, yellowish-green foliage.

The BALSAM POPLAR (*P. balsamifera*) is a coarse, rank grower of erect habit, with large, shiny leaves; it sprouts, *B.* There are several handsome Weeping Poplars : namely, the Weeping, Large American Aspen (*P. grandidentata pendula*), a beautiful and very rapid grower, with slender branches that droop gracefully to the ground; valuable, *B.* Athenian Weeping Poplar (*P. Græca pendula*), a fine, weeping tree, with dark-colored catkins ; and the Parasol de St. Julien, a new drooping variety from France. The American Aspen (*P. tremuloides*) is a species with long, slender leaf-stalks, which cause the leaves to quiver in the slightest breeze.

THE TULIP TREE. *Liriodendron. A.*

The TULIP TREE (*L. Tulipifera*) is a beautiful tree wherever it grows and flowers well. The trunk is straight, covered with grayish-brown bark ; leaves round-ish, ovate, with two lobes near the base, and two at the apex, which appears as if cut off, of a charming light-green tint, and smooth. The flowers resemble single tulips. It requires a deep, loamy soil, and must be transplanted while young. The Gold-margined-leaved Tulip Tree is a recent introduction, with most beautifully margined leaves. May prove tender in the North.

THE HICKORIES AND OTHER NUT-BEARING TREES. *A. B.*

The COMMON HICKORY, or SHELL BARK (*Carya alba*), is an ornamental tree of noble dimensions and a spread-ing habit, with the branches starting low down; excellent where the space admits. Handsome compound leaves of a rich, glossy green—darker than those of most other trees —and frequently measure twelve to fifteen inches long on vigorous specimens.

The BLACK WALNUT (*Juglans nigra*) is one of the grandest and most massive of trees, and well suited for embellishing large grounds. The bark is very dark in color, and deeply furrowed ; leaves compound, with thir-teen to seventeen leaflets, and exceedingly handsome, *A.*

The BUTTERNUT (*J. cinerea*) is another fine ornament-al tree, somewhat resembling the last, but rarely as hand-some, *B.*

The EUROPEAN WALNUT, or MADEIRA NUT (*J. regia*), forms a fine, well-balanced tree, thickly clad with warm, russet-lined foliage, *A.* There is also a Cut-leaved variety (var. *lacinata*) and a Dwarf variety (var. *praeparturiens*) of this.

THE PLANE, OR BUTTONWOOD. *Platanus.* *A.*

In Paris and other large European cities, our native
AMERICAN PLANE, or BUTTONWOOD (*P. occidentalis*),
is esteemed above all other trees for street planting, but,
strange as it may seem, in this, its native country, it
suffers badly in most places from a fungus which destroys
the young growth.

The ORIENTAL PLANE (*P. orientalis*) is less liable to
the same trouble, though not free from it. As they are
of great value, they are nevertheless worthy of trial by
planters.

THE MAPLE. *Acer* and *Negundo.* *A–F.*

The Maples, in their many species and varieties, possess
a value as ornamental trees of the very highest order.
The trees are of free, in some kinds of rapid growth, and
healthy; they are adapted to all soils, and are seldom
troubled by insects. Their foliage is handsome, appears
early, and goes out in the fall, in various gorgeous tints.
Some maples have richly-colored leaves all through the
season, and the leaves of others are of singular shape,
while a few bear attractive blossoms.

The SUGAR MAPLE (*A. saccharinum*) is a well-known
native species, admirable in form, foliage, and habit. It
is one of the best for street and lawn-planting, *A.* The
Black Sugar Maple (var. *nigrum*), a variety of the last,
has darker leaves, with their lobes more rounded, *A.*

The RED, or SWAMP MAPLE (*A. rubrum*), also a native,
is noted in early spring for its showy, red blossoms, and
in autumn for the extreme brilliancy of its foliage, *B.*
There is a fine dwarf form of this, called the Dwarf
Scarlet Maple (var. *fulgens* of some, and var. *tomentosum*
of other authors.)

The NORWAY MAPLE (*A. platanoides*) is a tree of spreading, rounded form, broad, shining leaves, producing dense

shade, and of free growth ; is worthy a place in every roomy garden, *A.* The Curled-leaf Maple (var. *cucullatum*) is a variety of the Norway, with leaves more or less curled, giving the tree a curious appearance. There are, at least, three cut-leaved varieties of this species, all valuable; the Cut-leaved Norway Maple (var. *dissectum*), has its leaves so deeply cut as to almost divide them into three parts; the Eagle-claw Maple (var. *laciniatum*), with leaves deeply cut, pointed and curled ; and the Lorberg's, Norway Maple (var. *Lorbergii*), which has very deeply cut leaves, of a bright, reddish hue when young ; Schwerdler's Norway Maple (var. *Schwerdlerii*) is a promising new variety, with leaves that are richly variegated in the spring with purple and crimson.

The SILVER-LEAVED MAPLE (*A. dasycarpum*), gives a number of valuable varieties, mostly of open, slender growth. The tree is a rapid grower, the foliage bright-green above and silvery white beneath. New Cut-leaved Silver Maple (var. *heterophyllum laciniatum*), very distinct and fine; somewhat inclined to "sport," *C.* Wagner's Cut-leaved Silver Maple (var. *Wagneri*), of great value ; drooping gracefully, and with deeply dissected leaves. The Crisp-leaved Silver Maple (var. *crispum novum*), with leaves that are deeply-cut as well as curled, rendering the tree singularly attractive.

The EUROPEAN SYCAMORE MAPLE (*A. Pseudo-Platanus*) is a handsome, strong-growing tree, with large leaves, which have long, reddish leaf stalks. Valuable for the sea-shore and exposed places, as it will grow erect where the winds would cause other trees to lean, *A.* Douglas's Sycamore Maple (var. *Douglasi*) has smaller and more pointed leaves than the type. There are two beautiful varieties, with peculiar leaf coloration, that render them valuable for creating contrasts of foliage in plantations. The Golden-leaved Sycamore Maple (var. *aureo-variegata*), a handsome ornamental tree, with the leaves distinctly and permanently marked with yellow, *B*, and the Purple-leaved Sycamore Maple (var. *purpurea*), with greenish-purple foliage, the under side of which is singularly handsome. The Velvety Maple (var. *velutinum*) is a rapid-growing form, with large, dark-green, five-lobed leaves.

In recent years the Maples, with richly-colored leaves introduced from Japan, have attracted much attention. At first the indications seemed to be against their hardiness, but as the trees attain more age, and as the stock is propagated in this country, they appear to be more hardy, and they will undoubtedly prove valuable under careful culture. Thus far, the wonderfully rich colors of the leaves have faded in summer, but even this defect promises to be remedied as the trees grow older. The species itself, *Acer polymorphum*, is very showy and of comparatively free growth; it is the parent of many varieties, of which the following five are perhaps the best of the many Japanese Maples thus far introduced :—The Blood-red-leaved Japanese Maple (var. *sanguineum*), with purple or rich red leaves ; the Dark Purple-leaved Japanese Maple (var. *atropurpureum*), of deep-claret tint ; leaves very deeply cut ; Various-colored Japanese Maple (var. *versicolor*), of free growth, as compared with others, and picturesquely spotted with white, pink, and green ; Cut-leaved Purple Japanese Maple (var. *dissectum*), beautiful rose-colored leaves and branches in the new growth, changing to deep purple later; leaves delicately-cut, giving them a fern-like appearance ; of dwarf, weeping and graceful form ; Netted-leaved Japanese Maple (var. *reticulatum*), deeply-lobed, greenish-whitish leaves, traversed by a network of light, yellowish veins. There is also a variety with whitish leaves. There are two other distinct Japanese Maples worthy of mention :

The RED COLCHICUM MAPLE (*A. Colchicum rubrum*), of bright, crimson color in the young leaves and wood; rather tender; and the

PALMATE-LEAVED MAPLE (*A. palmatum*), with small leaves, having reddish leaf-stalks and veins, the tree in time assuming a weeping form.

The ENGLISH, or CORK-BARKED MAPLE (*A. campestre*), is a remarkably handsome, slow-growing tree of compact habit, with very dark-green leaves; sometimes grown in a shrub-like form.

The LARGE-LEAVED MAPLE (*A. macrophyllum*) is a stately tree with immense leaves, but rather tender in the North while young.

STRIPED MAPLE (*A. Pennsylvanicum*) is an elegant tree with light-green foliage and distinctly striped bark.

TARTARIAN MAPLE (*A. Tartaricum*) is of irregular habit, but making a handsome tree, with small, light-green leaves and light-colored, smooth bark.

The Ash-leaved Maple belongs in a distinct genus (*Negundo*), but closely related to the common Maple. ASH-LEAVED MAPLE, or BOX-ELDER (*Negundo aceroides*), is of rapid growth, with small, light-green foliage, resembling that of the Ash, and Maple-like fruit. The bark on the young wood is greenish-yellow, *C.* Curled Ash-leaved Maple (var. *crispum*), has the foliage curled and somewhat cut. Variegated Ash-leaved Maple (var. *foliis argenteis variegatis*), a variety distinctly marked with white, more so, perhaps, than any other white-leaved tree in cultivation. Extensively used in French gardens, but liable to be sun-burned here, *F.*

THE BEECH. *Fagus. A. C.*

The Beeches are highly esteemed, picturesque trees, with rich, glossy leaves and smooth bark which, in some, is of a very light color. The light and shade of the verdure is usually disposed horizontally, giving to the trees a distinct appearance. They prefer light, loamy soils; the roots keep near the surface, on which account grass does not thrive well under them, unless it is kept well watered. All the Beeches can be kept closely pruned, to adapt them to small grounds, or for use as hedges.

The AMERICAN BEECH (*F. ferruginea*) is an elegant tree of fine form, with rich leaves, and smooth, light-colored bark, *B*.

The EUROPEAN BEECH (*F. sylvatica*) is very ornamental, with spreading branches, which in time often droop gracefully almost to the ground; leaves thin, ovate, and obscurely toothed, *A*. Among the fine varieties that have sprung from the European Beech, those with purple leaves stand very high, as being the most attractive trees with purple foliage in cultivation.

The COMMON PURPLE-LEAVED BEECH (var. *purpurea*) has dark, reddish-purple foliage in the spring, changing to crimson and then to purplish-green during the season, *B*. Rivers' Purple-leaved Beech (var. *purpurea Riversii*) is darker and more effective than the common purple-leaved variety, *B*. Large-leaved Purple Beech (var. *purpurea major*) is a variety with large, shining, dark-purple leaves, which are exceedingly rich and effective, *C*. The Copper-colored Beech (var. *cuprea*) resembles the Common Purple Beech somewhat, but has lighter-colored leaves, with darker-colored young shoots. Another variegated Beech, widely different in the color of its leaves from those described, and one that contrasts markedly with them, is the Golden Variegated Beech (var. *aurea variegata*), with leaves deeply margined with yellow, rendering the tree very distinct and handsome. Among other valuable sorts belonging to the European, are the Weeping Beech (var. *pendula*), a most picturesque tree, with long, tortuous branches, upon which the foliage is apparently piled in masses; the tree often seems to be deformed when young, but in time becomes very ornamental, *B*; the Broad-leaved Beech (var. *macrophylla*), of vigorous habit, with large, handsome foliage, *C;* the Cut-leaved Beech (var. *lacinata*), of medium size, compact, pyramidal form, and possessing great elegance, *B;* the Fern-leaved Beech (var. *aspleniifolia*), somewhat resembling the last, but more rounded in form, and with fern-like leaves, delicately cut,

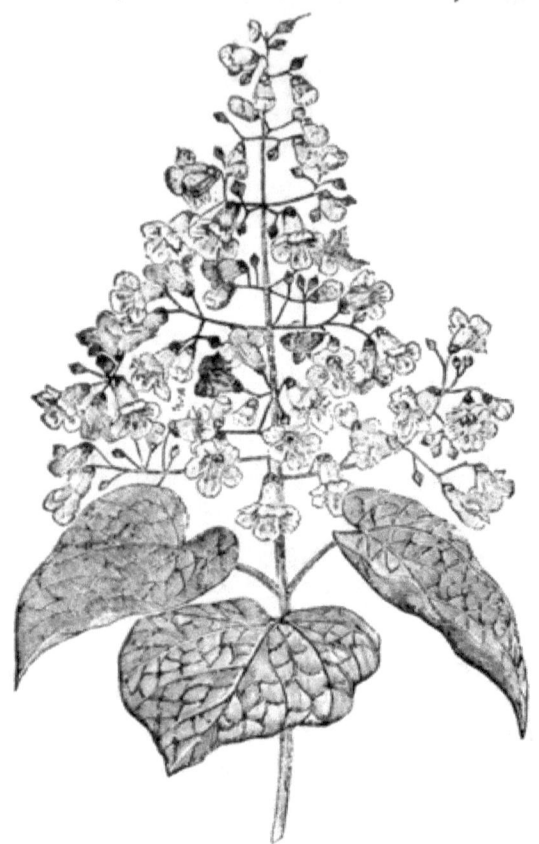

Fig. 3.—CATALPA BIGNONIOIDES.

B; the Crested-leaved Beech (var. *cristata*), a curious variety, with small, curled leaves, not remarkable for beauty.

THE CATALPA. *Catalpa. A–E.*

Trees at maturity of different sizes, conspicuous on account of their large leaves of a soft hue, with showy flowers, which are followed by long seed pods which often hang until spring; noted for the rapid growth of the large native kinds.

The COMMON CATALPA, or INDIAN BEAN (*C. bignonioides*, sometimes called *C. syringæfolia*), is a native of the Southern States, but does well in some parts of the North if protected when young; leaves large, showy, heart-shaped, presenting a peculiar, tropical appearance; flowers white, tinged with purple and yellow, *A*. The Golden Catalpa (var. *aurea*) somewhat resembles the common species, but with the young leaves tinged with gold for a time. There is a Dwarf American Catalpa (var. *nana*), resembling most of the others, but of a bushy growth, and attractive, *E*.

The HARDY CATALPA (*C. speciosa*), while less remarkable in appearance than the common, is hardier, and flowers earlier, *A*.

Other dwarf kinds have been introduced from Asia, which are valuable. One of these is *C. Kæmpferi*, and another *C. Bungei*, but confusion prevails at present as to their identity.

THE LARCH. *Larix. A.*

The Larches are cone-bearing trees, without being "evergreens," like the Spruces, Pines, and most other conifers. They mainly have a peculiar grace and beauty, with delicate, soft foliage, that contrasts well with that of most other trees and shrubs. They are valuable for adding to the effect and variety of grounds, and are adapted to all soils, but should be planted very early in the spring, or in the fall.

The EUROPEAN LARCH (*L. Europæa*) is of erect form, tapering very delicately; is the kind most commonly planted, *A*. There are several desirable variations: the Glaucous European Larch (var. *glauca*), of fine appearance; and the Weeping European Larch (var. *pendula*), the branches of which assume most grotesque forms, and being clothed with fine glaucous foliage, the tree has a very picturesque appearance.

The AMERICAN LARCH, TAMARACK and HACKMATACK (*L. Americana*), is a tall, pyramidal tree, with a very slender trunk ; less desirable than the European species.

The JAPAN LARCH (*L. leptolepis*) is a slender-growing kind, with reddish-brown shoots, and leaves that turn to a rich yellow in the autumn.

THE ASH.   *Fraxinus.*   A–D.

While some of the Ashes do not rank high as ornamental trees, there are a number of most excellent species and varieties which are entitled to be classed among the finest trees in cultivation.

The AMERICAN WHITE ASH (*F. Americana*) is a fair shade tree, thriving in almost any location, with broad, round head, straight, clean trunk and compound pinnate leaves, *A*.   Bosc's Ash (var. *Boscii*) is a fine and distinct American variety with dark, glossy foliage, *B*. There are some valuable variegated sorts, among which are the Gold Spotted-leaved Ash (var. *punctata*), the leaves of which are strongly marked, and blotched with golden yellow, giving the tree a very effective appearance —in this respect exceeding all other trees with golden-hued foliage.   The Aucuba-leaved Ash (var. *aucubæfolia*), with distinct splashes and spots of yellow on the leaves, remaining through the season, *C*.   The Walnut-leaved Ash (var. *juglandifolia*) strongly resembles the walnut in the form of leaves ; valuable only in large collections, *B*.   The Cloth-like-leaved Ash (var. *pannosa*), a native of the Carolinas, has beautiful foliage, somewhat resembling that of Bosc's Ash but larger, *B*.   Rufous-haired Ash (var. *rufa*) is a distinct and ornamental variety, of upright habit and dark green leaves, *B*.   The

Showy Ash (var. *spectabilis*) has large, glossy, leathery leaves, of dark green color.

The EUROPEAN ASH (*F. excelsior*) is a spreading tree, with a handsome head, a short thick trunk and beautiful pinnate leaves, *B*. There are two pendulous varieties, the Weeping European Ash (var. *pendula*), a valuable, rapid grower, that may serve as an arbor on the lawn, *C*; and the Golden-barked Weeping Ash (var. *aurea pendula*), an elegant but quite tender tree, with bark as yellow as gold, *C*. The common Golden-barked Ash (var. *aurea*) is also a conspicuous tree on account of its yellow bark, twisted branches and fine foliage, and it is hardier than the last named, *C*. The varieties with peculiar leaf forms are interesting: Dwarf Crisp-leaved Ash (var. *atrovirens*), with dark green, curled foliage, arranged closely along the stem, *D*. Hooded-leaved Ash (var. *cucullata*), with singularly curled and twisted leaves, of pyramidal growth, *C*. Dwarf Globe-headed Ash (var. *globosa*), a pretty round-headed tree when worked six or eight feet high, with small myrtle-like leaves, *D*. Willow-like-leaved Ash (var. *salicifolia*), with narrow willow-like leaflets of pleasing habit, *D*. Another variety called *scolopendrifolia* has leaflets as narrow as grass blades, and which droop curiously, *D*. The Single-leaved Ash (var. *monophylla*) is a fine tree, with broad leaves, *B*. There is a beautiful variety of the Single-leaved (var. *monophylla laciniata*) in which the margins of the leaves are finely cut. The Variegated-leaved Ash (var. *concavæfolia variegata*) is said to be striking on account of its silvery white young leaves, tinged with pink, changing later to light green.

The FLOWERING ASH (*F. Ornus*) is a small tree which produces a profusion of pale or greenish-white flowers in clusters on the terminal branches in spring, on which account it is valuable for ornament, *C*. There are several Japanese Ashes offered, but which it is feared are too tender to become generally useful.

THE LINDEN, BASSWOOD, OR LIME. *Tilia.* A–B.

Generally graceful, handsome trees of good size, with heart-shaped, serrate leaves, and producing heavy shade. The flowers, which are inconspicuous, are in some species much sought by the honey bee.

The AMERICAN LINDEN OR BASSWOOD (*T. Americana*) is a native of rapid growth, with very large leaves and fragrant flowers, *A.* The Broad-leaved Basswood (var. *macrophylla*) is less common, and has yet larger leaves than the last. Both are desirable in large grounds. The European Linden and its varieties are quite distinct in appearance.

The common EUROPEAN LINDEN (*T. Europea*) is well shaped, inclined to be pyramidal in form, thriving in almost any soil, and well adapted for lawns and avenues; leaves are smaller and darker than those of the American Linden, *A.* European White-leaved Linden (var. *alba*) is a handsome, dense-growing variety, the leaves of which are downy beneath and smooth above, giving the tree a striking appearance, and constrasting strongly with other kinds. There is also the White-leaved Weeping Linden (var. *alba-pendula*), a valuable tree with large leaves and slender branches that incline to droop, *B.* The Cut or Fern-leaved Linden (var. *laciniata*) is a tree of good habit with rather small leaves that are deeply cut and twisted, *B.* Another cut-leaved variety is the Red Cut-leaved Linden (var. *laciniata rubra*), the young shoots of which are of a bright rose color. The Broad-leaved Linden (var. *platyphylla*), with massive leaves; the Small-leaved Linden (var. *microphylla*) with leaves quite the reverse of the last as to size; and the Grape-leaved Linden (var. *vitifolia*), with deeply-lobed leaves, are all valuable. Among the European Lindens are some with attractive bark as follows: Pyramidal Linden (var. *pyramidalis*), and Red-twigged Linden (var. *rubra*), with young branches of reddish color; and the Yellow-twigged Linden (var. *sulphurea*), the Golden Broad-leaved Linden (var. *platyphylla aurea*), and the Hairy-styled Linden (var. *dasystyla*), with golden-hued bark, showy in winter.

The JAPAN LINDEN (*T. cordata*) is yet rare, it is of medium size, and has heart-shaped leaves.

THE WILLOW. *Salix.* *A. D.*

The Willow is a very large genus, having among its species many fine ornamental trees. Most of them are easily transplanted, thrive in any soil, and are of rapid growth.

The BABYLONIAN OR WEEPING WILLOW (*S. Babylonica*) is a very common species, a graceful tree of large size, its fresh, bright green, wavy foliage making it attractive, particularly in conjunction with water scenery, *A*. A variety of this from France (var. *Salamonii*) is more upright in habit, while retaining the weeping style of growth.

The GOLDEN WILLOW (*S. alba* var. *vitellina*) is a distinct variety of the White Willow, with yellow bark, very attractive both in summer and winter, *B*.

The GOAT WILLOW (*S. Caprea*), and some of its varieties are valuable; the common kind being a medium-sized tree of spreading form with broad leaves, *C*. The excellent, and well-known Kilmarnock Weeping Willow is a variety of the last (var. *pendula*), when grafted low this forms a fountain-like tree of great beauty, with the branches reaching to the ground; when grafted six or eight feet high, it forms an exceedingly graceful tree of umbrella shape; its foliage is glossy; habit vigorous,

thriving in any soil; excellent for small grounds, *D*.
Three-Colored Goat Willow (var. *tricolor*), has blotched
foliage of three distinct colors, it is usually grafted from
five to seven feet high, when it forms a handsome, small,
round-headed tree, *D*.

The AMERICAN WEEPING OR FOUNTAIN WILLOW
(*S. purpurea-pendula*), a variety of an European species,
is a small, slender-growing willow of European origin,
which forms a remarkably handsome weeping tree when
grafted on a large stem, *D*.

The ROSEMARY-LEAVED WILLOW (*S. rosmarinifolia*),
with small, silvery leaves so arranged on the branches as
to give them a feathery appearance, *D*.

The ROYAL WILLOW (*S. regalis*), is an elegant tree with
silvery leaves, which are larger than those of the last
named, both are of great value for contrasting with
other trees, on account of their whitish appearance and
handsome growth, *D*.   .

The LAUREL-LEAVED WILLOW (*S. laurifolia*), and the
Shiny-leaved Willow (*S. lucida*), are both rapid growing
trees, usually kept in a bush form, both have dark, glossy
leaves; those of the former species being the largest, *C*.

Other Willows worthy of note, are the Silky Weeping
Willow (*S. sericea pendula*), with small leaves and long,
slender branches; Wolsey's Weeping Willow (*S. Wolsey-
ana pendula*), a small leaved, dwarf species; Wisconsin
Weeping Willow, highly recommended in the West; Japan Weeping Willow (*S. Japonica pendula*), Palm-leaved
Willow (*S. palmæfolia*), a distinct-red stemmed tree
with large leaves, and the Ring-leaved Willow (*S. Babylonica*, var. *annularis*), a useful variety of the Weeping
Willow, the leaves of which are curiously curled.

THE MAIDEN-HAIR OR GINKGO.   *Ginkgo*.   *A*.

The common species (*G. adiantifolia*), an introduction
from Japan, is a remarkable and elegant tree; the leaves

resemble in shape the fronds of the Maiden-hair ferns (*Adiantum*), but are about three inches broad. The growth is naturally rapid and upright, but it can be trained against a house or over a trellis like a climber, and in this way presents a most singular appearance. It is hardy as far north as Buffalo, in partially sheltered situations. There is a Broad-leaved Ginkgo (var. *macrophylla*), with leaves somewhat broader than those of the species, and a Varigated-leaved Ginkgo (var. *variegata*), a kind that sometimes only shows variegation in the leaves. The genus has been called (*Salisburia*), a name which must give way to the older Ginkgo.

THE MAGNOLIA. *Magnolia.* *A.-E.*

Wherever the Magnolias are known they are highly prized as ornamental trees. The large-leaved, native species are grand in their foliage and produce showy flowers ; while the Asiatic and hybrid sorts are magnificent when in flower. They may be planted either as single specimens or in open groups on the lawn with good effect, and they contrast well with evergreens. One drawback to their popularity is the difficulty of transplanting them. On this point the well-known nurserymen, Ellwanger & Barry, of Rochester, N. Y., say: " To insure success in the transplanting they should be moved in the spring, never in the fall, and the Chinese varieties at that period when they are coming into bloom, and consequently before the leaves have made their appearance. Great care should be exercised in their removal, the fibrous roots being preserved as nearly as possible, and carefully guarded from any exposure to wind or sun. While almost any good soil is sufficient to insure their growth, they succeed best in a soil which is warm, rich, and dry." Among the native species which may be named as valuable are the

CUCUMBER TREE (*M. acuminata*), a rapid, upright grower, reaching size *A*, with oblong-pointed leaves, often

3

nine or ten inches long ; bell-shaped, greenish yellow flowers ; the fruit, when green, resembling a cucumber.

The HEART-SHAPED MAGNOLIA (*M. cordata*) blooms usually in May and August, producing tulip-shaped yellow flowers ; the oval, slightly cordate leaves are downy beneath, *E*.

UMBRELLA MAGNOLIA (*M. Umbrella*), a rapid-growing tree, with immense, long, light-green leaves; creamy-white flowers, which are often a foot across, *D*.

GREAT-LEAVED MAGNOLIA (*M. macrophylla*), has enormous leaves, two to three feet long; white, bell-shaped flowers, nine or ten inches across ; requires protection in the North, *C*.

EAR-LEAVED MAGNOLIA (*M. Fraseri*), leaves eight to twelve inches long, with ear-like lobes at the base; the white flowers are six inches across, *B*.

The SWEET BAY (*M. glauca*), with glossy leaves, whitish beneath ; flowers pure white, very fragrant ; if carefully trained forms a beautiful small tree, *E. D.* Long-leaved Sweet Bay (var. *longifolia*), is a variety of the preceding, with larger leaves, and of stronger growth.

GREAT LAUREL MAGNOLIA (*M. grandiflora*) is the Magnolia of the Southern States, not hardy north of Washington ; remarkable for its large, fragrant flowers and evergreen leaves.

The Chinese and Japanese Magnolias, with their varieties and hybrids, are the kinds noted chiefly for their attractive flowering qualities.

The YULAN, or CHINESE WHITE MAGNOLIA (*M. conspicua*), has bright, obovate leaves, pure white, fragrant, medium-sized flowers, which appear before the leaves, *E*.

PURPLE MAGNOLIA (*M. purpurea*) resembles the last-named, but the flowers are dark-purple on the outside, and white within, *E*.

SLENDER-GROWING MAGNOLIA (var. *gracilis*), a graceful and finer formed variety of the above, with a more slender, fastigiate growth, *E.*

VERY DARK-PURPLE JAPAN MAGNOLIA (*M. atropurpurea*), has the darkest flowers of all the Magnolias; later in bloom than the Chinese, *E.*

HALL'S JAPAN MAGNOLIA (*M. stellata*), a very early-

Fig. 4.—MAGNOLIA STELLATA.

flowering sort, with pure white flowers, the petals arranged in double rows. *M. hypoleuca* and *M. parviflora*, are comparatively recent introductions of promise.

The hybrids produced between the species possess high

merits. One of the finest and hardiest of all in this section of Asiatic Magnolias is SOULANGE'S MAGNOLIA (*M. Soulangeana*), which closely resembles the White Chinese; flowers cup-shaped, white and purple; foliage large and massive, *C.* The Showy-flowering Magnolia (*M. speciosa*), differs from the last-named in having smaller and somewhat paler flowers, but producing them in great profusion, and they remain longer on the tree than those of any other variety; forms a conspicuous specimen tree, *C.* Norbert's Magnolia (*M. Norbertiana*), resembles Soulange's, but is lighter colored. Lenne's Red-flowering Magnolia (*M. Lennei*), very large, deep-reddish-purple flowers, and good-sized showy leaves, *C.* Thompson's Magnolia (var. *Thompsoniana*), is a hybrid between the American Umbrella Magnolia and the Sweet Bay, partaking mostly of the character of the latter; it has large leaves; large, fragrant, creamy-white flowers, but it is tender in the North.

DECIDUOUS CYPRESS. *Taxodium.* A–C.

The several trees that go by this name, are conifers, that shed their leaves every autumn like the Larches. They somewhat resemble the Larches in form of growth and the small size of their leaves; but are less hardy, and thriving only in protected localities in the North.

The DECIDUOUS SWAMP CYPRESS (*Taxodium distichum*) is a stately tree of the Southern States, but succeeds in the North in protected places, *A.* There is a variety, known as the Weeping Deciduous Cypress (var. *pendulum*), which is a fine tree.

The CHINESE WEEPING DECIDUOUS CYPRESS (*T. Sinense pendulum* and *Glyptostrobus pendulus* of the catalogues), is now, by the best authorities, regarded as a variety of the above. It is a beautiful, perfectly straight tree, with slightly drooping, horizontal branches and twisted foliage in tufts; sheds its lower branches with age.

THE KENTUCKY COFFEE TREE. *Gymnocladus Canadensis.* B.

A rapid-growing native tree, with charming, feathery foliage, of twice-pinnate leaves, and bark that is singularly rough, even in small trees.

THE AILANTHUS. *Ailanthus glandulosus.* B.

A rapid-growing tree, with elegant, long, feathery foliage, exempt from all diseases and from nearly all insects. This tree may be employed to great advantage in "subtropical gardening," by cutting it down to the ground annually. Each spring a vigorous shoot will appear, furnished with most luxuriant leaves of a tropical aspect. The sole objection to the tree is its unpleasant odor at flowering time. This may be avoided by propagating (by means of root-cuttings) from those trees that have pistillate, or female, flowers only.

THE LIQUIDAMBAR, OR SWEET GUM, OR BILSTED. *Liquidambar.* B.

A genus of but two species, one growing in tropical Asia, and the other in our own country. *L. Styraciflua* is a desirable tree, somewhat resembling the Maples in the shape of its leaves, and the Walnuts in the roughness of its bark. The foliage, when bruised, gives off a fragrant odor. In autumn the tree assumes a most brilliant appearance, the leaves turning red and yellow.

THE YELLOW-WOOD. *Cladrastis tinctoria.* B.

This is generally conceded to be the finest, hardy-flowering tree known. In June its white, pea-like, fragrant flowers appear in long, hanging clusters that almost cover the tree, giving to it an exceedingly handsome appearance. The tree is of medium size, with a peculiar graceful sweep to the branches. Leaves compound, of a delightful green, changing to yellow in the autumn. A slow grower for several years after planting. The tree is sometimes called *Virgilia*, a name that by priority belongs to an African tree.

THE PEPPERIDGE, OR SOUR GUM. *Nyssa. B.*

This is a picturesque tree, with fine, glossy foliage, arranged in distinct, horizontal lines of light and shade, something like the American Beech, and turning to deep crimson in the autumn. The northern species is *N. multiflora.*

THE SOPHORA. *Sophora. B–D.*

There are two Sophoras grown for ornament, namely, the common JAPAN SOPHORA (*S. Japonica*), and the WEEPING SOPHORA (var. *pendula*), both of which bear a resemblance in delicacy of leaf and flowers to the Robinias, or Locusts. The former is a round-headed, upright grower of much beauty, producing in summer small, cream-colored flowers in racemes, *B.* The latter is naturally a strong-growing, trailing shrub, but if grafted on the common kind at seven or twelve feet high, forms a small weeping tree of picturesque appearance. The young branches of both are green, and singularly contorted. They should be planted on well drained soil, and only in sheltered places throughout the North.

THE ALDER. *Alnus. B.*

A genus of rapid growing trees, especially valuable for planting in moist places, although all do well on dry land. While some possess but little beauty, others are hardly excelled in attractiveness for lawn decoration. Among valuable of the Alders are :

The EUROPEAN ALDER (*A. glutinosa*), with showy, roundish foliage, *B.* Of this there are three cut-leaved varieties known respectively as the Imperial Cut-leaved Alder (var. *laciniata imperialis*), a stately tree of vigorous and graceful growth, and large deeply-cut leaves, very elegant for the lawn, *B.* The Common Cut-leaved Alder (var. *laciniata*), less attractive than the last ; and the Hawthorn-leaved Alder. There are also the Oak-leaved Alder (var. *quercifolia*), and the Red-leaved Alder (var. *rubronervis*), the latter having large leaves on striking red leaf-stalks.

The HOARY OR SPECKLED ALDER (*A. incana*) is a distinct native species of vigorous growth. Its leaves are broad, somewhat toothed, and whitish underneath. A cut-leaved variety of this (var. *laciniata*) makes a handsome tree, with its broad, deeply-cut leaves.

The LINDEN-LEAVED ALDER (*A. tiliacea*) is a fine kind, with large, deep-green, hearted-shaped, glossy leaves. There are also several Japanese species in cultivation.

THE MULBERRY. *Morus. B. C.*

Trees mostly with large, shining leaves, that have a singularly fresh and luxuriant appearance, even in the dryest of seasons, on which account they are favorites wherever they do well. Unfortunately the trees are apt to take on a bad, open style of growth some years after planting, which greatly mars their beauty. Some produce edible fruit.

The RED MULBERRY (*Morus rubra*) is an American species with large, luxuriant, heart-shaped, rarely-lobed leaves.

The WHITE MULBERRY (*M. alba*) is more slender, and has smaller leaves than the Red ; it is grown as food for silk worms. Fruit pinkish-white, *C.* There is a variety of the last with larger leaves, sweeter and darker fruit, and of a compact, pyramidal habit, called var. *fastigiata.* Downing's Ever-bearing Mulberry is a fine variety, yielding delicious fruit, *B.*

Several Asiatic species are also grown, such as the Black Mulberry (*Morus nigra*), of moderate growth.

Japan Mulberry (*M. Tokwa*), a stronger grower than the last, with large, shining leaves, often curled and crimped when developed.

PAPER MULBERRY. *Broussonetia.*

The PAPER MULBERRY (*B. papyrifera*) is so called because the Japanese and other orientals make a substitute for paper from its inner bark. The species and its varieties are handsome, small-sized trees, of rapid growth, with smaller leaves than those of the common Mulberries. A little tender north of Pennsylvania, *C.*

THE PAULOWNIA. *Paulownia imperialis. B.*

This, also known as the Empress Tree, presents a most striking appearance under favorable circumstances. It has immense leaves, a foot or more across, and beautiful, gloxinia-like flowers, in upright panicles in May. Being somewhat tender in the North when young, and the wood becoming brittle and easily broken by winds when old, the tree should be planted in a partially sheltered place, and if the soil is poor, the growth will be the finer for it. Suitable for the sub-tropical garden, with annual cutting down.

THE BIRCH. *Betula. B. C.*

The Birches possess a grace and elegance in their light, airy foliage, and slender, clean, often white, branches, that is without equal among trees. Most of them are specially valuable in small places where large shade trees are objectionable, but where some tree verdure is needed to break the lines of buildings or give balance to a place, as well as for shade. They thrive in any soil, even the poorest.

The EUROPEAN WHITE BIRCH (*B. alba*) and its varieties are especially valuable. The typical form is an elegant tree of pyramidal outline, and the small branches are pendant.   These latter, of a reddish color, contrast finely against the whiteness of the trunk and main branches, *B.*   The Cut-leaved Weeping Birch (var. *pendula laciniata*). this popular and charming tree resembles the species in many respects, but has delicately-cut foliage, and a most graceful appearance, which makes it a tree of the very first importance in ornamental planting, *B.*   Two other varieties : Young's Weeping Birch (var. *pendula Youngii*), considered by some the finest of all the Birches, being of rounded, picturesque form, with graceful, thread-like shoots, several feet long.   The Elegant Weeping Birch (var. *pendula elegans*) has the branches pendant towards the ground, and directly parallel with the trunk, both have the white bark of the species, and are remarkable for their elegance, *D.*   The graceful Weeping Birch (var. *tristis*) is a variety of picturesque habit with light branches, arranged in clumps, and reaching almost to the ground.   The Purple-leaved Birch (var. *foliis purpureis*), an effective kind with foliage that is tinged with purple, *C.*   The Nettle-leaved Birch (var. *urticifolia*) with leaves of dark-green, slightly cut, and presenting a distinct appearance, *D.*   The Downy-leaved B.rch (var. *pubescens*). with roundish leaves, and slightly drooping habit ; and the Pyramidal Birch (var. *fastigiata*) of very erect columnar form.   All the foregoing are varieties of the European White Birch, and possess marked value.   Among American Birches the following are desirable for ornamental planting :

SWEET OR CHERRY BIRCH (*B. lenta*), of rapid growth, with large leaves that come out early, and dark-brown bark, *B.*

PAPER OR CANOE BIRCH (*B. papyracea*), very distinct, with brilliant white bark, which may be easily separated into thin layers.

POPLAR-LEAVED OR AMERICAN WHITE BIRCH (*B. alba*

var. *populifolia*), a rapid grower, with glossy, triangular leaves, *B.*

YELLOW BIRCH (*B. lutea*), with golden-yellow bark, *B.* The Low Birch (*B. pumila*), a shruby form, has numerous, round, sharply-crenated leaves.

The newly introduced species (*B. costata*), is a fine tree of erect habit, with the branches somewhat drooping, and with dark, heart-shaped leaves.

The INDIAN PAPER BIRCH (*B. Bhojpaltra*) is distinct, of upright habit and with large, heart-shaped leaves. *B.*

LOCUST. (Often called Acacia.) *Robinia. B.–D.*

The BLACK OR YELLOW LOCUST (*R. Pseudacacia*) is a well-known native tree, with soft, graceful foliage, of refreshing tint and yellowish-white, fragrant flowers; of only common value, *B.* There are a number of excellent varieties of this, such as the Golden Locust (var. *aurea*), a fine tree with golden-tinted foliage. Besson's Locust (var. *Bessoniana*) is considered the best of the Locusts, of upright growth, with luxuriant, dark-green foliage, and is thornless, *B.* A variety called *bullata* is more compact in growth, *B.* *Bella-rosea* is a thornless variety of vigorous habit, with delicate, flesh-colored flowers, tinged with yellow, *B.* There are several varieties which have a characteristically erect habit, among these are the Pyramidal Locust (var *pyramidalis*), with dark foliage, and one called *fastigiata*, resembling the Lombardy Poplar in form of growth. The variety *spectabilis* is a sort with straight, vigorous shoots and large leaves. There are some varieties of a gobular form of growth, which are quite distinct in appearance, namely: Globe or Parasol Locust (var. *inermis*) is a remarkably handsome, thornless tree, that may by clipping be kept as round as a ball, *D.*; var. *inermis rubra monstrosa*, a tree of dwarf growth with blush flowers; var. *inermis rubra*, globe-headed, with white flowers tinged with pink.

The ROSE OR MOSS LOCUST (*R. hispida*) is a native species of low irregular habit, but producing elegant racemes of rose-colored flowers in June and later, *C.* The variety *grandiflora* is extremely attractive when in bloom, the flowers, as well as the foliage, being much larger than those of the species.

The Clammy Locust (*R. viscosa*), a native, is a beautiful, compact grower, with fine foliage, and pale-pink, odorless flowers; slightly tender in the far North, *D.* A kind offered in some catalogues as the

JAPANESE ACACIA (*Acacia Nemu*) is said to be entirely distinct, and described as having handsome rose-colored flowers and delicate foliage.

THE HONEY LOCUST. *Gleditschia.* B.

The COMMON HONEY LOCUST (*G. triacanthos*) is a tree with elegant foliage, and which, with proper shearing, is one of our best hardy hedge plants. *B.*

There are several Asiatic species, embracing the Caspian Honey Locust (*G. Caspica*), of strong growth and irregular habit, with large foliage and white flowers, *B;* and the Chinese Honey Locust (*G. Sinensis*).

The THORNLESS HONEY LOCUST (*G. triacanthos*, var. *inermis*) is a small, globe-headed tree, with elegant foliage, *D.*

The WEEPING HONEY LOCUST (var. *Bujotii*) is a variety of the common three-thorned species, of graceful, slightly pendulous habit; liable to winter-kill in the North, unless growing where well protected.

THE PERSIMMON. *Diospyros.*

The AMERICAN PERSIMMON (*D. Virginiana*) is the hardiest of the Persimmons, and this needs protection when young, in the North. Large, smooth, thickish leaves, and crab-apple-like fruit, that is edible after being severely frosted.

The JAPAN PERSIMMON (*D. Kaki*), and the European Persimmon (*D. Lotus*), both possess fine ornamental qualities, but are not to be considered as hardy north of Richmond. The former has a reputation for affording good edible fruit.

THE NETTLE TREE. *Celtis.* B.

The AMERICAN NETTLE TREE OR HACKBERRY (*C. occidentalis*) is a desirable tree for ornament, with leaves resembling, in part, both the Elm and Apple, *B.* There are also several varieties of this.

The EUROPEAN NETTLE TREE (*C. australis*) is an interesting tree of vigorous habit, with long, slender branches and dark-green leaves.

THE CERCIDIPHYLLUM. *Cercidiphyllum.* B.

C. JAPONICUM, the only species in cultivation, is a recent introduction from Northern Japan, and related to the Magnolias. Prof. Sargent says that it is perfectly hardy about Boston, and of great promise. Foliage small, compact, and graceful. Flowers small and inconspicuous.

THE FLOWERING APPLE AND MOUNTAIN ASH. *Pyrus.* B.–C.

The Flowering Apple and the Mountain Ash, both belonging to the same genus, are herewith placed under one head. Of the former,

The CHINESE DOUBLE ROSE-FLOWERING CRAB (*P. spectabilis*) is a handsome growing tree, with attractive, fragrant flowers in May. *C.* There is a variety of this with pale, semi-double flowers.

The GARLAND FLOWERING CRAB (*P. coronaria*) is one of our most delightful, small, native trees. Covered in the spring with blush-colored flowers, which load the air with delicious fragrance for a long distance.

Other ornamental forms are Rivers' Semi-double Crab, the Aucuba-leaved, and the Double-flowering Apple.

The Mountain Ash section of the genus affords a number of fine ornamental trees.

The EUROPEAN MOUNTAIN ASH (*P. aucuparia*) is an excellent, handsome tree, of compact form, showing an abundance of scarlet berries from July until winter, *C.* There are several varieties of this, including the Weeping Mountain Ash (var. *pendula*), a valuable sort on account of its curious habit of growth, *D.,* and two dwarfs that are handsome.

The AMERICAN MOUNTAIN ASH (*P. Americana*) resembles the European in many respects, but is less desirable on the whole, *B.* The Elder-leaved Mountain Ash (*P. sambucifolia*) is another native, with pleasing foliage, *B.* The Hybrid Mountain Ash (*P. hybrida*) is a choice tree, with fine, large, grayish leaves, which produce a handsome effect.

The OAK-LEAVED MOUNTAIN ASH (*P. quercifolia*) is a handsome sort of vigorous habit, and with beautiful lobed leaves of bright green, *B.* The Golden-striped and the Golden Hybrid Mountain Ash, and some other varieties not included here, are valuable only in large collections.

THE OSAGE ORANGE. *Maclura aurantiaca. B.*

A native tree of spreading, picturesque habit, and handsome, orange-like foliage, which gives to it a pleasing appearance. Well suited for making hedges in any but the northernmost parts of the country.

THE SASSAFRAS. *Sassafras officinale. B.*

This tree, well known for its spicy bark, is very handsome for small pleasure grounds, if grown in a warm, rich soil. The foliage, which is small and usually two and three-lobed, is of a soft texture and has a warm green color. There is a peculiar beauty in the soft outlines, and lights and shades of this tree, that renders it quite distinct in appearance.

AMELANCHIER. *Mespilus, Medlar.* B.–F.

To simplify matters, I bring together here the ornamental species of the kinds above named in the head. They are all closely related to, and somewhat resemble, the apple and thorns in leaf and forms of growth.

SERVICE-BERRY, SNOWY MESPILUS, SHAD-FLOWER AND JUNE-BERRY, are names used in different localities for *Amelanchier Canadensis*. A small native tree, which is especially variable in size, character of its leaves, and abundance of its flowers; the var. *Botryapium* is one of the most pleasing, and in spring is covered with a profusion of snow-white flowers. The Common European species (*A. vulgaris*) is sometimes cultivated. It has smooth leaves and small, white flowers.

The MEDLAR (*Mespilus Germanica*) is a small tree with curious tortuous branches, and large, white flowers. It is sometimes grown in hedges in Europe, and produces a fruit of little value, *C.*

ORNAMENTAL CHERRIES, PLUMS, ALMONDS, AND PEACHES. *Prunus.* B.–F.

Formerly the Cherry, Plum, Almond, and Peach were placed in different genera. Sometime ago, botanists united the Cherry (*Cerasus*) with the Plum under *Prunus*, and the more modern authors have placed the Almond (*Amygdalus*), the Peach (*Persica*), and Apricot (*Armeniaca*) all under *Prunus*. All of these have double-flowered varieties, which are highly ornamental and deserve more attention from planters than they have yet received.

The DOUBLE FLOWERING CHERRY (*P. avium, fl. pl.*), is extremely handsome when in bloom, being so densely covered with large, pure white, double flowers as to hide the branches.

The WEEPING CHERRIES.—The Common Weeping Cherry belongs to the preceding species, and is a pleasing variety with drooping branches. The Weeping Bigarreau Cherry is a good sized, handsome tree, with graceful, pendant branches. The Dwarf Weeping Cherry is a very small, beautiful tree, suited to small plots. The Weeping Sour Cherry is a fine drooping variety, and a new double Cherry from Japan with rose-colored flowers, is regarded as a promising ornamental tree.

The EUROPEAN BIRD CHERRY (*P. Padus*), belonging to the same section of the genus as our Wild Cherries, is an admirable lawn tree. It has a handsome form, good foliage, and a profusion of white flowers in long racemes in May, *C.*

There are two fine forms with variegated leaves:

The AUCUBA-LEAVED CHERRY with deep-green leaves, speckled and splashed with yellowish-white, *C.;* and the Variegated Bird Cherry, with leaves dotted and blotched with yellow ; both have a slender drooping habit, *C.*

Of the FLOWERING PLUMS, those bearing the most resemblance to the common Plum are : the Double Flowering Sloe (*P. spinosa, flore pleno*), from Japan, with daisy-like, white flowers in spring, followed by purple fruit, *E.;* and the Common Double Flowering Plum (*P. domestica, fl. pl.*), *E.*

Some dwarf Plums are among our best ornamental shrubs. The Double Flowering Plum (*P. triloba*) is a very fine, hardy shrub, with beautiful, delicate-pink, semi-double flowers, arranged closely along the branches, and forming compact spikes. *P. tomentosa*, from Japan, is a fine shrub, with plaited leaves, but inconspicuous flowers, *G. P. Sinensis*, of some, is a distinct species, with small flowers early in the spring, followed by nectarine-like fruit.

The Flowering Almonds belong here. Some of the so-called Flowering Almonds are properly plums or cherries. One of the best known is the

Double White Flowering Almond, a small tree with a great profusion of double white flowers in early spring. It has very rich foliage. The Rose-flowered Almond resembles the preceding, except in the color of its flowers.

The Dwarf Flowering Almonds (*Prunus* [*amygdalus*] *nana*) are very old garden favorites, their double flowers are rose-colored or white, and produced in great profusion.

The Flowering Peaches, when properly pruned, are very handsome, but if left to grow at will, form unsightly broad heads. There is a double white and a double rose-colored variety, and one in which the flowers are curiously variegated, being white and rose-colored upon the same tree. The Blood-leaved Peach has its foliage in spring and early summer of a bright, crimsom color, but later it turns to a dull green.

THE LABURNUM OR GOLDEN CHAIN. *Laburnum.* C.

Ornamental, profuse-flowering, small trees and shrubs, which succeed in almost any soil, but at the North are apt to be injured in winter.

The Common Laburnum or Golden Chain (*Laburnum vulgare*) has glossy, trifoliate leaves and drooping racemes of yellow flowers, which give the tree a very rich appearance.

Alschinger's Laburnum (*L. Alschingeri*), and Park's Laburnum (*L. vulgare*, var. *Parkii*), are distinct forms, and produce similar racemes of yellow flowers. The Oak-leaved Laburnum (var. *quercifolia*), and the Large-leaved (var. *macrophylla*), are other varieties of merit.

The PURPLE-FLOWERED LABURNUM, so called, belongs to the closely related genus *Cytisus* (*C. purpureus*). It produces racemes of golden flowers. The Alpine, or Scotch Laburnum (*L. alpinum*), is regarded as the hardiest of the genus; of dense, irregular, spreading form, reaching size *B* in good soil. Foliage large, smooth, and dark. Flowers golden-yellow, in long racemes.

THE HORNBEAM. *Carpinus.* *C.*

The AMERICAN HORNBEAM (*C. Americana*) is a small, neat-looking tree, with wiry branches and leaves that resemble those of the Beech. Handsome whether planted singly or in groups. It is also a good hedge plant.

The ENGLISH HORNBEAM (*C. Betulus*) resembles the above, but is of stronger growth, *C*. There is a dwarf variety of this (var. *pendula*), which, when grafted standard high, makes a beautiful, round-headed tree.

The HOP-HORNBEAM OR IRON-WOOD, belongs to a closely-related genus (*Ostrya Virginica*). It has a resemblance to the foregoing, but is more upright and slender, with smaller leaves. It is valuable as an ornamental tree on account of its light, graceful spray.

THE KŒLREUTERIA. *Kœlreuteria paniculata.*

A low-growing tree, with fine, brilliant-green, pinnate foliage, which turns to a rich yellow in the autumn. Flowers golden-yellow, produced in spreading clusters in mid-summer, and with showy, inflated seed-pods in autumn. A native of China.

THE JUDAS-TREE OR RED-BUD. *Cercis.* *C.–E.*

The AMERICAN JUDAS-TREE (*C. Canadensis*) is a small tree, with large, glossy, heart-shaped leaves, and in spring, before the foliage comes, is covered all along the branches with delicate pink flowers in great profusion, *C.*

The ORIENTAL JUDAS-TREE (*C. Chinensis; C. Japonica* in some catalogues), is another valuable kind, more dwarf and compact than the American, with thick, roundish leaves, of a dark-green color, and has larger and brighter flowers, *E.*

THE VIRGINIAN OR WHITE FRINGE.   *Chionanthus Virginica.   C.*

This is a handsome small tree or bush, with large, glossy, acutely-elliptical leaves, and drooping racemes of fringe-like, white flowers in the spring ; a great favorite generally.

THE DOGWOOD.   *Cornus.   C.–G.*

The FLOWERING DOGWOOD (*C. florida*) is a fine, small tree, with glossy, grayish-green foliage, that turns to a most attractive red in autumn. Its chief charm is its large, pure-white flowers, produced in spring before the leaves appear. The showy portion of the flowers is really the bracts or appendages surrounding the clusters, the real flowers being small and inconspicuous. Delights in a well-drained, rich soil, *C.*

The WEEPING DOGWOOD, said to be a variety of *C. florida,* is described as being handsome, of upright growth, and pendulous branches, with flowers and foliage resembling the parent.

The ROUND-LEAVED DOGWOOD (*C. circinata*) has roundish leaves, downy beneath ; young shoots green, blotched with purple ; small, white flowers in flat cymes, *G.*

ALTERNATE-LEAVED DOGWOOD (*C. alternifolia*), a beautiful shrub, but it may be trained in a tree form ;

it has yellowish-white flowers, in May and June, and blue-black fruit in autumn, *E.*

The RED-BRANCHED OR OSIER DOGWOOD (*C. sanguinea*), a species from Europe. It is a large, spreading bush, with blood-red bark that is conspicuous in winter, and especially so in early spring. White flowers, *G.*

The RED SIBERIAN DOGWOOD, (*C. Sibirica,* var. *variegata*), is a remarkable new shrub, with richer colored bark than the last named, and with leaves slightly margined with a silvery color ; undoubtedly a great acquisition.

The CORNELIAN CHERRY (*C. Mas.*), an European species, somewhat resembling the Flowering Dogwood, and bearing yellowish flowers early in the spring, with edible fruit later. The Variegated Cornelian Cherry (var. *variegata*) has richly variegated leaves, more than one half of their surface being of a clear silvery-white, giving the shrub an exceedingly handsome and distinct appearance, which renders it unequalled as a silvery-hued shrub, *F.*

THE THORN. *Cratægus. C. H.*

There are many species of thorns in cultivation, not one of which is undesirable where room is abundant. All are well adapted for growing in lawns of small area. Some of the best are the double-flowering varieties, with red, pink, and white flowers.

The COMMON HAWTHORN (*C. Oxyacantha*) is the celebrated English hedge plant. The Arbutus-leaved, Apple-leaved, Pear-leaved, Glossy-leaved, Parsley-leaved, and many others are varieties of this species. Nearly all are of compact growth, and will grow in any soil and situation, producing their very attractive flowers most freely. They readily bear pruning, and are well adapted for hedges.

The EVERGREEN THORN (*C. Pyracantha*) is a handsome, small species, that retains its dark-green foliage through the winter, it has purplish and white flowers, and red fruit ; there is a variety with white fruit.

THE BUCKTHORN. *Rhamnus catharticus.*

Is a fine shrub for hedges. It has small, dark leaves, and inconspicuous greenish-white flowers. There is a variety of Buckthorn (var. *latifolius*) with larger leaves.

THE WITCH HAZEL. *Hamamelis Virginica.*

A native, tall shrub, with somewhat downy leaves, in appearance resembling those of the Hazel. It is notable for producing its curious yellow flowers late in autumn, just as the leaves are falling, at the same time the capsules from the flowers of the previous year open and eject their seeds. Some recent introductions from Japan belonging to this genus are little known as yet.

THE SUMACH. *Rhus. E.*

The PURPLE FRINGE (*R. Cotinus*), known also as the Venetian Sumach, Smoke-Tree, Mist-Tree, Wig-Tree, etc., is an old favorite, which is prized for its handsome appearance at mid-summer and later, when it is covered with its large, cloud-like, masses of "fringe." These are really the enlarged branching and very hairy flower-stalks of abortive flowers. They are often tinged with red, and are very ornamental. The foliage has a fresh appearance and in autumn takes on rich colors. It should be grown in the form of a shrub, *E.*

OSBECK'S CHINESE SUMACH (*R. Osbeckii*) is a new species with handsome foliage, that turns to attractive colors in autumn.

The FRAGRANT SUMACH (*R. aromatica*) is a showy, early-flowering shrub, the flowers of which are succeeded by showy berries. Several other native Sumachs are desirable for ornamental planting. Of these the

STAGHORN SUMACH (*R. typhina*) is especially note-worthy on account of its elegant, compound leaves, which assume colors of great brilliancy in autumn, at which time it bears its bunches of crimson berries, *C.*

The CUT-LEAVED SUMACH (*R. glabra,* var. *laciniata*) is a variety of our most common native species, with re-markably handsome, fern-like leaves, which are dark-green above, and glaucous below.

THE LILAC. *Syringa. E.*

The Lilac, represented by a large number of species, and innumerable varieties, is one of our most valuable ornamental shrubs. Of the easiest culture in any or-dinarily good soil, with attractive foliage and very fragrant flowers, it is rarely the case in adorning grounds, what-ever may be their size, that some of the Lilacs cannot be used to good advantage. Some are disposed to send up sprouts from the roots, but these may be easily kept down. They can be grown to a tree form with careful pruning, but should generally be trained with a low head. The well-known

COMMON LILAC (*S. vulgaris*), with purple and white flowers, still ranks high in value. From this have sprung many varieties, some of which are improvements on the species. Some of these have larger flowers than the parent, or differently colored ; others vary in their habit of growth, there being both dwarf and stronger growing sorts, and there is one variety called Golden-leaved Lilac (var. *variegata*), with large, yellowish-green foliage, which is valuable for creating contrasts of color. The Asiatic species possess great value, being, as a rule, more graceful and delicate in form, and with smaller leaves than those of the Common Lilac.

The PERSIAN LILAC (*S. Persica*) has large panicles of somewhat loosely arranged, dark lilac flowers. This forms a bush of great beauty when grown where it has a chance to develop.   The Persian White Lilac (var. *alba*) is like the preceding, except in the color of the flowers.   There is also a Cut-leaved variety.

The CHINESE LILAC (*S. dubia*, also *S. Chinensis* of some), is a species resembling the Persian, but with longer leaves, and of which there are several varieties, including reddish, purple, and white.

EMOD'S LILAC (*S. Emodi*) is a distinct and choice Chinese species, which assumes a tree-like form, and has white flowers, *D*.

The ROUEN OR FRENCH RED LILAC (*S. dubia*, var. *Rothomagensis*), is said to be a hybrid between the Common Lilac and the Persian, and embodies perhaps more good qualities than any other Lilac.   The flowers are reddish, in numerous, large panicles, *C*.

JOSIKA'S OR CHIONANTHUS-LEAVED LILAC (*S. Josikæa*) is a distinct and remarkably handsome variety, of strong, upright growth, and with long, rich, shining leaves.   Flowers purple, appearing after other kinds have flowered.

VERSCHAFFELT'S LILAC (*S. Verschaffelti*) is another distinct variety, with flowers in large compact panicles, dark-red in the bud, changing to lilac as they open.

THE CARAGANA OR PEA-TREE.   *Caragana*.   *E*.

Low growing trees or shrubs from Asia, with peculiar acacia-like, light-green leaves, with a golden hue, and which contrast in a marked manner with most other shrubs.   Flowers yellowish.

The SIBERIAN PEA-TREE (*C. Altagana*) is of pleasing habit and quite hardy.

The CHINESE PEA-TREE (*C. Chamlagu*) throws up erect branches at first, but later they droop.

The ARBORESCENT PEA-TREE (*C. arborescens*) is upright in habit, but always remains small. There are still other kinds named in some lists.

THE ELDER. *Sambucus.* *E.–G.*

Large shrubs, with ornamental foliage, flowers and fruit, that entitle them to a place in large collections of shrubs. With the exception of the Cut-leaved they are rather coarse for small lawns.

EUROPEAN ELDER (*S. nigra*), of large, irregular, picturesque growth, with broad cymes of white flowers in mid-summer. Very popular in European parks, *E.* Golden-leaved Elder (var. *aurea*), a handsome, but rather coarse shrub, with bright, golden-splashed foliage, and sweet, white flowers in July. Variegated-leaved Elder (var. *variegata*), leaves edged and mottled with yellowish-white. Improved by severe pruning occasionally, as the variegation on the young growth is the most attractive, *G.* Cut-leaved Elder (var. *laciniata*), a valuable cut-leaved shrub, with elegantly divided leaves, *G.*

The COMMON AMERICAN ELDER (*S. Canadensis*) is useful for ornament in large grounds, and can usually be procured without cost.

SNOWDROP OR SILVER-BELL TREE. *Halesia.* *E.*

The FOUR-WINGED SNOWDROP OR SILVER-BELL (*H. tetraptera*) is a graceful shrub, bearing a profusion of pretty, white, bell-shaped flowers, resembling somewhat those of the little snowdrop, in May, and are followed by curious four-winged fruit. Thrives in poor soil and does not object to moist places.

The TWO-WINGED SNOWDROP (*H. diptera*) has larger leaves than the last named, and is less common.

THE HOP-TREE OR SHRUBBY TREFOIL.   *Ptelea trifoliata.* E.

A large shrub or small tree of rapid growth, with handsome, smooth, trifoliate leaves in June, clustered whitish flowers followed by seed-pods, which in taste and odor resemble hops. Makes a handsome low tree, if trained with a single stem.

THE TAMARISK.   *Tamarix.   E.*

Shrubs of strong, irregular growth, with delicate, feathery foliage, somewhat resembling the Juniper, and with the branches covered with fine, pink flowers in June. The general growth is coarse. There are several species which do not differ much in appearance. The most generally cultivated is *T. Gallica.*

THE SPICEBUSH.   *Lindera Benzoin.   E.*

A large and rather pleasing native shrub, with light-green foliage, and small clusters of yellowish flowers, appearing in early spring before the leaves.

THE ARALIA.   *Aralia.*

A genus comprising small, singular-looking trees, with large, showy, and much divided leaves. Useful for creating "tropical" effects in gardens. Of free growth, but needing a little protection in exposed places.

The ORIENTAL ARALIA (*A. Chinensis,* also called *A. Japonica*), is of dwarf, spreading form, with prickly stems and shoots, large feathery leaves, and white flowers.

The MANDSCHURIAN ARALIA is a variety of the foregoing (*A. Chinensis,* var. *elata,* which has been called *Dimorphanthus Mandshuricus*), is a Chinese species, with hairy and prickly bipinnate leaves.

ANGELICA TREE or HERCULES' CLUB (*A. spinosa*), a native kind, with stout stems, and very large leaves; throws up suckers from the roots.

SPINDLE-TREE OR BURNING-BUSH. *Euonymus.* E.–G.

A genus with mostly pleasing foliage of a fresh green color, showing to fine advantage among other shrubs. They nearly all bear a profusion of crimson and scarlet or ornamental fruit, which renders the trees very attractive in the autumn, and it is to this that most of them owe their common names.

The STRAWBERRY BUSH (*E. Americanus*), a small bush, rarely over five feet high, with rich, shining leaves, and medium-sized scarlet berries, *E.*

The BURNING-BUSH or SPINDLE-TREE (*E. atropurpureus*), a handsome native species, of erect habit and fresh, green foliage, with bright crimson, or purplish fruit.

The BROAD-LEAVED EUONYMUS (*E. latifolius*) is an exceedingly fine European species, with broad, glossy leaves, and large, deep-red fruit.

The WINGED EUONYMUS (*E. alatus*) from Japan is interesting on account of the wings, that extend down the stems.

The EUROPEAN BURNING-BUSH (*E. Europæus*) is a a large species, with handsome foliage and fruit. Of this one there are several varieties that are quite ornamental, such as the Purple-leaved Euonymus (var. *atropurpureus*), with purple leaves in autumn; the White-fruited Euonymus; the Linear-leaved Euonymus, with narrow, dark-colored foliage, and of small size; the Dwarf Euonymus, of dwarfish form, with dark-green leaves, *G.*

The handsome, evergreen, Japanese kinds are very desirable where they will stand the winters uninjured.

4

THE ROSE OF SHARON OR SHRUBBY ALTHÆA. *Hibiscus.*
E.–G.

Mostly free-growing shrubs of upright forms, producing showy flowers resembling hollyhocks, in the late summer season, and at a time when few hardy trees and

Fig. 5.—ROSE OF SHARON, VARIEGATED (*Hibiscus Syriacus*, var.)

shrubs are in bloom. To keep them in good shape, they should be closely headed-in annually. The first two winters after planting there should be a liberal coat of coarse litter applied over the roots in the North, to protect them from cold, and after that they will prove very hardy.

All of the many varieties that are now offered in

nurseries, are descendents of *H. Syriacus*, a free flowering, but rather coarse grower. There are single and double flowering varieties of white, red, purple, pink, rose, violet, and other colors, and some are beautifully striped or blotched. The double flowering sorts are generally the handsomest shrubs. One of the most valuable of the double flowering kinds is the Variegated-leaved Hibiscus (fig. 5), with leaves which are conspicuously marked with light-yellow, on a green ground, and one of the very best variegated-leaved shrubs; flowers purple, but not showy, *F.*

THE MOCK ORANGE OR SYRINGA. *Philadelphus.* *E.–H.*

How the name Syringa ever came to stand so improperly, yet generally for this genus, it is hard to tell, and its use both for these shrubs, and for the Lilac, where it rightly belongs, tends to confusion in names. However, it may be said that no collection of shrubs can be considered complete without the presence of the Mock Oranges. They are noted for their sweet and showy, white, or nearly white, flowers, single and double, their handsome and free growth, and their remarkable adaptability to any place and soil.

The COMMON or GARLAND MOCK ORANGE (*P. coronarius*), also called Garland Syringa, is a rapid-growing, slightly coarse shrub, well known for its showy and fragrant, white flowers, *E.* Double-flowering Mock Orange is an attractive semi-double-flowering form of the above. The Dwarf Mock Orange (var. *nana*) is a handsome, and very dwarf-growing variety, more valued for its generally fine and cleanly appearance, than for its flowers, which are shyly produced, *H.* The Golden-leaved Mock Orange is a very pretty dwarf variety, with yellow-tinged foliage; valuable for single specimens, clumps, or for contrasts of foliage, *H.* The Dwarf Double-flowering

Mock Orange (*P. dianthiflora*) is another low-growing variety of great beauty, with fine, double, creamy-white, fragrant flowers.

There are several other species and varieties not varying greatly in general respects from the sorts above described. The Large-flowering Mock Orange (*P. grandiflorus*). Gordon's Late-flowering Mock Orange (*P. Gordonianus*). Red-twigged Mock Orange (*P. sanguineus*), among older sorts, and *P. laxus* with very large flowers; *P. nivalis*, with snowy-white flowers, among recent introductions, are perhaps entitled to special mention on account of their merits.

THE VIBURNUM.　*Viburnum.*　E.–G.

This genus gives us a number of our most valuable and interesting ornamental shrubs. They are perfectly hardy, of easy growth in most any soil, and produce both handsome foliage and flowers. For the sake of variety some may readily be grown to a tree form.

The Common Snowball or Guelder Rose (*V. Opulus sterilis*) is a well known variety, with large, globular cymes of pure-white, sterile flowers, of a very showy character, *E.* The High or Bush Cranberry (*V. Opulus*) is the original form of the Snowball, with coarser foliage and habit of growth, and less showy flowers, the clusters of which have only sterile flowers around the margin; those in the interior of the cyme are not showy, but are followed by scarlet, acid fruit, sometimes used as a substitute for cranberries, *E.* A dwarf variety (var. *nana*) forms a much smaller bush, *H.*

The Japan or Dwarf Snowball (*V. plicatum*) is a shrub of great merit, and is much finer than the common Snowball, with whiter flowers of the same form, a dwarf habit of growth and much handsomer foliage. The leaves are firm, plaited, of a rich green, and contrast finely with the handsome, pure-white flowers, G. Several other introductions from Japan are announced, which are well spoken of.

The NEPAL VIBURNUM (V. Nepalense) is a robust-growing species, with white flowers appearing later than most others.

ROUGH-LEAVED VIBURNUM (V. rugosum) has large, dark-green, rough leaves, and white flowers in cymes, G.

The LANTANA-LEAVED VIBURNUM or HOBBLE BUSH (V. lantanoides), also called the Way-faring Tree ; the Plum-leaved Viburnum (V. prunifolium), the Withe-Rod (V. nudum), and several other native species are also suitable for ornamental planting.

THE BUSH HONEYSUCKLE. *Lonicera.* E.-H.

The Bush Honeysuckles are mostly strong-growing shrubs, of good habit, producing a profusion of fragrant flowers, which are generally followed by ornamental fruit. They thrive in any soil and situation.

The TARTARIAN HONEYSUCKLE (L. Tartarica) is a well-known shrub with pink, and there is a variety with almost white, flowers, E. Varieties of the Tartarian, known as the Large-flowering Honeysuckles, both pink and white, resemble the common, but are more robust in habit and have larger flowers. There is also one with variegated foliage (fig. 6), E.

The FRAGRANT BUSH HONEYSUCKLE (L. fragrantissima) is of low spreading growth, with branches thickly studded, before the leaves appear, with clusters of whitish flowers, having a delicious fragrance, G.

LEDEBOUR'S HONEYSUCKLE (L. Ledebourii) is a distinct and very fine species. The flowers, which are yellow, appear in June, and are followed by showy red bracts, which bear the appearance of flowers ; foliage a rich deep green; a shapely grower, E. Standish's Honeysuckle (*L. Standishii*) has large leaves with April flowers, that are reddish outside and white within, E. The English Fly Honeysuckle (*L. Xylosteum*) has very

Fig. 6.—TARTARIAN HONEYSUCKLE, VARIEGATED (*Lonicera Tartarica* var.)

sweet, pinkish flowers before the leaves come. A dwarf, native species with oval, downy leaves and blue berries, is called the Mountain Honeysuckle (*L. cærulea*), H.

THE STUARTIA.   (*Stuartia*).   E–G.

S. pentagyna is a charming low tree or shrub, resembling the Dogwood somewhat in its foliage, and producing creamy-white, saucer-shaped flowers in summer. A native of the southern mountains, it should be planted only in sheltered places in the Northern States, *E.*

The VIRGINIAN STUARTIA (*S. Virginica*) is another fine species, more dwarf than the preceding kind, but

Fig. 7.—STUARTIA (*Stuartia pentagyna*).

resembling it in form, foliage, and time of flowering. Not hardy north of Virginia, *G.* Several recent introductions from Japan have been reported, which have not been well tested as yet.

THE WEIGELA. *Diervilla.* *E-H.*

A much esteemed genus of flowering shrubs which, while represented by a few natives of little value for any ornament, owes its fame to the handsome introductions from China and Japan, and varieties of these. The Weigelas are good growers, profuse bloomers, and in their foliage always present a rich glow of vigor, that is most pleasing. Mostly erect-growing when young, but changing later to a drooping form. The well-known and handsome

ROSE-COLORED WEIGELA (*D. rosea*), which bears lovely, rose-colored flowers in the greatest profusion in June, is the species from which have sprung either directly or by hybridization with others, most of the excellent sorts now cultivated. Its habit is all that could be desired, *G.* Of the varieties and hybrids there are many, which range in colors from the lightest pink—almost white—through rose and red down to dark reddish-purple and brownish-black, and all are of excellent habit, producing their beautiful flowers with great freedom, and would be sure to prove satisfactory to planters.

The VARIEGATED-LEAVED DWARF WEIGELA is a variety quite similar to the parent in the shape of the leaves and flowers, but of dwarfish habit, and with the foliage variegated with a golden tint, which gives to it a distinct and handsome appearance.

Among other valuable and distinct kinds are several white-flowered sorts, embracing the old White-flowered Weigela (*D. hortensis nivea*), which produces fine blossoms, but is a rather unsatisfactory grower; and the charming New White-flowered Weigela (*D. candida*), which, with its freely produced, pure white flowers and vigorous habit, is destined to rank as one of the best of the Weigelas. The *D. arborea-grandiflora* is a late blooming sort, producing long, tubular, pale-yellow flowers, which change to rose-color, of strong growth with large leaves.

THE BLADDER-NUT. *Staphylea.* *E.*

The AMERICAN BLADDER-NUT (*S. trifolia*) is a native upright shrub, with greenish-striped branches, pinnate leaves, of three to five leaflets each, and small, white flowers in drooping racemes.

ASIATIC BLADDER-NUT (*S. Colchica*) is a handsome spring-flowering shrub, with clusters of fragrant white flowers. The European Bladder-nut (*S. pinnata*) is a native of the south of Europe, resembles our native species in a general way, but rather more vigorous.

THE BLADDER SENNA. *Colutea.* *E.*

The COMMON BLADDER SENNA (*C. arborescens*) is a quick-growing shrub, with fine, light-green, compound leaves, and bright, yellowish, pea-shaped flowers in June and July, followed by bladder-like pods, *E.* The Oriental Bladder Senna (*C. cruenta*) is a smaller species than the last, with reddish-colored flowers. Aleppo Bladder Senna (*C. Halepica*) bears a general resemblance to the first-named; flowers orange-colored.

To keep the Coluteas furnished with branches and foliage at the bottom, they should be freely cut back at times. *C. arborescens* may, however, be readily trained into a very pretty tree.

THE PRIVET. *Ligustrum.* *E.*

The Privets are handsome shrubs, with rich, dark-green leaves of waxy texture, and which come early and hang until the winter; they also produce attractive flowers in early summer. They are well adapted for hedges, and possess the valuable quality of growing and flowering well in partial shade and even under trees. A good, strong soil is preferred by them.

The COMMON PRIVET (*L. vulgare*) has small, shining, dark-green leaves and white flowers in terminal panicles, which are succeeded by small, black berries. Among the varieties of the Common Privet with smallish leaves, are the Box-leaved Privet (var. *buxifolia*), with short, thick leaves. White-berried Privet (var. *leucocarpa*), with white fruit, and the Weeping Privet (var. *pendula*), of weeping habit and quite ornamental, when grafted on other stocks.

There are several varieties with much larger leaves than the common, such as the Oval-leaved Privet (*L. ovalifolium*), and the Laurel-leaved Privet (*L. laurifolium*), all of which are very attractive with rich, waxy-looking foliage, and are pleasing either when grown singly, in groups, or in hedges.

THE OLEASTER, OR WILD OLIVE. *Elæagnus.* E.

The SILVER-LEAVED OLEASTER (*E. argentea*) is a strong-growing, spreading shrub, with delicate, narrow, silvery leaves, that give it a peculiar appearance, and make it very desirable for contrasting with other trees and shrubs. Small yellow flowers in summer.

GARDEN or EUROPEAN OLEASTER (*E. hortensis*) is an elegant species of stronger growth than the former one, and with wider leaves, of a striking silvery color. It is covered in June with small yellow flowers, having bright, silvered calyxes, which give to the shrub increased whiteness at this season. The sweetness of the flowers, which is very pleasant and marked, is wafted for some distance on the air. Very desirable for contrasts; does well on the sea-shore. The Small-flowered Oleaster (var. *nivea*) is a variety of the last, forming a fine compact bush with silvery leaves, and bearing showy fruit. Sometimes used for hedges.

There are several Japanese species, among them *E. longipes*, and other desirable sorts, possessing the general characteristics of the genus.

THE FALSE INDIGO. *Amorpha.* *G–H.*

Large shrubs of open-growing, almost ungainly habit, which are susceptible, however, of improvement in this respect by pruning, and with pleasing, pinnate foliage, that contrasts well with that of most other shrubs. The Common False Indigo (*A. fruticosa*) is a native of the Southern and Western States, but hardy at the North, producing spikes of dark-purple flowers in June, *G.* Fragrant Amorpha (var. *angustifolia*), a hairy shrub, bearing dark-colored flowers in the summer, *G.* The Lead-plant (*A. canescens*), of low growth, has dark-blue flowers in July and August, *H.*

THE WINTERBERRY. *Ilex,* § *Prinos.* *E-G.*

The COMMON WINTERBERRY, or BLACK ALDER (*I. verticillata*), is a fine native shrub, related to the Holly, with glossy-red berries in autumn and early winter; should be planted in peaty soil, *E.* Another species, the Smooth-leaved Winterberry (*I. lævigata*), has berries similar to the preceding, but larger and earlier, *E.* There is also a dwarf evergreen species, known as the Inkberry (*I. glabra*), the fruit of which is black; leaves small and lance-shaped, *G.*

THE BUTTON-BUSH. *Cephalanthus occidentalis.* *G.*

A native shrub, growing in moist places, of rounded form, with thick, glossy leaves, and globular clusters of yellowish-white flowers in July and August. Desirable for planting at the water's edge.

THE CALYCANTHUS. *Calycanthus.* G.

Shrubs of good habit, with handsome, rich foliage ; fragrant wood and flowers, that are prized for their peculiar sweetness, color, and form.

The COMMON CALYCANTHUS (*C. floridus*), also called Carolina Allspice and Sweet-scented Shrub, has soft leaves, downy beneath; double chocolate-colored flowers in June, which possess a rich, strawberry-like fragrance, G.

Of other species, the following are grown for ornament : Glaucous-leaved Calycanthus (*C. glaucus*), with larger and handsomer leaves than the last. Smooth-leaved Calycanthus (*C. lævigatus*); Long-leaved Calycanthus (*C. elongatus*); Large-fruited Calycanthus (*C. macrocarpus*), a Californian species, tender while young.

THE FORSYTHIA OR GOLDEN BELL. *Forsythia.* G.

FORTUNE'S FORSYTHIA (*F. Fortunei*) is one of our best hardy shrubs, of strong-growing habit, handsome foliage, which hangs until late in the autumn, and delightful, yellow, drooping flowers very early in the spring, G. The Weeping Forsythia (*F. suspensa*) is of slender, straggling growth, the branches curving to the ground, or they may be trained like a climber. *F. viridissima* resembles Fortune's in its flowers, but blooms a little earlier, and is of a neat habit, with rich-looking, dark-green foliage, G.

THE HAZEL-NUT OR FILBERT. *Corylus.* G.

The PURPLE-LEAVED HAZEL (*C. Avellana*, var. *purpurea*), is a vigorous shrub, with large purple leaves, which give it a fine appearance, making it valuable for contrasts, G. The American Hazel (*C. Americana*) is an ornamental shrub, producing delicious nuts, and suitable for any large collection of shrubs. The Cut-leaved

Hazel (*C. Avellana laciniata*) has deeply cut foliage, that renders the shrub very ornamental. The Constantinople Hazel (*C. Colurna*) is a strong grower, with large leaves.

THE WHITE ALDER OR CLETHRA. *Clethra.* *G.–H.*

The ALDER-LEAVED CLETHRA (*C. alnifolia*), also called the Sweet Pepper-bush, is a dense-growing, native shrub, with light-green foliage, resembling the Alder, and spikes of sweet, white flowers in mid-summer, of which the honey-bee is fond, *H.* Acuminate-leaved Clethra (*C. acuminata*) is of stronger growth and has larger leaves than the last, *G.*

THE CEANOTHUS. *Ceanothus.* *G.–H.*

Shrubs of rather small value, except for the sake of variety. The New Jersey Tea or American Ceanothus (*C. Americanus*) has small racemes of white flowers from June to August, *H.* *C. thyrsiflorus* and *C. velutinus* are natives of California and Oregon, of sub-evergreen character, *G.*

THE CALLICARPA. *Callicarpa.* *G.*

A genus of low-growing shrubs, mostly tender ever-greens. *C. Americana,* also called the "French Mulberry," is a handsome, somewhat coarse, deciduous shrub, with inconspicuous flowers. followed by violet-colored berries. The Purple Callicarpa (*C. purpurea*) is a species from China and Japan, with rather brilliant, but small, purple flowers in summer. There are others from Asia which must be classed among plants too tender for general planting.

THE BARBERRY. *Berberis.* *G.–H.*

The Barberries are a useful class of shrubs, attractive in their style of growth, their foliage and their fruit. Sometimes they are used in ornamental hedges.

The AMERICAN BARBERRY (*B. Canadensis*) is of erect habit when young, but in time the branches droop. Yellow flowers in spring, followed by showy red berries.

The COMMON EUROPEAN BARBERRY (*B. vulgaris*) is a handsome shrub, the branches of which curve outwards and downwards with exquisite grace. Small, rounded leaves; yellow flowers in the spring, followed by clusters of brilliant fruit, *G.* The Purple-leaved Barberry (var. *purpurea*) resembles the last named kind, but in addition the foliage is of a reddish-violet color throughout the season, serving to make this the most valuable, purple-leaved shrub in cultivation, *H.* There is also a Violet-fruited Barberry (var. *fructu violacea*). The Evergreen Barberries will be found under Mahonia.

THE HYDRANGEA. *Hydrangea.* *G.*

A genus embracing some of the most attractive, large-flowering shrubs in cultivation. The Japanese species are the most valuable for flowers. Of these the following is placed first on the list, because hardy throughout the United States.

The PANICLED HYDRANGEA (*H. paniculata*) is a vigorous-growing species, with upright panicles of white flowers, standing well above the foliage in July. The Large-flowered variety of this, *H. paniculata grandiflora,* is of vigorous, spreading form, with immense pyramidal panicles, a foot or more long, of white flowers that change to pink. The plant delights in rich soil, and when well provided for in this respect, a large bush will sometimes bear from one to two hundred of these large panicles—many bending gracefully downwards.

The other Japanese species, of which the Common or Changeable Hydrangea (*H. Hortensia*) is a type, are not hardy in the North, but are easily grown in boxes, while further South they thrive without protection.

The native Hydrangeas are vigorous, somewhat coarse growers and hardy, with large leaves and showy heads of flowers. They delight in deep soil and moisture. Of these the Oak-leaved Hydrangea (*H. quercifolia*) is a vigorous, shapely grower, with large leaves, downy beneath, and richly tinted in the autumn; white flowers in spikes. *H. arborescens* has ovate, rarely heart-shaped leaves, and white flowers in flattened heads. *H. radiata*, formerly *H. nivea*, is a vigorous grower, with the leaves very white underneath.

THE FLOWERING CURRANT. *Ribes.* G.

Hardy, vigorous, profusely-flowering shrubs, very attractive early in the spring when in bloom, and again in autumn, from the brilliant colors which the foliage assumes.

The YELLOW-FLOWERING or MISSOURI CURRANT (*R. aureum*) is a well known species, with gay and sweet-scented flowers early in the spring and shining leaves.

The CRIMSON-FLOWERING CURRANT (*R. sanguineum*) is a species producing many deep-red flowers in early spring. Of this kind there are several varieties, namely: var. *albidum* with slightly pinkish-white flowers; var. *carnea* with flesh-colored flowers; Double Crimson-flowering Currant (*flore pleno*) with double crimson flowers.

GORDON'S CURRANT (*R. Gordonianum*) a hybrid between the yellow and the crimson sorts, has flowers that combine both yellow and crimson colors, and produced in hanging bunches in May.

THE JAPAN QUINCE. *Pyrus.* G.

The Japan Quinces possess a number of qualities, than which nothing more desirable could be wished for in ornamental shrubs. They are handsome growers and assume fine forms, with rich glossy foliage and flowers, that in point of brilliancy, are unequalled. Whether the shrubs are grown as single specimens, in masses, or mingled with other shrubs, the effect is certain to be fine. They are perfectly adapted for making hedges. The flowers come very early in the spring, covering the entire plant, while the foliage retains its beauty until late in the fall.

THE SCARLET JAPAN QUINCE (*P. Japonica*) is the species, and produces bright scarlet-crimson flowers, with great freedom. Of this there are numerous varieties, which are equally valuable with and closely resemble the parent, except in variation of the colors of the flowers, which range from light-blush to the most brilliant orange-scarlet. A Variegated-leaved sort is mentioned, which I have not seen.

THE COTONEASTER. *Cotoneaster.* *G.–H.*

Attractive shrubs when well grown, but they must be introduced with caution in the Northern States, as most of them would be liable to suffer in winter, unless greatly favored in regard to shelter.

The DOWNY or NEPAUL COTONEASTER (*C. affinis*) is one of the hardiest, with smooth, soft leaves, somewhat resembling those of the pear-tree, and producing white flowers in May.

The FRIGID COTONEASTER (*C. frigida*) is only half hardy; smooth, pointed leaves, and panicles of small, white flowers. The Moneywort-leaved Cotoneaster (*C. nummularia*) is quite hardy as well as handsome. Some nurseries furnish it grafted on Mountain Ash, in which form it makes a beautiful, small, lawn tree. The Round-leaved Cotoneaster (*C. rotundifolia*) is of fine, spreading habit, white flowers, *H.* The Loose-flowering Cotoneaster (*C. laxiflora*) is also a dwarf sort, and has pinkish flowers.

Some of the species are evergreen and of prostrate growth, very suitable for edgings and rock-work, but rather tender. Of these the Box-leaved Cotoneaster (*C. buxifolia*) is very dwarf, producing white flowers; and the Small-leaved Cotoneaster (*C. microphylla*) with attractive dark-green leaves.

ST. JOHN'S WORT. *Hypericum.* G.

Pretty, low shrubs, flowering in July and later, and have the merit of succeeding well in the shade and under the drip of trees.

KALM'S HYPERICUM (*H. Kalmianum*) is a fine, low shrub, with small, oblanceolate leaves, and bright yellow flowers. Shrubby Hypericum (*H. prolificum*), varying but slightly from the above, having clusters of larger flowers. *H. calycinum* is of trailing habit, with yellow flowers. *H. patulum* is a Japanese species, said to be attractive.

THE STYRAX. *Styrax.* G.

The JAPAN STYRAX (*S. Japonica*) is a low-growing shrub of picturesque appearance, with small, Dogwood-like leaves, and white, bell-shaped flowers. Hardy as far north as New York City.

THE EXOCHORDA. *Exochorda grandiflora.* G.

This is a beautiful, hardy shrub from China, closely related to the Spiræas, but distinct from them in habit and appearance. The leaves are a tender-green in color, and the flowers pure white, opening in May.

SPIRÆA. *Spiræa.* E.–H.

A genus containing many species, among which, and their varieties, are a number of fine, ornamental shrubs. Only the most valuable kinds are here noticed.

REEVES' SPIRÆA (*S. Reevesiana*, *S. lanceolata* of some), is one of the best flowering shrubs in cultivation. It has a graceful, slightly drooping habit, and narrow, pointed leaves of good color. The plant in June is covered with clusters of pure-white flowers, making it highly attractive, *H*.

FORTUNE'S SPIRÆA (*S. callosa*). It was at one time supposed that this, *S. callosa*, and *S. Fortunei* were the same, but they are now regarded as distinct. Fortune's name has become in the catalogues well fixed to this plant, though it really belongs to *S. Fortunei*. All confusion may be avoided by the use of the scientific name, *S. callosa*. It is a fine species, bearing large corymbs of rose-colored flowers for a long time. There is a white-flowered variety which is more dwarf, and flowers at intervals all through the season, *H*.

DOUGLAS'S SPIRÆA (*S. Douglasii*. S. Menziesii, and S. Eximia of the catalogues, are at most varieties of this). A fine species of upright habit, with long panicles of rose-colored flowers in June, *G*.

PLUM-LEAVED SPIRÆA, DOUBLE. (*S. prunifolia, fl. pl.*), a highly esteemed shrub from Japan, densely covered in spring with double-white, daisy-like flowers. Its fine, glossy leaves assume brilliant tints in autumn, *G*.

THUNBERG'S SPIRÆA (*S. Thunbergii*), a distinct and remarkably fine species of picturesque habit. The delicate, very narrow leaves, are of a tender green color, which in autumn change to reddish shades. Produces an abundance of white flowers in May, *H*.

GOLDEN-LEAVED SPIRÆA (a variety of *S. opulifolia*, as it was formerly called, but the species is now placed in the genus *Neillia*). A robust variety of the well-known Nine-bark; the foliage has a yellow tinge especially early in the season, *E*.

BILLARD'S SPIRÆA (*S. salicifolia,* var. *Billardi*), a

golden variety of our well-known Meadow-sweet, with very showy, pink flowers all summer, *F*.

MOUNTAIN ASH-LEAVED SPIRÆA (*S. sorbifolia*) a vigorous species, with large, light-green, pinnate leaves, and immense, plume-like panicles of white flowers, very ornamental in the bud. Early summer, *E*. Other species of Spiræa are given under Herbaceous Plants.

THE ROSE. *Rosa.* *G–H.*

It is impossible within the limits of the present work, to touch very fully on the Rose, for it is a subject that might well occupy an entire book. As there are a number of excellent works devoted exclusively to Rose culture, the necessary information respecting kinds and culture is easily found. Still I present some notes on the various classes of Roses in cultivation, and also throughout the book give such brief hints on culture and other points, as may be useful to amateurs.

It may be remarked, that provided the soil is sufficiently well drained to be free from standing water, almost any garden soil, with good preparation, (see Part IV), will answer for Roses. All budded roses should, in planting, be set so deep that the junction of the stock and the rose will be two or three inches below the surface of the soil, so that the root may give the least amount of trouble from sprouting. The Tree Roses, which are so popular in Europe, are comparatively worthless in America, owing to the bad effects of our hot summers on the long stem.

As to insects, "these are the bugbears," as Mr. H. B. Ellwanger, a leading American authority on the Rose, says, " which prevent many from cultivating the Queen of Flowers, but they offer little discouragement to loyal subjects, for generally it is only the careless and indolent who suffer from these pests." In Part V of this book directions are given for destroying insects on Roses.

The HYBRID PERPETUAL, or HYBRID REMONTANT ROSES (*R. Damascena*). These are, all things considered, the most desirable class of hardy Roses for garden culture. The plants are, as a rule, when fairly treated, vigorous in habit, and producing flowers, that for perfect form, fragrance, handsome and brilliant colors are unequalled. Although the name would indicate that they are perpetual bloomers, this is not strictly the case. All bloom profusely in June, and some of the more prolific ones yield a scattering crop of flowers later in the season, with an increase in the autumn. Although quite hardy, it is best to protect with straw in the winter. They should be planted in a rich soil. Of this class, there are more than one thousand named varieties now in existence.

The MOSS ROSES (*R. centifolia muscosa*), a well-known and much esteemed class, which receive their name from the delicate, mossy growth, that appears on the calyx or flower-cup. The flowers are most prized when in the bud state, but some of the kinds are very attractive when open. The so-called Perpetual Moss Roses, are as a class inferior, with the perpetual quality lacking. All delight in liberal culture.

The YELLOW, or AUSTRIAN ROSES (*R. lutea*), are a distinct and attractive class, numbering but few varieties. These are usually budded on the stock of some strong growing kinds.

The COMMON JUNE, or SUMMER ROSES, a class of hardy Roses, which yield an abundant crop of flowers in many colors in June. Some of the best White Roses come under this head. As a rule, these produce flowers under circumstances that would be unfavorable to other kinds; still they will repay good treatment in the matter of soil and cultivation.

The CLIMBING ROSES. There are a number of differ-

ent species of these, which possess a well-known value
for covering walls, trellises, etc. The Prairie Roses (*R.
rubifolia*), are the most valuable class of climbers, and,
unlike most others, are perfectly hardy in the Northern
States.

The BOURBON ROSES (*R. Bourboniana*) belong to
the half-hardy division of the so-called Monthly Roses;
being the hardiest class of these, and usually living
through the winter with slight protection, in all but the
more northern parts of the country, if growing on dry
soil. Of vigorous growth, rich, luxuriant foliage, and
large, well-shaped, fragrant flowers of good colors, and
produced in clusters nearly all summer.

The HYBRID TEA ROSES (*R. Indica odorata hybrida*).
These are hybrids between the tender Tea Roses and the
Hybrid Perpetuals, which have only lately been brought
out. Originating from such sources, much is to be expected from them, and so far the flowers have certainly
proved very fine, while in hardiness it is believed they
may equal the Bourbons, or perhaps the more tender Hybrid Perpetuals.

The HYBRID NOISETTE ROSES (*R. Noisettiana hybrida*), mostly crosses between Remontant, Bourbon, and
Noisette Roses, and of the same general hardiness as the
Bourbons. The flowers are mostly white, or tinted, of
small size but good form, and very freely produced in
quickly succeeding crops throughout the growing season.

The BENGAL, or CHINA ROSES (*R. Indica*), a class
of free Summer-flowering or Monthly Roses, with small,
bright-colored flowers and buds, which show up brilliant-
ly as seen from a distance, as well as near by. The
flowers are usually semi-double to double. Require protection in the North.

The TEA ROSES (*R. Indica odorata*). These are more
tender than any of the previously named classes, and can-

not be depended upon for keeping over winter in the Northern States, no matter how well protected. But the plants may be potted and housed in the green-house, or a cold pit at the approach of winter, and then be set out again in the next spring with good results. The Teas are in many respects the most delightful of all Roses, and it is well worth while to be at some trouble in thus keeping them over. They are almost perpetually in bloom when in a growing condition.

THE BRAMBLE. *Rubus.* *H.*

Clumps of Bramble-bushes, while they might seem out of place in small grounds where everything introduced should be of the choicest kind, still they look very well in the Wild Garden, with their free wild habits and really attractive flowers.

The PURPLE BRAMBLE (*R. odoratus*), also called Flowering Raspberry, forms a clump of vigorous canes, which produce showy, fragrant flowers of a rich purple color for a long time in summer, *H.*

The WHITE BRAMBLE (*R. Nutkanus*) has coarse, toothed leaves, and fewer flowers than the above; the petals are narrow and white, *H.*

The DOUBLE BLACKBERRY (*R. fruticosus*) has curious, fine, double flowers, or masses of narrow petals. The Cut, or Parsley-leaved Bramble (var. *laciniatus*), is of low trailing habit, and produces palatable fruit. *R. cratægifolius* is of robust erect habit, with large leaves of a deep-green color, turning to a dark-red in autumn.

THE AZALEA. *Azalea.* *G–H.*

The Native Azaleas are attractive shrubs, producing umbelled clusters of showy flowers; they are most effective in the garden when planted in clumps. These plants are much prized abroad, being especially very common in English and Dutch gardens. They require a soil containing a good share of leaf mould or muck, and do not object to partial shade. Some of the foreign varieties are only half-hardy.

Of natives, all of which flower early in the season, the SMOOTH AZALEA (*A. arborea*) has thickish leaves, and sweet, white and rose-colored flowers. *H. G.*

The CLAMMY or SWAMP AZALEA (*A. viscosa*), also called White Swamp Honeysuckle, has rich, green foliage, and rose-tinted flowers. There is a variation of the common type with paler, often whitish green leaves, and a dwarfish growth, *H.*

The PURPLE AZALEA, or PINXTER FLOWER (*A. nudiflora*), is of dwarf habit, with showy flowers, varying from flesh-color to pink and purple, *H.*

The FLAME-COLORED AZALEA (*A. calendulacea*) has large, changeable, orange-colored blossoms. *H.*

A. mollis, and *A. Pontica*, are Asiatic species, the former with numerous varieties, and yielding large, showy flowers, and the latter with yellow flowers. These need thorough protection in the North in winter. The Belgian or Ghent Azaleas are a beautiful class of hybrids, between *A. Pontica* and the American species. There are a multitude of handsome varieties, mostly in the line of yellow, orange, scarlet, crimson, rose, pink, and white colors, and some are fragrant. This class are nearly hardy in the North.

THE DEUTZIA. *Deutzia. G–H.*

The Deutzias are valuable low shrubs from Japan, that are universally esteemed for their hardiness, good forms, and free-flowering habits, producing a great profusion of delicately-formed, white, or tinted flowers in June.

The GRACEFUL, or SLENDER DEUTZIA (*D. gracilis*),

is of low, compact growth, with pure white flowers; may be sheared to a perfect globe, *H.* There is a variegated form of this that possesses but little value.

The CRENATE-LEAVED DEUTZIA (*D. crenata*) is of stronger growth than the last named species, with white flowers tinged with pink, *H.* The Double-flowering Deutzia (var. *flore pleno*), a variety of the last, with handsome double-white flowers tinged with pink, in racemes four or five inches long, and coming in bloom somewhat late, *H.* There are several other varieties of this valuable species, var. *flore albo pleno*, with pure white, double flowers; var. *purpureo pleno*, with double, purple-tinged flowers ; the variety, Pride of Rochester, has larger and more double white flowers than the common double.

The ROUGH-LEAVED DEUTZIA (*D. scabra*) is the strongest grower of the genus, with pure white flowers freely produced. It is much less common than *D. crenata*, which is often sent out for it, *G.* There are some others, but they vary little from those described.

THE SNOWBERRY, OR WAXBERRY. *Symphoricarpus. G-H.*

The Snowberry, or the White-fruited Waxberry (*S. racemosus*), is a well-known shrub of good quality, but valued chiefly for the snow-white waxy berries it bears in the latter part of the season.

The RED-FRUITED WAXBERRY, or INDIAN CURRANT (*S. vulgaris*), is a handsomer shrub than the last, with gracefully curving branches, small, round leaves, but with inconspicuous reddish fruit. There is a pleasing Variegated-leaved Waxberry, a form of the last, with golden mottled foliage, rendering the plant very effective for contrasting with other shrubs, *H.*

THE JAPAN GLOBE-FLOWER, OR CORCHORUS. *Kerria.* H.

Very desirable small shrubs of compact growth, if occasionally pruned. The Japan Corchorus (*K. Japonica*) is a slender green-branched shrub, with pointed leaves and globular, double, yellow flowers. The Silver-leaved Corchorus (var. *foliis variegatis*) is a handsome, low, variegated-leaved shrub, of excellent quality, and producing a fine effect when planted to contrast with other shrubs.

THE ANDROMEDA. *Andromeda.* H.

A genus of deciduous and evergreen native shrubs, seldom seen in our gardens, but highly esteemed in European collections of "American Plants." By using some muck in the soil—aiming to imitate the soils of their natural habitats—they may be made to thrive very successfully almost anywhere.

A. Mariana, known as the Stagger-Bush, has glossy oval leaves, and nodding clusters of white flowers; grows wild in sandy, low places.

The FREE-BLOOMING ANDROMEDA (*A. floribunda*), and the Marsh Andromeda (*A. polifolia*) are evergreen species, but differing greatly. The former is a very leafy and charming evergreen shrub, bearing an abundance of white flowers, *G–H*; the latter a very small bush, rarely exceeding a foot and a half in hight, with thick linear leaves, white beneath. Both are hardy.

CATESBY'S ANDROMEDA, botanically separated from Andromeda, and now *Leucothoë Catesbæi*, is also evergreen, with long, recurving branches, ovate-lanceolate leaves and white flowers.

The LEATHER-LEAF (*Cassandra calyculata*) is closely related to the Andromedas, and still classed with them by some. It is a small branching shrub, with dusty-

5

looking, oblong leaves, and pretty, white flowers in a one-sided cluster, *H.*

THE DAPHNE. *Daphne. H.*

The MEZERON (*Daphne Mezerum*) is the earliest flowering of all our shrubs; of pleasing growth; with many small, fragrant, pinkish flowers. There is a White-flowering, and also a Purple-leaved variety of this, the latter with showy foliage.

The GARLAND FLOWER (*Daphne Cneorum*) is an ever-green species, a native of the mountains of Switzerland, of dwarf trailing habit, adapted to use on rock-work; light crimson flowers early in the spring; requires protection in winter at the North in severe localities.

THE SHRUBBY CINQUEFOIL. *Potentilla fruticosa. H.*

A much branching, low shrub, with small, pinnate leaves, the leaflets closely crowded, which give the plant a singular appearance. Flowers bright-yellow, produced freely in summer.

THE BAYBERRY OR WAX MYRTLE. *Myrica cerifera. H.*

A native shrub, of low, irregular growth, and dark, shining green, slightly notched, very fragrant leaves, which are almost evergreen. Grows best in moist places.

CHAPTER VII.

EVERGREEN TREES AND SHRUBS.

Under this head are embraced the conifers or cone-bearing, and other trees and shrubs that hold the leaves over winter. The conifers, as a rule, will thrive in any well-drained, loamy soil, that is moderately rich, but they mostly prefer a light one that is porous and open. If the more delicate and half-hardy species cannot be given such soil, it is scarcely worth while to plant them, for in any other, the growth will not be completed early enough in the season to ensure the proper ripening of the wood to enable them to endure the winter. A few evergreen shrubs have been described under Thorn, Cotoneaster, Daphne, Andromeda, and Winterberry, with the deciduous species of the same genera.

THE PINE. *Pinus.* *A.–E.*

Many of the Pines, in their numerous species and varieties, are unsurpassed in beauty for ornamental planting, being especially effective in masses, while most of them are hardy. Being somewhat difficult to transplant, a preference should always be given, if possible, to trees that have been root-pruned in the nurseries where they were grown.

Of those Pines that have two leaves in a sheath, the following, among large growers, are considered the best :

The AUSTRIAN or BLACK PINE (*P. Austriaca*), of robust, spreading habit and luxuriant growth, with long, dark-green, leaves, *A.*

The CORSICAN PINE (*P. Laricio*), a distinct, handsome grower, with long, dark-green, twisted leaves; generally hardy, *A.*

TAURIAN PINE (*P. Pallasiana*), of roundish, compact form, with bluish-green leaves; generally hardy, *A.*

CLUSTER PINE (*P. Pinaster*), a beautiful species, with the leaves in dense whorls; not reliable in the Northern States, succeeds well near the sea, *A.*

PYRENEAN PINE (*P. Pyrenaica*), a beautiful, hardy species, with long, soft leaves; of picturesque spreading growth, *A.*

SCOTCH PINE (*P. sylvestris*), very hardy, of rapid growth in any soil, making it valuable for screens; short, rigid, light-green leaves, *A.*

HIGHLAND PINE (var. *horizontalis*), a variety of the Scotch Pine, with the branches more horizontal, and with broader leaves, covered with bloom.

SHORT-LEAVED YELLOW PINE (*P. mitis*), a handsome native, forming a fine specimen tree, with slender leaves often of a bright, bluish-green color.

Of dwarf sorts, with two leaves in a sheath, may be named the

MUGHO PINE (*P. Mugho*), a superior species for small grounds, with handsome, short, stiff, dark-green foliage, *E.*; var. *compacta* is a very symmetrical compact variety of this; var. *rotunda* is another variety of more rounded habit than the parent.

DWARF or MOUNTAIN PINE (*P. pumilio*), of small, often bushy, or creeping habit, with silvery-green foliage, *G.*

TABLE MOUNTAIN PINE (*P. pungens*), a handsome, hardy species, with rigid, stout, pale-green leaves, and producing many cones in masses.

The species of Pine with three leaves in a sheath usually become large trees in time.

BENTHAM'S PINE (*P. Benthamiana*), a handsome, rapid grower, with long, dark-green, slender, drooping leaves, *A.*

The HEAVY-WOODED PINE (*P. ponderosa*), with leaves almost as long as the last, but more erect and of a silvery-green color ; an attractive and imposing tree, *A.*

The JEFFREY'S PINE (*P. Jeffreyii*) is a vigorous, tall species, with long, deep, bluish-green leaves, *A.*

SABINE'S PINE (*P. Sabiniana*) is a majestic tree, valuable as a single specimen, with long, twisted, drooping leaves of a silvery-gray color, *A.*

The PITCH PINE (*P. rigida*) is a tall tree, with rigid, dark-green foliage and dark bark, *B.*

Of Pines with five leaves in a sheath, those immediately following are tall, and the others dwarfish.

The WHITE or WEYMOUTH PINE (*P. Strobus*), the most ornamental of all our native Pines, and especially valuable on account of bearing the shears well ; of quiet grandeur, with light, glistening, silvery-green foliage, flourishes in any soil, *A. D.*   The Compact White Pine · (*P. Strobus compacta*), a valuable dwarf, forming a rounded head of light-green foliage, excellent for massing, *G.*   Silver-white Pine (var. *alba*, syn. *nivea*), a handsome dwarf variety of the White Pine, with shorter leaves, silvery-white when young, changing to dark-green.

CALIFORNIA MOUNTAIN PINE (*P. monticola*) resembles the last somewhat, but the leaves are slightly shorter and obtuse, of a glaucous green.

LAMBERT'S PINE (*P. Lambertiana*), a large tree, with stiff, yellowish-green leaves four to six inches long.

LOFTY BHOTAN PINE (*P. excelsa*), a hardy, vigorous species from India, resembling the White Pine, but with larger and more pendulous foliage ; sometimes affected by our hot suns, *A.*

There are several desirable varieties given in the nursery catalogues.

The Swiss-stone Pine (*P. Cembra*) is a handsome,
slow-growing, cone-shaped tree, with dense and remark-
bly dark-green foliage, *G*. Var. *pygmæa* is a desirable
little dwarf, with very short leaves, *H*.

There are many other Pines, including some from
Japan, but the above lists, it is believed, embrace about
all that are desirable for general culture.

THE SPRUCE, HEMLOCK, AND FIR. *Abies.* *A. H.*

The trees known by these names are all now classed
under the one genus, *Abies*. All things considered, they
are together the most valuable genus of ornamental evergreens for the American climate. Mostly of rapid
growth, handsome forms, and excellent colors, they
thrive in almost any place and soil, and are well adapted
for growing either as single specimens, in masses, or in
hedges. Of the Spruce section the

Norway Spruce (*A. excelsa*) is the best known
species, being an elegant tree of great hardiness, and free
growth ; at fifteen or twenty feet in hight the branches
droop gracefully, but the tree assumes a somewhat coarse
appearance at such an age, which, while appearing to
good effect in large areas, is not so pleasing in small
grounds, and this may be prevented by controlling the
growth to a much smaller hight by clipping ; it is one
of the best hedge plants known, *A*. Of this species
there are many valuable varieties, embracing, among
others, the following : Barry's Spruce (var. *Barryii*), elegant, and smaller growing than the parent form. Fine-
don Hall Spruce (var. *Finedonensis*), compact, with
yellow-tinged leaves on the upper sides of the shoots.
Inverted-branched Spruce (var. *inverta*), very desirable,
with large, bright foliage and weeping branches. Pyramidal Spruce (var. *pyramidalis*). of a symmetrical pyramidal form, without pruning. Clanbrasil's Dwarf Spruce

(var. *Clanbrasiliana*), very dwarf and symmetrical, with small foliage, one of the most valuable of the very small Spruces. Ellwanger's Dwarf Spruce (var. *Ellwangeriana*), a distinct and valuable variety ; the leaves project in a bristle-like manner. Gregory's Dwarf Spruce (var. *Gregoriana*), hemispherical, very dense, an excellent small dwarf. Maxwell's Dwarf Spruce (var. *Maxwelliana*), dwarf, compact and regular, forms a dense, hemispherical mass. Small-formed Spruce (var. *parviformis*), small and distinct. Conical Spruce (var. *conica*), dense, conical-form ; valuable. Pigmy Dwarf Spruce (var. *pygmæa*), the dwarfest form of the Spruces. The var. *tortuosa compacta* is of dwarf, spreading habit, with the young branches curiously twisted.

The WHITE SPRUCE (*A. alba*) is another species of compact growth, with light-colored bark, and foliage of a light glaucous green, *B*. There are several varieties embracing the Glaucous Spruce (var. *cærulea*), a small and beautiful tree, with bluish-green foliage, and spreading habit. Dwarf White Spruce (var. *nana*), of small, compact form, but resembling the species in other respects.

The BLACK SPRUCE (*A. nigra*) is a native species, of no high merit for ornament. The Dwarf Black Spruce (var. *pumila*) is a fine dwarf variety, forming a cushion or ball of small, dark-green foliage, *H*. Doumet's Spruce (*Doumeti*) is another handsome dwarf variety, of compact growth and bluish leaves.

ALCOCK'S SPRUCE (*A. Alcoquiana*) is a distinct species from Japan, not thoroughly tested yet, but promising well ; deep-green, glaucous leaves.

MENZIES' SPRUCE or COLORADO BLUE SPRUCE (*A. Menziesii*), one of the hardiest and most beautiful species, until it attains to about thirty feet in hight ; compact, with broad, sharply-pointed, bright, bluish-gray leaves, *A*.

DOUGLAS' SPRUCE (*A. Douglasii*), of pyramidal habit, and in foliage resembling the Hemlock; said to improve with age for generations, *A.*

HIMALAYAN or SMITH'S SPRUCE (*A. Smithiana*), variable as to hardiness in the Northern States, habit singularly graceful, and with light-green, glaucous foliage. Obovate-coned Spruce (*A. obovata*), resembles the Norway Spruce, but slower growing and more slender. Oriental or Eastern Spruce (*A. orientalis*) somewhat resembling the last, and remarkable for its graceful habit; needs protection in northern localities while young. *Abies polita*, from Japan, is a very handsome tree of erect habit, with sharply-pointed, bright-green leaves.

In the Hemlock section of this genus are a number of valuable ornamental sorts.

The HEMLOCK SPRUCE (*A. Canadensis*) is a well-known native species, of excellent quality for the lawn, and as a hedge plant. The drooping branches give the tree a graceful appearance. Foliage delicate and dark, like that of the Yew; delights in deep, moist loam, and does not object to some shade, *B.* Of varieties of the above there are the Dwarf Hemlock Spruce (var. *nana*), forming a compact, conical bush; the Dense Hemlock Spruce (var. *densa*), of handsome, dwarf, dense form; Sargent's Weeping Hemlock (var. *Sargentii*), a dense, irregularly, weeping form, with graceful, spray-like branches, like an evergreen fountain; remarkably handsome and hardy; the Small-leaved Hemlock Spruce (var. *microphylla*), a slow grower, compact, picturesque, and full of deep shadows; heavy, dark-green leaves. There are several other varieties of no marked merit.

Among the Firs are many fine ornamental trees.

The BALSAM FIR (*A. balsamea*) is a well-known species of most handsome appearance while young, with dark-green foliage.

NORDMANN'S SILVER FIR (*A. Nordmanniana*), an exceedingly handsome and stately tree, with massive, shiny, dark-green verdure, the under sides of the leaves slightly glaucous. Hardy in Buffalo, *A.*

NOBLE FIR (*A. nobilis*), a noble tree of symmetrical growth, and regular, spreading branches ; foliage of a rich, glaucous green on both sides. Hardy at Philadelphia, *A.*

The GREAT SILVER FIR (*A. grandis*), of lofty pyramidal form, and dark-green leaves, *A.*

CEPHALONIAN SILVER FIR (*A. Cephalonica*), a beautiful, vigorous species, broad for its hight, when young; leaves silvery and dagger-shaped ; of doubtful hardiness in the Northern States.

SIBERIAN SILVER FIR (*A. Pichta*) is a handsome, hardy, medium-sized tree of conical growth, and dense, dark-green foliage, *B.*

CILICIAN SILVER FIR (*A. Cilicica*), of compact growth, and dark foliage.

HUDSON'S BAY DWARF FIR (*A. Fraseri*, var. *Hudsonica*), a very dwarf and hardy species, with the leaves of a charming dark-green, and glaucous underneath, valuable for rock-work, *H.*

The following named Firs are also desirable for ornament. Lovely Silver Fir (*A. amabilis*), with bushy branches and dark-green leaves, silvery beneath, *A;* Pinsapo Fir (*A. Pinsapo*), of handsome, compact growth, with deep, shining green, very pointed leaves; not hardy in the North. The European Silver Fir (*A. pectinata*) is a fine species, with spreading, horizontal branches, and broad silvery foliage, somewhat tender in the North. The Dwarf Silver Fir (var. *compacta*), and the Weeping Silver Fir (var. *pendula*), both varieties of the European, are handsome trees, but rather tender in the North.

THE CYPRESS.   *Cupressus.*   A.

A genus not generally hardy north of Philadelphia, but of great value wherever they stand the winters. They may be tried, however, throughout the North on high, dry spots, with some hopes of success with them.

LAWSON'S CYPRESS (*C. Lawsoniana*) is of rapid growth and delicate beauty, with drooping branches and slender branchlets, that look like glaucous-green plumes, A.   Pyramidal Lawson's Cypress (var. *pyramidalis*), a variety more heavily furnished with foliage, and more erect than the above, A.   Upright Lawson's Cypress (var. *erecta*), of very erect, dense habit of growth. Weeping Lawson's Cypress (var. *pendula*), of graceful, drooping habit, and shining, silvery foliage.   Silver Lawson's Cypress (var. *argentea*), a handsome, compact grower, with glaucous leaves, slightly drooping.   Variegated-leaved Lawson's Cypress (var. *variegata*), foliage dotted and blotched with golden yellow; should have partial shade.

The NOOTKA SOUND CYPRESS (*C. Nutkaënsis*) ; by some classed as *Thujopsis borealis*, is the hardiest of the genus; a free pyramidal grower, with light, glossy foliage.

The WHITE CEDAR (*C. thyoides*) is a hardy native species, forming a fair lawn tree, and useful for hedges; has fine, glaucous-green foliage. There are several varieties of this ; the Dwarf White Cedar (var. *nana*) is of diminutive form, and the Variegated White Cedar (var. *variegata*) has branches of a green and golden color.

THE CEDAR.   *Cedrus.*   A.

The true Cedars, of which the Cedar of Lebanon, mentioned in Sacred History, is a representative, are all too tender to be thoroughly reliable in the Northern States, but form noble trees south of Philadelphia.

Sometimes, however, they succeed in favorable situations north of this. What are known commonly as the Red Cedar and White Cedar do not belong to the genus *Cedrus*.

The CEDAR OF LEBANON (*C. Libani*) is a grand, spreading tree, with massive, dark-green foliage. Although tender when young, its hardiness increases with age, *A.*

MOUNT ATLAS CEDAR (*C. Atlantica*) is of pyramidal form, with light, silvery foliage, and is quite hardy.

DEODAR or INDIAN CEDAR (*C. Deodara*) is a charming evergreen of pyramidal form, but with graceful drooping branches, and glaucous green foliage. A fine tree for the Southern States.

The JAPAN CEDAR (*Cryptomeria Japonica*), belonging to another genus, is a beautiful conifer, only suitable for culture at Baltimore and southward, *B.*

The CALIFORNIA WHITE CEDAR (*Libocedrus decurrens*) is also of a distinct genus. It is from California, and too tender for general culture in the North, but one of the finest evergreens for the South, *B.*

THE ARBOR VITÆS and RETINISPORAS. *Thuja and Biota.*
A–C.

The members of the two genera, *Thuja* and *Biota*, are both popularly known by the name of Arbor Vitæ. The Retinisporas, formerly classed as a distinct genus, have been added to *Thuja*, as they are not botanically distinct. As they were introduced as Retinisporas, and are under that name in all the catalogues, it is convenient to retain it as a garden name.

AMERICAN ARBOR VITÆ (*Thuja occidentalis*), also called in some localities White Cedar, is a perfectly hardy tree, of rapid growth under favorable conditions, assuming a conical form, but possessing less beauty than some of its varieties, owing to the tame color of its foliage;

valuable for screens and hedges. Among its varieties, the Siberian Arbor Vitæ (var. *Sibirica*. syn. *Warreana*), is one of the best, and scarcely excelled as a fine evergreen; very hardy, of conical growth, with dark-green foliage, *C;* Nee's Plicate Arbor Vitæ (var. *plicata*) resembles the last, but the branches are so disposed in pairs, as to give the spray a massive plaited and twisted look; hardy and excellent, *C;* Upright Arbor Vitæ (var. *pyramidalis*), remarkably erect and compact, dark-green, and almost as conspicuous as an Irish Yew, *C;* Weeping Arbor Vitæ (var. *pendula*), of handsome, rapid growth, the branches drooping gracefully. Buist's Arbor Vitæ (var. *cristata*) resembles the last somewhat; with dense, short, twisted foliage, of a very dark-green color.

There are many varieties of the American Arbor Vitæ, with golden and silvery-hued foliage, making them desirable for creating contrasts with trees of other colors, and also numerous sorts of distinctly dwarf habit, highly esteemed for massing and lines in small gardens, some of which are also of the golden-leaved type. Among these, the following may be named as representative varieties and some of the best. Geo. Peabody's Arbor Vitæ (var. *aurea*), of small size, with the foliage of a bright golden color, which is retained throughout the summer; *H;* Burrow's Arbor Vitæ (var. *Burrowii*), of very fine habit with golden-yellow foliage; Parsons' Arbor Vitæ (var. *compacta*), of globular form, yellowish-green foliage, *H;* Hovey's Arbor Vitæ (var. *Hoveyi*), compact and globular, with bright, yellowish-green foliage; one of the best, *H.* Vervæne's Arbor Vitæ (var. *Vervæneana*), a distinct and handsome yellow-marked variety. Queen Victoria's Arbor Vitæ (var. *alba*), with silver-tipped foliage. Dwarf Dense Arbor Vitæ (var. *conica densa*), dark-green, compact, and handsome in outline. Heath-leaved Arbor Vitæ (var. *ericoides*), linear, sharp-pointed leaves; very dense, *H.* Globe-headed

Arbor Vitæ (var. *globosa*), dense, and globular, *H.* Hacker's Arbor Vitæ (var. *Hackerii*), of dwarf habit, with very dark foliage, *H.* Hoopes' Dwarf Arbor Vitæ (var. *nana*), of conical form, and very compact in its growth, *H.* Dwarf Round-headed Arbor Vitæ (var. *rotundata*), very dwarf; deep green, with a crested appearance, *H.* The variety Tom Thumb is a miniature variety, of slow growth, with sharp-pointed, dark-green leaves, valuable for bold edgings or low hedge, *H.*

The RETINISPORAS, or JAPANESE ARBOR VITÆ, also known as the Japan Cypress, are among the handsomest and most easily grown evergreens in cultivation. Some of them are rather tender, but the hardier ones will thrive over nearly the entire country, and possess such positive excellence, as to be worthy of frequent use.

The PLUME-LIKE RETINISPORA (*T. Plumosa*) is one of the hardiest species; a rapid grower, with pretty, small, bright-green leaves, and short, slender branches, *G.* There are several varieties of this. The Silver-spotted Retinispora (var. *argentea*) has the young shoots sprinkled with silvery white. The Golden-tipped Retinispora (var. *aurea*) has a bright golden hue at the ends of the branches; one of the hardiest, *H.*

The OBTUSE-LEAVED RETINISPORA (*T. obtusa*) is of remarkable beauty, and one of the hardiest; leaves glossy-green above and silvery-white beneath, *A.*

The PEA-FRUITED RETINISPORA (*T. pisifera*) is of small size and slender habit, with sharp-pointed, green leaves. There are several dwarf varieties of this last named species.

The THREAD-BRANCHED RETINISPORA (var. *filifera*), of elegant pyramidal form, with the ends of the shoots drooping gracefully; bright-green foliage. The Golden Thread-branched Retinispora (var. *aurea*), with the branches of a beautiful golden color. The Heath-like

Retinispora (var. *ericoides*) is a compact, cone-shaped bush, the leaves of which turn to a violet-red in winter. The Squarrose Retinispora (*R. squarrosa*) is round-headed and bushy in its style of growth, with light, bluish-green foliage. *R. leptoclada* is of a bright, glaucous-green color; hardy in England, but perhaps not reliable in this country.

The CHINESE or EASTERN ARBOR VITÆ (*Biota*) are, as a class, too tender for the northern parts of our country, unless, as sometimes happens, they may find a place that is well sheltered, or otherwise favorable to them. The species (*B. orientalis*) is of erect growth, with flat, light-green foliage. Of its varieties, the Golden Chinese Arbor Vitæ (var. *aurea*) is an excellent sort, of globular form and bright, golden-tinged foliage. Rollinson's Golden Chinese Arbor Vitæ (var. *elegantissima*), of pyramidal form, and golden-hued foliage. Golden Arbor Vitæ (var. *semper aurea*), a dwarf variety, of fine growth, with the golden tint remaining constant throughout the year. There is also a weeping variety (var. *filiformis pendula*), and some others.

THE JUNIPERS. *Juniperus.* *B* to trailing.

The Junipers are a beautiful and reliable class of hardy evergreens, and of such a range of adaptability, as influenced by size and habit in the different species and varieties, that nearly every garden can employ some of them to great advantage. Among the smaller-growing species may be named :

The COMMON JUNIPER (*J. communis*), with its varieties. The common one is a well-known native of America, Europe, and Asia, assuming a variety of forms, but generally pyramidal, and with some attention to shearing, makes a handsome specimen, *E.* The Canadian Trailing Juniper (var. *alpina*, syn. *J. Canadensis*) is of dense, spreading habit, with silvery-hued foliage; fine for rockwork. The Dwarf Juniper (var. *alpina nana*) is a sort that does not grow over a foot high, and spreading. The American Pyramidal Juniper (var. *a'pina pyramidalis*) is a distinct form of the common species of upright habit. Polish Juniper (var. *Cracorica*), a robust, erect grower, with yellowish-green foliage. The Irish Juniper (var. *Hibernica*), a compact, free-growing variety of great popularity; the growth is upright and formal, producing a fine columnar effect, *E*. Robust Irish Juniper (var. *Hibernica robusta*) is more vigorous, but less dense than the Irish. Swedish Juniper (var. *Suecica*), of pyramidial form with yellowish-green foliage.

The SAVIN JUNIPER (*J. Sabina*) is another well-known low-growing species, with wide-spreading, sombre, thickly clothed branches; thrives in the poorest soil; admirable for hillsides and rockwork, and also bears the shears well, *H*. The Tamarisk-leaved Savin (var. *tamariscifolia*) is a distinct and handsome variety of the last, *H*. The Cypress-leaved Savin (var. *cupressifolia*) is another variety with light-green, and sometimes silvery-glaucous leaves. The Variegated-leaved Savin (var. *variegata*) shows some distinct white and pale-yellow markings on the leaves ; less vigorous than the species. Var. *alpina* is a low trailer in habit and quite distinct.

The RED CEDAR (*J. Virginiana*), with its varieties, are Junipers of great hardiness and indispensable in all good collections of considerable extent; the parent form is a well-known native, with bright-green, compact foliage, *C–D*.

SILVERY, or GRAY-LEAVED RED CEDAR (var. *glauca*), is a handsome, free-growing variety, with silvery foliage, that contrasts well with other evergreens, *E*. Weeping Red Cedar (var. *pendula*) is a variety with a weeping tendency; the young shoots being long and slender, and reaching to the ground. There are two Variegated Red

Cedars, the one with white spots and stripes on the foliage (var. *variegata alba*); the other one with golden marblings (var. *variegata aurea*), both of fair merit, if not especially valuable. The Light-green Red Cedar (var. *Schottii*), and also Bedford's Red Cedar (var. *Bedfordiana*, syn. *Barbadensis*), are varieties with lighter colored foliage than the species.

One of the finest Junipers is the Chinese (*J. Chinensis*), belonging to the Cypress-like section. The foliage is of a handsome dark-green, presenting a peculiar, lively appearance, and the tree has an erect habit. The sexes are in separate trees, there being a sterile and a fertile form, this last has a lighter foliage, and is somewhat pendant, *C.* Reeves' Chinese Juniper (var. *Reevesiana*) is of remarkable hardiness, and has a fine habit, with somewhat drooping and spreading branches. Lee's Chinese Juniper (var. *Leeana*) is a variety with long, bright-green leaves, and vigorous and dense habit.

The JAPANESE JUNIPER (*J. Chinensis,* var. *Japonica, J. Japonica* of some authors), is a pleasing shrub of very small size, and suitable for rockwork; it has bright, lively-green foliage; it is not perfectly hardy at the North, *H.* There are also several variegated-leaved varieties of this.

There are still several other desirable Junipers which might be named here, such as the Prostrate Juniper (*J. prostrata*), of trailing habit, with shining, dark-green foliage; hardy, and well adapted for rockwork and edgings. The Scaled Juniper (*J. squamata*), also of low-spreading habit, with foliage of a delicate, glaucous hue. Globular Juniper (*J. hemisphærica*), very dwarf and dense, with whitish foliage. Lovely Juniper (*J. occidentalis,* var. *venusta*), a handsome, hardy variety of erect-waving, torch-like form, and fine glaucous, bluish foliage. Daurian Juniper (*J. Daurica*), a low tree, with the leaves whitish on their upper surface.

THE TORREYA. *Torreya.* *C.*

A genus of evergreens, near relatives of the Yew, and natives of our Southern States, California, and Asia. They are not considered hardy generally in the North, but are desirable for garden planting throughout the South. Among the species are the California Nutmeg Tree (*T. Californica*), with long, pale-green leaves. Nut-bearing Torreya (*T. nucifera*) from Japan. Yew-leaved Torreya (*T. taxifolia*), a Florida species, with shiny green leaves, which give off a disagreeable odor if bruised. This is hardy in New York City.

THE HOLLY. *Ilex.* *C.*

The AMERICAN HOLLY (*I. opaca*) is the only true Holly that is reliable in the United States. It has large, tough, smooth leaves, with scattered spiny teeth along the wavy margin, and ornamental red berries in winter. Should be severely pruned when transplanted.

THE UMBRELLA PINE. *Sciadopitys.*

S. verticilla'a, the only species, is a remarkable tree from Japan, with curious, shining, dark-green foliage, arranged in whorls of umbrella-like tufts. It is hardy in New England.

THE LAUREL. *Kalmia.* *E. H.*

Beautiful native shrubs, with shining foliage and large clusters of flowers. Will thrive in a moist, light soil, that is well supplied with vegetable matter, like leaf-mould, or muck, and in partial shade.

The MOUNTAIN. or BROAD-LEAVED LAUREL (*K. latifolia*), has medium-sized, shining green leaves, and white and rose-colored flowers, *E. G.*

The NARROW-LEAVED, or SHEEP LAUREL (*K. angustifolia*), of much smaller size than the last named, has small, light-green leaves and crimson flowers, *H.*

THE YEW.   *Taxus.*   C. H.

A genus of evergreens, with handsome, generally dark-green foliage, that are very popular in England, but are not so reliable in our climate, owing to the injury the foliage is apt to receive from the sun in winter.   Particularly fine for cemetery planting.

The ENGLISH YEW (*T. baccata*) is a handsome bush, densely branched and can be trimmed to any shape. *C.* The American Yew or Ground Hemlock (var. *Canadensis*) is brought under the foregoing species by Prof. Gray; perfectly hardy, of dwarf, spreading habit, and growing readily in the shade.   There is also a variegated-leaved form of this, with the young shoots marked with yellow.

Of other fine varieties may be named Dovaston's or Weeping Yew (var. *Dovastoni*), with pendulous, straggling branches, and long dark leaves ; one of the hardiest.   Beautiful Yew (var. *elegantissima*), of erect, rapid growth, and foliage marked with yellow.   Erect Yew (var. *erecta*), one of the hardiest and finest, with slender branches and small, shining, dark leaves.   Fox's Dwarf Yew (var. *nana*), a diminutive form, with handsome, very dark leaves, *H.*   The Golden Yew (var. *aurea*), with gold-colored foliage ;   the Irish Yew (var. *fastigiata*), an upright grower, with very dark foliage, and of which there are also several sub-varieties.

The JAPANESE YEW (*T. adpressa*) is one of the hardiest, most beautiful, and least liable to receive injury from the sun in winter of the entire genus ; of low, spreading form, with short dark-green leaves, *H.* Upright Japan Yew (var. *stricta*) is a variety of the above, of erect habit, but less hardy.   The Abrupt-pointed Yew (*T. cuspidata*) is a distinct and handsome species from Japan, with large, glossy, dark-green leaves, and compact habit, one of the hardiest.

The JAPAN YEW or PODOCARPUS (*Podocarpus Japon-*

ica) is of a distinct genus, but somewhat resembles the Irish Yew. Tender in the North, *C.*

THE THUIOPSIS. *Thuiopsis.*

Evergreens from Japan, sometimes called Japanese Arbor Vitæ, too tender to be considered reliable with us, excepting in central and southern portions of our country, and here they should have the benefit of some shade. Of different kinds there is the Hatchet-leaved Thuiopsis (*T. dolabrata*), of conical form, with slightly pendulous branches, and flat leaves. Standish's Thuiopsis (*T. Standishii*) is somewhat like the last, but said to be hardier ; and a Variegated-leaved Thuiopsis (*T. dolabrata variegata*), has bright-green foliage, silvery beneath.

THE CEPHALOTAXUS. *Cephalotaxus.* *C.*

The PLUM-FRUITED CEPHALOTAXUS (var. *C. drupacea*) is a compact growing, rather tender, ornamental evergreen, with short leaves. Fortune's Cephalotaxus (*C. Fortunei*) is a species of which there are two forms, male and female trees ; the former with long leaves, and of a spreading habit of growth ; the latter with smallish, dark-green leaves, and slender drooping branches.

THE RHODODENDRON. *Rhododendron.* *E. H.*

Wherever they will do well, it is hard to find any other shrubby plants that will give equal satisfaction with the Rhododendrons, especially the improved hybrid sorts. They are of a handsome form, with glossy, evergreen leaves, and are covered in June with immense clusters of the most attractively colored and handsomely formed flowers. The plants will not thrive in heavy clay, and a limey soil seems to be about as bad for them, while any light loam that is well supplied with decayed leaf-mould or other similar vegetable matter, will suit them well. They like coolness and moisture at the roots in summer, which may be secured by mulching them before hot weather comes on. A temperature fifteen degrees below zero, if not too long continued, or too frequent, does not hurt them, provided they have shelter from wind and sun, and they may be planted near buildings or trees to receive this. For some further directions in preparation of the soil and their management, see Divisions IV and V.

The AMERICAN RHODODENDRON (*R. maximum*), also called the Great Laurel, is a native species, and found growing wild from Maine to Ohio, and southward, as a straggling bush, with thick, smooth leaves, and small, green-spotted, rose-colored or white flowers.

PONTIC RHODODENDRON (*R. Ponticum*) is an European species, almost valueless in America, from the liability of the flower buds to be winter killed.

The CATAWBA RHODODENDRON (*R. Catawbiensis*), the Rose Bay of the Southern States, is found growing on the mountains of Virginia and southward. From this species have sprung nearly all the fine hardy hybrids of the gardens. There are many named varieties of these, the colors of which are exceedingly handsome, and varying through pure-white, light-pink, cherry-red, rose, lilac, purple, and brilliant-scarlet, and crimson. There are some other distinct species also, which are of little consequence, hence I omit them.

THE BOX. *Buxus. E. H.*

A genus of beautiful evergreens, suitable for lawn decoration, and the dwarf varieties for edgings to walks, etc. The trees may be grown to any desirable shape by shearing. Although hardy, they sometimes suffer from sun-scald in winter, and from harsh sweeping winds, but as they do not object to partial shade, by planting them where they will receive this, the first named difficulty is avoided, and shelter from winds is the remedy for the other.

The COMMON TREE BOX (*B. sempervirens*) is the well known European species, with beautiful glossy foliage, *E.* The following are some of the varieties of this : Dwarf Box (var. *suffruticosa*), is the sort usually employed for edgings ; forms a pretty bush when planted alone. Handsworth's Box (var. *Handsworthii*) is a vigorous, upright grower of great hardiness. Jackson's Weeping Box (var. *Jacksonii*) has pendulous branches, which habit gives the tree a fine appearance. The Broadleaved Box (var. *latifolia*), and the Myrtle-leaved Box (var. *myrtifolia*), are both fine sorts. There are a number of varieties, the leaves of which are marked and splashed with gold and silver colors, such as the Goldstriped Box, Silver-striped Box, Elegantly-variegated Box, and others.

THE MAHONIAS. *Berberis. H.*

The evergreen species of Barberry were formerly placed in the genus *Mahonia*, but they are now arranged as a section of *Berberis.* It is convenient to retain Mahonia as a popular or garden name.

The HOLLY-LEAVED MAHONIA (*B. Aquifolium*) is one of the hardiest and finest low-growing evergreens we have. It is liable to receive spots from the sun in winter, on which account it should be protected somewhat, a thing easily done with evergreen boughs or otherwise, as the plant is of low growth ; or it may be planted in the shade. It has handsome, thick, glossy leaves, with prickly and scalloped edges, which somewhat resemble those of the Holly ; clusters of yellow flowers in the spring. There are several other rather unimportant species.

CHAPTER VIII.

CLIMBERS AND TRAILERS.

As found growing wild, the hard-wooded climbers and trailers afford some of the most delightful bits of natural scenery to be met with. Many of these serve valuable purposes for embellishments in ornamental gardening, as shown in Part III. Some kinds, and conspicuously the Clematis, have been improved much by cultivation since first brought into the gardens.

THE VIRGINIA CREEPER. *Ampelopsis.*

A genus of climbers of the first rank for general culture. The VIRGINIA CREEPER (*A. quinquefolia*), also called " American Ivy," and incorrectly, " Woodbine," is the common native species. It is a rapid grower, producing dense masses of splendid, digitate foliage, and attaching itself firmly to wood, stone, or the trunks of trees. There is, however, a form not possessing this last named quality, which should be avoided. The foliage of this species turns to a beautiful crimson in autumn.

VEITCH'S AMPELOPSIS (*A. tricuspidata*, syn. *A. Veitchii*), from Japan, possesses great merit as a hardy climber, and particularly for covering brick and stone walls. The leaves are smaller than the common kind, lobed instead of divided, and of a clear green, changing to crimson-scarlet in the fall. They possess the pleasing peculiarity of regularly overlapping one another, literally forming an even sheet of green, if growing on any smooth surface like a building. Perfectly hardy if protected for one or two winters until well established.

Among other ornamental species may be named the Pepper Vine (*A. bipinnata*), of vigorous, picturesque growth, with compound, pinnate leaves. Royle's Ampelopsis (*A. Roylii*), of rapid growth, with large foliage, that colors up richly in the autumn. *A. indicisa* has leaves less deeply cut than the others.

THE WISTARIA. *Wistaria.*

Usually, for several years after planting, the Wistarias make but little growth, but after being once well established, they grow rapidly and to a great length. Besides their free growing qualities, they are prized for their picturesque appearance in general, and the profusion of showy flowers they bear.

The CHINESE WISTARIA (*W. Sinensis*) is one of the best known and most vigorous species, attaining to an immense size with age; long pendulous clusters of pale lilac flowers in the spring, and sometimes again in the fall. There are several varieties of this species, namely the Chinese White Wistaria (var. *alba*), with charming white flowers. Double Purple Wistaria (var. *flore pleno*), said to produce long racemes of double flowers, but it is very slow to come into bloom.

There are a number of Japanese species and varieties (*W. brachybotrys*), with fragrant, light, rosy-purple flowers; var. *rubra,* a variety of the last named, with darker red flowers. *W. Japonica alba nana,* of dwarfish growth with white flowers; *W. multijuga* and *multijuga alba*), are of another species, with very large racemes of flowers, in the first named of purple color, in the last white. .

The AMERICAN, or SHRUBBY WISTARIA (*W. frutescens*), is a native, less attractive and strong growing than the Chinese; pale-blue flowers in short clusters. The White American Wistaria (var. *alba*) is a white-flowered variety of the species. Var. *magnifica* is said to have the flowers in dense drooping racemes.

THE HONEYSUCKLE OR WOODBINE. *Lonicera.*

A rather extensive genus, the more ornamental species and varieties of which are much valued for their fine flowers. Their nature is to twine about any support, hence they are more useful for adorning pillars, veranda posts, etc., than for covering walls. Excellent about rockwork. By stopping the leading shoots at four to six feet, most of the kinds form handsome standards if supported by a stake.

Among native species and their varieties are the following :

SCARLET TRUMPET HONEYSUCKLE (*L. sempervirens*), a strong grower, with handsome, scarlet flowers, about two inches long, produced all summer; dark-green leaves. Brown's Scarlet Trumpet Honeysuckle (var. *Brownii*), a variety of the last with large dark-scarlet flowers. Small Red Honeysuckle (var. *minus*), a variety with small flowers, slightly darker than in the species.

YELLOW TRUMPET HONEYSUCKLE (*L. flava*), very fragrant, bright-yellow and orange flowers. What is known in the nurseries as the Canadian Honeysuckle (var. *Canadensis*), probably a variety of this, is a distinct and striking form, of robust growth, with large, bluish-green leaves, united in pairs at the base around the stem ; yellow flowers in June; readily grown as a standard.

The Asiatic species are a class of great value, Hall's Japan Honeysuckle (*L. Halleana*), a species with fine, nearly evergreen leaves, and very sweet flowers, at first pure white, and then changing to yellow, and produced all summer, a superb sort. Japan-Evergreen Honeysuckle (*L. brachypoda*), of remarkably vigorous growth, with white and yellow fragrant flowers. Golden-Veined Honeysuckle (var. *reticulata*), a variety of the last, the small, rounded leaves of which are elegantly netted and veined with yellow. Among other meritorious kinds may be named

The COMMON WOODBINE (*L. Periclymenum*), a rapid

grower, with showy flowers, red outside, white within. Monthly Dutch Honeysuckle (var. *Belgica*), a superior variety, blooming throughout the season, with red and yellow, fragrant flowers.

MANGEVILLE'S HONEYSUCKLE (*L. Caprifolium*, var. *pallida*), an evergreen species, with yellowish-white, fragrant flowers. Standish's Honeysuckle (*L. Standishii*), light pink and yellow flowers.

THE CLEMATIS. *Clematis.*

The species of Clematis are most attractive and valuable climbers, being easily grown, of graceful habits, and possessing magnificent flowering qualities. They will thrive in any good soil which is well enriched, and by protecting the roots by a slight covering over them each fall, they stand the severest winters safely. Besides their great value for decorating verandas and arbors, they are admirably suited for growing in pots or tubs, training the vines on a trellis, or balloon frame, for adorning verandas, roof gardens, conservatories, etc.

The species are divisible into two classes, namely : those that flower on the last year's growth in the early part of the season, and those flowering on the present season's growth in summer and autumn, either continuously or in successive crops. There are many varieties of both these classes described in the catalogues, ranging in color from white through lavender, reddish-purple, violet, mauve, etc., to the most intense violet-blue, and blackish mulberry.

JACKMAN'S CLEMATIS (*C. Jackmanii*) is one of the best sorts, and well known, being of free growth, and a most abundant bloomer, the flowers being of a rich, violet-blue color.

The SCARLET CLEMATIS (*C. coccinea*) is a quite distinct species, with scarlet flowers, having yellow centers.

The COMMON WILD CLEMATIS (*C. Virginiana*) is a

6

species of free growth, with smooth leaves and white flowers in profusion.

TRUMPET FLOWERS. *Tecoma.*

AMERICAN TRUMPET VINE (*T. radicans*) is a vigorous, hardy climber, with large, trumpet-shaped, scarlet flowers in August, excellent to cover stumps and stones, or to train as a standard.   Dark-red or Purple Trumpet Flower (var. *astrosanguinea*), a variety with purplish-crimson flowers, and more shrub-like in habit than the last.

GREAT TRUMPET FLOWER (*T. grandiflora*) has large, showy, pale-orange flowers.

OTHER ORNAMENTAL CLIMBERS.

The DUTCHMAN'S PIPE (*Aristolochia Sipho*), a valuable native climber of rapid growth, with immense leaves ten to twelve inches across, and pipe-shaped, yellowish-brown flowers.   There are several other species, but not equal to the one named.

The CLIMBING BITTER-SWEET or STAFF-TREE (*Celastrus scandens*), a native, and one of the most elegant climbers or twiners, and worthy of being generally used ; exceedingly fine for verandas ; rich, glossy leaves, and beautiful, pendant branches, with clusters of orange capsules. The Bitter-Sweet may be grown in the form of a shrub, by cutting back to three or four feet. There are also several Japanese species.

The *Akebia quinata*, a neat and most attractive climber from Japan, with small leaves and fragrant purple flowers in early summer, followed by ornamental fruit.

The *Actinidia polygama*, another climber from Japan, is of vigorous and elegant habit, and has white and purple flowers.

A VINE with variegated leaves (*Vitis heterophylla, Cissus variegata* of some catalogues), is a very pleasing plant. Of rapid, slender growth, with small leaves, resembling those of the grape vine, but beautifully marbled, and variegated with white, pink and green.

The CAROLINA COCCULUS (*C. Carolinus*), a native vine, with small, heart-shaped leaves, greenish flowers in summer, and small, red fruit, the size of a pea.

The CANADIAN MOONSEED (*Menispermum Canadense*), a pretty, slender-branched, twining plant, with small, yellow flowers and black fruit, resembling small frost grapes.

The GRAPE (*Vitis*). There are situations, and especially about the Wild Garden, where the native species of grapes are most attractive climbers. They are neat, free growers, with foliage well adapted to making shade for arbors, for overhanging ledges, bridges, etc.; some have fragrant flowers. Among the best for ornament, may be named the Summer Grape (*V. æstivalis*); the Frost Grape (*V. cordifolia*), with very sweet flowers, and the species *V. indivisa*, and *V. vulpina* for the more southern sections of our country.

The WHITE JESSAMINE (*Jasminum officinale*) is an elegant climber, that has long been in cultivation, but is too tender for the North, unless well protected in winter. There are several other species and varieties belonging to the genus.

The GRECIAN SILK VINE (*Periploca Græca*), a rapid growing climber of no high order of beauty, with pointed leaves, and purplish-brown flowers.

The EUROPEAN IVY (*Hedera*). Owing to our bright sunshiny winters, in which it suffers if the sun comes to it, the Ivy can never become popular in this country to the extent it has in Europe. The hardiest kinds, however, do well, when planted against the north side of buildings or walls. They may also be thickly planted in beds to produce a mass of foliage over the bed, or be used as

edgings, as when grown thus they can be easily protected.
The Irish Ivy (*H. Helix*, var. *Hibernica*), is about the
best for general planting. There are a number of interesting varieties with variegated and striking forms of
foliage, all more or less useful.

CHAPTER IX.

HARDY HERBACEOUS PLANTS.

Let me introduce the plants that come under this head
as the Hardy Wild Plants of the temperate regions of
the earth, and then it may be known at once what they
are. The lists embrace such as are perennial, having
roots that live from year to year, producing new growths
above ground annually, but which die down as often,
either soon after flowering, or in the fall. Many of the
kinds have been much improved in the gardens, affording numerous varieties that greatly exceed the parents in
value.

It is a pleasure to note the increasing attention this
class of plants is now attracting in ornamental gardening in this country and ʼEurope. As a rule they are
easily grown, very ornamental and inexpensive, for, unlike most other kinds of flowers, when once they are
planted, they remain.

Pains have been taken in this chapter, to classify these
plants somewhat, according to their adaptability and
value. To save space, I have generally, in the descriptions, merely separated the distinguishing qualities of the
plants by the semicolon, giving color of flowers first, season of flowering next, with the hight in inches or feet
last. The word "protect," indicates that the sort which
it follows, must be protected in the Northern States in
winter.

CLASS I.—HARDY PLANTS, MOSTLY IMPROVED SORTS, OF THE HIGHEST ATTRACTIVENESS.

Adonis, Spring (*Adonis vernalis*).—Yellow; spring; 8 to 12 inches.

Anemone or Wind-Flower (*Anemone*).—Japan Anemone (*A. Japonica*).—Bluish-rose; autumn; 2'/₂ feet.

> White Japan Anemone (var. *alba*).—White, golden center; autumn; 2'/₂ feet.
>
> Apennine Anemone (*A. apennina*).—Bright blue; early spring; 6 inches.
>
> Double White Wind-Flower (*A. nemorosa fl. pl.*).—Early spring; 6 inches.

Anthericum (*Anthericum*).—Branching Anthericum (*A. ramosum*).—White; spring; 18 inches.

> St. Bruno's Lily (*A. liliastrum*).—White; June; 18 inches.

Columbine (*Aquilegia*).—Rocky Mountain Columbine (*A. cærulea*).—White and cærulean blue; spring; 2 to 3 feet.

> Golden-spurred Columbine (*A. chrysantha*).—Yellow; summer; 2 to 3 feet.
>
> Siberian Columbine (*A. glandulosa*). — Blue and white; summer; 2 feet.
>
> Skinner's Columbine (*A. Skinneri*).—Distinct, red and yellow.
>
> Striped Columbine (*A. caryophylloides*).—Striped.
>
> Common Columbine (*A. vulgaris*).—There are many varieties.

Woodruff (*Asperula odorata*).—Pure white; spring; 6 inches.

Astilbe, Japan (*Astilbe Japonica*). — White; cut-leaves; May; 2 feet. Often called *Spiræa Japonica*.

Daisy (*Bellis perennis*).—White, pink, etc.; spring; 3 inches; protect.

Bell-Flower, Harebell (*Campanula*).—The following are the names of a few species among many :

Peach-leaved Campanula (*C. persicæfolia*).—Blue; June; 2 to 3 feet. There is a variety with white flowers. Var. *coronata,* has double flowers, both white and blue.

Nettle-leaved Campanula (*C. Trachelium*).—Blue ; with a white variety ; 3 feet.

Betony-leaved Campanula (*C. sarmatica*). — Pale blue ; July ; 2 feet.

The catalogues give other species and varieties of Campanula. The normal color is blue, but nearly all have varieties with white flowers.

Large Bell-flower (*Platycodon grandiflorum.* Syn. *Campanula grandiflora, Wahlenbergia grandiflora*). — Very large blue flowers ; summer ; 1 to 2 feet. There is a white semi-double variety.

Meadow Saffron (*Colchicum*).—*C. autumnale.* Light-purplish, mottled ; autumn ; 4 inches. There are varieties with white and with rose-colored flowers. *C. variegatum,* with rose and purplish-violet flowers, is probably a variety also. Autumn ; 4 inches.

Lily of the Valley (*Convallaria majalis*).—White ; fragrant ; May ; 8 inches.

Hollyhock (*Althæa rosea*).—Many colors, single and double ; summer ; 4 to 6 feet.

Crocus (*Crocus*).—Many colors ; early spring ; 4 inches.

Larkspur (*Delphinium*).—The following are excellent kinds :

D. formosum.—Rich, dark blue, tinged purple ; summer ; 2 to 3 feet.

D. cœlestinum.—Light blue, double ; June, Sept.; 3 to 4 feet.

D. pyramidalis.—Blue ; fine grower ; June ; 4 to 5
feet.

D. azureum.—Light blue ; single ; July ; 2 to 3
feet.

D. grandiflorum.—Of different colors.

Pink (*Dianthus*).—Garden Pink (*D. plumarius*).—
Pink, with a white variety ; 12 to 15 inches.

Maiden Pink (*D. deltoides*).—Rose and white ; 6 to
9 inches.

Amoor Pink (*D. dentosus*).—Lilac ; dwarf in habit.

Sweet William (*D. barbatus*). —Many colors and
forms.

D. Querterii.—Deep crimson ; clove fragrance ;
spring ; 1 foot.

Bleeding Heart (*Dicentra spectabilis*).—Rosy crimson;
spring ; 2 to 4 feet.

Plumy Bleeding Heart (*D. eximia*).—Rose ; summer ; 9 to 18 inches.

Fraxinella (*Dictamnus Fraxinella*).—Both pink and
white ; June ; 18 inches.

Foxglove (*Digitalis*).—White, purple, etc.; summer ;
2 to 3 feet.

Adder's Tongue, Dog's Tooth Violet (*Erythronium*).—

Yellow Adder's Tongue (*E. Americanum*).—Yellow;
May ; 6 to 9 inches.

White Dog's Tooth Violet (*E. albidum*).—Bluish-
white ; May.

European Dog's Tooth Violet (*E. Dens-canis*).—

Crown Imperial (*Fritillaria imperialis*).—Different
colors ; spring ; 3 feet.

Plantain Lily (*Funkia*) : As the species of *Funkia*
and of *Hemerocallis* are both known as Day Lilies, and
much confusion results, it has been proposed in England,
to call the *Funkias* Plantain-lilies, an appropriate name,
having reference to their plantain-like leaves.

White Plantain Lily (*F. alba*).—White ; summer ; 15 inches.

Blue Plantain Lily (*F. cærulea*).—Light blue ; June and July ; 1 foot.

Japan Plantain Lily (*F. Japonica*).—Lavender ; narrow leaves ; 2 feet.

Siebold's Plantain Lily (*F. Sieboldii*).—Pale pink ; 12 to 18 inches.

Day Lily (*Hemerocallis*) :

Yellow Day Lily (*H. flava*).—June ; 2 to 4 feet.

Copper-colored Day Lily (*H. fulva*).—Yellowish copper-color ; July.

Double Day Lily, of several species.

Snowdrop (*Galanthus*). — Common Snowdrop (*G. nivalis*).—White ; early spring ; 4 inches ; also a double variety.

Canada Tick-Trefoil (*Desmodium Canadense*).—Bluish-purple ; all summer ; 1 to 2 feet.

Rocket Flower (*Hesperis*).—Dame's Violet (*H. matronalis*).—Purple ; June ; 1 to 2 feet ; also white and double white varieties.

Hyacinth (*Hyacinthus*).—Common Hyacinth (*H. orientalis*).—Single and double in many colors ; May.

Grape Hyacinth (*Muscari*).—Common Grape Hyacinth (*M. botryoides*).—Deep sky-blue ; spring ; 9 inches ; also a pure white variety.

Feathery Hyacinth (*M. comosum*).—Blue ; feathery ; 12 to 18 inches.

Musk Hyacinth (*M. moschatum*).—Purplish green.

Candy-tuft, Perennial (*Iberis*) : Evergreen Candy-tuft (*I. sempervirens*).—White ; May.

Coris-leaved Candy-tuft (*I. corræfolia*). — White ; dwarf ; early summer ; 6 to 9 inches.

Gibraltar Candy-tuft (*I. Gibraltarica*).—White and purplish ; June ; 1 foot.

Iris, Fleur de Lis, Flag (*Iris*).—Of the numerous species and hybrids, the following are among the best :

    Florentine Iris (*I. Florentina*).—White, blue and yellow ; early summer ; 18 inches.

    German Iris (*I. Germanica*).—The old " Blue Flag," of which there are many fine named varieties.

    Japan or Clematis-flowered Iris (*I. lævigata*, Syn. *I. Kæmpferi*).—Flowers distinct in form, and presenting a wonderful variety of colors and shades in the named sorts ; 3 to 4 feet.

    Dwarf Iris (*I. pumila*).—Deep violet, yellow, etc. ; spring ; 3 to 6 inches.

    Iberian Iris (*I. Ibirica*).—Purple and black ; spring.

    Peacock Iris (*I. Pavonia*).—Pure white and deep blue.

    Netted Iris (*I. reticulata*).—Blue, netted yellow ; spring ; 6 inches.

    English Iris (*I. xiphioides*).—White, blue, etc.; summer.

    Spanish Iris (*I. Xiphium*). — Resembles the last ; many colors.

Jonquil (*Narcissus Jonquilla*).—Double and single ; yellow ; spring.

Pea, Perennial (*Lathyrus latifolius*).—Rose and white sorts ; summer ; 4 to 8 feet.

Everblooming Pea (*L. grandiflorus*).—Purple ; summer ; 3 to 4 feet.

Blazing-Star (*Liatris*).—Spiked Blazing-Star (*L. spicata*).—Purple ; summer ; 2 to 4 feet.

    Elegant Blazing-Star (*L. elegans*).—Bluish purple ; summer ; 1 foot.

    Dwarf Blazing-Star (*L. pumila*).—Handsome purple ; July ; 1 foot.

Loose-strife (*Lythrum*).—Spiked Loose-strife (*L. Salicaria*).—Rosy-scarlet ; summer ; 3 feet ; there is also a variety with rosy-purple flowers.

Snowflake (*Leucojum*).—Spring Snowflake (*L. vernum*).—White; very early spring; 9 inches.

> Summer Snowflake (*L. æstivum*).—White; June; 1½ feet.
>
> Autumn Snowflake (*L. autumnalis*). — White or pale rose; 6 inches.

Lilies (*Lilium*).—The following are a few of the best from among many species :

> Golden-Banded Lily (*L. auratum*).—White, maroon and yellow; 2 to 5 feet.
>
> White Lily (*L. candidum*).—Pure white; summer; 3 to 4 feet.
>
> Buff Lily (*L. excelsum*).—Nankeen, shaded red; 4 to 6 feet.
>
> Long - flowered Lily (*L. longiflorum*). — White; 12 to 20 inches; protect.
>
> Turban Lily (*L. Pomponium*).—Red, dotted black; summer; 1 to 2 feet; and a variety with yellow flowers, dotted black.
>
> Rose-colored Japan Lily (*L. speciosum roseum*).—Rose; spotted; summer; 1 to 2 feet.
>
> Slender-leaved Lily (*L. tenuifolium*).—Small; scarlet; June; about 1 foot; protect.
>
> Turk's Cap Lily (*L. superbum*).—Bright orange; summer; 4 to 7 feet.
>
> Umbelled Lily (*L. umbellatum*).—Bright red; July; 1½ to 2½ feet.
>
> Splendid Tiger Lily (*L. tigrinum splendens*).—Orange-scarlet; spotted.
>
> Thunberg's Lily (*L. Thunbergianum*).—Blood red; 1 to 2 feet.
>
> Kramer's Lily (*L. Krameri*).—Suffused delicate pink; 2 feet.
>
> Wild Yellow Lily (*L. Canadense*).—Yellow; summer; 2 to 5 feet.
>
> Southern Red Lily (*L. Catesbæi*).—Scarlet; 1 to 2 feet; protect.

Lychnis (*Lychnis*).—Scarlet Lychnis (*L. Chalcedonica*).
—Double and single ; various colors ; summer ; 2 to 3
feet.

> Double German Catchfly (*L. Viscaria, fl. pl.*).—
> Bright red ; 12 to 18 inches.
>
> Flower of Jove (*L. Fos-Jovis*).—Large, deep red.
>
> Ragged Robin (*L. Fos-cuculi*).—Fine, deep pink ;
> summer ; 1 foot ; also a white variety.
>
> Haage's Lychnis (*L. Haageana*).—Red, of various
> shades ; large.

Forget-me-not (*Myosotis dissitiflora*). — Sky-blue ;
May ; 6 to 12 inches.

Daffodil (*Narcissus*). — This well known genus of
hardy bulbs now embraces many fine sorts. One
establishment at Passaic, N. J., alone offering in their
catalogue almost two hundred distinct species and varieties ; mostly yellow, orange, scarlet, and white colors ;
double and single ; spring.

Star of Bethlehem (*Ornithogalum umbellatum*).—
Satiny-white ; spring ; 6 to 9 inches.

> Pyramidal Star of Bethlehem (*O. pyramidale*).—
> White; summer ; 1 to 2 feet.

Bitter Vetch, Spring (*Orobus vernus*).—Dark purple ;
spring ; 1 foot.

Pæony (*Pæonia*).—Of this grand genus there are a
number of species, and a great many improved named
varieties.

> Tree Pæony (*P. Moutan*).—Superb flowers in many
> varieties ; 5 to 8 feet.
>
> Chinese Double Blush Tree Pæony.—Rose and pur-
> ple.
>
> Common Garden Pæony (*P. officinalis*).—Many va-
> rieties ; mostly large and double ; June ; 2 to 4
> feet.

Fennel-leaved Pæony (*P. tenuifolia*).—Double and single ; dark crimson ; May ; 1¹/₂ to 2 feet.

Poppy, Perennial (*Papaver*).—Golden Poppy (*P. croceum*).—Orange yellow ; early ; 8 to 15 inches.

Oriental Poppy (*P. orientale*). — Bright scarlet ; June ; 18 inches.

Pentstemon (*Pentstemon*).—There are a number of species and varieties, with scarlet, purple, white, and other colored flowers.

Phlox, Perennial (*Phlox*).—Hybrid Garden Phlox.— These have mostly originated from *P. paniculata* and *P. maculata,* and are represented by a long list of excellent named sorts ; summer ; 2 to 4 feet.

Spreading Phlox (*P. divaricata*).—Lilac-blue ; 9 to 18 inches.

Creeping Phlox (*P. reptans*).—Rosy-purple ; May and June ; 4 to 8 inches.

Moss Pink (*P. subulata*).—Rose, white, and purple varieties ; spring ; 4 inches.

Greek Valerian (*Polemonium cœruleum*).—Pale blue ; 18 inches ; and a form with variegated leaves.

Jacob's Ladder (*P. reptans*).—Bright blue ; spreading; 10 to 12 inches.

Primrose (*Primula*).—Common Primrose (*P. vulgaris*).—Many colors ; protect. Polyanthus Primrose.— Yellow, sulphur brown, etc.; spring ; 4 to 6 inches.

Lungwort (*Pulmonaria*).—Narrow-leaved.—(*P. angustifolia*).—Bright blue; April; 1 foot. Spotted-leaved Lungwort (*P. maculata*).—Showy foliage; blue; spring; 1 foot.

Feverfew, Hardy (*Pyrethrum*). — Scarlet, crimson, rose, and other colored varieties ; spring ; 15 inches.

Sage, Southern (*Salvia azurea*).—Deep blue ; 2 to 3 feet ; protect ; some other species are desirable.

Wood-Hyacinth, Squill (*Scilla*).—A charming genus of plants, embracing numerous species and varieties, showing many shades of blue flowers, some flowering early, and others late.

Sedum or Stone-crop.—See Rock Plants.

Catchfly (*Silene*): Sea Catchfly (*S. maritima*).— White; June; 2 to 4 inches.

> Pennsylvania Catchfly (*S. Pennsylvanica*).—Showy, pink; June; 4 to 6 inches.
>
> Autumn Catchfly (*S. Schafta*). — Purplish-rose; June; 6 inches.
>
> Oriental Catchfly (*S. orientalis*). — Deep rose; showy: 1 to 2 feet.

Pink Root (*Spigelia Marilandica*).—Scarlet; June; 6 to 18 inches; protect.

Meadow-Sweet (*Spiræa*): Goat's Beard (*S. Aruncus*). —White; 4 feet.

> Dropwort (*S. filipendula*).—White; fern-like foliage; June; 1 to 2 feet.
>
> Purity (*S. Ulmaria, fl. pl.*).—White ; handsome ; June; 2 feet ; there is also a variety of this with golden variegated foliage.
>
> Queen of the Prairie (*S. venusta*).—Soft rose; summer; 2 to 4 feet.

Stokesia, Blue (*Stokesia cyanea*).—Blue ; August and later; 2 feet.

Spiderwort (*Tradescantia*).—Blue Spiderwort (*T. Virginica*).—Fine blue ; of this species there are a number of varieties, including white; May; 1 to 2 feet.

Flame-flower, or Red-hot Poker Plant (*Tritoma Uvaria*).—There are a number of varieties, scarlet, yellow, etc.; September; 2 to 4 feet.

Tulips (*Tulipa*).—The varieties are very numerous, of many colors and shades, single and double; April and May.

Speedwell (*Veronica*): *V. amethystina.*—Amethyst blue; summer; 12 to 18 inches.

    Gentian-leaved Speedwell (*V. gentianoides*).—Pale blue; 12 to 18 inches.

    Japanese Speedwell (*V. longifolia*).—Blue; summer; 1 to 2 feet.

Periwinkle (*Vinca*).—Lesser Periwinkle (*V. minor*).—Blue and white varieties, also one with variegated leaves; summer; trailing; 1 to 2 feet.

    Greater Periwinkle (*V. major*).—Blue; summer; 1 to 2 feet.

Violet (*Viola*): Sweet Violet (*V. odorata*).—Violet; early spring; 6 inches.

    White Violet (*V. blanda*).—Whitish.

    Birdfoot Violet (*V. pedata*).—Bluish-lilac; sandy soils.

    Horned Violet (*V. cornuta*).—Blue; summer; 3 to 6 inches.

Heart's-ease or Pansy (*Viola tricolor*).—Many beautiful colors.

CLASS II.—HARDY PLANTS, POSSESSING SHOWY FOLIAGE AND FORMS, WHICH RENDER THEM PICTURESQUE IN APPEARANCE, AND WELL SUITED FOR GROUPS ON THE LAWN, OR FOR SUB-TROPICAL EFFECTS.

Acanthus (*Acanthus*).—Broad-leaved Acanthus (*A. latifolius*).—White; thick leaves; 2 to 4 feet; protect. Soft Acanthus (*A. mollis*).—Rose; showy leaves; 3 feet; protect.

Monkshood, Autumn (*Aconitum autumnale*).—Pale blue; 6 feet.

Acorus gramineus, var.—2 to 6 inches.

Grass, Ribbon (*Phalaris arundinacea, var.*).—3 to 5 feet.

Grass, Fescue (*Festuca glauca*).—Blue-leaved ; low; for edgings.

Dactylis—Orchard Grass (*D. glomerata*). — A variegated form with striped foliage, of good habit.

Grass, Pampas (*Gynerium argenteum*).—Grand in rich soil; 6 to 9 feet ; protect.

Grass, Panic (*Panicum virgatum*).—Stately ; 4 to 6 feet.

Bugle, Red-leaved (*Ajuga reptans*).—Purple leaves; 6 inches.

Alfredia, Nodding (*Alfredia cernua*).—Yellow ; cut leaves; 6 feet.

Wormwood (*Artemisia*).—*A. Stelleriana*, silvery foliage; 9 to 18 inches. *A. vulgaris*, delicately cut leaves; 3 feet.

Reed (*Arundo Donax*).—A handsome gigantic grass, forming clumps; 8 to 12 feet.

The Variegated Reed is a variety of the above, with foliage striped with white.

Bocconia (*B. cordata*).—Whitish leaves ; flowers in August; 6 to 8 feet.

Bupthalmum (*B. speciosum*).—Large leaves ; yellow flowers; summer; 2 feet.

Thistle, Globe (*Echinops Ritro*).—Blue; showy leaves; summer; 2 to 3 feet.

Lyme Grass (*Elymus arenaria*).—Very narrow, gray grass; 2 feet.

Erianthus Ravennæ.—Valuable showy grass; 6 to 12 feet.

Eringo (*Eringium*).—Amethystine Eringo (*E. amethystinum*).—Blue; showy cut foliage; summer; 2 feet. Yucca-leaved Eringo (*E. yuccæfolium*).—White ; yucca-like leaves.

Eulalia, Variegated (*Eulalia Japonica variegata*).—Striped grass; 4 to 6 feet; protect. Zebra Eulalia (*var. Zebrina*).—Leaves striped crosswise; protect.

Plantain Lily, Variegated (*Funkia undulata medio-picta*).—Yellow-striped; 6 to 12 inches.

Sunflower, Graceful (*Helianthus orgyalis*).—Yellow; handsome leaves; 8 to 10 feet.

Day Lily, Variegated (*Hemerocallis Kwanso var.*).—White striped foliage.

Fig. 8.—YUCCA.

Mint, Variegated (*Mentha rotundifolia var.*).—Foliage blotched with yellow.

Whorl Flower (*Morina longifolia*).—Rose; large leaves; 2 to 3 feet; protect.

Rhubarb, Indian (*Rheum Emodi*). — Large, showy leaves; 2 to 3 feet.—Palm-leaved Rhubarb (*R. palmatum*). Deeply lobed, showy leaves; 6 to 8 feet.

Clary, Silver (*Salvia argentea*).—Large, white, woolly leaves; 2 to 3 feet.

Sage, Variegated (*Salvia officinalis tricolor*).—Leaves blotched, white; 1 foot.

Lavender Cotton (*Santolina Chamæcyparissus*). — Silvery leaves; 1 foot.

Sedum.—There are several species with showy foliage, such as *S. spectabile; S. cruciatum;* the Live-for-ever, etc. See Rock Plants.

Compass Plant (*Silphium laciniatum*).—Large pinnate leaves.—Cup Plant (*S. perfoliatum*).—Yellow, of strong growth; 4 to 6 feet.

Comfrey, Variegated (*Symphytum officinale var.*).— Gold variegated; 1 to 2 feet.

Thyme, Lemon, Variegated-leaved (*Thymus citriodorus*).—Golden Variegated.—Common Variegated-leaved Thyme (*T. Serpyllum*).—White variegated.

Yucca, or Adam's Needle (*Yucca filamentosa*). — White; 3 to 4 feet.

  Narrow-leaved Yucca (*Y. angustifolia*).—White ; 2 to 4 feet.

  Date Yucca (*Y. baccata*).—Large throughout ; 2 to 10 feet; protect.

CLASS III.—HARDY PLANTS, MOSTLY AS FOUND IN THEIR WILD STATE, AND COMPARATIVELY LACKING SOMEWHAT IN ATTRACTIVENESS.

The plants of this list, while not averaging as fine in general quality as those of preceding classes, would still, in most instances, be prized if given a place in the border, while all are desirable for naturalization in the Wild-garden. With many the flowers are handsome, but the foliage or the habit of the plants may be comparatively coarse, while sometimes just the reverse is the case.   Then again a single plant of this class makes no show, but a mass of them is very attractive.

Yarrow or Milfoil (*Achillea*).—Rose-flowered Yarrow (*A. millefolium roseum*).—Rose ; summer ; 18 inches ; there is also a deep-red variety of this,

> Double-flowering Sneezewort (*A. Ptarmica, fl. pl.*). —White; 15 inches.
>
> Hoary-leaved Yarrow (*A. filipendula*).— Yellow ; summer; 2 feet.

May Apple, Oregon (*Achlys triphylla*).—White; fragrant; 15 inches.

Monkshood, or Wolfsbane (*Aconitum*).—These have poisonous roots.

> Japan Monkshood (*A. Japonicum*).—Deep blue ; August; 18 inches.
>
> Common Monkshood (*A. Napellus*).—Blue ; summer; 2 feet.

Baneberry (*Actæa*), White Baneberry (*A. alba*).— Summer; 2 to 3 feet.

> Cut-leaved Baneberry (*A. spicata*).—Neat and graceful; 18 inches.
>
> Red Baneberry, a variety of the above, with red berries; 2 feet.

Bugle, Blue-flowered (*Ajuga pyramidalis*). — Blue ; spring; 3 inches.

Star Grass, Yellow (*Aletris aurea*).—Yellow ; July ; 2 to 3 feet. Colic Root Star Grass (*A farinosa*).— White; July; 2 to 3 feet.

Allium, Golden (*Allium Moly*).—Golden; summer; 1 foot. There are various other species of Allium of different colors, such as white, rose, lilac, etc.

Alstræmeria (*A. aurantiaca*).—Orange, lily-like flowers; summer and autumn; 2 to 4 feet.

Amianthium (*A. muscætoxicum*). — White ; broad leaves ; summer.

Amsonia, Hairy (*Amsonia angustifolia*).—Pale blue; protect.

Willow-leaved Amsonia (*A. Tabernæmontana*).—Pale blue; May; 2 feet.

Anemone, or Windflower, Yellow (*Anemone ranunculoides*).—Spring; 6 inches.

> Snowdrop Anemone (*A. sylvestris*).—Pure white; spring; 1 foot.
>
> Long-fruited Anemone (*A. cylindrica*).—Greenish-white; spring.
>
> Pennsylvania Anemone (*A. Pennsylvanica*).—White and pink; 12 inches.
>
> American Pasque Flower (*A. patens*, var. *Nuttaliana*).—White or purplish; spring.

Mountain Everlasting (*Antennaria dioica*).—White; summer; trails.

Butterfly Weed (*Asclepias tuberosa*).—Orange; July; 2 feet. Milkweed (*A. verticillata*).—Greenish-white; 1 to 2 feet.

Asphodel (*Asphodelus*).—There are a number of species, mostly with yellow and white flowers; May to July; 2 to 4 feet.

Aster (*Aster*).—Of many species, the following are noteworthy here:

> New England Aster (*A. Novæ-Angliæ*).—Violet purple; 4 feet.
>
> New Belgian Aster (*A. Novi-Belgii*).—Dark crimson.
>
> Oblong-leaved Aster (*A. oblongifolius*).—Purple and yellow; 2 to 3 feet.
>
> Long-leaved Aster (*A. longifolius*).—Handsome form and foliage; 2 feet.

False Indigo (*Baptisia*): Blue False Indigo (*B. australis.*—Blue; June; 2 to 5 feet. White False Indigo (*B. alba*).—Purplish tinged; 2 to 3 feet.

Berlandiera (*B. tomentosa*).—Yellow ; downy leaves ; 1 to 3 feet.

Betonica (*B. officinalis*).—Purple; July; 2 feet.

Boltonia (*B. glastifolia*).—White; 3 to 5 feet.

Brodiæa, Allium-like (*Brodiæa congesta*).—Lilac; summer ; 18 inches. Large-flowered Brodiæa (*B. grandiflora*).—Bluish-purple; 1 foot.

Brunella, Large-flowered (*Brunella grandiflora*).— Purplish-blue; summer; 9 inches.

Callirrhoë, Crimson (*Callirrhoë involucrata*).—Crimson; summer; 1 foot.

> Callirrhoë, Large-rooted (*C. alcæoides*). — White ; summer ; 2 feet ; protect. Callirrhoë, Triangular (*C. triangulata*).—Purple; 2 feet.

Butterfly Tulip (*Colochortus Gunnisoni*).—White; 6 to 8 inches.

Senna, American (*Cassia Marilandica*). — Yellow ; summer; 3 to 4 feet.

Cupidone, Blue (*Catananche cærulea*). — Sky-blue ; summer; 2 to 3 feet.

Centaurea, Mountain (*Centaurea montana*).—Blue ; showy; June and July; 3 feet. Centaurea, Giant-headed (*C. macrocephala*).—Bright yellow ; June and July ; 2 feet.

Valerian, Red (*Centranthus ruber*).—Red; June; 2 feet; also a white variety.

Chelone, Snake's-Head (*Chelone glabra*).—White and rose; 1 to 2 feet.

Clematis, Erect (*Clematis erecta*).—Whitish ; small ; June; 3 to 4 feet. Clematis, Entire-leaved (*C. integrifolia*).—Blue and white; June; 2 feet.

Clintonia, Northern (*Clintonia borealis*).—Yellowish ; 6 inches.

Coreopsis (*Coreopsis*).—There are several species ; yellow; June; 1 to 3 feet.

Coronilla (*Coronilla varia*). — Deep rose to white; June; 2 feet.

Golden Aster (*Chrysopsis Mariana*).—Golden yellow; late summer; 6 to 12 inches.

Crosswort, Long-styled (*Crucianella stylosa*).—Pink; summer; 12 to 18 inches.

Fig. 9.—RUDBECKIA MAXIMA.

Leopard's Bane (*Doronicum Caucasicum*).—Yellow; spring; 1 foot.

Cone Flower, Purple (*Echinacea purpurea*).—Maroon and purple; 4 feet.

Cone Flower, Great (*Rudbeckia maxima*). — Large; yellow; 6 feet; protect.

Cone Flower, Shining (*R. nitida*). — Large golden rays; showy.

Fleabane Rose (*Erigeron macranthum*).—Purple; July; 2 feet.

Stork's Bill, Showy (*Erodium Manescavi*).—Purplish-red; summer; early spring; 15 inches.

Aconite, Winter (*Eranthis hyemalis*).—Pale yellow ; early spring; 3 to 6 inches.

Eupatorium, White Snake-root (*Eupatorium ager-atoides*).—Late summer; 3 feet. There are a number of other desirable species.

Spurge, Flowering.—(*Euphorbia corollata*).—White ; July to October; 2 to 3 feet.

Spurge, Glaucous (*E. Myrsinites*).—Yellow; prostrate; July.

Gaura, Narrow-leaved (*Gaura angustifolia*).—From the Southern States; white; summer; 3 feet.

Gentian. Closed (*Gentiana Andrewsii*).—Azure blue ; 12 to 18 inches.

Gentian, Crosswort (*G. cruciata*).—Brilliant blue; 6 inches.

Geranium, or Cranesbill, Blood-red (*Geranium sangui-neum*).—Purplish-red ; summer ; 6 inches. Geranium, Broad-petaled (*G. platypetalum*).—Violet and red ; 18 inches.

Avens, Scarlet (*Geum coccineum*).—Bright scarlet ; summer; 1 to 2 feet; also a double variety.

Bowman's Root (*Gillenia trifoliata*). — Rosy-white ; July; 1 to 2 feet.

Gypsophila, Acute-leaved (*Gypsophila acutifolia*). — White; summer; 12 to 20 inches. Gypsophila, Panicled (*G. paniculata*).—White; summer; 2 to 4 feet.

Sunflower, Narrow-leaved (*Helianthus angustifolius*). Yellow ; autumn ; 3 feet. Sunflower, Soft-leaved (*H. mollis*).—Autumn; 2 to 4 feet.

Rose Mallow, Swamp (*Hibiscus Moscheutos*).—Pale rose; late summer; 2 to 4 feet.

> Rose Mallow, Large-flowered (*H. grandiflorus*).—Both white and red; 4 to 5 feet.

> Rose Mallow, Californian (*H. Californicus*).—White, with purple centre; 3 to 5 feet.

Hawkweed, Orange-colored (*Hieracium aurantiacum*). —Bright orange; June; 1 foot.

Hyssop (*Hyssopus officinalis*).—Blue and white sorts; summer; 2 feet.

Hyssop, Giant (*Lophanthus anisatus*).—Lavender; fragrant leaves; 2 feet.

Flax, Perennial (*Linum perenne*).—Fine blue; summer; 12 to 18 inches. There are also varieties of white, rose, and lilac colors.

Lobelia, Great Blue (*Lobelia syphilitica*).—Purplish-blue; 1 to 2 feet. Cardinal Flower (*L. cardinalis*).—Fine scarlet; late summer; 2 to 4 feet.

Trefoil, Bird's-foot (*Lotus corniculatus*).— Yellow; summer; trailing. Also a double variety.

Lupine, Many-leaved (*Lupinus polyphyllus*).—Blue; summer; 1 to 4 feet; protect.

Loosestrife, Yellow (*Lysimachia vulgaris*).—Yellow; June, July; 2 feet.

> Loosestrife, Clethra-like (*L. clethroides*).—White; autumn; 1½ to 2 feet.

Moneywort (*L. nummularia*).—Yellow; late summer; prostrate.

Mallow, Moren's (*Malva Morenii*).— Reddish; late summer; 2 to 3 feet.

Lungwort, Panicled (*Mertensia paniculata*).—Blue; July; 1 to 2 feet.

> Virginia Cowslip, or Lungwort (*M. Virginica*).—Fine blue; spring; 1 to 3 feet.

Monkey Flower, Cardinal (*Mimulus cardinalis*).—Scarlet; 1 to 2 feet; protect.

Bee-Balm, or Horsemint (*Monarda didyma*).—Bright red ; summer; 2 to 3 feet; protect.

Catnip, Mussin's (*Nepeta Mussini*). — Azure blue ; downy; fragrant leaves; June; 1 foot.

White Cup (*Nierembergia rivularis*).—Creamy white; June; 3 inches.

Evening Primrose, Missouri (*Œnothera Missouriensis*). —Yellow; prostrate. Evening Primrose, Tall White (*Œ. speciosa*).—White and purple; 6 inches to 2 feet.

Mountain Spurge (*Pachysandra procumbens*).—Purple and white; prostrate.

St. Bernard's Lily (*Anthericum Liliago*).—White in spikes; summer; 1 foot.

Dragon Head (*Physostegia Virginiana*).— Purplish red; 4 feet.

Knotweed, Giant (*Polygonum cuspidatum*).—White ; summer ; 3½ to 8 feet. Knotweed, Red (*P. vaccinifolium*).—Rose; autumn; 6 to 10 inches.

Pentstemon, Scarlet (*P. barbatus*).—Scarlet; summer; 3 feet.

Cinquefoil, Pyrenian (*Potentilla pyrenaica*).—Yellow; May; dwarf.

Turfing Daisy (*Pyrethrum Tchihatchewii*).—For covering poor soils; 3 inches.

Buttercup, or Crowfoot, Double (*Ranunculus bulbosus*).—Yellow; spring; 18 inches.

    Buttercup, Rhomboid (*R. rhomboideus*).—Deep yellow; spring; 3 to 6 inches.

    Crowfoot, Early (*R. fascicularis*).—Bright yellow ; 5 to 9 inches.

Skullcap (*Scutellaria*).—Numerous species ; purplish; summer.

Groundsel (*Senecio*).—A few of the Groundsels **are**

quite ornamental. Golden Ragweed (*S. aureus*).—Yellow; cut leaves; 1 to 2 feet.

Satin Flower (*Sisyrinchium grandiflorum*).—Purple; spring; 6 to 10 inches.

Golden Rod (*Solidago*).—A number of species; yellow; autumn; 3 to 8 feet.

Solomon's Seal (*Polygonatum vulgare*).—White; 2 to 3 feet. Solomon's Seal, Japan (var. *macranthum*).—White; May; 2 to 4 feet.

Hedge-Nettle, Woolly (*Stachys lanata*).—Purple; July; 1 foot. Hedge-Nettle, Scarlet (*coccinea*).—Scarlet; July; 3 to 4 feet.

Sea Pink, or Thrift (*Armeria vulgaris*).—Rosy-lilac; summer; 6 inches.

Costmary (*Tanacetum Balsamita*). — Pale yellow; autumn.

Meadow Rue, Showy (*Thalictrum speciosum*).—Showy; yellow; 3 to 4 feet. Meadow Rue, Columbine (*T. aquilegifolium*.—Purplish; 2 to 3 feet.

Star Flower, Spring (*Triteleia uniflora*).—Whitish; spring; 4 to 6 inches; protect.

Bellwort (*Uvularia*).—A number of sorts; yellowish; 6 inches to 2 feet.

Valerian (*Valeriana officinalis*).—Blush white; June; 3 feet.

Verbena, Hardy (*Verbena bipinnatifida*, also called *V. montana*).—Rosy-lilac; summer; 9 inches.

CLASS IV.—ALPINES AND ROCK PLANTS.

The plants under this head are mostly natives of high elevations, and lovers of dry, sandy, or stony soil, hence perfectly at home on rockwork. Nearly all do well in the border, but being of small stature, they should be planted at the front.

7

Thrift, Prickly (*Acantholimon glumaceum*).—Rose; summer; 6 inches.

Thrift, Common (*Armeria vulgaris*).—Pink; summer; 6 inches.

Thrift, Plantain-like (*A. plantaginea*). — Purplish-red.

Milfoil, Woolly (*Achillea tomentosa*).—Yellow; summer; 8 inches.

Golden Tuft (*Alyssum saxatile*).—Yellow; grayish leaves; spring; 1 foot.

Golden Tuft, Dense (var. *compactum*).—More compact than the parent.

Kidney Vetch, Mountain (*Anthyllis montana*).—Pink; summer; 6 inches.

Columbine, Wild (*Aquilegia Canadensis*).—Scarlet and yellow; May; 1 foot to 18 inches.

Rock Cress (*Arabis*).—Several species; white; spring; dwarf.

Sandwort (*Arenaria*).—Several species; white; early summer; low.

Meadow Saffron, Spring (*Bulbocodium vernum*).—Violet; early spring; 6 inches.

Aubrietia (*Aubrietia*).—Several species; white and purple; spring and summer; 3 inches.

Quamash (*Camassia*).—Several species; blue; purple, etc.; 12 to 15 inches.

Harebell, Common (*Campanula rotundifolia*).—Deep blue; 6 to 12 inches.

Harebell, Ligurian (*C. isophylla*).—Blue; 4 inches.

Harebell, Carpathian (*C. Carpatica*). — Large, showy; blue; 9 inches.

Mouse-ear Chickweed, Woolly (*Cerastium tomentosum*).—White; summer; 2 to 6 inches.

Mouse-ear Chickweed, Boissier's (*C. Boissieri*).

Wallflower, Alpine (*Cheiranthus alpinus*).—Yellow; spring; 9 inches.

Spring Beauty (*Claytonia Virginica*).— Rose; early spring; 6 inches.

Clematis, Herbaceous (*Clematis*). — Several ornamental species; purplish; 6 to 12 inches.

Barrenwort, Alpine (*Epimedium alpinum*).—Purplish; May; 6 to 9 inches.

Barrenwort, Large yellow (*E. pinnatum*).

Erinus, Alpine (*Erinus alpinus*). — Purplish and white; 3 to 6 inches.

Gentian, Stemless (*Gentiana acaulis*).—Velvet blue; May; 1 to 3 inches.

Geum, Mountain (*Geum montanum*).—Bright yellow; 9 to 18 inches.

Ground Ivy (*Nepeta Glechoma*). — Robust, dense creeper.

Bluets, Common (*Houstonia cœrulea*). — Shade of blue; early spring; 3 to 6 inches.

Bluets, Thyme-leaved (*H. serpyllifolia*).

Toadflax, Alpine (*Linaria alpina*).—Violet and yellow; 3 to 6 inches.

Lychnis, Rock (*Lychnis Lagascœ*).—Bright rose; summer; 3 to 6 inches.

Catchfly, German (*L. Viscaria*, var. *splendens*).— Bright red; 12 to 18 inches.

Prickly Pear (*Opuntia Rafinesquii*).—Hardy Cactus; yellow; 6 to 10 inches.

Wood Sorrel, Violet (*Oxalis violacea*).—Violet; spring; 5 to 9 inches.

Partridge, or Squaw Berry (*Mitchella repens*).—White; scarlet fruit; trailing.

Pentstemon, Acute-leaved (*Pentstemon acuminatus*).— Lilac; 6 to 20 inches; protect.

Phlox, Douglas's (*Phlox Douglasii* —Whitish purple; 6 to 12 inches.

Phlox, Lovely (*P. amœna*).—Pinkish; 6 to 12 inches.

Pine-barren Beauty (*Pyxidanthera barbulata*).—Pinkish white; spring; prostrate.

Soapwort, Rock (*Soponaria ocymoides*).—Rosy-pink; summer; 6 to 12 inches.

Fig. 10.—THICK-LEAVED SAXIFRAGE (*Saxifraga crassifolia*).

Saxifrage, Early (*Saxifraga Virginiensis*).—White; 6 inches.

Saxifrage, Heart-leaved (*S. cordifolia*).—Blush-red; April and May; 6 to 9 inches.

Saxifrage, Thick-leaved (*S. crassifolia*).—Resembles the last.

Saxifrage, Strap-leaved (*S. ligulata*).—Red; dark-red foliage; spring; 6 to 9 inches.

Stonecrop or Sedum (*Sedum*).—There are many species and varieties, of which but a few are named here; all do equally well in the border.

Love Entangle (*S. acre*).—Several forms; yellow; 3 inches.

Stonecrop, Orange-flowering (*S. Kamtschaticum*).— Yellow; fine; July; 6 inches.

Sedum, Beautiful (*S. pulchellum*).— Pink; July; 6 inches.

Sedum, Poplar-leaved (*S. populifolium*).—Creamy-white; August; 6 inches.

Sedum, Siebold's (*S. Sieboldii*).— Rosy-purple; autumn; also a variegated form.

Sedum, Showy (*S. spectabile*). — Rosy purple; autumn.

Live-for-ever (*S. Telephium*).—Purple; summer; 2 feet.

Live-for-ever, Dark-red (var. *hybridum*). — Very showy foliage and flowers.

Houseleek (*Sempervivum*).—Numerous species; showy in flowers and leaves.

Catchfly, Alpine (*Silene alpestris*).—White; 3 to 6 inches.

Tunica, Rock (*Tunica Saxifraga*).—Whitish; summer; 3 to 4 inches.

Speedwell, Alpine (*Veronica alpina*).—Bluish; 2 to 12 inches.

Strawberry, Barren (*Waldsteinia fragarioides*).—Yellow; summer; 2 to 6 inches.

CLASS V.—FERNS AND SHADE-LOVING PLANTS.

This list embraces such plants, as are usually met in partly open woods, exiting our admiration by their simple beauty, and often by the sweetness of their flowers. Directions are given in Part IV for preparing a soil that will suit them. While all love moisture, they will not do well where it is exceedingly wet. Some prefer the elevation that rockwork in the shade affords. In these cases the fact is stated along with the descriptions.

Anemone, Wood (*Anemone nemorosa*).—White; early spring; 6 inches. Double Wood Anemone.—Double; white; 6 inches. Double Bracted Anemone (var. *bracteata*).—Double; white; green bracts. Double Rose-colored Anemone.—Double; red.

Apennine Anemone (*A. Apennina*).—Bright blue; early spring; 6 inches.

Adam and Eve (*Aplectrum hyemale*).—A hardy native orchid.

Jack in the Pulpit (*Arisæma triphyllum*).—Purple and white; 18 inches.

Snakeroot, Virginian (*Aristolochia Serpentaria*).—Purple; summer; 18 inches.

Snakeroot, Canadian (*Asarum Canadense*).—Brownish-purple; spring.

Snakeroot, Heart-leaved (*A. Virginicum*).—Purple and green; April; low.

Tailed Snakeroot (*A. caudatum*).—Brownish-purple.

Cornus, Dwarf, or Bunch Berry (*Cornus Canadensis*). White; June; 5 to 7 inches.

Lady's Slipper, Stemless (*Cypripedium acaule*).—Rosy-purple; May; 10 inches.

Lady's Slipper, European (*C. Calceolus*). — Dark-brown; 2 feet.

Cowslip, American or Shooting Star (*Dodecatheon Meadia*.—Rose; spring; 8 to 12 inches.

Cowslip, American, Jaffray's (var. *lancifolium*).—A larger variety.

Trailing Arbutus, or Mayflower (*Epigæa repens*).—White and pink; prostrate.

Ferns and Brakes.—The following are some of the most useful hardy species :

Maiden-hair Fern, Hardy (*Adiantum pedatum*).—9 to 15 inches.

Fragrant Wood Fern (*Aspidium fragrans*).—4 to 12 inches.

Shield Fern (*A. acrostichioides*).—1 to 2 feet.

Chamisso's Shield Fern (*A. munitum*).—1 to 5 feet.

Spleenwort (*Asplenium ebeneum*).—8 inches and upward.

Moonwort (*Botrychium*).—There are several species.

Walking Fern (*Camptosorus rhizophyllus*).—Prostrate.

Lip Fern, Hairy (*Cheilanthes vestita*).–6 to 15 inches.

Fig. 11.—DOWNY LIP FERN (*Cheilanthes tomentosa*).

Lip Fern, Downy (*C. tomentosa*).—Rather stout; 12 to 20 inches; protect.

Deer Fern (*Lomaria Spicant*).—Evergreen; 6 to 30 inches.

Flowering Fern (*Osmunda*).—Several species; 2 to 5 feet.

Polypod Fern (*Polypodium vulgare*).—Evergreen; 4 to 10 inches.

Chain Fern (*Woodsia Ilvensis*).—2 to 6 inches.

Cliff Brake (*Pellæa atropurpurea*).—2 to 6 inches.

Common Brake (*Pteris aquilina*).—2 feet.

Fritillaria, Lance-leaved (*Fritillaria lanceolata*). — Purple; summer; 6 inches.

Fritillaria, Purple (*F. atropurpurea*).—Purplish ; 4 to 20 inches.

Rattlesnake Plantain (*Goodyera*).—Several species with fine leaves; shaded rocky.

Christmas Rose, Common (*Helleborus niger*).—Greenish-white; early spring; 1 foot.

Christmas Rose, Dark Purple (*H. atrorubens*).—Purplish-red; 1 foot.

Helonias, Spiked (*Helonias bullata*).—Showy purple; May; 1 to 2 feet.

Hepatica, or Liverleaf (*Hepatica*).—Shades of blue; early spring.   There are various colors, and single and double varieties.

Orchis, Showy (*Orchis spectabilis*).—Pink, purple, white lip ; 4 to 8 inches.

Polygala, Fringed (*Polygala paucifolia*).—Purple; 3 to 4 inches.

Rosette Mullein (*Ramondia Pyrenaica*).—Purple and orange; 2 to 6 inches.

Meadow Beauty (*Rhexia Virginica*).—Reddish-purple; neat; 8 to 12 inches.

Bloodroot (*Sanguinaria Canadensis*).—Purple; white; early spring; 3 to 8 inches.

Club Moss (*Selaginella*).—Several useful native species.

False Solomon's Seal (*Smilacina stellata*).—White ; summer; 1 to 2 feet.

Wake Robin, Nodding (*Trillium cernuum*).—White ; nodding; spring; 12 to 18 inches.

Wake Robin, Painted (*T. erythrocarpum*).—White and purple; spring; 8 to 12 inches.

Wake Robin, Snowy (*T. nivale*).—Small; white; early spring; 2 to 4 inches.

Wood Lily (*T. grandiflorum*).—Large; white, changing to rose.

Violet, Canada (*Viola Canadensis*).—Whitish; summer; 1 foot.

Violet, Yellow (*V. pubescens*).—Yellow; spring; 6 to 12 inches.

Violet, Arrow-leaved (*V. sagittata*).—Purplish blue; spring.

May Apple (*Podophyllum peltatum*).—White; May; 1 foot.

CLASS VI.—AQUATIC AND BOG PLANTS.

An interesting class of plants, and quite easy to grow, where attention to their simple requirements is paid; respecting these, some information is given in Part IV as to place and soil.

Sweet Flag (*Acorus Calamus*).—Greenish; sword-like leaves; 2 to 3 feet.

Green Dragon (*Arisœma Dracontium*). — Greenish; divided leaves.

Water Shield (*Brasenia peltata*).—Dark purple; July.

Calopogon (*C. pulchellus*).—An orchid; purple; 1 foot.

Marsh Marigold (*Caltha palustris*).—Yellow; spring; 1 foot. Marsh Marigold, Double.—A variety of the above.

Calypso, Northern (*Calypso borealis*).—An orchid; pink and yellow.

Lady's Slipper, Showy (*Cypripedium spectabile*).—White, crimson; July; 1 to 2 feet.

Lady's Slipper, Small White (*C. candidum*).—Greenish-white; 1 foot.

Lady's Slipper, Small Yellow (*C. parviflorum*).—
Yellow; spring; 1 to 2 feet.

Lady's Slipper, Ram's Head (*C. arietinum*).—Red
and white; June; 6 to 10 inches.

Pitcher Plant, California (*Darlingtonia Californica*).
Purplish; 1 to 3 feet; protect.

Marsh Calla (*Calla palustris*).—White; summer; 6 to
9 inches.

Sundew, Thread-leaved (*Drosera filiformis*).—Rose;
summer; 6 to 12 inches.

Sundew, Round-leaved (*D. rotundifolia*).—White;
summer; 6 inches.

Fringed Orchis, Yellow (*Habenaria ciliaris*).—Yellow;
summer; 1 to 2 feet.

Fringed Orchis, White (*H. blephariglottis*).—White;
12 to 15 inches.

Fringed Orchis, Purple (*H. fimbriata*). — Lilac,
purple; 1 to 2 feet.

Fringed Orchis, Small Purple (*H. psycodes*). —
Purple; fragrant; 12 to 18 inches.

Cardinal Flower (*Lobelia cardinalis*).—Intense scarlet;
1 to 3 feet.

Water Lily, White (*Nymphæa odorata*). — White,
changing to rose.

Water Lily, Yellow (*Nuphar advena*). — Yellow;
summer.

Golden Club (*Orontium aquaticum*).—Elliptic leaves;
fine for ponds.

Grass of Parnassus (*Parnassia asarifolia*).—White;
summer; 3 to 6 inches.

Pogonia (*Pogonia*).—A hardy orchid; a number of
species.

Centaury, American (*Sabbatia chloroides*). — Rose;
summer; 12 to 18 inches.

Centaury, Lance-leaved (*S. lanceolata*).—White; 1
to 3 feet.

Arrow Head (*Sagittaria variabilis*).—Aquatic, with pretty leaves.

Pitcher-Plant, Side-Saddle Flower (*Sarracenia purpurea*).—Purple; 1 foot. There are several other interesting species of *Sarracenia*.

Fig. 12.—ARROW HEAD (*Sagittaria variabilis*).

Globe Flower, American (*Trollius laxus*).—Greenish-yellow; May; 1 foot.

Cat-tail, or Reed Mace (*Typha latifolia*).—Brown; summer; 3 to 5 feet.

Cat-tail, Narrow-leaved (*T. angustifolia*). — More slender and smaller.

Pickerel Weed (*Pontederia caudata*).—Blue; July; a fine water-plant.

CHAPTER X.

ANNUAL PLANTS.

What are known as Annuals, are those plants which owe their perpetuation, especially in the North, to seeds, or to bulbs which are taken up in the fall and started newly with every year. The plants grow up, flower, produce a new crop of seed or bulbs, and then die, all in one season. Although the lists of annual flowers in the catalogues are usually very extensive—some German catalogues containing lists of no less than three thousand different sorts—it is found that the number of those which really possess a high order of attractiveness is not very large. As the catalogues of dealers usually treat elaborately on the matter of varieties, merits, and adaptability, in the present book, I only take space to give some select lists to guide planters, referring the reader to the catalogues for additional matter.

Some kinds embraced in the lists below, are perennials or biennials, but as they flower the first season from the seed, they are brought into this selection.

In the lists, *h* stands for hardy annual, or sorts that may be treated as such; *h*, *h*, stands for half hardy annuals; *t*, for tender annuals. Directions for sowing are given in Part V.

A SELECTION OF THE CHOICER KINDS OF BEDDING AN-
NUALS.

Aster, *h, h.*	Petunia, *h, h.*
Balsam, *h, h.*	Phlox Drummondi, *h.*
Candytuft, *h,*	Portulaca, *t.*
Cockscomb, *t.*	Snap Dragon, *h.*
Larkspur, *h.*	Stocks, *h, h.*
Marigold, *h.*	Sweet Alyssum, *h.*
Mignonette, *h.*	Verbena, *h, h.*
Dwarf Nasturtium, *h, h.*	Zinnia, *h.*
Pansy, *h.*	Sweet Pea, *h.*

A SELECTION OF BEDDING ANNUALS OF SECONDARY MERIT.

Abronia, *h.*	Sunflower, *h.*
Calliopsis, *h.*	Lychnis, *h, h.*
Callirrhoë, *h.*	Lupine, *h.*
Campanula, *h.*	Flora's Paint Brush, *h.*
Batchelor's Button, *h.*	Gaillardia, *h.*
Collinsia, *h.*	Browallia, *h, h.*
Dwarf Morning Glory, *h.*	Four O'Clocks, *t.*
Centranthus, *h.*	Nigella, *h.*
Clarkia, *h.*	Salpiglossis, *h, h.*
Ageratum, *h.*	Salvia, *t.*
Eschscholtzia, *h.*	Mourning Bride, *h.*
Erysimum, *h.*	Sensitive Plant, *t.*
Godetia, *h.*	Sweet Rocket, *h.*

Swan River Daisy, *h, h.*

A SELECTION OF ANNUALS OF CLIMBING AND RUNNING HABIT.

Morning Glory, *h.*	Maurandia, *t.*
Cobæa scandens, *t.*	Nasturtium, *h, h.*
Hyacinth Bean, *t.*	Canary Bird Flower, *h, h.*
Gourds, *t.*	Thunbergia, *t.*
Cypress Vine, *t.*	Scarlet Runner, *t.*

A SELECTION OF ANNUALS WITH SHOWY FOLIAGE SUITABLE FOR TROPICAL EFFECTS.

Amaranthus, *t.*	Perilla, *h, h.*
Canna, *h, h.*	Castor Oil Bean, *t.*
Chamæpeuce, *h, h.*	Golden Feather, *h.*
Centaurea, *h, h.*	Tobacco, *t.*
Glaucium, *h, h.*	Striped Maize, *t.*

A SELECTION OF ANNUALS SUITABLE FOR NATURALIZATION IN THE WILD GARDEN.

Clarkia.	Leptosiphon.
Collomia.	Portulaca.
Erisymum.	Gilia.
Eucharidium.	Poppy.
Candytuft.	Platystemon.
Gypsophila,	Silene.
Godetia.	Saponaria.

A SELECTION OF ANNUAL BULBS, TUBERS, AND ROOTS.

Caladium.	Madeira Vine.
Canna.	Oxalis.
Dahlia.	Tuberose.
Erythrina.	Tigridia.
Gladiolus.	Richardia.

CHAPTER XI.

TENDER PERENNIAL PLANTS.

By the help of artificial heat in green-houses, the list of natural materials for ornamental gardening is much enlarged. We go towards the equator and collect attractive species, and by preserving them from the cold in winter, can turn them out in summer, and thus are able to enjoy something of tropical vegetation in the North. Lack of space forbids giving much attention to this subject here, but several lists are introduced, in which are named the leading kinds of plants used for adorning pleasure grounds, and where further information is wanted, the reader is referred to books on floriculture, and to the catalogues of florists.

Alyssum, Variegated.
Alyssum, Double flowering.
Abutilon.
Century Plant.
Ageratum.
Alternanthera.
Carnation.
Cigar Plant (*Cuphea*).
Coleus.
Dusty Miller (*Centaurea*).
Echeveria.
Geranium, single, double, and variegated-leaved.
Dew Plant (*Mesembryan-themum*).

Gnaphalium lanatum.
Heliotrope.
Hibiscus.
Lantana.
Lobelia.
Leucophyton.
Othonna sedifolia.
Salvia splendens.
Verbena.
Achyranthes.
Sedums.
Variegated Thyme.
Variegated Stevia.
Cannas.
Caladiums.

A SELECTION OF PLANTS WITH SHOWY FOLIAGE SUITABLE FOR EFFECTS IN SUB-TROPICAL GARDENS.

Acacia lophantha.
Agaves in variety.
Alsophila australis.
Aralia macrophylla.
Aralia papyrifera.
Araucaria excelsa.
Caladium.
Canna.
Chamæpeuce diacantha.
Dracenas in variety.
Echeveria Metallica.
Erythina Crista-galli.
Ferdinanda eminens.
Ficus elastica.
Dicksonia antarctica.
Melianthus major.

Musa Ensete.
Papyrus antiquorum.
Phormium tenax.
Polymnia grandis.
Solanum Warscewiczii.
Wigandia macrophylla.
Ricinus in variety.

PALMS.

Corypha australis.
Carludovica palmata.
Caryota in variety.
Chamærops in variety.
Cycas revoluta.
Latania Borbonica.
Phoenix in variety.
Seaforthia elegans.

CHAPTER XII.

MISCELLANEOUS NATURAL MATERIAL.

Rocks and stones are not, like soil, absolutely necessary to garden making, yet the frequency with which
these are met in attractive natural scenery, and their power
in contributing to picturesqueness, entitle them, at
the least, to be named among available garden materials.
In other parts of this book, considerable attention is
paid to their use in ornamental gardening.

What is true of the ornamental value of rocks, is mainly and in an enlarged degree true of water in garden
and landscape scenery.   Remove the sparkling river,
lake, and spring, the gurgling rill, swift rapids and waterfalls, out of nature, and she would be devoid of some
of her most attractive charms.   It is well, therefore, to consider the ornamental value of water, when
gardens are large enough to admit of it in some form.

Some kinds of beasts, birds, and fishes add much to
the charms of natural scenery.   Cattle, sheep, and deer,
grazing or else reclining in the shade, contribute an
effect to scenes that without them would be tame.   The
sweet-voiced birds in the trees, the graceful water-fowl
in the lake, or the schools of tame fishes within its
bosom, are all of great value for adding to the interest
of pleasure grounds.   While in the majority of places it
may not be practicable to do much in the way of introducing these, yet their value should not be lost sight of
where circumstances will allow of them.

In addition to the natural garden making materials which have now been named in this book, there
are many other things, from the gravel of walks to the
slate on the roof, that might be enumerated.   But as
these are used mostly as mere constructive material,
there is little need of so doing.

PART III.

ARRANGEMENT.

CHAPTER XIII.

GENERAL PRINCIPLES.

NATURE AS A TEACHER.

As nature supplies the materials for making gardens, so also we may take lessons from her in arranging them. Still the primitive, natural style of arrangement can seldom be closely followed in the majority of places that are to be improved. The horticulturist takes the wild plants from fields and woods, and in improving them always finds in nature herself a co-worker, and succeeds in rearing some plants that are more beautiful than the wild. So natural arrangement may be studied, and in planning our comparatively restricted garden plats, the lessons thus gained may be modified to meet the wants of every case. Indeed, just so far as our improved plants and flowers are more ornamental than the parental wild forms, so do we possess more and richer material for creating garden effects, than is seen in nature. We may aim in ornamental gardening to exhibit nature idealized, rather than nature real.

The fundamental difference between natural landscapes, and made gardens, is, that in the former only natural materials exist, while in the latter much that is artificial, houses, walks, streets, etc., enters in, as a rule, exerting a strong influence on effects. Such being the case we are often led to a different course of action in gardening, than if we dealt solely with natural effects.

(161)

MAJOR AND MINOR FEATURES OF EMBELLISHMENT.

It is important to observe that the nearer the materials used for making ornamental gardens are to their natural condition, the more freely may they be used, if generally appropriate without offending good taste and *vice versa*. A town lot, for example, might be unadorned, except with grass and not look distasteful, but if we plant every foot solid with the brightest art-improved flowers, the effect would then be shocking. Use a large proportion of grass—because it is a material near the natural condition, and a few improved flowers—because they are more or less distantly removed from their primitive forms by culture, and both are better for these proportions. In the same class with grass are trees, shrubs, wild flowers, rocks, and water, and these, when not in a general way inappropriate, and are arranged naturally, may be used almost without limit as major features of adornment in landscape gardening. But arrange trees and shrubs formally, or clip them into unnatural shapes, or make "geometrical" beds of improved flowers, or artifical terraces, walks and drives, or bring statuary, fountains, and the like into gardens, and it must, as a rule, be on a moderate scale or bad effects result. Such productions in gardening, like jewels in dress, must be used with discretion, having an appropriate setting, or their power to gratify is weakened.

The famous gardens of Versailles, France, are only great in the respect that millions of francs have been spent in the stupid attempt to enlarge what should serve as minor embellishments into leading features, crowding the place with semi-natural and artificially clipped trees, formal beds, fountains, water-works, avenues, terraces, etc., until nothing is left to embellish.

But a garden may be so essentially artificial, owing to smallness or the proximity of large buildings, etc., that an artificial style of embellishment may fitly prevail to a considerable degree, on the principle that the introduced garden features are yet decidedly subordinate in degree, to the general features—in this case strongly artificial. Thus urns and boxes filled with the brightest flowers may be used in roof, portico, or window gardening, to a degree that would be utterly out of place in the same proportions in general gardening. So too, conspicuous terraces and slopes are in better taste in close conjunction with buildings—especially large ones, than in the midst of a garden not naturally very undulating.

VARIETY.

In natural landscapes, it is the variety afforded by woodland, meadow, mountain and water, the light and shade in trees and plants, the sunshine and shadow, the cheerfulness in forms, foliage and flowers, the sparkling of water, the sound of rills, and other of nature's attractions that charm us. And then in such a distribution of these, as to render no two scenes alike, we find great delight for our love of variety. This should lead us to aim in gardening at introducing first, the peculiar natural and other beauty each garden can best support in good variety. Secondly, to act on nature's suggestion, and vary the effects of different gardens as they may allow. As no two natural landscapes are exactly alike, so no two gardens ever need be.

CHARACTER AND EXPRESSION.

Individual character and positive qualities are as desirable in gardens as in architecture, or as they are in persons. In the garden, these chiefly depend on the shape of surface, the natural lay of the land, outlines, size and character of the buildings, size and arrangement of trees, walks, drives, etc. Some grounds are like some men,

hard and abrupt in character, naturally, and will bear
cultivation and a toning down of some of the projections.
Others are found that possess grace of outlines, and an
air of polish that will need little improving.   Some lands
are tame, flat, and spiritless, requiring all the gardener's
arts to render them pleasing.   Outside influences, such
as the sea, trees, buildings, etc., in sight, also affect the
character and appearance of the place.   These in a sense
are subject to our control, as respects giving them a setting, so to speak, by opening vistas towards them between plantations as viewed from the interior, or shutting them out of view entirely.   This is a matter requiring much attention when arranging a garden.

One piece of ground may resemble another in general
character, and yet be greatly varied in expression and
tone.   With the use of different styles and colors of
trees, shrubs, and plants—in both foliage and flowers,
we may control and vary expression in gardening to a
marked degree, and change the appearance of different
gardens otherwise essentially alike.   We have power to
clothe these, as we do our bodies with materials, styles,
and colors to suit every taste.

ORDER AND SIMPLICITY.

These are chief elements of all true beauty.   It is not
uncommon to see gardens of pretence, that are complete
muddles of grass, trees, walks, drives, arbors, etc.   In
nothing will order and simplicity count for more than when
using garden-making materials with a view to creating
beautiful effects about our homes and grounds.   Through
a desire for display, one is liable to overdo, by bringing
too many objects into the garden and scattering them
unduly.   Simplicity implies neither poverty in materials
or in design.   A garden, or the parts of a garden, may
be essentially simple in design, and elaborate in detail.

UNITY AND HARMONY.

A unity of the objects of a garden for contributing to
a complete whole, a harmonizing of these, one with another, and a balance of the different features and sections,
are important things to secure in planning an ornamental
garden. Where marked features and bold contrasts are
sought, there should also be agreeable, easy transition
from one to another, without abrupt breaks to interfere
with the harmony. In all large works abounding in details, we crave for some such comprehensive plan, where-
by the total may be retained while surveying the part.

BREADTH AND EXTENT.

Nothing is more desirable to secure in a garden than
an air of breadth and repose, such as nature so often re-
veals in her attractive landscapes. This can be done by
keeping some conspicuous areas clear in their center, excepting grass, and skirting them about with masses of
woody and other growths. Natural landscapes usually
suggest the idea of unlimited extent beyond what the
eye sees at any point. The same thing is quite possible
to secure in our gardens, by managing them to show
ample breadth in parts, and some extended vistas between the farthest limits, and then breaking the views
along the outlines, by so planting that there may seem
to be large areas unseen beyond projecting groups.
There is such a thing as so managing an acre, that it
shall seem as large as two or more acres.

Where outside scenery, like mountains, water, neigh-
boring landscapes, etc., can be "appropriated" to contribute to one's own garden, by so arranging the interior
as to allow such scenery to show at its best from the garden, or even seem to be a part of it. This can often
easily be accomplished, and by all means let it be done.

RICHNESS AND FINISH.

A certain air of richness and finish in the arrangement and keeping of the pleasure grounds, goes far towards raising them up to the highest ideal of such a place. Gracefulness of lines, elegance of ornaments, and a general appearance of finish in the composition and the effect of groups, are among the features that delight us. A place in even a partial state of disorder and neglect, shocks our sense of beauty. Due regard to the little matters of mown lawns, clean walks, carefully attended edges, absence of weeds and litter, cultivated borders, clean and well-painted architectural features, have such a marked effect on the pleasure a place may afford that they can not be lightly disregarded.

CONVENIENCE.

Let it be remembered that gardens are for use as well as ornament, hence they should be accessible and convenient, and this should always be kept in mind in locating different objects, walks, and drives. There is no more conflict between utility and beauty in the garden than elsewhere, and we may always aim to have it very convenient, and at the same time very handsome.

CHAPTER XIV.

THE HOME BUILDINGS.

The house, because of its crowning importance, and for sanitary reasons also, should stand somewhat elevated above the common surface. The same is true in a somewhat less degree of other buildings also. If grounds are level, or if the most suitable place for the building is not as high as would be desirable, the foundation walls may be carried to a proper elevation, then by using the soil excavated for cellars and foundations, and more if needed, for filling in, the surface may be brought as high as desirable, allowing properly for settling. As finished, the surface should slope away from every building, so that water from heavy rains and snows will be led from, instead of towards the walls, to cause dampness.

The windows and verandas should be so situated as to command good views of the garden, and especially from the living rooms. We want the benefit of garden beauty in the home, when the state of the weather forbids walking out, and at all other times. There is no more delightful time for enjoying the garden than during, or just after a rain, or in twilight, when approaching nightfall softens the outlines and casts a mellowness and quietness over the scene. The house and garden should both be planned with reference to the enjoyment of the view at such times as these. When buildings are too low, as seen from the street, or from the garden itself, they have a depressing influence on the surroundings, robbing the scene of much of the fine effect which belongs to every well designed structure, and not allowing the purely ornamental features of it to show for all they are worth.

CHAPTER XV.

THE SURFACE.

That which may be called character, in an ornamental garden, is largely owing to the contour of its surface. It is realized at once that a flattish garden, which happens to be lower through its center, has a tame look, while a similar piece, but slightly crowning along the middle, seems to possess character. Sometimes, however, a plot perfectly straight in its surface line is pleasing, and seems to fit a place better than any other could, but, as a rule, some variation from the straight line is preferable.

In nature we find more delight in the bold hills and valleys than in level stretches of plain. This is because we love variety, and in undulations of the surface, we find a form of this, independent of the variety afforded by that which grows upon it. This fact suggests the desirability of introducing undulations, wherever the size of grounds and other circumstances will allow.

For small grounds of a third of an acre and less, aside from buildings, the even or slightly crowning center is, as regards shape, the best. But even in these, in many

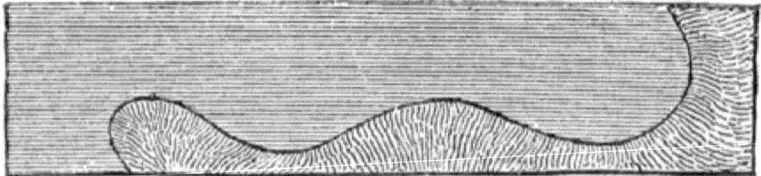

Fig. 13.—AN UNDULATING BORDER.

cases a decided departure may be made which, without destroying the identity of the style, will afford scope for bringing in not only considerable variety of surface in places, but also the means for greatly increasing the beauty in other ways. I refer to the making of a series of undulations which are to be treated as cultivated borders, for some years at least, to be planted with small trees, flowering and evergreen shrubs and plants.

These borders should come mostly along the boundaries, and may vary in width according to the size of the place. Figure 13 illustrates the outlines of one of these.

The merits of such borders in creating interest and variety in a place, however small, are several. Firstly, by making them of varying widths throughout their length, the ground in them may be made more crowning in the wide parts than where they are narrower, thus causing a marked variation of the surface in the center lengthwise. Then the wavy outlines give variety in the shape of the border on the grounds, where it meets the grass. Further still, with affording room for planting numerous trees, shrubs and plants, of different forms, habits and seasons of attractiveness, a great addition to the interest and beauty of a place is possible. Besides these, if selections of trees, shrubs, etc., for planting, the size they attain at maturity is kept in view, by placing tall-growing subjects in the highest parts, and dwarf kinds in the lower and narrower places, a still further means of creating variety is gained.

Fig. 14.—A RAISED BORDER AGAINST THE HOUSE.

Something similar to the boundary borders may also be made next to the house, at junctions of walks and other places, for the sake of having more of this feature, and to preserve a proper balance throughout the grounds.

Fig. 15.—UNDULATED BORDER PLANTED WITH SHRUBBERY AND FLOWERS.

Those next to the house may come along the foundation in front of the piazza, around bay windows, or in corners made by angles in the shape of the house, somewhat

8

as indicated in figure 14, while the same method of arranging the plants indicated for the marginal borders,
may be employed here.

Figure 15 shows the appearance of these planted undulations, with the effect of the variations in the size of
growths alluded to. It will be seen that with all the
advantages of this style for creating interest, there may
still be maintained, even in small places, the open area
of lawn, essential for imparting an air of breadth and
repose.

Another gain by such borders is, that with good arrangement, they hide the natural limits of a place, thus
giving an idea of increased largeness of the garden
area. Instead of the conspicuous sharp line caused
by the fence meeting the ground, we may have an actually longer, because wavy line, at the front for the eye

Fig. 16.   Fig. 17.   Fig. 18.
ADJUSTING GROUNDS TO THE LEVEL OF THE STREET.

to rest upon, by this means ridding the place of an air of
narrowness and angularity, and having instead, graceful
lines of increased length, decidedly conducive to pleasing effect.

No two places should receive the same treatment, as
regards shape and planting of undulating borders. The
plans figure 30 to 35 will give some idea regarding different ways of arrangement. It is surprising what an
effect small rises and depressions, of even a few inches,
will have in removing dullness, and imparting an air of
grace and freedom to such borders or to mounds. In
some places along the boundary there should be breaks
extending to the fence. In selecting shrubs, pains should
be taken to employ those of strikingly different appearance

in leaf, flowers, and forms, for the sake of contrast, and to place those with beautiful foliage and habits, near the house, and other conspicuous places.

Sometimes undulated borders may be employed to advantage in another way. A case of a two-acre garden on a corner, where there was a continuous fall in the streets in a south and eastern direction, amounting to about fifteen feet, may be used to illustrate. It was considered desirable, owing to the natural lay of the land, to keep the surface of the garden nearly level, notwithstanding the fall in the street. Figures 16, 17, 18, representing cross sections of the boundary undulations at these points, namely, where the street was a little higher than the general garden level, (figure 16). Where it was uniform with it (figure 17), and where considerably lower (figure 18), will explain how the case was satisfactorily managed; the

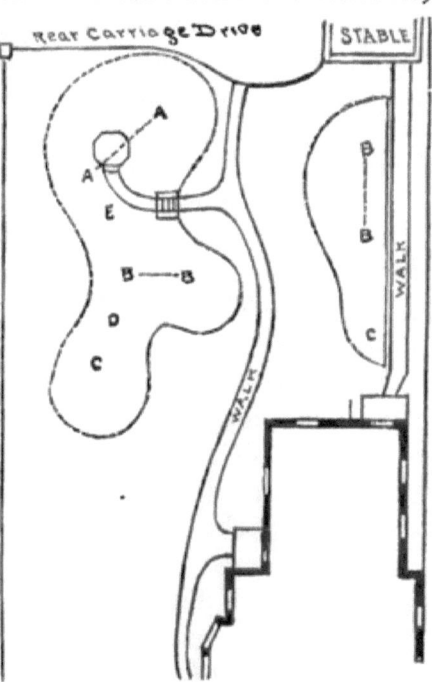

Fig. 19.—PLAN OR MOUND FOR TREES.

dotted lines in the engraving representing the garden surface. From the interior of the garden, hardly any idea of the descent outside, or of the streets themselves, can be gathered, which in this case was desirable, owing to the heavy traffic going on through one of them.

Another effective style of surface variation sometimes introduced, consists of one or more mounds somewhat centrally located, and away from house and boundaries

to be planted with trees and shrubs. The object may be
the mere formation of a new style of garden variety, to
hide a near approach or some unsightly object. Figure
19 illustrates the idea, *A* representing the highest point,
in this instance crowned with an arbor, and the other
letters below, show lower levels downward. Such mounds
introduced into grounds where the prevailing character
of the surface is even, are more difficult to manage than
the boundary mounds, or these against buildings, on
account of their standing out in bold relief. The emer-
gence of the elevation into the general level should be
soft and gradual, a point respecting which too great care
cannot be taken. Indeed it requires a great degree of
good taste to manage these so they may appear natural.

In gardens the surfaces of which are generally even,
there is not that absolute necessity to have the grade
strictly even over the whole lawn, that many seem to
think. Certain gentle variations here and there, and especially if trees and shrubs are set on the higher points, are
in place in almost any grounds. But attention to smooth-
ness and finish in minor respects is as much in order in
such cases, as if the whole were made uniformly and
precisely straight.

In larged sized grounds, from an acre upwards, with
rare exceptions, a departure from a surface of a generally level character is to be preferred. Of three different kinds of surface usually to be met, namely : the
level, the abruptly hilly, and a mean between these two,
the latter is considered the best for making a large area
interesting, and abounding in pleasing garden effects.
The objection to the plane as a style of surface for a
large garden is, that it yields no variety to the eye, independent of what is brought upon it. If strong, bold
effects, either in the planting or in undulating the surface are desired here, they are from the nature of things
very expensive to make. As regards the other extreme,

a Park may be so entirely composed of large hills, that the very sight of the place, and the thought of following the up and down courses of the paths is enough to tire any but a strong person. With a mean between these two, we have the advantage of variety as afforded by the hills and vales without much inconvenience of ascent and descent.

Where grounds of this preferred character are to be improved, it is often easy to increase their effectiveness by drawing out some existing features more strongly. A prominence may be added to, at the expense of the valley bottom at the side, or one mound removed to increase the strength of another, or a lake be excavated to the advantage of the surroundings. Naturally such improvements suggest heavy expenses at the outset. But let it be considered that every load of material moved in such operations counts for two, because a depression of one foot here, added to an elevation elsewhere, effects an actual change in both of two feet at the expense of moving one foot of earth.

In every fair sized garden, prominent elevations to support shady arbors, and from which to get a bird's eye view of the scenery, and to catch cool breezes in hot weather are worth aiming to secure. For guidance in every kind of mound construction the brief suggestions accompanying figure 19 are in a general way applicable.

In earlier times, as many European gardens yet bear evidence, it was thought that pleasure grounds to be beautiful, must present a very artificial appearance. Surfaces that were naturally quite level were so managed as to present a series of terraces and slopes. Trees were not only all of them planted in formal lines, but they were by hundreds distorted into outrageous patterns by clipping. The world moves, and landscape gardeners to-day, although not disposed to set aside the old formal style in every case, as a rule insist that the nearer they can keep to nature's ways of using nature's materials, the more pleasing will be the result. What is admired most in nature is the very freedom and informality, which in by-gone times was avoided. In severely formal gardens the picture may strike us with delight at first sight, but being unchangeable, we tire of it in time, unless there are counter-balancing features to offset the formality.

Where a garden is on a hillside, and the natural contour is too abrupt for beauty or convenience, the terrace and slope arrangement, with stairways in the walks, sometimes come in use to advantage. We recall an admirable illustration of the use of this style in the terraces and slopes in the Queen's Park at Glasgow. Partly for convenience, and partly for effect in relieving the sameness that would exist in a not very large park, by the presence of too many natural hills, there was contructed a series of these on a large scale, which for their general fitness, simplicity and beauty, are most charming. There is a well-known and most delightful Italian garden at Wellesley, the estate of H. H. Hunnewell, Esq., near Boston, Mass., constructed at the head of a lake on a steep bluff, which very strikingly shows that in some places a contribution of formal terraces, slopes, clipped trees, balustrades, stairways, and vases may be introduced as a minor feature of an extensive private park, with very pleasing effect. Small plats in towns, or even small public squares, hemmed in with buildings, may, with fountains or other artificial objects, walks, etc., be so essentially artificial in appearance, and strongly influenced by architectural lines, as to very properly admit of considerable formality in the arrangement.

The guiding principle in every instance where the making of terraces and slopes is invited, should be to introduce them only as objects of embellishment, and where the surroundings show some other features of great boldness and strength. They should seem to be secondary

in importance and effect to something else, be that something buildings, towers, monuments, prominent hills, or
large adjacent areas devoted to a natural style of effects.

Terrace and slope combinations should, with rare exceptions, be characterized by a great degree of simplicity
in their arrangement. The complicated pretty productions in this line, sometimes met with in old school gardens in Europe, are intolerable to every one of correct

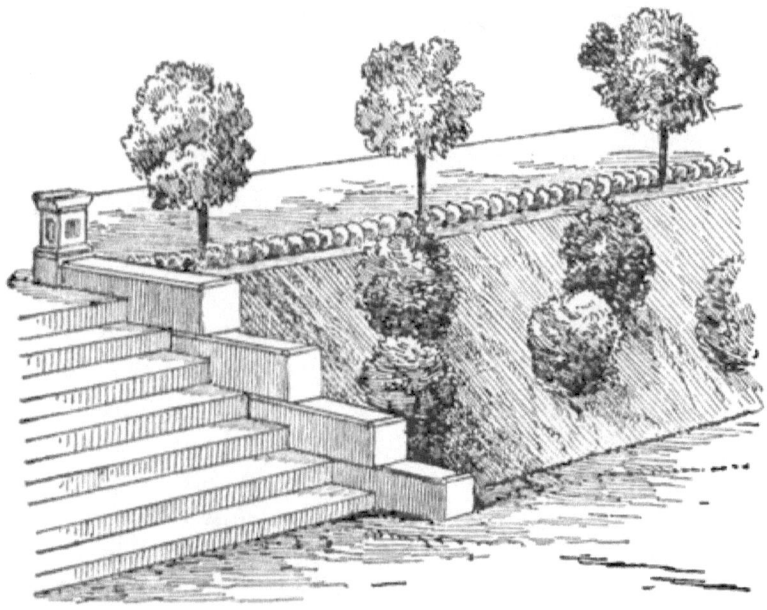

Fig. 20.—TERRACE WORK ADORNED WITH TREES, SHRUBS, AND FLOWERS.

taste. The use of trees and shrubs in different places
for balancing the parts and relieving the geometrical
lines, is very desirable, provided they are dispersed with
taste. Figure 20 shows a simple terrace slope, embellished with roses or other shrubs with good effect.
There is also shown a row of trees and a line of geraniums, or other showy plants, on the level above in front
of the balustrade. Such a method of embellishment
goes far towards ridding these constructions, of what is

to many persons one of the greatest objections, namely, the prevailing blankness of the slopes as frequently seen.

What is called a Sunken Garden consists of depressed terraces of one or more levels—square, round or other shape—constructed lower than the general surface, and meeting with it by some well-formed, easy slopes. On these lower levels flowers, shrubs, vases, fountains and so forth are displayed, all designed to be viewed from above. Sometimes there are walks and stairs leading down to the lower levels. The making of such gardens is recommended only with caution, as rarely can they be made to serve as good a purpose, even for the sake of increased variety, as the same area and conditions treated more naturally.

I have sometimes employed a style of small terraces retained by a stone coping with good effect, as shown in

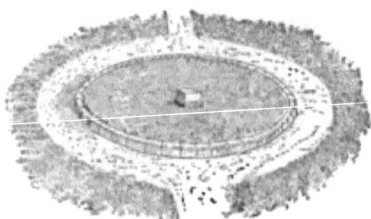

Fig. 21.—CIRCULAR TERRACE IN A WALK RETAINED BY A STONE COPING.

figure 21. Where some bold object in a town or other garden seems essential, to counteract the influence of large buildings, this terrace placed in the center of a walk or elsewhere serves a good purpose. The center may support a vase, or piece of statuary placed on a base or a fountain. Properly the ground should be rounded up a little towards the object in the center. A bed of brilliant flowers extending around the terrace next to the coping, save a narrow strip of grass between, produces a fine effect. The remainder of the surface should be in grass.

There are ways of treating boundary lines and fences often met with in Europe, which might at times be adopted in improving our own grounds. I refer to the plan of contriving to keep the boundary and other fences out of sight, as shown in figures 22 and 23. By such means, large outside areas may often be appropriated in effect, and a garden of a few acres seems to embrace large outside areas because the boundaries are not visible. Carrying with them as they do the idea of being works of art, terraces, and slopes of all kinds should be made with exactness in their levels, and with as straight lines and

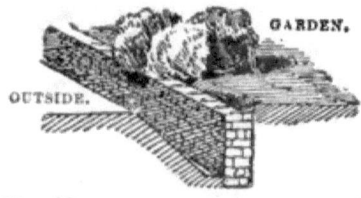

Fig. 22.—BOUNDARY WALL SET OUT OF SIGHT FROM THE GARDEN.

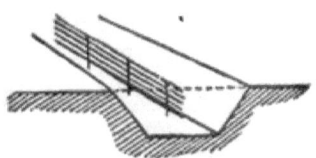

Fig. 23.—A SUNKEN CROSS-FENCE.

as true curves as possible, and for the same reason it is necessary to bestow a greater degree of care upon their keeping than is required by most other styles of garden work. Scarcely anything in the way of a garden is more intolerable than the pretentious, formal work, in a state of slovenly neglect.

CHAPTER XVI.

WALKS AND DRIVES.

When well located, walks and drives convey the idea of habitableness, imparting an air of welcome and freedom to a home and grounds, and in no slight degree seem to promote the beauty of a place.

The most important walks and drives are those at the entrance. If these can be laid out, to approach the home or buildings from such a direction, that more than one side of the building will strike the eye at once, it should always be done. Architects ask that a house be

thus seen to show it at its best.   We should aim to make
the first view of a residence and grounds as favorable as
possible.

In places of the smallest size, where the door is near
the street, a straight walk is about the only one that can
be devised, and so of a drive to the stable.   When the
door of the house is twenty or more feet from the
entrance gate, curves may usually be introduced by
having the gate not directly in front of the door, but a
little to one side.   Such an arrangement tends to keep

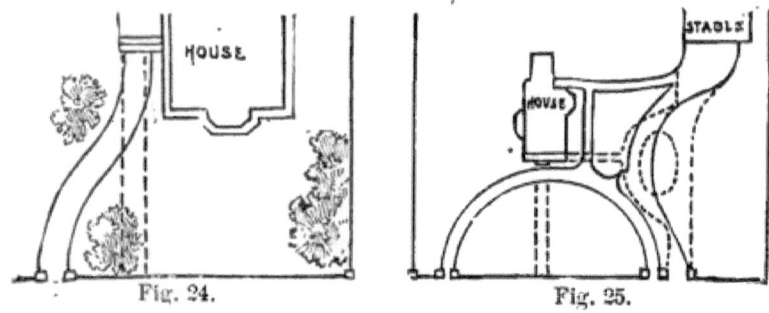

Fig. 24.   Fig. 25.

SHOWING ADVANTAGE OF CURVED WALKS AND DRIVES OVER STRAIGHT.

the area in front of the house larger, when the walk is
set to one side ; as a result, the house shows to better
advantage, than if the main front plat were kept smaller
by a straight walk encroaching upon it.   The house in
figure 24, it is at once seen to have a finer setting with a
curved approach, than if the part in front of it were to
be narrowed by a straight walk, as shown by the dotted
lines.

This principle is also illustrated in figure 25, both in
walks and carriage-drives.   Although here, by making
curved walks, there is one more leading to the house than
if they were straight ; still with the foreground thus
arranged, the buildings are seen to much better advantage over the stretch of lawn, embellished with trees,
shrubs, and flowers (omitted in the engraving), than if
the scene were cut up by the hard lines of a straight walk.

And the general improvement in the appearance of the grounds is also much better, for instead of increasing the angular outlines—strong enough already in the buildings and boundaries—by making the walks straight, we curve them gracefully, and thus induce variety in the lines. The curves are brought in such a way, that we secure that most desirable of all garden qualities, breadth just where it is most needed, namely: in the foreground of the main building. This simple point is one that accounts for much of that indescribable difference in places, which makes some appear much finer than others, with the use of about the same advantages and materials in both.

But if on the one hand there may be a liability to not employ curves often enough for good effect, on the other

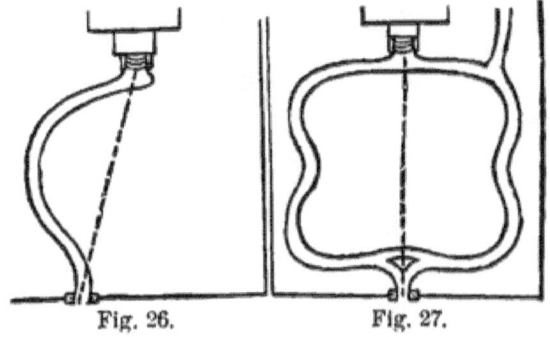

Fig. 26.　　　　Fig. 27.

POORLY ARRANGED CURVED WALKS, SKETCHED FROM ACTUAL EXAMPLES.

there is danger, when curves are used, of making them ungraceful or indirect, in a way to serve neither beauty or convenience. Figures 26 and 27 illustrate two examples of this kind. Tortuous walks like these prove worse than useless in one sense, for there will be a constant inclination, if not very frequent practice, to cut across the lot, as indicated by the dotted lines, instead of using the walks. People when they are in hurry, and especially children, have little respect for long, winding, inconvenient curves, introduced for beauty, but in such cases sadly lacking it, because they lack utility.

One of the best possible remedies for the common
trouble of having grass verges walked upon in private
and public grounds, is to place the walks just where they
are needed, and whether curved or otherwise, let them
run as directly from point to point as possible, and then
to make them of a material comfortable to the foot.   It
may be stated, however, that should this bad practice be
persisted in, a protector made like a croquet arch, only
much heavier and larger, and set either lengthwise, or at
short distances apart crosswise, along the edge, will effectually break it up.

In figures 24 and 25 it may be observed that the curves
are so direct, graceful, and easy, that there would be no
inducement to leave them, for gaining a more direct route
from point to point.   The drive in figure 25 is curved
considerably towards the house it is true, but it is used
chiefly for carriages, and under the circumstances this is
allowable.

A walk or drive of serpentine form, like the one on the
right-hand side of figure 27, is very faulty.   Any series
of bends closely together like these, showing two bays or
projections of about the same size, from any one point
are poor in effect.   Every curve should be continuous,
and easy to be kept by pedestrian or horse.   If the bends
are too short, the projections of drives are sure to be
shaved by wheels, while weeds will spring up in their
inner portions.

While, as a rule, walks should never be put down except where there is a real or apparent need of them, still
it is sometimes the case that they may be made to serve
largely for adornment.   Figure 28 shows a case of this
kind of a small garden of square outlines, lying adjacent
to a large public building.   The plat is skirted in its
border by a belt of trees and shrubs, and a conspicuous
circular bed of evergreens occupies a central position.
This simple arrangement of neat, well-kept walks, **cut**

into the level sward, harmonizes with the strong angular features that exist in the surroundings—which are, it may be said, too strong to be overcome in effect, by ordinary natural arrangements. In this way is found a pleasing kind of ornamentation for the place, which it would be hard to equal by any other means. It should be observed in this case, that the walks are not so prominent or so close together, but that they convey the idea of subordination to buildings, trees, grass, and

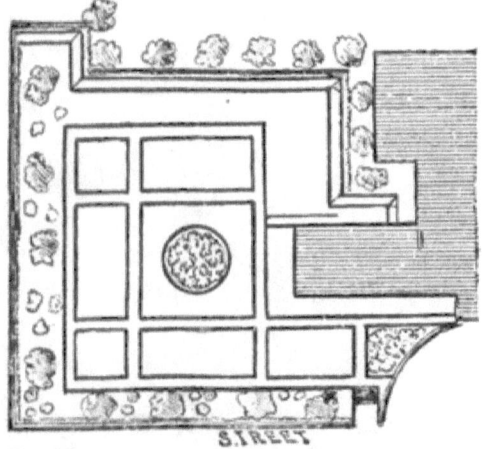

Fig. 28.—WALKS USED FOR EMBELLISHMENT.

streets, hence their fitness is easily accounted for. Were the square plats between walks filled with flowers or numerous vases, etc., instead of, as at present, mostly plain grass, the present fine effect would be largely lacking.

Where the lawn throughout the grounds is kept closely mowed, so that walking is always comfortable, except in wet weather or during a heavy dew, there is little call for walks besides those leading to and between chief points of interest. Shady grass walks kept well mown, with masses of shrubs and flowers at the sides, are really as pleasurable parts of a garden as can well be provided.

Sometimes one or more straight walks, or avenues, are in place in gardens or parks, as for instance along the

top of an extended, formal slope.   There are places
where such a walk or drive, if following a nice grade and
showing its entire length from the end, presents a magnificent appearance, especially if there is enough grass at
the sides to give it an ample setting; and trees and
flowers are used in abundance some distance back from
the edge, to be seen over the intervening grass.   Walks
or avenues of this character can hardly be considered
complete, without some striking objective point near or
distant, either real or apparent at each end, such as a
building, monument, fountain, or it may be only a piece
of statuary, or a large vase.   Small objects, like the last

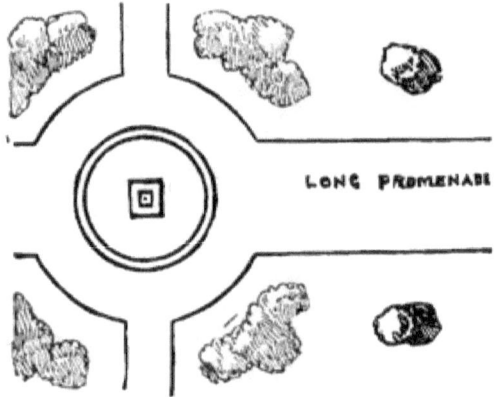

Fig. 29.—OBJECTIVE POINTS IN WALKS.

named, may be given a suitable setting near the ends of
such walks, or at junctions with cross-walks, as shown in
figure 29, by placing the object on a low, circular terrace
of green sward, retained either by a stone coping, or by
turf sloping sharply down to the common level.   For
smaller and short, straight walks, a tree of striking foliage or form, or an evergreen clipped into pleasing shape,
a flower-bed, arbor, vase, or seat, may serve as a terminal
object.   Such objects may also, if the walk or avenue be
long, be brought in at points, not too close together,
along the sides, to break monotony.

As regards width, long, straight walks or drives should be wider than curved ones, because their beauty depends in a measure upon boldness, and this is secured by breadth.   Ordinary walks are made anywhere from three feet wide (and sometimes as narrow as two feet), upwards, according to their place and the size of the garden. Rear private walks may be the narrowest. General garden walks, if curved, may be four to six feet wide, and straight approach walks, four to eight feet, while terrace or principal walks in large pleasure grounds and parks, may be eight to fifteen feet or more in width. Five feet is considered a good width for ordinary purposes. Drives may range all the way from eight to fifty feet or more in width, according to purpose and size of grounds. Ten to fourteen feet for ordinary drives in private grounds, with branches or back drives at eight to ten feet is about right. In large grounds, cemeteries, and parks, twenty to thirty-five feet, are the usual widths of drives.

CHAPTER XVII.

THE USE AND COMBINATIONS OF GRASS, TREES, SHRUBS, ETC.

In natural landscapes the common grasses serve the important purpose of supporting or affording a setting for other growths. They thus fill a place for which no other plants could serve so well. It would be better for the soil to be clothed with a carpet of green sward and treeless, than to be covered with trees and plants, to the exclusion of grass. Still, the custom that prevails in some places, of having only grass to ornament the grounds, is by no means to be commended, because of the better effect and greater interest attainable, through using some of the endless array of beautiful natural materials at our service, together with the grasses. Grass to the ground, is as carpets or tiles to a floor, indispensable in themselves, yet no one considers a room furnished without the addition of furniture and decorated walls. Neither should we be content with simply a carpet on our grounds, when handsome leafy furniture is so easily procured.

The lawn, to be most satisfactory, should present a green, velvety appearance throughout the season, and this is gained through a suitable condition of the soil, properly stocking it with grass, and attention to mowing, watering, etc. Instructions respecting these matters are given in other parts of this book. A common error in garden arrangement is found, where trees are planted close and never thinned, causing in time by their shade death to the grass underneath. The only remedy in such a case is the removal of a sufficient number of trees, to admit enough air to supply the wants of the grass. Good lawns will bear considerable shade, and enough trees can remain to afford ample shelter for comfort, and have fine grass besides.

For ornamental purposes in roof, and all kinds of architectural gardening, the lawn grasses are undervalued. A good illustration of their utility for such purposes, is seen in a public roof-garden over the market in Edinburgh, Scotland, where a large bed of grass, or in other words a patch of lawn, is employed, along with elaborate flower-beds, all surrounded by low stone copings. While the flowers are more showy, the presence of some cleanly mown grass in such a place tends to form a more perfect whole, than would otherwise be possible.

It is upon trees, shrubs, and flowering plants, that we depend for the chief attractions of our pleasure grounds. No garden can be considered properly furnished without some of these. Imagine our earth robbed of her arboreal beauty, and its appearance would be little better than that of a desert.

Starting out to use trees, shrubs, and flowering plants to embellish our grounds, it is a matter of first importance to gain an adequate idea of the kinds and nature of the materials. No one can enter upon a full examination of this subject, without being impressed with the large number of, and the great variety in natural and improved growths, suitable for such purposes. In Part II may be found lists and descriptions of most kinds of these that are adapted to the American climate.

To compose fine garden effects, we must take into account the prevailing and strongly marked characteristics possessed by the different materials at hand. I refer more especially to the differences found in the colors, sizes, and forms of foliage and flowers, and the great variety in the habit of growth of different trees and shrubs.

As alluded to in Chapter XIII, we have advantages in making beautiful garden scenes, unpossessed by nature, in her most charming compositions, owing to the greatly increased number and beauty of kinds obtained through culture. We find nothing similar to and as strikingly attractive in nature as an improved Purple-leaved Beech, a Cut-leaved Oak, a Variegated Cornelian Cherry, or any of hundreds of other improved trees and shrubs. Not only is nature's own ample storehouse at our command, but there are besides a multitude of variations from the best she possesses, that have been obtained through culture.

As between the two forms of woody growth, trees and shrubs, too little regard is yet paid by planters to the great value of the latter class. This is especially the case as regards their eminent fitness for embellishing small grounds. In beauty and diversity of form and foliage, they equal the larger trees. Most of them, in addition to other merits, produce an abundance of flowers of great beauty and sweetness, and in the different species, yield a succession throughout the whole season, while the ever-green kinds are attractive both summer and winter. As a rule, all the shrubs grow easily, and after transplanting develop a full measure of beauty in half the time required by trees. With all these qualities, their adaptability by nature to the limited areas of the majority of American home gardens, may be added as a leading recommendation of this class.

In employing trees and shrubs for ornament, such a selection and arrangement should be aimed at, as will, for the number used, ensure the greatest possible degree of beauty and interest attainable.

As we come to the matter of arranging these, we may receive useful lessons from nature. In a study of natural landscapes, it may be observed that trees, shrubs, and plants bear relation to each other here, about as follows : First, in the form of groups and thickets; second, in open or somewhat scattered arrangements ; third, as single, isolated specimens ; and then fourth, as being wholly absent in places. If these points are kept in mind when arranging our pleasure grounds, we need not diverge far from a right course in the main features of the work. Indeed, it is the attempt, either unconscious or otherwise, to make a garden by limitation to some one or other uses or non-uses of material as specified, that causes so much unsatisfactory work in this line.

Let it be noted at the outset, that the partly open feature of a landscape is most essential, if we would have beautiful gardens. Without this, there can never be anything but a confused effect, and without it the beauty and dignity of the rich woody and other plants used is also largely lost. The open area affords a field for viewing the garden-beauty, a space for admitting cool breezes and sunshine; a play-ground for shadows, and then, most important of all, that degree of general repose and breadth, without which no garden can be satisfactory.

Next to the open area in gardens, the group easily holds a first place, as an effective means of employing embellishing plant material, and has been called the key-note of modern natural gardening. Whether as found in nature, or as it may be formed, the chief merits of the group consists in its boldness; the power gained for augmenting individual beauty of kinds, by clustering to-

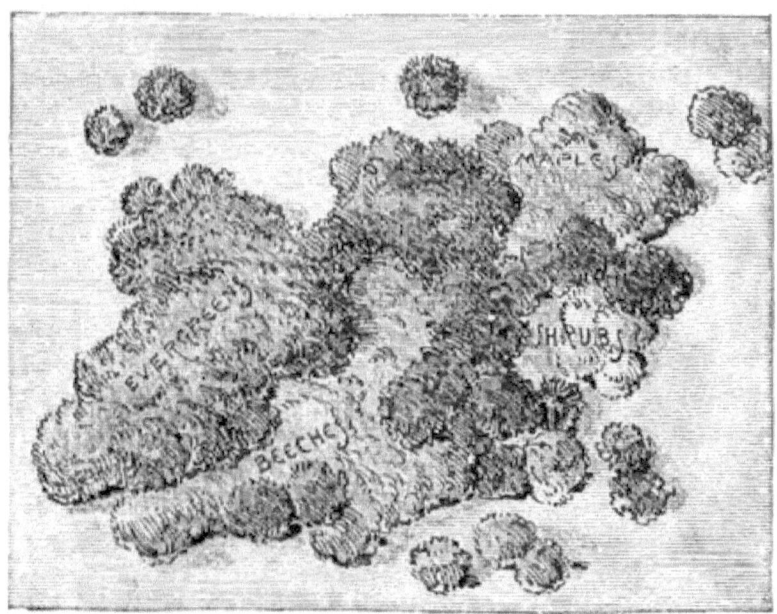

Fig. 30.—NATURAL GROUPING OF DECIDUOUS AND EVERGREEN TREES AND SHRUBS.

gether of numbers of subjects alike or nearly so, and the picturesqueness which may be created by contrasting groups of one class, with similar groups or marked individuals of other classes, in what may be called compound groups. To analyze the beauty of natural masses, it may be seen that this comes largely from the peculiar way in which different kinds are combined. It may be observed that in such groups individual kinds generally gravitate towards one or more centers, with usually a scattering and intermingling of these between such group-centers, something as is shown in figure 30, which illustrates a natural arrangement.

From this largely results the impressive beauty so commonly found in nature, arising from strong individual effects and marked contrasts, as different kinds blend with each other.

This principle of minor groups within large groups, should often be adopted in garden arrangements. Under most circumstances a dozen or a hundred trees, shrubs, or plants, if arranged on some such basis, will be productive of immeasurably better effects than the same scattered about or else mixed promiscuously.

The right idea in the garden is, to bring together such kinds as possess contrasting qualities, arranging these group against group, with a scattering of individuals here and there, but all done for making the distinguishing and often strongly marked characteristic of one kind, relieve and offset those of others. As shown in the natural group of figure 30. dark Evergreens may offset the Beeches of lighter foliage, while the colored bark has its effect of contrast, or projecting masses of the former stand against the Maples with finely contrasting shrubs to the front.

Purple Beeches might be brought in conjunction with the light-colored Silver Maples, with dark-green English Elms near by for heavy effect. Some Weeping Willows along the margin of water, may be backed by a few spiry Lombardy Poplars ; pyramidal Spruces, clustered with trees having low, round heads, and so on.

In shrubs. the small-leaved Privet, or cut-leaved Elder, could go against the large-leaved Viburnums or Weigelas, or we might use the light-green Thunberg's Spiræa, next to the dark-leaved Japan Quince, with the Virginia Fringe, with its large foliage at the back. The pure white flowers of Thunberg's Spiræa also contrast well

with the brilliant scarlet of the quince flowers, both
coming in together.   Beautiful effects spring from com-
bining differently tinted species and varieties of the same
genus, for instance: the light and dark Spruces, Pines,
and others, may be contrasted with one another, and so
on with other different kinds indefinitely.

In the matter of general style and location of groups,
it is obvious, as we consider the importance of retaining
certain open stretches of lawn, that as a rule the masses
must, in all small places, be set along the margins of the
grass plat, keeping the center open.

But such arrangements correspond in principle with
nature's most effective groupings.   The most delightful

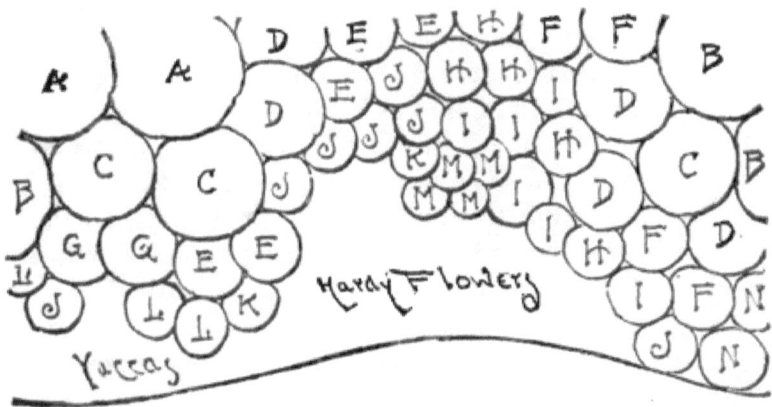

Fig. 31.—ARRANGEMENT OF TREES, SHRUBS, AND FLOWERS, THE
LETTERS INDICATING THE KINDS.

natural landscapes show open vistas, skirted by margins
of woody growth, either near or distant, which limit and
support the former.   On the laying out of marginal
borders, some attention has been given in Chapter XV,
as illustrated by figures 13 to 18.

Figure 31, illustrating a section of such a border,
shows the method of arranging the different materials.
In this figure it may be noticed that the outside line of
woody growths is less regular than that of the border

margins, and the spaces between are filled with hardy flowering plants.

While the grouping of trees and shrubs, and herbaceous plants in marginal borders finds a wide adaptability, it is of special value in embellishing small gardens, even the very smallest.

There are numerous shrubs, both deciduous and evergreen, that are highly ornamental, but which seldom grow more than a few feet high (see figure 1 and explanations), that are ordinarily adapted for creating bold and pleasing effects in the smallest grounds by properly grouping them. With the use of these, striking effects may be secured in the planting, to give a fine setting to the architecture of the place, whatever the style of this may be. They should be massed somewhat closely, always taking future size into account in marginal borders, and also next to the house as before alluded to. Then if there is room, one or two shade trees of moderate size may also be set in some part of the open area. By such means it is possible to secure, even in small gardens, about every feature that enters into the most extensive natural landscape, and with proportionally as good an effect.

In pleasure grounds of larger size, there is increased scope for introducing variety both as to the style of the groups and their materials. Here we may have a larger selection of kinds, for the increased space also allows the use of larger growers. In grounds of the largest size, trees and shrubs of every kind and size may be admitted, and here the most varied effects, from very delicate to bold, are possible.

In all fair-sized places, the boundary masses may jut inwards to a considerable distance here and there, and some isolated clumps be introduced for creating minor vistas. Views opening to the longest possible distance in some directions, and then broken by projections and masses in others, hiding some parts of the grounds, produce some of the most desirable effects that can be attained in landscape gardening. It is a special merit of the grouping system, that it tends to give an enlarged idea of the size of the place. Grounds with the boundary shut off by masses, and these arranged with irregular outlines, will look larger than they would if the boundary line were plainly in sight.

Figure 32 illustrates an irregular group upon the lawn. This form and arrangement is adapted to trees

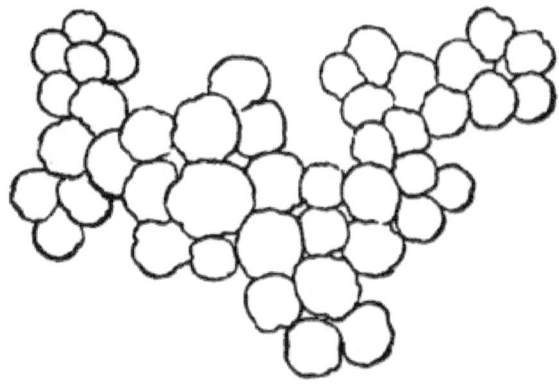

Fig. 32.—GROUPING OF LARGE AND SMALL GROWTHS.

or shrubs of any size, but especially to the formation of a thicket with small shrubs.

It is usually the case that, no matter how few trees, shrubs, or plants may be employed in any place, they will be more effective if brought together in groups. Three, four, or six, for instance, will serve a better purpose thus treated, than if set in a row or scattered as far apart as possible. Figure 33 shows some different ways of arranging a small number of shrubs in groups, and these will readily suggest the making of groups of a larger or smaller number. It may be said that Roses, Rhododendrons, Pæonies, and many other things, should hardly ever be used in any other way than in masses.

In all work of·grouping, a leading aim should be to

invest the compositions with an air of grace and freedom. This is a point which the inexperienced would do well to heed, for it is easy to fail right here. In nature, bushes and trees, herbs and shrubs, blend together in the freest manner, while the edges of the group commonly round off with exquisite finish; a good example which we should strive to imitate.

Where a beautiful garden fronts on a public highway, it is as commendable in the owner to allow passers on the street to get glimpses of the interior, as it is to have

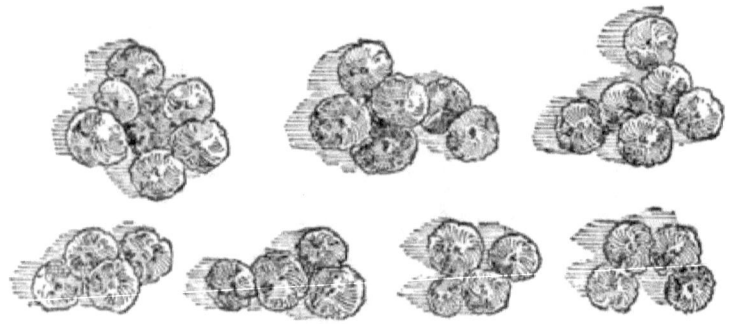

Fig. 33.—DIFFERENT WAYS OF ARRANGING A SMALL NUMBER OF PLANTS.

thought of the effect of a fine house upon a neighborhood. But then a garden is designed chiefly for the pleasure of the owner's family and friends, and he likes to enjoy it in seclusion. It is a luxury to sit at ease, or swing in a hammock on a summer's day, and drink in the sights, sounds, and perfumes peculiar to a garden, without fear of interruption, and this seclusion should be provided for. Figure 34 shows how masses may be set so as to give the public some benefit of a garden, and yet render portions of it secluded.

By grouping, complete effects may be produced more quickly than in any other manner of planting. Whether dealing with trees or shrubs, we may plant very thickly at the start, by using at first twice or three times as many shrubs of each kind as will finally be needed, or else by locating the choicer and long-enduring kinds at distances that will accommodate their increase for many years, and then fill out more or less between these with some of the cheap kinds of rapid growth, which are at the same time very handsome. The extra shrubs in both cases to be removed as the others demand the space. In this way masses will be made to look solid and complete immediately after setting.

The planting of trees and shrubs in groups affords the means of promoting rapid development and beauty. The ground under them may, in fact, ought to be, for some

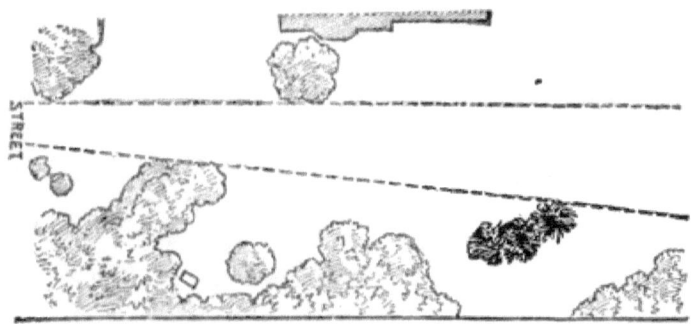

Fig. 34.—PLANTING FOR BOTH OPENNESS AND SECLUSION.

years at least, kept cultivated, and if this is well done and an application of manure be made occasionally, they will reach a large size in half the time they would if standing in the grass. Then, too, we may feel safe against summer drouths, if conveniences for watering are not at hand, for in such cultivated borders trees suffer little from dryness in the severest seasons of drouth.

Clumps are desirable for breaking the transitions from terrace banks to natural slopes, and in other ways to reconcile discrepancies in the surface. They may also well be introduced for breaking the outlines of garden or foundation walls, or for hiding unsightly objects.

9

The gain that comes from massing evergreens and other trees in a way to shelter the grounds and buildings, is worth considering. It is really surprising to see what effect Spruces, Pines, Hemlocks, etc., planted freely in the direction of prevailing winds has, both on the comfort of the home in winter, and on the ability of many choice kinds of trees and shrubs to withstand the severity of the cold ; these, if exposed, would die outright. By thus giving shelter, the number of kinds of trees that will thrive in the North is greatly increased. Many of our beautiful native trees and shrubs, that in their wild state thrive in the shelter of forests, are erroneously called tender in the North, simply because they will not succeed in the absence of the shelter of trees.

From the close grouping it is but a short step to the open or scattered arrangement in planting. A type of this style is to be found in an open, light, and breezy grove, where there is almost as much of sunshine as of shade. This style may often be brought in as the termination of one or more points of closer groups, and in gardening the two may often be closely associated. While irregularity and rugged picturesqueness easily become characteristics of the close group, a different form of beauty, embracing greater gentleness, marks the scattering system, for in this, each tree or plant is allowed to more fully develop its individual beauty and form. Most of the instruction and ideas advanced, and illustrations given, respecting ordinary groupings are, however, applicable to the open groups, by merely making allowance for the peculiarities of each member as regards compactness and openness.

The scattered cluster is not so well adapted to small gardens as is the closer group, because its characteristic beauty depends largely upon ample space, yet by confining the selections to the smaller growing kinds, very complete effects are attainable by this pleasing system, even in a limited space. Figure 35 shows some of the smaller growing Pines, Yucca filamentosa, and Deutzia gracilis, the latter kept clipped to a rounded form, arranged in this style on a lawn.

Where there are mounds, a scattering of either evergreens or deciduous shrubs in open clumps over conspicuous slopes is proper. It is the free scattering of Junipers and Firs over the mountain sides skirting the Hudson River, in some places, that lends to the scenery it great charm. A rise in the garden may support half a dozen

Fig. 35.—SCATTERINGS OF DWARF PINES, YUCCAS, AND DEUTZIA GRACILIS IN CITY LAWNS.

or more Savins or other evergreens, or some plants of striking foliage like the Wild Olive or Weigela, planted near the crown, and in this way produce a good effect. At the edge of an abrupt bluff may be placed two or three Camperdown Elms or other bold weeping trees. Such kinds as love moisture, like the Willows and Alders may be effectively disposed by planting in similar clumps along the water's edge or in low places.

Where it is desirable to plant trees along the sides of long garden walks and avenues, for shade, scattering them along irregularly, allowing some complete breaks here

and there, will produce a better effect than to make
formal lines with the trees at uniform distances apart.
There is a striking illustration of this in the strong contrast afforded between the irregularly wooded north
drives in Hyde Park, London, where along the sides
for miles the trees are arranged in scattered groups, and
similar avenues in other parks with formal lines of
trees at their sides. The same idea is true generally of
trees to be planted along the boundaries of large grounds.
They will create a much better effect if grouped openly,
as in figure 36, than if set, as is often done, in a straight

Fig. 36.—PLANTING ON BOUNDARIES AND MOUNDS.

line. It is seldom indeed the case, anywhere outside
of narrow streets, that formal lines might not well give
way to informal scattering clusters.

Throughout the grounds, open groups of large trees
may jut out from heavy marginal plantations, or occupy
places by themselves surrounded by the open lawn, or
they may be in some parts brought in to form groves.
Near the junctions of walks and drives, or in bends of
these, are also suitable places for trees thus disposed.
But the open grouping system of planting should never
be confounded with the faulty "dot-a-tree-everywhere"
system sometimes met with, and in which such essential
garden features as open areas and vistas seem to never
have been even thought of by the planters.

The planting of trees, shrubs, etc., as isolated specimens, either singly or two or three near each other, is often
desirable. It may be observed that in nature isolated
specimens generally are, in effect, subordinate to masses

either near, as if broken away from them, or farther off.
Usually they occupy a place somewhat central, with
masses skirting the horizon around, and it will be safe to
have regard to this point in similarly bringing trees and
shrubs into our gardens.   In selecting single specimens
we should be governed by the size of the grounds to be
planted.   An Oak makes a grand tree for a large garden,
but a Kilmarnock or Rosemary-leaved Willow would be
more suitable for a small town lot, while the effect of
one of the latter would be almost lost in the larger area.
A few Austrian or White Pines make a splendid show in

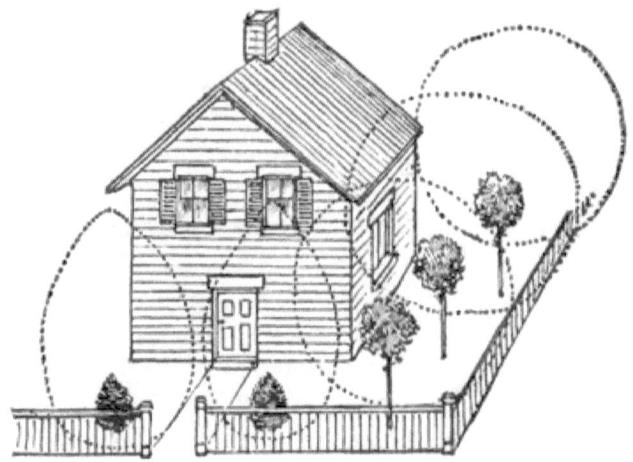

Fig. 37.—ILLUSTRATING THE ERROR OF NOT TAKING FUTURE GROWTH
INTO CONSIDERATION.

a roomy cemetery, or any place of broad area, but the
small Junipers, Spruces, or Mahonias are greatly preferable for small grounds.   Some of the most common mis-
takes in choosing trees is in such unsuitable selections.
We often see young trees, and evergreens particularly, of
strong growing kinds, planted so near to walks or buildings that after some years they encroach upon them, and
for the sake of room have to be mutilated by severe cutting, impairing their beauty forever.   An illustration of
this mistake is shown in figure 37, where the size of the

trees, as they appeared at planting and their size fifteen years later is outlined.   Such a condition of things is deplorable, because wholly without adequate remedy, and of course owes its origin to the fact, that the planter only considered the beauty and the size of the tree at planting, and not its appearance in later years.

The classification of trees according to the size they reach at maturity, as explained in connection with figure 1, and the letters throughout the description in Part II, will help one to a right idea of the size of trees and shrubs.   As a rule, no tree properly belongs in grounds that are too small to admit of its full development or which will intrude too much upon space when full grown.

In some places where planting is done for shade, an error is seen in the setting of not only larger growers than were needed for the place, but so many of them as to defeat the very idea of comfortable shade, by shutting out the access of cool breezes and retaining the heat of the sun's rays that may penetrate here and there.   What is wanted in our hot climate, is not so much excessive shade, as open shade that allows the air to circulate freely through and under the trees.   The character of trees has something to do with their forming a comfortable shade.   For example, the shade of open-headed Silver Maples, Willows, Walnut, etc., is cooler than that of dense, close-headed kinds, for the simple reason that the heads of the former cause but a slight barrier to the entrance of cool breezes underneath.

As distinct means for increasing variety, the forming of Shrubbery-walks, Rosaries, Pinetums, etc., may be mentioned.   These, as their names would imply, consist of a collection of members of the same family, or style of growth, so arranged as to facilitate the study of them and to develop the beauty that springs from bringing together in numbers the different species of the same family.

In everything pertaining to the arrangment of trees, shrubs and plants, there is room for the exercise of a great deal of knowledge, taste and skill. As canvas, brushes and paints do not in themselves make the painter, so it cannot be expected that inexperience and lack of close acquaintance with kinds, will accomplish as good results in garden arrangment as arise from the labors of the trained arboriculturist and landscape gardener. Still, where the number to be planted is limited, and close attention is given to selections, being guided by descriptions, and then with proper forethought as to the arrangement, there need be little fear of really bad results.

CHAPTER XVIII.

CLIMBERS AND THEIR USES.

The value of the climbing and twining plants is entitled to higher appreciation than it now receives from Americans. In Europe they are used more freely than with us. The adaptability of the hardy Ivy to the European climate, and its common use for ages, for mantling the walls of castles and kirks, may have had much to do with cultivating in Europeans a love for climbers. The Ivy, however, is by no means used exclusively abroad. As a climber of free habits, our own Virginia Creeper seems to find preference over it for most ordinary purposes, and in many respects it is greatly its superior.

The adaptability of climbers is perhaps without equal among plants. Rarely can a building be found, even in the heart of a city, and where there is no room for shrubs or grass, that may not be gracefully adorned with the verdure and flowers of one or another of these.   They are inexpensive as regards first cost, of easy and rapid growth, adapted to a great variety of soils, and as appro-

Fig. 38.—FENCE AND GATE POSTS COVERED BY CLIMBERS.

priate for decorating a laborer's cottage as the mansion of the millionaire.

Figure 38 represents a fence and gate posts covered with climbers.   For such a purpose, the Virginian Creep-

Fig. 39.—SMALL CITY COTTAGE FRONT COVERED WITH CRÉEPERS.

er is as well adapted in America as any, and with attention to pinching and training, may be made to serve most admirably.

Figure 39 shows a small cottage, one of a row with a free growing climber running over its front. The beautiful manner in which the Virginia Creeper, if thus used, may be made to partially curtain the windows is delightful; no better illustration of the value of plant life in making a town or any other home attractive can be found, than in such a use of climbers. By means of one or two plants, a blank house front is converted into a scene of interest and beauty that at once attracts the eye of every passer. How readily beauty of this kind is at-

Fig. 40.—SETTING OF GREEN FOR   Fig. 41.—BASE OF BAY WINDOW AND
        BAY WINDOW.   PROJECTION COVERED WITH LONICERA.

tainable, and what a wonderful influence for good would be exerted by its general prevalence throughout our cities, especially in portions where the poorer classes reside.

Figures 40 and 41 show two bay windows decorated with climbers, each different as regards shape of windows, kind of plant and form of training. Figure 42 shows the end wall of a house with bay window, where climbers, shrubs and flowers are used to make a pretty garden picture, whether as seen from without or within. For this purpose the climbers may be Wistaria, Celastrus, Virginia Creeper, or other free growers with Weigela, Japan Quince, Reeves's Spiræa, or other shrubs of shapely growth and good foliage; and Geraniums, Coleus, and similar bright plants between the shrubs.

The climbers may be used to good advantage in con-nection with trees in several ways. Sometimes very picturesque combinations are met in nature, which are worthy of imitation in the garden. Trees fifteen to

Fig. 42.—SHRUBS, FLOWERS, AND CLIMBERS ABOUT A BAY WINDOW.   Fig. 43.—VERANDA COVERED WITH CELASTRUS.

twenty feet high may be so covered and weighed down with Virginia Creeper or the Wild Grape, as to form per-fect arbors of green, the branches falling in garlands to the ground. Nothing can be more delightful than such natural arbors. If a tree is of considerable size when such a climber is planted at the root, little harm to it can arise from the combination.

A strong plant of the Dutchman's Pipe, or the Virginia Creeper running up one tree trunk about ten feet high, and then carried in a festoon across to another tree, veranda, or some other object near by, makes a novel and pleasing object in a garden. A wire must be stretched across from tree to tree to support the vine at first.

The value of climbers for covering arbors, verandas, and the like is generally known. Figure 43 represents a veranda wreathed with Celastrus for which particular purpose there can be no better plant. The effect is best in such places if the branches are trained along in one line near the edge of the roof. For adorning all kinds of arbors and similar structures, the climbers are well fitted. If a simple, light, frame-work trellis of any de-

Fig. 44.—PLAN FOR ARBOR OVER A GARDEN SEAT.

sired form is made, somewhat after the plan shown in figure 44, and climbers be planted to run over it, the affair will be so completely covered in time, that nothing but the green will show, and an exceedingly pretty, cheap, and complete shelter from the sun will be the result.

It is often desirable to have a screen of climbers over some portions of the side of a veranda for protection from the sun. A neat and cheap trellis to support the vine, may be made of No. 12 or 14 wire, by putting a row of common screw eyes, such as can be bought at hardware stores, at six or eight inches apart along the

upper and lower lines of the space to be covered, and
then running wire between them, top and bottom obliquely to form diamond shaped interstices. Where they
strike the posts, eyes must be put in to fasten the wires,
they may then be bound together at points of crossing,
strengthening the whole. A rather better contrivance
with the wires crimped to prevent them slipping where
crossed and the ends attached to a frame work of iron
rod, shaped to fit the space, may with some increased expense be purchased of wire workers.

Screens to serve as fences may be made in a similar
way, by running the wires from top to bottom rails supported by posts. These made to take the place of fences
or hedges, around divisions of the garden, prove very attractive when covered with vines.

Figure 45 shows a screen of this character with an

Fig. 45.—SCREEN OF VINES,
WITH ARCHWAY.

archway carried over the walk,
and all covered with one or
two climbers. For such purposes nothing can be superior
to that valuable and common
climber, the Virginia Creeper.
For the sake of variety, however, the Flowering Honey-
suckles, Clematis, Wistaria, or others may also be used.

A use to which climbers may be put in many gardens
is represented by figure 46. Light posts of any hight,
from eighteen inches upwards, may be set in line and
connected by a wire running from one to another
through the posts near the top. By keeping up a narrow border on the line of the posts, and planting a climber at each, the whole structure will become beautifully
covered in time. A line of this kind at the edge of a
terrace in place of a balustrade, proves pleasing and inexpensive.

A dead tree trunk, an oak post ten or twelve feet high,

or a large boulder covered over with free growing climbers are handsome objects in gardens. Honeysuckles or other climbers may be made to form handsome altars of green and flowers in the lawn, if five or six stakes are put about the plants, say four feet high, surrounding them with about three hoops at equal distances and allowing the vine to cover them. If the Gold-Netted Honeysuckle be used it will give a splendid golden effect. Other forms of trellis may also be used similarly for adorning lawns.

Mantles and festoons of greenery over walls, railings, bridges, arbors, and the buildings generally, are so pleas-

Fig. 46.—POSTS WITH GARLANDS BETWEEN.

ing to the eye that the use of climbers should be very common. Plants of trailing habit, such as Periwinkle, Ivy and prostrate Junipers, are useful as edgings to plats of grass or shrubbery groups, or the former for covering terrace banks, shady places against buildings, or under trees where nothing else will grow. Single lines of Periwinkle or Ivy, a foot or more wide between walks and the lawn, are effective, as there is a pleasing contrast between the dark-green foliage of the former, and the lighter green of the grass. With a little attention to trimming, either of these plants may be made to form a shapely rounded line. The Gold-netted Honeysuckle may also be thus used, and in that case the color is much lighter than that of the grass.

CHAPTER XIX.

FLOWERING AND ORNAMENTAL PLANTS.

The effectiveness of hardy perennial or annual flowering plants in the garden depends, as with woody plants, much upon their position and arrangement. In the natural style of garden making, the front parts of tree and shrubbery borders, as well as in the midst of these, in the bare spaces, are suitable places for these or flowers of every kind. Some lines of bright annuals, or low, hardy, variegated grass, or any other low growing plants that are suitable for edging, may be placed next to the grass, while in the bays of the shrubbery line, and also further back, showy, hardy plants, bulbs, bright, seed-grown things, as well as tender, perpetual blooming flowers may be set. There are many little hardy flowers that thrive directly under the shade of shrubs, and some of these may be introduced to become naturalized in such places. All kinds may be grouped promiscuously, or for the sake of variety in some places, be arranged in lines lengthwise or in any other direction. Combinations of different classes of ornamental plants may easily be so managed in borders, as to render them very attractive in flowers and foliage from early spring until freezing weather in the fall. Different borders and beds on the same ground may be planned to differ in arrangement and style of expression. Even if the free-flowering, tender plants that must be newly bedded each year, were omitted from these collections, a selection of hardy plants alone could be employed, that would, together with flowering shrubs, never allow the beds to be without flowers or attractiveness during the growing season.

In the use of seed-grown plants in such places, or in any place, if the massing plan were more generally observed in setting them, these flowers would have a better reputation in fine gardens. Candytuft, Clarkia, Erysimum, and all kinds, in fact, if sown in round, triangular, or other shaped drills, the ends of which meet, and about eighteen inches or upwards across, so as to form a clump of foliage and flowers when grown, prove, as a rule, much finer than the same plants scattered in driblets too small to make an impression.

The more common use of the many attractive hardy flowers, is recommended in every kind of ornamental gardening. Admitting that there is something of a lack in the constancy of bloom afforded, as compared with the tender bedders, it should be remembered that they are inexpensive to get at the start, and once planted are almost as permanent as Oak trees, growing and increasing indefinitely. They come up each spring with little care, many of them are unequalled for beauty, and selections can be made that will, by succession, afford in different kinds a constant show of flowers during the summer season. Some of this class are very fine if arranged in clumps, either alone, or several kinds together on the lawn. Lily of the Valley, Plantain Lilies, Crocus, Colchicums, Yuccas, Pampas, and other grasses, Pæonies and some others possessing attractive flowers and foliage are effective when so planted.

The more formal style of arranging flowers and plants —sometimes called carpet bedding—in which mostly tender kinds, such as are planted anew every spring, and produce richly colored flowers or foliage, are used, is a very effective as well as popular means of embellishing pleasure grounds. Bright flowers and showy foliage, if brought together in tasteful designs, with regard for harmony and contrasts, are susceptible of producing most attractive results.

Some excellent and elaborate work in this line is now to be seen everywhere in gardens both private and public, as well as in cemeteries.   The managers of Lincoln Park, Chicago, and in Battersea Park, London, England, easily take the lead in this style of adornment, and the display now annually made in each of these, as well as in some other parks that could be named, would be difficult to excel.   That these embellishments are in the main well conceived and find appreciation from the public is easily seen in the fact, that in these parks, which abound in a variety of interesting garden and other features—the former both in the natural and other styles—the parts devoted to these showy arrangements of flowers are those among all competing ones in interest, that are the most constantly thronged by admirers.

I am well aware that some advocates of a strictly natural style of garden making, pronounce against the bedding or massing system as being wrong both in principle and taste.   But it will be difficult to ever educate the people to have none of it, for that it has a legitimate place in the ornamentation of grounds is obvious to most gardeners and other persons.   When the mass of the people may be brought to see that there is more real beauty in the coarse primitive Zinnia, Balsam, or Iris, than in the splendid improvements on these that have been accomplished by art, then they may also learn to despise art in the arrangement of flowers.   And as to the use of geometrical lines and outlines, delicate tints and rich colors combined in contrasts, where can be found more suggestive examples, in such arrangements, than in nature's own work-shop, in the mutiplicity of such forms and combinations as are everywhere in the flowers, fruits and foliage of the vegetable kingdom.

That disagreeable effects often do arise in this, as in other uses of flowers, is very true, but a chief cause for this, it should be understood, comes from disregarding the true relation of flowers and plants in such arrangments to garden scenery generally.   It should be remembered that the sphere of such a style of ornamentation is in the line of what has elsewhere been termed minor embellishments, hence it follows, that the use of striking and fanciful compositions like these must be limited accordingly. If nature shows many fanciful forms, and varied colors in her attractive flowers, she also teaches by example, that these in order to be most beautiful need an appropriate setting, hence we find every flower usually borne above or brought in close conjunction with masses of foliage, which give it needed relief. So too, diamonds and rich ribbons in dress, are only used with their full power for conveying pleasure to the eye, when they find an appropriate setting in connection with something that possesses less capacity for ornamentation.

Mr. De Vry's great success in using flowers and plants in the Chicago Park, lies largely in the fact, that although a multitude of beds are filled, they are so seated on ample areas of lawn, and these skirted by trees, that notwithstanding their abundance, they seem only to richly embellish the parts where they are introduced. In marked contrast with his success, is a conspicuous flower garden annually made in the West End Park of Glasgow, Scotland. Here is a garden of flowers instead of a garden (or a part of it) embellished with flowers. The arrangement consists of a circular plat, one hundred and thirty feet across, bounded by a gravel walk, and divided by others into about fifty different sized flower beds, which are closely planted, and there is little or nothing else besides. The entire absence of grass and other features that deserve to be termed major features of adornment, the numerous walks and the sameness that exists in the form of the beds, all serve to produce a very weak effect, with a great abundance of very excellent plant material.

In a public garden near New York, I met recently a

marked example of the misuse of flowers in embellishing
grounds as shown in figure 47.   The beauty of a conspicuous but not large plat was almost destroyed, and at large
cost, by immense, long, glaring masses of a single color

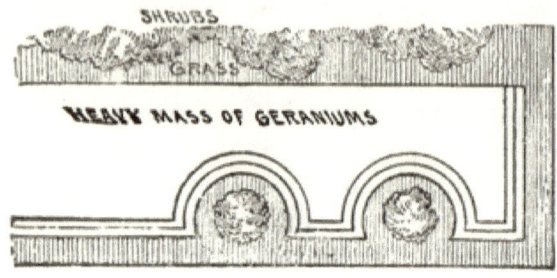

Fig. 47.—TOO MANY FLOWERS FOR GOOD EFFECT.

of geranium, with only the relief of a few lines of other
plants at the edge.

   Figure 48 shows the improvement of which the same
spot was susceptible, if less than one-fourth as many
plants had been used, but on the principle of employing
them as minor features in the adornment, with a corres-

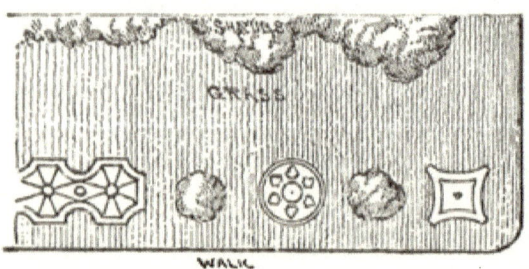

Fig. 48.—THE SAME PLAT WITH FEWER FLOWERS.

ponding increase of grass, and the former arranged by
introducing a little pleasing variety into the designs.

   Let bright flowers and plants be used in planting the
garden, being guided by the same principle upon which
growing flowers or plants are set to be surrounded and
supported by a profusion of foliage, or that which gov-

erns the tasteful use of ornaments in dress, never using them in excess. Thus employed, whether the ground to be embellished is a square rod or many acres, there will be little room for complaint of the formal style of

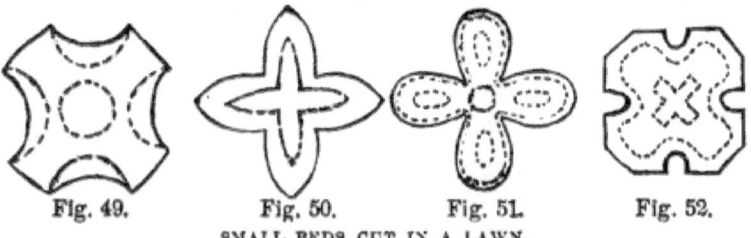

Fig. 49.   Fig. 50.   Fig. 51.   Fig. 52.

SMALL BEDS CUT IN A LAWN.

arrangement, provided the designs after which the flowers are planted be in themselves good and tasteful.

The character of the designs which are followed in setting out plants in formal or geometric bedding has

Fig. 53.   Fig. 54.   Fig. 55.

Fig. 56.   Fig. 57.   Fig. 58.

LARGE CIRCULAR BEDS IN A LAWN.

much to do with their beauty. In the accompanying engraving are shown numerous tasteful plans, which may serve as a guide in this kind of work. Figures 49 to 52 show four beds of irregular outline, suitable for planting with different kinds or colors as indicated by dotted lines, or the same shaped beds may be planted with a single kind. If such beds of any desired size, say from four to eight feet across, are cut into the lawn, and planted with Coleus, Geraniums, Cannas, Alternantheras, or other showy plants, they will be very pleasing.

For larger beds of circular outline, from ten to twenty feet across, the designs from figures 53 to 58 are any of them handsome for garden lawns, if well planted with a good selection of kinds. The central figures alone of several of these might be laid out in the lawn, depending on the grass for ground work with capital effect.

Two beds of oval shape are shown in figures 59 and 60. In some places such a form is required in preference to

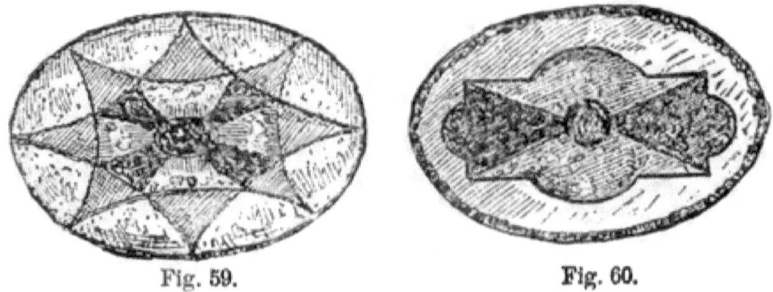

Fig. 59.   Fig. 60.

ELABORATE BEDS OF OVAL FORM.

the round. The various designs here given may be the means of suggesting others to the inventive mind. I have not taken space to illustrate plain circles, stars, crescents, squares, triangles, and other simple designs, all of which look attractive in the lawn, and are easily made by any one. In all cases, whatever designs are used, let them be quite simple. While it is easy to draught an elaborate plan that will be satisfactory in pen or pencil marks upon paper, the same might be very difficult to work out in plants.

PLANTS FOR CARPET BEDS.

In choosing these, those of contrasting colors should be brought together. The parts appearing dark and lighter in the engravings, just given, will readily suggest how colors may be used in different parts. No precise rule, however, can be laid down for this, and variations without end are allowable if made with good taste.

Where a hight of nine inches and upwards of a solid mass of color is desired, the Coleus, Achyranthes, Geranium, Centaurea, Variegated Stevia, Gnaphalium, Abutilon Thompsoni, and so forth, are among the best that can be used. When plants of a lower growth are desired, say from four to eight inches, the following are suitable: Alternantheras, Golden-Feather Pyrethrums, Variegated Thyme of several kinds, Alyssum in several varieties, Lobelia, Dwarf Ageratum, Cigar plant (*Cuphea*) and Golden and Silver-edged Geraniums.

For forming a low carpet, Othonna sedifolia (*crassifolia* of some), Dew Plant (*Mesembryanthemum*) in two varieties, Echeveria (*Cotyledon*) secunda glauca, Pilea serpyllifolia, Moneywort, Leucophyton, the prostrate Sedums, all of low-trailing habit, rarely growing more than two inches high, are the most valuable.

For low edgings the Alternantheras, Thymes, Alyssums, Golden Feather, Leucophyton, Echeverias and others are suitable. Sometimes these kinds are used in beds like those of figures 58 and 59, and also others for making single lines or to mark divisions through plants of low growth.

For the center of beds, or to place at points in the design, the Agaves, Echeverias, Yuccas, Dracenas, Palms, etc., may be used, while something taller yet to occupy a space in the middle of beds is found in Caladiums, Cannas, Ricinus, Striped Maize, and others.

The modern style of raised geometric beds, one of which is represented by figure 61, are ornamental in the highest degree when well designed and planted and properly cared for. The one shown in the engraving, sketched in Mt. Auburn Cemetery, near Boston, was about two and a half feet high at the foot of the plant vase, and all parts of it thickly planted with Echeverias, Othonna, Dracenas, Sedums and a few other low plants.

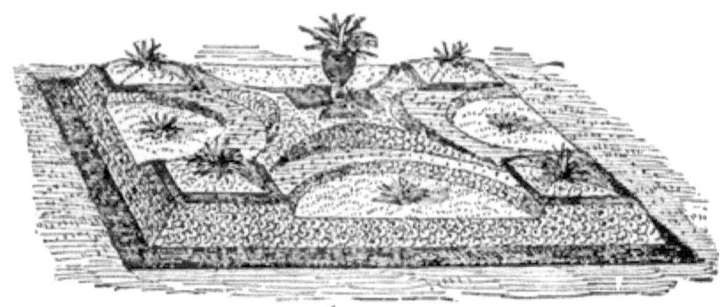

Fig. 61.—AN ELABORATE, ELEVATED BED.

The graceful outlines and excellent proportions, the slopes and surfaces of various forms and angles, and the contrast between delicate colors, shown in the compositions, together contributed to an effect at once quietly pleasing, rich and beautiful.

There is no limit to the variety and pleasing effects that may be secured in this style, in designs marked either by simplicity or by elaboration. A very simple, yet effective form, consists of a series of circular terraces placed stair-like, one above another, each a foot high with the bottom one eight, the next six and a half, then five feet, three and a half and two feet across respectively, with a large Dracena or Agave at the top, crowning all. The level parts planted with Alternantheras, and the almost perpendicular slopes with Echeverias, produce a very fine result.

In a still more simple style, the bed is raised six inches or more above the common surface, with an abruptly sloping edge. The surface of the bed is occupied as any ordinary bed, while the slope may be planted with Echeverias or other plants that lie close to the ground. If the

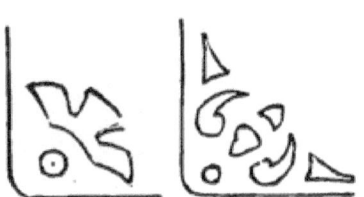

Fig. 62.—DESIGNS FOR CORNERS.   Fig. 63.—SECTION OF RIBBON BORDER.

slope is covered with grass kept nicely clipped, instead of Echeverias, etc., the effect is also good. The outline of such beds may be of any other form than circular, such as a star, crescent, oval, etc.

DESIGNS FOR CORNERS AND BORDERS.

Figure 62 represents two designs of flower beds for the corners formed by the intersections of walks or drives at right angles; where two corners directly opposite are to be thus occupied, the same design ought to be used in both.

Figure 63 shows a section of border in the ribbon style. Commencing with line *a*, low plants are used, and with this the hight is increased with each letter, and the *d* may contain the highest plants, from this they decrease in size, and those in *g* and *a* being alike in hight. The effect of a long border of this kind is very striking.

Fig.64.—PORTION OF SCROLL BORDER.

A scroll pattern for a border is shown in figure 64.

A beautiful narrow border in an arabesque arrangement, all the plants of which should be fine, low-growing kinds, is shown in figure 65. In carrying out any of the designs given, it is hardly possible in transferring the pattern to the ground to take too great pains with all lines, to have them of proper shape and in graceful curves. Beds are often seen which were intended to be copies of

Fig. 65.—ARABESQUE PATTERN IN PART FOR BORDER.

excellent patterns, but the work of laying out and planting was done in such an inferior manner as to deprive it wholly of its due effect.

LOCATION OF FLOWER BEDS.

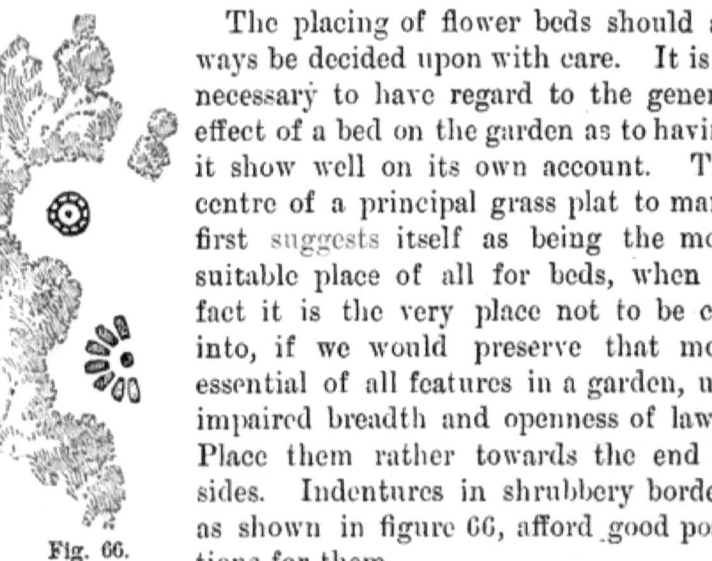

Fig. 66.

The placing of flower beds should always be decided upon with care. It is as necessary to have regard to the general effect of a bed on the garden as to having it show well on its own account. The centre of a principal grass plat to many first suggests itself as being the most suitable place of all for beds, when in fact it is the very place not to be cut into, if we would preserve that most essential of all features in a garden, unimpaired breadth and openness of lawn. Place them rather towards the end or sides. Indentures in shrubbery borders as shown in figure 66, afford good positions for them.

It is well, when grading the grounds, to have some

such points as these made slightly elevated, or mound-
like, expressly for accommodating showy flower-beds.   In
this way a desirable degree of boldness may be secured,
while the means by which it was acquired would ordinarily
escape detection.   But be careful not to make such elevations too high, else they may appear unnatural.

The Parisians have a pleasing mode of using flowers in
decorating their lawns worth noticing.   It consists of
running a narrow border several feet in from the edge of
grass plats, on four sides, with some openings to the
centre, as shown in figure 67.   These borders are usually
from three to six feet wide, with the plants arranged

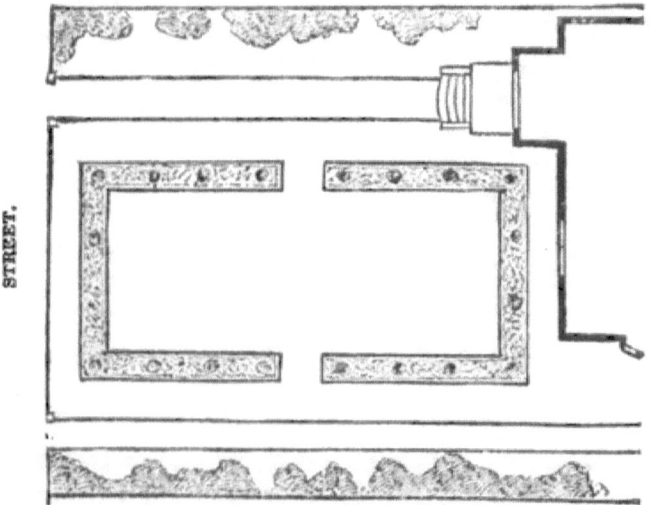

Fig. 67.—FRENCH METHOD OF ADORNING LAWNS.

in the mixed irregular style and quite uncrowded, with
usually an edging of some bright low plants.   It is a
charming style, and the effect is largely due to preserving
an ample central plat of grass.   A pleasing feature is
the introduction of some handsome shrubs, along the
centre of the borders at equal distances apart.   Altogether
the arrangement is satisfactory to the eye, and worthy
of adoption in our gardens when of sufficient area.

10

SUB-TROPICAL GARDENS.

Sub-tropical gardens are those in which tropical and sub-tropical plants of showy foliage, like the Palms, Cycas, Dracenas, Agaves, and many others, or else kinds of a different nature that bear some resemblance to these, or both, are used with a view to introducing some of the picturesqueness of tropical vegetation into the gardens of the North. Under the head of Hardy Plants in Part II are named some of that class, which possess qualities that suit them to this style of gardening. These possess a special value for the purpose, because while very effective along with others, unlike the Palms and other tender tropicals, they can be had in any garden, without requiring a conservatory in which to winter them. To such also may be added some hardy trees and shrubs that have a picturesque appearance, like the Ailanthus, Cut-leaved Sumach, Aralias, Magnolias, Honey Locusts, and others. The first two named, when used for this purpose, should be subjected to the peculiar treatment of cutting them down to near the ground every year, and then depending upon the new growth for effect. Some plants grown from seed and tubers, such as Ricinus, Japanese Maize, Sunflower, Caladiums, Cannas, etc., are also very suitable here. If with a good collection of such kinds, only a few real tropicals can be used, a decidedly good effect may be created. These latter kinds will be growing in pots, which should be sunk in the soil of the bed. Even if the true tropicals are entirely lacking, the effect may still be very satisfactory. The sub-tropical garden should be in a place somewhat protected from sweeping winds, for these play havoc with the foliage of some kinds.

HARDY FERNS AND THE WILD GARDEN.

The hardy Ferns are a class of plants of peculiar beauty, and an out-door fernery is very desirable. Delight-

ing in shade, as most of them do, there are many town
lots so hedged in by high buildings as to forbid the
growth of other plants, but which are well adapted to
growing ferns. Beds for these may be treated as low
rockeries. In Part IV directions are given for preparing
soil for them.

The Wild Garden is a place where interesting wild and
cultivated plants are brought together in the most natural manner, and allowed to live and struggle, much
as they do when wild. In small grounds a place in the
midst of groups of trees and shrubs, or in large grounds
a number of acres partly wood and partly open, treated
thus for revealing the wildness peculiar to woods and
clearings, may be rendered a most enjoyable place. Where
space will admit, hardy flowers. grasses, ferns, and creepers should be scattered about, and thickets be formed of
shrubs, including brambles. Some clumps of the more
graceful wild-looking plants of the garden should be
placed here, together with those gathered from woods
and clearings. Here is a place where the Fennel-leaved
Pæony will be enjoyed more than would an improved
variety with large gobular flowers ; the single Briar Rose
more than the best improved Hybrid Perpetual. Some
annuals may be scattered over the soil in spots, to come
along as they can, and some of these will live for years
by self-seeding.

Rocks, stumps, and mounds, clothed with Mosses,
Lichens, Winter-green, Partridge-berry, and many other
little wild things are well in such a place, and could
there be a small brook with aquatic plants, trees, and
rocky cliffs festooned with climbers, little would be lacking to render the spot constantly attractive. The loveli-
ness and ceaselessly varying charms of such scenes are
indeed difficult to describe, and something of the kind
would prove to be one of the most gratifying spots in
any place, no matter what other features of adornment

might be introduced.   Then such a wild garden has the great merit of permanence and inexpensiveness, for if arranged with some judgment at first, the colony may almost be left to take care of itself.   If the owner were to go away for ten years, time would so add to its attractions, that he might on his return find it more beautiful than ever.

CHAPTER XX.

ROCKWORK.

That there is a general love for the rough picturesqueness of rocks and crags, is shown by the frequency with which the former, in either good taste or bad, are used

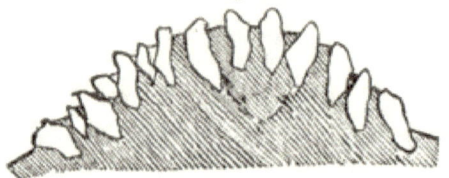

Fig. 68.—SIMPLE FORM OF ROCKWORK.

for adorning home grounds.   With rocks we may transfer material for garden embellishment from nature that remains wholly unchanged with the removal.

The effectiveness of rockwork depends largely upon the manner in which it is formed.   Figure 68 represents one of the simplest ways of using rocks and stones for garden adornment.   Stones of most any size that can be handled are set a part of their length in the soil of a bed, somewhat mound-like in shape, and at such distances apart as to allow some plants to grow between them. They are better for being elongated, mostly setting them then with their longest way at right angles with the surface of the soil.

Chips of building stone from the cutter's yard are excellent. If their diameters are nearly alike, they may vary considerably in length without deteriment. If kinds of two or more different colors and shades can be selected for the same, or different beds, a pleasing kind of variety is thus secured.

Such a rockery is well suited to ferns or any plants that in order to flourish need moisture at the roots. The stones aid the retention of moisture in the soil, and it may be remarked that the nearer flat the bed is kept the

Fig. 69.—A ROCK-BORDER WITH ROCK-PLANTS, CLIMBERS, EVER-
GREENS, ETC.

less trouble there will be from drying out. A rockery is well adapted to situations which are difficult to embellish otherwise. such as narrow spaces between the walks and fence or house, or in angles formed by buildings and walls, or at junctions of walks, and sometimes they may be even used effectually in simple circular mounds.

Figure 69 shows a rock-border suitable to be placed next to the boundary of lots, against buildings, or to be used as a low screen. The engraving will give suggestions for arranging such mound rockeries. It is seen that there is first an edging of stones mostly set on their ends, retaining the soil of the mounds. Then there are more or less stones, large and small, partly imbedded in the soil all over the surface. The mound should, for the sake of variety, vary somewhat in its hight in different parts. As shown here, the front line is supposed to vary from one to three feet in hight. The ground outline may be waved or straight, as may be preferred, or space will allow. In some places pockets are arranged among the stones in laying them up, for holding soil and plants,

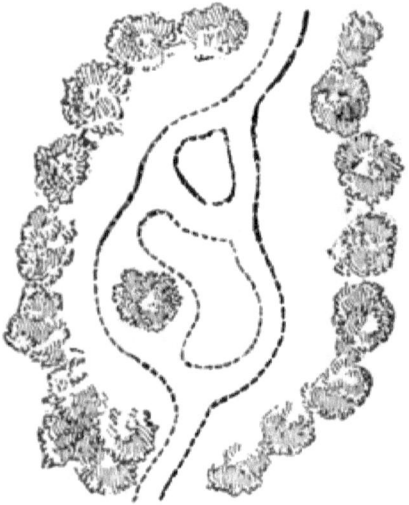

Fig. 70.—IDEA FOR WALKS IN A ROCK-GARDEN.

and in these trailers, like Moneywort, Vinca or Peri-winkle, etc., may be set.

This engraving represents a rockery which is fully ex-posed to the sun. Such, if made fifteen to twenty feet wide, will accommodate a large variety of hardy and tender plants, dwarf, deciduous, and evergreen shrubs, etc. It is an excellent place for some of the slightly tender ever-greens, for the soil being elevated, is never wet, and al-lows the annual growth to ripen so thoroughly that they can endure severe cold with impunity.

In grounds of large extent, and especially on places

where large stones abound, rock-gardens can be formed
with many variations. An idea for walks in such a garden is given in figure 70, the rock-faced line of the
mound as shown in figure 69, forming the edge of the
walk all around. The outer edge of the outside mounds,
and also beyond, may be planted with shrubs and trees,
but these, especially the trees, should not be so dense all
around as to shut out the cool breezes in summer. If
such a rock-garden is formed where one or several
large shade trees stand, and the walks are carried near
or under these, and seats provided in the shade, and then
if a small stream of water can be had to pass through it,
about every requirement for a very complete rock-garden
would be met, and one suited to plants that like shade,
moisture, and dry places.

Sometimes instead of sowing a slope in the pleasure
garden with grass, its surface may be converted into a
rockery. There is a chance in large rock-gardens for introducing an almost endless variety in the shape of
grottos, steps, archways, springs, pools, cascades,
bridges, ledges, shelves, etc., and it is not a difficult matter to render these remarkably interesting and attractive.

In planting, the principles governing the arrangement
of groups of trees and shrubs, touched upon in previous
chapters, may be observed here. One part of the construction may have trailers predominating, another evergreens, from the spiry dwarf Spruces and Junipers to
the Creeping Junipers and Ivies, still others may be devoted to alpine plants, upland and shade-loving ferns,
wild flowers, and even showy tender tropicals and green-
house plants may be introduced. In moist, shady places,
the grotesque Rex Begonias, Marantas, Dracenas,
Tradescantias, etc., would be effective. Cobæa scandens
is a climber of special value for such places. By using
good taste in the arrangement of the surface, rocks,
plants, and trees, and avoiding every thing like stiffness

and formality in the work, there is no reason why such rockeries should not prove very pleasing in any garden that can accommodate them.

An arch constructed of rough stones, and covered with climbers, is represented by figure 71. This makes an appropriate entrance to a rock-garden, or it may be introduced independently as an entrance to other divisions of the grounds. Even small lots will allow such an object to be brought in very fitly. This may be, because there are but few steps of transition between rocks, as they come

Fig. 71.—AN ARCHWAY OF ROCKWORK.

from nature, and as they are used in buildings. At any rate, I have observed that we may have, even in a small and highly finished garden, a bit of some such picturesque roughness, where other kinds of natural material used to a marked extent would seem out of place.

Rock Grottos often prove interesting features in gardens. They need not necessarily be dark, damp, or unhealthy, and may, from the very nature of the material, and the manner of their construction, be made comfortable places in the heat of summer. Figures 72 to 74 give a ground outline, a cross section and a stairway of a simple form of Grotto. There are in this two places of entrance and exit on the level of the floor, and stairs leading from the interior to the summit, thus providing for free circulation of air. In the one figured there is a bubbling spring of water, giving rise to a lively rill which crosses

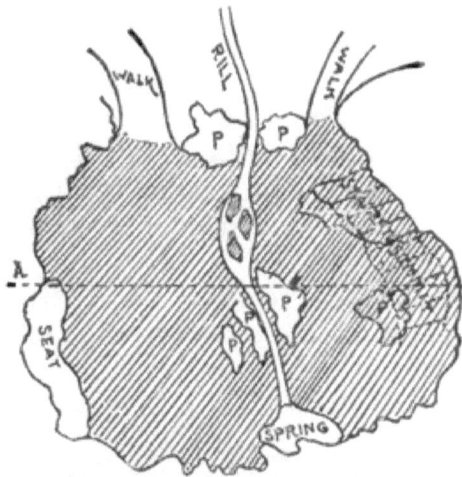

Fig. 72.— GROUND OUTLINE OF ARTIFICIAL GROTTO—*P, P*, REPRESENT ROCK PILLARS.

the floor, and an ample stone seat. There is a large field for variety and for displaying taste and knowledge of building in the construction of rockwork of this kind.

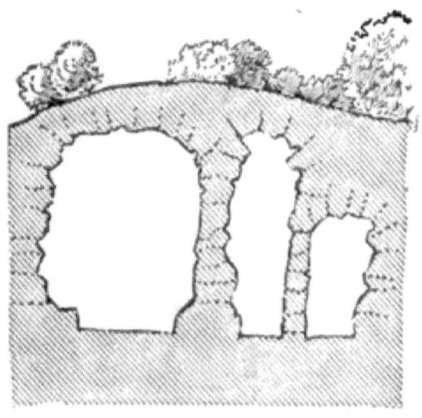

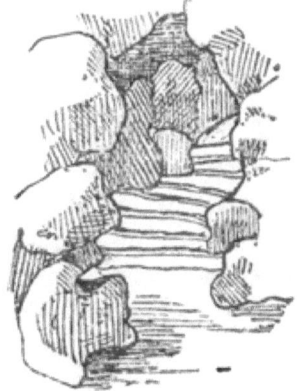

Fig. 73.—CROSS-SECTION OF ARTIFICIAL GROTTO ABOVE, AT CROSS LINE *A*.

Fig. 74.—STAIRWAY IN ARTIFICIAL GROTTO.

In the Paris public gardens one may see that the construction of Grottos may amount to quite an art. Great skill is brought to bear in imitating natural grottos, even to the introduction of imposing artificial stalactites and stalagmites, also in introducing cascades and other forms of water in connection with them.

The imitation of castles or their ruins, and draping them with climbers, is sometimes engaged in with favorable results. But caution should be observed as regards the materials, designs, and location of such work, else it may prove a blemish rather than an ornament in the grounds.

It is elsewhere suggested that a large boulder may be converted into an ornamental feature by draping it with

Fig. 75.—BRIDGE OF ROCKS.

the Virginia Creeper or other climber. There is propriety in introducing some of these sparingly, with or without the drapery of foliage, into gardens, especially such as are laid out in the natural style. Placed in groups in a corner of a plat, or at the side of knolls, or singly at junctions, or along the sides of walks and drives, the effect of these is generally good.

Sometimes shapely stones, uniform in size, may be used as edgings to walks or flower beds throughout a place. Such should be large enough to admit of sinking them part way into the ground, so that they will not easily become displaced, yet they should not be so large as to be very conspicuous.

Figure 75 represents a bridge of rocks for private or

public grounds, either crossing over water, or another walk on a lower level as through a gully. With the right materials at hand, such a bridge is easily laid up and quite sure to look well.

Very fair substitutes for natural rocks in rockwork are the odd shaped clinkers that come from furnaces, and the distorted burned bricks from kilns, which are often cemented together in masses. Some of these can be selected which, at a little distance, can not be distinguished from rocks.

In introducing rockwork into the garden, let everything like overdoing be guarded against. Where one meets with success beyond expectations in work of this kind, enthusiasm is usually aroused, and enthusiasm here, if it should blind the eye of correct taste and discretion is liable to lead to very objectionable excesses.

CHAPTER XXI.

WATER IN ORNAMENTAL GARDENING.

In many of the most attractive natural landscapes water holds a place of high importance, and this suggests its value in ornamental gardening. As a rule, unless it is supplied naturally, water effects produced in gardens prove somewhat costly, hence it will be only now and then employed, except perhaps in the shape of a fountain, tiny rill or lakelet. But where a natural rill, creek, or lake exists, it should be prized and so treated as to make the most of it.

A large stream or body of water may not be manageable in itself as a garden feature, but trees and shrubs can usually be introduced between the frequented parts of a garden bordering on the water, in such a manner as to afford most delightful glimpes of it. No large expanse of water is as pleasing if viewed all at once, as when seen by parts through openings between woody clumps. Where they can be used, tastefully built boat houses, landings, and bridges are pleasing features.

Small, natural lakes may sometimes be varied in outline to advantage. Figure 76 shows how a lakelet, represented by the dotted lines, which could be viewed at a glance in every part, was so varied by grading and planting as to be more ornamental, and to appear larger,

Fig. 76.—LAKELET IMPROVED.

because so arranged that all parts are never seen from any one point, thus conveying the idea of indefinite extent. In such work, regard should be paid to having the general outline simple rather than otherwise. The principle of partial concealment is an important one in managing all small bodies of water if we would make the most of them.

Islands add a pleasing variety to water scenery if happily placed. Usually they are better for being not far from the shore, to maintain an appearance of some connection with the main-land. They should be abundantly clothed with trees and shrubs. For every purpose of this kind, the Laurel-leaved and other free-growing Willows possess great value. Planted at the water's edge, their shrubby forms soon enlarge, and hanging in the water on one side, resting on the land on the other, they break the regular outline of the water delightfully.

Where a good living rill is found in gardens, or can be introduced, there need be little lack of the attractiveness water is susceptible of imparting. A lake may be formed by excavation or by damming, or a series of these may be made, or the course of the stream may be intercepted with rocks and earth, to produce small musical cascades or rapids, as shown in figure 77, provided there is a very slight fall in the land; or the water may be divided to meet again further on to form islets. Usually with a certain quantity of water at command, there is no more advantageous use to which it can be put for ornament than this of rills. Those European gardens, in which vast sums of money have been expended in constructing complicated fountains and water works, are poor examples to be followed in the use of water in gar-

Fig. 77.—A NATURAL RILL IMPROVED.

dens; for usually, if, instead, one-fourth of the water and one-tenth of the money had been employed in these in making rills, lakelets, waterfalls, etc., of natural appearance, the effects would have been far better.

One thing to be guarded against in the production of effects with artificial water, or, indeed, in artificial arrangements of rocks, trees, etc., is the investing of the work with an air of stiffness and a studied appearance so opposite to nature in her most pleasing moods. This defect is not unfrequently apparent in such compositions, and sometimes so bad that the general appearance of the grounds would have been better with no attempt whatever at ornamentation of the kind. A safe guide in this kind of work is to be found in fine natural scenes, and then, of course, experience, coupled with good taste on the part of the designer.

Unless adjacent grounds are elevated and hilly, the banks of lakes and streams should not generally be steep and regular. Usually in nature, the land meets the water gradually, unless in the case of streams, the sides of which are cut down by the wearing of the water, or where they run through gulleys or along hill sides. If walks are to be carried along the banks, they should not, as a rule, run close to the edge for long distances, but a strip of grass, however narrow in places, and then at some points clumps of trees and plants should be between them. Occasionally the walks may run down to the water and be widened into a beach for some distance and return again. Along winding rills, through gulleys, where the walks are carried along steep slopes, railings are sometimes needed and perhaps bridges now and then for crossing the stream. Large rocks set in the water to project boldly above the surface are appropriate in water scenery. Trees and shrubs in clumps, extending quite down to the water's edge in places, help greatly to produce an appearance of natural grace and freedom.

While no class of trees are more appropriate for enhancing water effects than Weeping and other Willows, still it is frequently demonstrated in the best landscape gardening, that no trees are more useful for planting with the Willows than the Poplars and other tapering kinds—trees the least likely to be thought of by many planters for such situations. In marked contrast, as such erect trees are with the weepers, they give strength to them, and create an improved effect throughout.

Water is often used in ornamental gardens in fountains and basins. By means of these, the refreshing beauty and music of moving water may be secured with quantities so limited, that the use of the element in any other manner would be impracticable. The beauty of a fountain depends largely upon having a sufficient water supply to make the streams strong and animated, and also upon its style and setting. The best fountain designs and figures can never make up for inadequate water supply. On the other hand, a fountain with no figure, and consisting only of one or more strong streams from nozzles placed at the surface of the water is usually very satisfactory.

Both stone and iron basins are used for fountains, but so far as appearances go, the former consisting of a cut stone coping, with a well constructed cement bottom, is to be perferred.

Where the water of a garden is suitable for fish and water fowl, it is desirable to introduce some of these for ornament. Water fowls soil a garden to some extent, on which account, if for no other, they must not be introduced too freely. Small garden ponds converted into washing pools for poultry are an abomination, and yet they may sometimes be met with looking quite as bad as this. The subject of Aquatic and Bog Plants is somewhat discussed in Parts II and IV.

CHAPTER XXII.

HEDGES AND CLIPPED TREES.

That peculiarity of some trees which allows of their being closely clipped with shears, and by this means kept compact and dense, when they would naturally reach a large size, is turned to account in the garden, particularly in making hedges. About all those known as hedge plants are of this nature.

Hedges, whether introduced for marking divisions, or

merely for ornament, are, when in good condition, and
it is easy to have them so, very useful for increasing
garden variety and effectiveness. Their forms may be
varied considerably, and in this way alone there is a
chance for a good deal of pleasing variety.

Figure 78 shows a number of forms of both plain and
ornamental hedges, including two passage ways through
them. The Norway Spruce and Hemlock, two of our

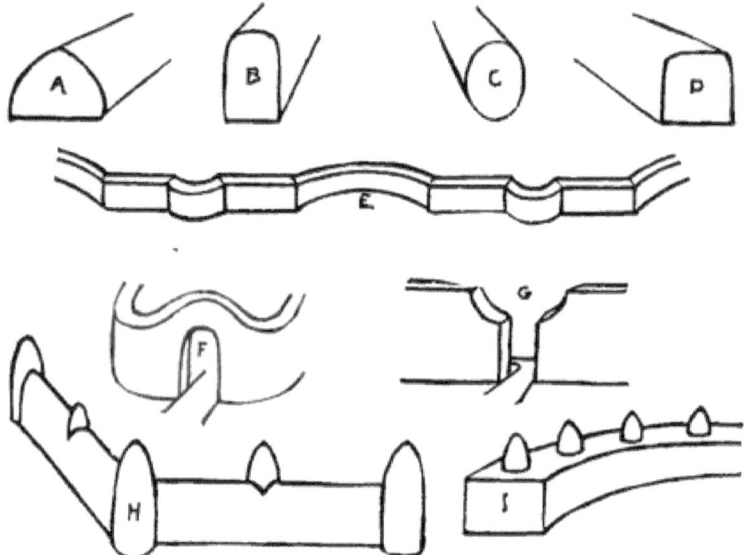

Fig. 78.—VARIOUS FORMS OF HEDGES.

most reliable and tractable hedge plants, and the Beech,
Hornbeam, and Holly, are suitable for the forms *A, D, H,
I.* Arbor Vitæ, Tree Box, Privets, Osage Orange, Honey
Locust, Japan Quince, and other shrubs may be trimmed
into forms *B, C.* and *E.* Entrances like *F* and *G* can be
worked out of any of the taller growing hedge plants.
Edgings to walks, borders, and clumps of plants and
shrubs may be made of the Dwarf Box, Tom Thumb
Arbor Vitæ, and Dwarf Spruce with good effect.

The distance apart for setting hedge plants, varies according to the size intended to be reached. For exam-

ple, if a fine, low Norway Spruce hedge is designed to be kept at three or four feet in hight, with perhaps five feet in view ultimately, the plants may be put eighteen or twenty inches apart, but if a screen, twelve or fifteen feet high is desired, they should not be closer than four feet, and six feet would be better. In cases like this they may be planted twice or three times as close at the start, to make a full row, and then remove those between as the others require the space. It is safe to say that from twelve to fourteen inches apart is a suitable distance for the majority of kinds where the hedge is to be low, with an increase to twice this distance for high hedges or screens.

The objection to hedges, that they cannot be crossed even when it is desirable to do so, at other places than

Fig. 79.—STILE FOR HEDGES.

gates, may be overcome by the use of a stile, as shown in figure 79.

Regarding clipped forms of trees, we hold in as great abhorrence as any one, the ludicrous extent to which these have been used in old-time gardening, especially in Europe, and which even to-day prevails in some places abroad. Still, in the same way as the formal terrace and slope, geometrical flower-beds, etc., may sometimes fit in the garden, as minor features of embellishment, so some clipped trees may properly be admitted. A number of acres closely covered with every conceivable pattern of these, such as can be seen in some old European places, may well fill us with disgust, but it does not follow that a few perfect globes, pyramids, urns, or trees in other shapes, well relieved by grass, in some parts of our gardens, would not afford genuine pleasure, or even that a larger number may not sometimes be employed with tasteful effect.

The charming garden of Mr. Hunnewell, Wellesley, Mass., owes its fame to no one thing, more than to an elaborate Italian garden at the head of a lake, which in excellent taste is made to support numerous trees clipped into pleasing forms. But here, let it be observed, that while the Italian garden is quite extensive itself, the grounds, as a whole, are so large and so generally conspicious is the natural style of gardening over extensive areas, that after all this fanciful feature is but a minor attraction of the place, and as such, certainly tends to add greatly to the charms of this private park.

In figure 80 a number of forms of clipped trees are given. The globular form A, is adapted to a number of shrubs such as Deutzia, Japan Quince, Dwarf Mock Orange, and other deciduous kinds, and Box, Dwarf Pines, Spruces, and Arbor Vitæ, in evergreens. Forms B, D, H, J, may be applied to the common Hemlock, American or Siberian Arbor Vitæ. E, D, H, or any other forms the beauty of which is nothing, unless attention is given to nicely shaping them, may be produced most perfectly from the Tree Box. The White Pine and Norway Spruce are well adapted to the styles shown in F and I, and the last named for C, G, K, and either this, Hemlock or Arbor Vitæ for the arbor L.

In producing forms like the arbor L, and archway J, after the trees have become well established in their places, a stay rod of iron or wood is required at a suitable hight against which to tie the bended tops and branches, as necessary during the first stages of the work.

The most suitable place for some clipped trees in gardens is in the vicinity of any portion devoted to the formal styles of planting. A pair of these on the sides of the walk near the entrance gate, or at the crossing of walks at right angles, or one placed as a

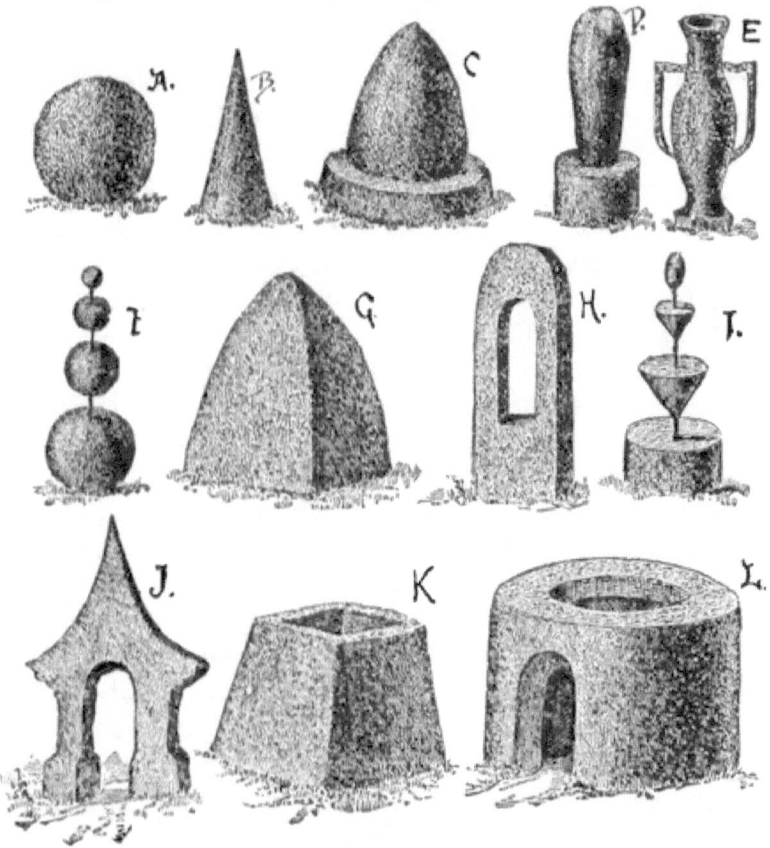

Fig. 80.—FORMS IN WHICH TREES MAY BE CLIPPED.

central or terminal object of a walk or drive, or a few along the sides of these, and on terraces, may be very ornamental, provided always they are well sustained by grass or by other prominent features. Yet it is proper to recommend great caution against introducing them too freely, for unquestionably it is easy to overdo the matter.

CHAPTER XXIII.

GARDEN STRUCTURES.

Whatever the size or nature of a garden, there is almost always need of some kind of architectural structures besides the main buildings, for adding to its comfort, security, and interest. Among these are fences, walls, railings, copings, seats, arbors, shelters, conservatories, lodges, tool houses, bird and animal houses, vases, trellises, fountains, statuary, terrace walls, sun dials, swings, bridges, boat houses, and sometimes aqueducts, viaducts, and in public parks, offices, museums, refectories, amusement halls, etc.

The guiding principles to the introduction of these should be, first their apparent need ; second their adaptiveness to the purpose and place in view ; third, appearance of stability and tasteful design, and lastly, due regard to a right balance of the features of the garden, and especially between made and natural ones, to see that the former, which may be introduced chiefly for ornament, are in a sense subordinate to the latter.

As to fences, walls, etc., it is apparent that gardens, and especially cemeteries, are more beautiful for excluding these from the scene. Usually the less we can have of them the better for pure garden effect, to say nothing of expense saved in their construction. Still we cannot get along entirely without them.

Where a guard is needed along streets and boundaries, the light ornamental iron fences now manufactured are excellent and interrupt the view but little. For many places hedges are very suitable instead of ordinary fences along the street, but if there would be an objection to a hedge in front of the house on account of its density, then just here an iron or other fence might take its place.

When wooden picket fences are used, as they commonly are, the lighter and more simple they are in design, the better their appearance. It is in poor taste to spend money on excessive ornamentation of these or any other kind of common fences of wood or iron in the manner often seen.

There might be much to recommend on the score of fine garden effect, in the custom common in some cities, of having no front fences even on large grounds. But their absence never allows the owner who thinks much of his garden surroundings, containing perhaps rare and prized specimens, to feel secure against intrusions from quadrupeds, children, etc. I observe that while a few years ago this custom seemed destined to prevail generally, now nearly all the best places of large size have some kind of fence or guard put up along the street.

Hurdle fences, made of light wrought iron posts and bars, as often seen in the gardens of the British Isles, can at

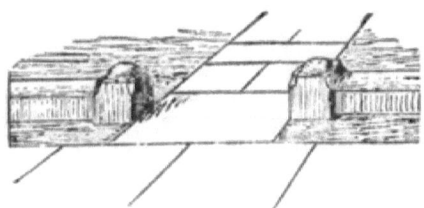

Fig. 81.—COPING AND ENTRANCE NEXT TO SIDEWALK.

times be advantageously used in parks and large grounds. Instead of mowing all parts, large plats some distance from the house or prominent drives, may be surrounded with these and cattle and sheep be allowed to pasture within. By this course, direct use may be had of some parts of the grounds without the expense of mowing, and yet, being closely cropped by the animals, these areas may have the same appearance as the mowed parts. The introduction of live stock in this way, engaged in feeding or resting, adds much to the interest and effect in large grounds. The hurdles may be so lightly constructed and yet strong, as to escape notice a short distance away. Where there are groups of trees or shrubs within the pastured plats, a line of hurdles may be used to enclose them, for protection from the animals. Wire fences can also be used for such purposes.

A simple stone coping, as shown in figure 81, is perhaps the best substitute for a street fence where the latter is not desired. Such a coping scarcely interferes with the garden effect, serves to mark the boundary and also to turn off intruders, be they brutes or persons. A very

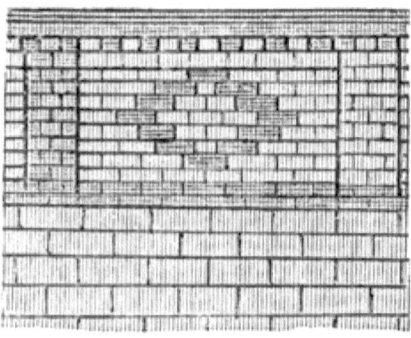

Fig. 82.—WALL OF STONE, AND RED AND YELLOW BRICK.

neat street guard may be made by running a low open iron fence along the top of a coping, like that illustrated in figure 81, or on a low brick wall one to two feet high.

In grounds it is sometimes desirable to separate the kitchen-yard or garden, or the cow-yard from other parts, by a close wall or fence ; or sometimes these are needed for shutting out unpleasant views on rear streets. Where a hedge for any reason is inappropriate, walls of brick or stone, or of both, may be built, or if something cheaper is preferred, a fence can be erected of boards, either rough or planed.

Figure 82 shows a wall of brick in two colors, and stone, and figure 83 a tight board fence, made of boards four to eight inches wide, lapped on each other as shown in the engraving. By planting Virginia Creepers, Wistarias or other climbers, or training fruit vines and

Fig. 83.—TIGHT BOARD FENCE, TOP VIEW.

trees against such walls, the blankness which would otherwise prevail is delightfully obviated.

Balustrades and railings may be introduced at the head of a terrace slope, in situations where such architectural decorations are warranted by proximity to the house, or by the general plan of the place.

SEATS, ARBORS, AND SHELTERS.

Seats, arbors, and shelters in pleasure grounds, are for both comfort and beauty, and to serve these ends should

Fig. 84.—GARDEN SEAT SHADED BY CLIMBERS.

be the first consideration in selecting them. Figure 84 shows a garden seat which is shaded by an arch covered with climbers. For a neat, cheap, and strong garden seat, what is called the " Central Park Settee," or some variation of it, made of two end frames of iron with ash slats for bottom and back, will answer well for almost any place. Rustic chairs and settees are very suitable for the garden. In selecting these, regard should be had to their being comfortable as seats and well made, for frequently they are not so; one of the great objections to every kind of rustic furniture, is the lack of durability, especially when it is carelessly put together.

Although expensive, perhaps the most beautiful, certainly the most durable material for garden seats, is stone, for one of which figure 85 gives a good design. They may be made curving or straight, and of a length to suit the place to be occupied.

A wooden seat, if well proportioned, neatly made, and kept thoroughly painted or oiled, answers very well for

Fig. 85.—A GARDEN SEAT OF STONE OR MARBLE.

Fig. 86. WOODEN FOLDING SEAT, END SECTION.

the garden. It may be made as shown by figure 86, with two pieces in the seat, the front half secured to the risers, and the back half so hinged that it can be turned over the front one, as the dotted lines indicate; with this there may always be a dry bench, unsoiled by birds and quadrupeds. Any good house-joiner could make such a seat in a short time. The corners of the hinges that project above the surface of the seat should be rounded off with a file. A four-inch strip should be nailed on the back half of the bottom, as shown in the engraving.

For a structure to afford shade, there can be nothing more appropriate, in most places, than a simple skeleton arbor, as shown in figure 44, covered with a heavy mass of some rapid growing climber like Virginia Creeper, Trumpet-vine, etc. If the pieces comprising the structure are put together with a view to replacing any when

Fig. 87.—A RUSTIC SUMMER-HOUSE.

they begin to decay, by taking out the old and slipping in new ones, they may be kept up for an indefinite time. Climbers however, that twine tightly around supports, like the Bitter Sweet, would not allow this plan to be carried out, but many others will.

There are instances where something more pretentious than the skeleton arbor is wanted, such as a rustic arbor; figure 87, which represents a type of garden architecture much liked when well made. In this six-sided arbor, three of the sides at the back are closed, and the interior surface of these as well as of the ceiling is covered with

11

small, straight branches an inch or so in diameter, nearly
uniform in appearance, arranged obliquely, as shown in
the engraving. The outside of these parts is covered
with sections of poles about three inches through or
more, split in halves, and arranged with the bark outwards,
obliquely or otherwise to suit the taste. One of the
front sides affords entrance, and two others are about half
open. The roof, in this instance, is heavily thatched
with straw, which not only affords perfect protection to
the structure, but being nine to twelve inches thick, it
serves to render the arbor cool under the rays of a mid-
summer sun. A seat is arranged against five sides of the
interior. Many variations from this style, both as regards material and form, will suggest themselves to the
ingenious.

BRIDGES.

Bridges across streams or ravines, afford a fine field
for the display of taste and ingenuity as to designs.

Fig. 88.—RUSTIC BRIDGE.

Those of rustic work are very appropriate, and where
taste is used in the selection and combination of materials, they are peculiarly effective. Figure 88 shows a
bridge of this style. This being raised in the centre,
not only allows boats to pass underneath where the banks

are somewhat low, but it gives a commanding appearance to the structure, and affords a good out-look over the grounds. The elevated portion may be furnished with seats, and even converted into an arbor by roofing it, as can easily be done by carrying the posts of the upper level to about eight feet high, to support the roof.

BIRD HOUSES AND OTHER SHELTERS.

The three bird houses represented in figure 89, are of rustic material, and suitable for placing on poles or in trees. The left hand one consists of a section of a tree trunk, dug or burned out, and capped with a roof turned in a lathe and painted. The centre one is made of bark-

Fig. 89.—RUSTIC BIRD HOUSES.

covered slabs. Houses after either of these two patterns, may be large enough to accommodate two or more families, by partitioning them off into apartments, with an entrance to each. The right hand cut shows a cluster of four houses, made of sections of branches. These are fitted up to accommodate occupants, by making a cavity in the side large enough for the nest, and to get in and out; afterwards replacing a shell of bark over the cavity to close it, and boring a hole from the end of the block for a door. In mounting these, the sides that are cut into should be placed downwards, to prevent water from entering. Nothing will better encourage the feathery songsters to be at home in the garden, than good houses like these and others they may suggest.

Where water fowl, deer, and other quadrupeds are introduced, the shelters for these look well constructed of rustic material. Rustic vases, window boxes, trellises, etc., are also desirable for ornament in certain places. There are a number of manufacturers of and dealers in rustic work in the country, who keep a regular stock of these and similar articles on hand. Every thing like overdoing in the introduction of rustic articles in the garden should be carefully avoided.

BOAT HOUSES.

Where the body of water in a garden is large enough and sufficiently deep for boats, these are generally intro-

Fig. 90.—DESIGN FOR A BOAT HOUSE.

duced. Figure 90 shows a boat house suitable for a lake or river side in a private garden, and may be built of either brick, stone, or wood. Such a structure affords shelter to the boats, a place for getting in and out of them, and in the above design, an observatory-room and veranda over the water. The upper floor is fitted for comfort by heating it with a stove, to be used as a look-out in the skating season.

PLANT HOUSES AND CONSERVATORIES.

The general desire to render our homes beautiful by the help of tender plants and cut flowers, makes one more or less dependent upon plant houses suited for their culture. If plants are not grown on the place, they are bought of the florists, and this is generally expensive, if a good showing is wanted. A plant conservatory in connection with the garden and home, may become, at a reasonable cost, a source of much beauty and pleasure, as well as profit the entire year through. The common bright flowers

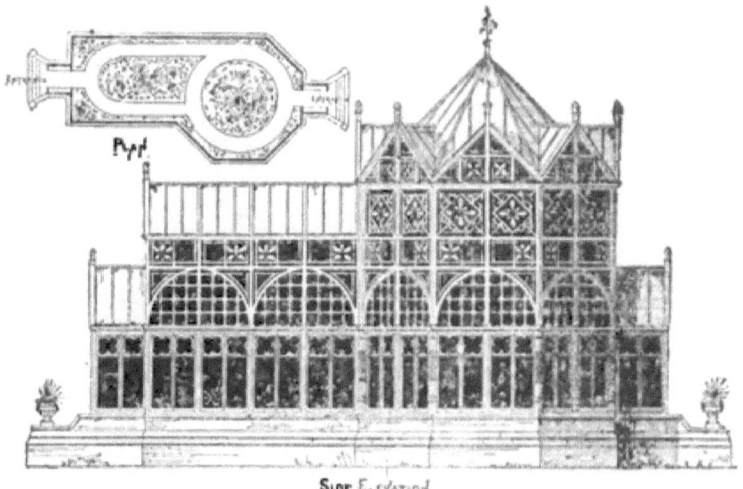

SIDE ELEVATION.

Fig. 91.—DETACHED CONSERVATORY IN GOTHIC STYLE, WITH PLAN.

may be had freely, and the rare exotics may also be grown for adorning the house in winter as well as the garden in summer. In addition to growing plants and flowers, glass structures possess an ornamental character of their own, as adjuncts of a house and garden, that make them very desirable. It has been well said: "Glass houses are like luminaries in pleasure grounds, they spread a sunshiny gladness over all the other improvements, and make them look more delightful."

A detached conservatory in the gothic style is shown in

figure 91, with also the ground plan. Such a conservatory might be sufficiently large to meet almost every demand of a complete plant house for a moderate sized garden. A recommendation for this particular style is, that although exceedingly handsome, all the glass surfaces are straight. It would be difficult to give such or a similar structure a place in any grounds large enough to properly hold it, and not have it contribute effectively to the general adornment. For small grounds, other conservatories

Fig. 92.—SMALL, CHEAP, LEAN-TO GREEN-HOUSE.

quite as pleasing in design as this, may be planned, but smaller and either detached like this, or connected with the house.

Figure 92 shows a small, cheap, lean-to green-house, which can be placed in almost any part of the grounds against a building. This is designed to meet the wants of those who like to have some means for growing plants, without any great outlay in the first cost, or who cannot readily so combine one with the house as to form a feature of its design. All conservatories attached to buildings should command a sheltered and sunny position.

Some of the other architectural objects named in the

beginning of this chapter, I pass by without giving them special attention. Some are articles that are purchasable, such as vases, statuary, sun dials, and the like, others are not in sufficient general demand to require space here, and when wanted, the landscape and building architect will be able to furnish suitable designs. On painting garden architecture see Part IV.

CHAPTER XXIV.

PLANS OF PRIVATE GROUNDS.

The materials used in, and principles governing ornamental garden-making, are mainly the same for every place, but different gardens, of course, vary in size, shape, and natural character. For these reasons, I propose in this work to pay special attention to describing materials, and the principles which should direct arranging them tastefully—so that one who has a place, whatever size or shape, to improve, may start on the right track for doing it well. I prefer to do this to giving many complete plans of grounds, and then perhaps it would be found, that not once in a thousand times would any of these fit this or that particular place. Still, some plans may serve a useful end, in suggesting the uniting of features with a view to complete effects, therefore I have chosen from a large collection such plans as I think will best answer this purpose.

Beginning with plans of very small plats, say from half a rod to two rods each, it may be said, that here is a class in which a greater degree of uniformity prevails, as to size and shape, than in larger grounds, hence a little more attention is given to complete plans. Moreover, this class greatly outnumbers all others everywhere, and are oftener totally neglected as regards embellishments than larger places.

The use of two shrubs only, is shown in figure 93 ; these may be chosen from Weigela, Althæa (Rose of Sharon), Japan Quince, Privet, and others. The shrubs are upon a grass plat, with a climber over the door. Figure 94 suggests the use of more shrubs than are employed in the last, and arranged in groups. The ground where they stand may be somewhat undulating for creating as much variety as possible with good taste. Only few shrubs being used, the selection should be choice, consisting of those that afford a good variety in tints, in foliage, flowers, and in their season of bloom. Some of

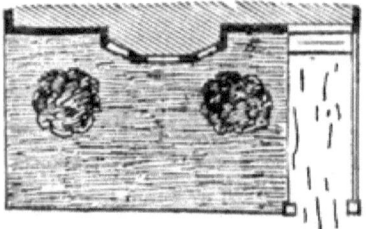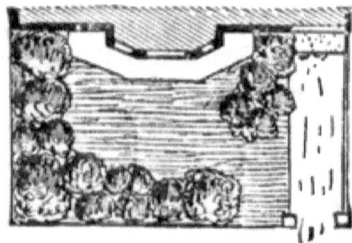

Figs. 93 and 94.—SMALL FRONT LOTS ADORNED WITH SHRUBS AND GRASS ONLY, WITH CLIMBERS OVER THE DOORS OF THE HOUSES.

the number might be dwarf evergreens, to give the eye something to rest on in winter. Small sized shrubs proportionate to the size of the grounds, are usually to be chosen for such places. The geometrical or straight lines of the house, street, and walks, have such an overpowering influence here, that there is little chance to work for the higher garden effects of breadth and freedom. And yet in these plans, the principle upon which such effects depend, is observed to the full degree allowable, and with good results.

Plans for laying out small lots, using flowers freely in addition to shrubs and grass, are given in figures 95 and 96. In both these lots, the ends farthest from the walks,

as well as the border projection towards the walks, may
be raised to be slightly mound-like.   When speaking
of giving a rounded elevation to such borders, I would
add the caution to not raise them too high.   From

Figs. 95 and 96.—SMALL FRONT LOTS ADORNED WITH GRASS, SHRUBS,
AND FLOWERS.

six to eighteen inches at the highest points may be
about right for the smallest sized lots thus laid out.

Two small lots planned for using more flowers than
anything else, are represented in figures 97 and 98.   The

Figs. 97 and 98.—SMALL FRONT LOTS WITH FLOWERS PREDOMINATING.

spaces between the flower-beds may be filled either with
grass or gravel, the former being decidedly preferable.
Such arrangements are particularly suitable for persons
who have a passion for growing flowers, and no other
space in which to grow them.

To carry out either of these plans in small places,
ought not as a rule to cost more than ten or fifteen dollars for each, especially if those who are to use them do

the work. Not much is thought of applying such amounts to the ornamentation of the house, yet if plans like these, or similar ones suggested, were applied to all the small lots of a neighborhood or a town, there would follow returns in the form of pure pleasure and healthfulness in such vicinities, not procurable in any other manner, or so cheaply.

In England, and elsewhere in Europe, the smallest sized cottage lots are oftener improved than with us. To pass along the streets of some English towns, and see rows of houses, the little front plats of each tastefully laid out, planted, and well kept, one can easily have faith in the favorable influences of such improvements on the happiness of these homes. Contrasting such cottage grounds with the neglected ones so general in our favored land, one is impressed with the wide field open for improvements in this class of places everywhere throughout America.

While the plans already given were designed for lots of the smallest sizes, several of them, for example those of figures 93, 94, and 96, would be adapted to front lots of a similar shape several times larger than those indicated, say from two to three square rods in each. Figure 94 would be the best of these, because the central portion of the lawn is open, tending to impart an air of breadth and repose, a matter, the importance of which increases with the larger size of the plats.

A long, narrow front yard is shown in figure 99 ; it is of moderate size, in which many shrubs are used, yet there is considerable open lawn, an arbor, several flower-beds, and a shade tree. Such an arrangement of borders and walks, the former planted with shrubs of all sizes and in large variety, with hardy and tender flowers, renders a small place exceedingly interesting to any lover of natural beauty in flowers, shrubs, and trees. Besides, such improvements may make a place seem far more ample, than if laid out, as are many similar front lots, with only a straight walk through the center from the entrance to the door of the house, and perhaps not a tree or shrub around. If desired, a vase might be placed

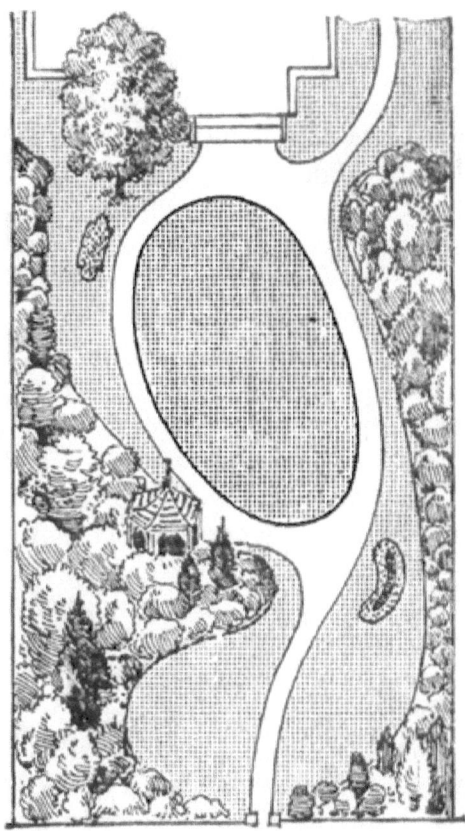

Fig. 90.—A DEEP FRONT LOT, LAID OUT TO ACCOMMODATE GRASS, FLOWERS, SHADE TREES, AND AN ARBOR.- Scale, 4 feet to ⅛ inch.

in the center of the oval plat, but this is by no means required for general good effect.

It may be observed by the plans presented in this chapter, that I am a strong advocate of the use of choice flowering and evergreen shrubs in groups, for embellishing home grounds, and particularly small ones. This is because it is found, that in such places good selections are certain of giving satisfaction, if they receive anything like fair treatment. Elsewhere I have called attention to the special merits of this class, and I here quote Mr. Thomas Meehan, of the "Gardener's Monthly," regarding the same point:

"Shrubs are not nearly enough employed in planting small places. By a judicious selection, a place may be had in a blooming state all the year; and they besides give it a greater interest by their variety, than is obtained by the too frequent error of filling up with two or three forest trees of gigantic growth. Plant thickly at first, to give a place a finished appearance, and thin out as they grow older. The average planter would have half a dozen plants scattered a dozen yards apart, because sometime in the future they would perhaps touch each other. We pass continually these weak conclusions, the little clumps near gate-ways will look like clumps some day; but why not have them now? It is as easy to have the perfect body as the ugly skeletons lying around. Masses of shrubs have a fine effect in a small place. The centers of such masses should be filled with evergreen shrubs, to prevent a too naked appearance in the winter."

Let it not be thought that belts or clumps of shrubs must make small grounds close and hot in summer for want of breeze. This might be, if these were wholly made up of tall shrubs planted thickly, but by having the margins varying in width, and then planting the narrowest parts with kinds, that in an age can not exceed a hight of a few feet, and the wide parts with large growers, this need not happen. More than that, by having enough tall kinds here and there, to break the force of the wind, diverting it in different directions through the garden, a place may be all the more agreeable.

An arrangement of shrubs in a town corner lot of

about half an acre, with straight stone walks and drives, is shown in figure 100. The walk leading to the side street is almost hidden as seen from the front by shrubs, while the back walk and the drive are entirely hidden from every part of the grounds, by shrubs and a hedge. While the arrangement provides for some long vistas, to give an idea of extent, the projection of masses in a measure divides the ground into front, rear, and side portions. Each part being managed in a separate style, with shrubs and trees of varied character, the entire plat

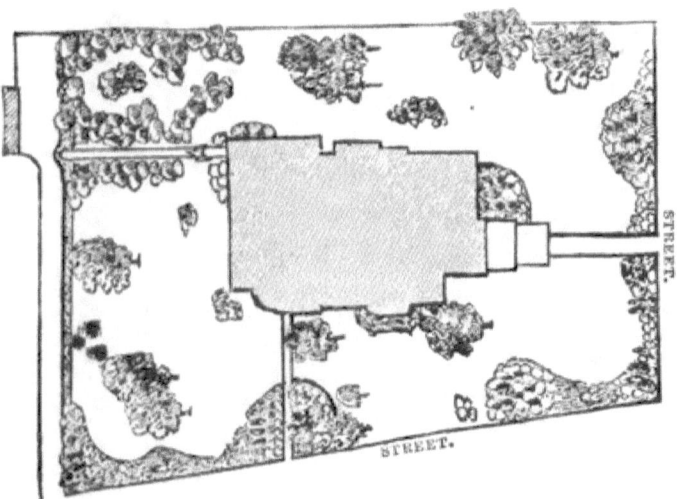

Fig. 100.—CORNER LOT, 110 BY 220 FEET, WITH STRAIGHT WALKS, PLANTED WITH A PROFUSION OF SHRUBS AND FLOWERS.

is made to yield a great degree of satisfaction. The lawn effects are ample; although the borders encroach upon these to some extent, there is much advantage gained in the relief and support that comes from trees and shrubs. Then in the long, wavy outlines of the grass-plat that meet the eye, being as long or longer than the boundary lines themselves, the idea is conveyed that the area is much larger than it really is, and larger than it would appear without the improvements.

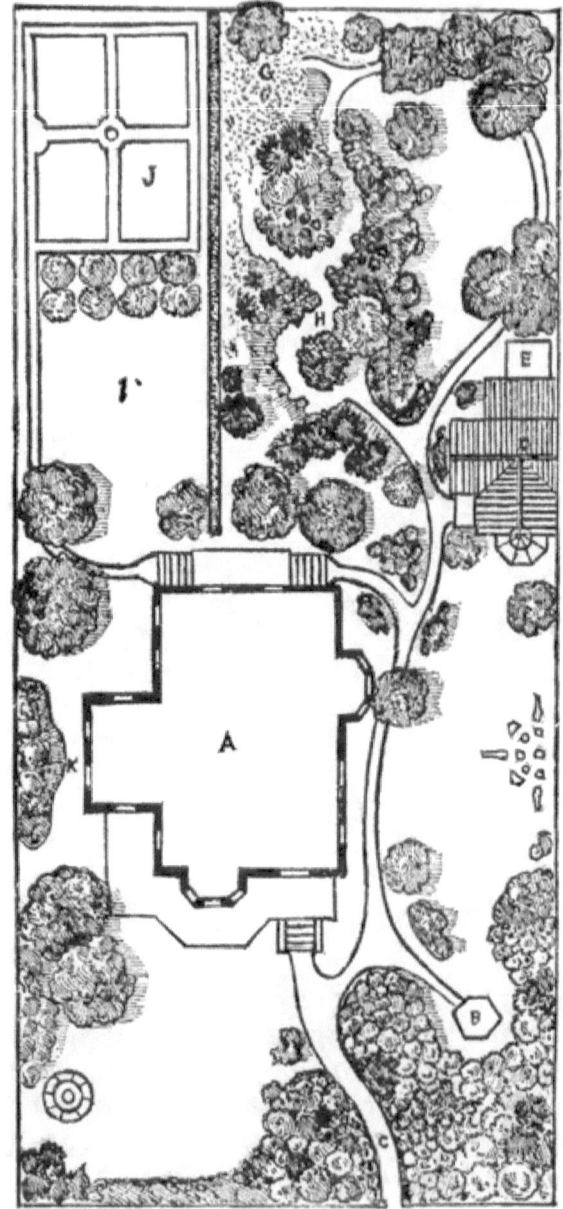

Fig. 101. — GROUNDS THREE-FOURTHS OF AN ACRE IN EXTENT. —

A, House; *B*, Front Arbor; *C*, Entrance Walk through Shrubbery; *D*, Conservatory; *E*, Shed; *F*, Rear Arbor covered with Climbers; *G*, Wild Garden; *H*, Rockery; *I*, Clothes-drying Ground; *J*, Fruits and Vegetables; *K*, Mixed Border.

Figure 101 represents a garden of about three-fourths of an acre, with the walks curving instead of straight, as seen in the last. As may be seen by the explanations, there are numerous features embodied in this plan.

The front arbor, *B*, might be surrounded with a display of flowers, and some of these could also be introduced all along the edges of most of the shrubbery masses. The entrance from the street might be edged with stones, which, especially if the ground of the shrubbery masses were raised to be mound-like, could be built up a foot or more to retain the raised earth, and thus creating an effect quite like that of a rockery. There are several fine open lawns adorned with flower-beds; there are shade trees throughout the grounds, and altogether just enough intricacy and scattered points of interest, to lead a visitor to its charms by giving him something new at every turn.

In figure 102 is shown a four-acre plat on a hillside, having a surface with a difference in elevation between the front and rear boundary lines of seventy-five feet—the rear being the highest. In these grounds rare opportunities were afforded for introducing a great variety of features, from the finished grass plats and Italian garden with its clipped trees, architectural embellishments and hedge, to a most picturesque wild garden, with thickets, bluffs, rill, waterfall, lakelet, winding wood paths, etc. A picturesque arbor on the hillside, not only adds a pleasing effect to the grounds, as seen from the front, but it affords a fine view of the lower parts of the garden and distant outside scenery, as do also the walks and seats of lookout plateau.

The plan on page 258, figure 103, is of a five and one-half acre garden. Here, in ground almost level throughout, there is sufficient area for introducing many attractive features, and yet preserving enough of openness for fine garden effects. A rill of water through the rear part,

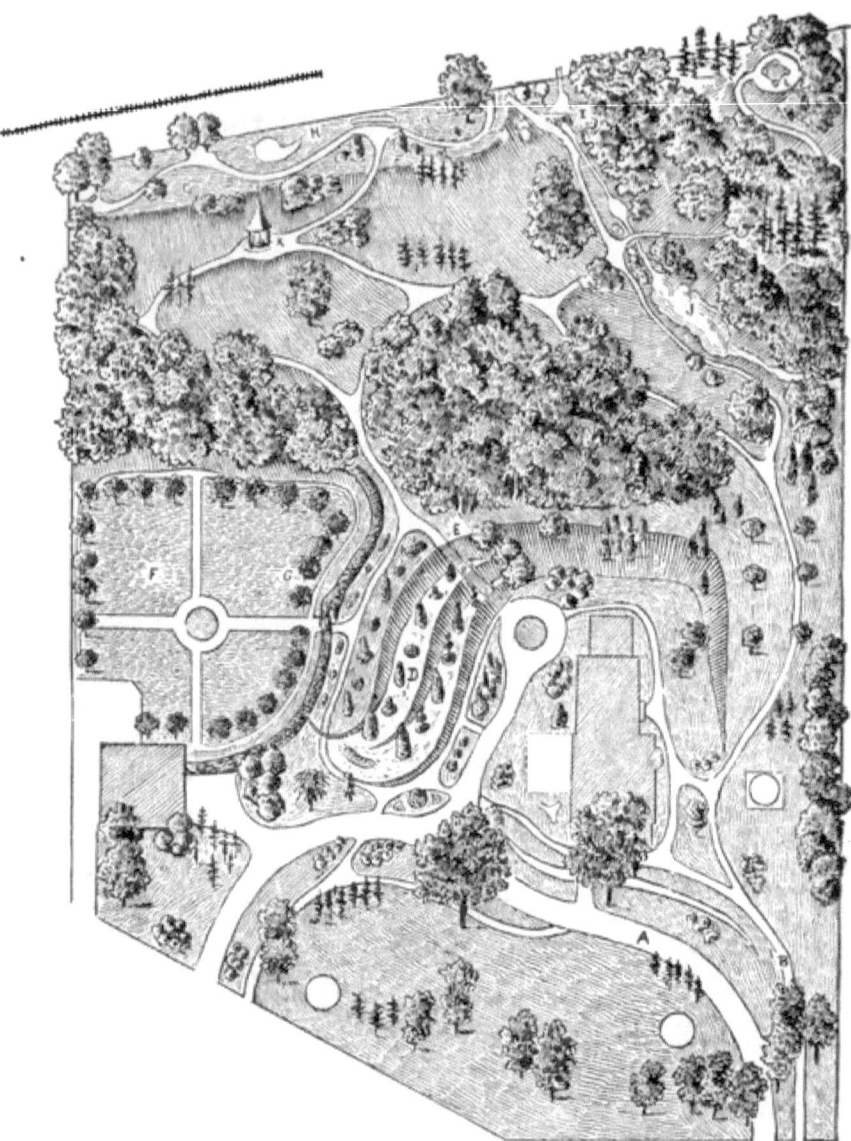

Fig. 102.—A FOUR ACRE FLAT ON A HILL-SIDE.

A, Carriage Drive; *B*, Front Walk; *D*, Italian Garden on Hillside; *E*, Stairs in Walk; *F*, Kitchen and Fruit Garden; *G*, Arbor Vitæ Hedge; *H*, Look-out Plateau, 75 feet above street level; *I*, Rill and Cascade; *J*, Lakelet; *K*, Summer-House; *L*, Seat on Elevated Point.

with considerable of an abrupt rise on each side, afforded opportunity for excavating a small lake. On the left-hand side beyond, but not far from the foot bridge, a picturesque rockery is formed, including a cave, through which extends a walk, that is broken by steps at the entrance, and with a seat in the middle. A sharp knoll is formed here on the edge of the water, partly by the help of the cave arch, and on this is located a shady rustic arbor, the top of which is seen from the street. This arbor is reached from the rear by a walk with steps. The knoll is faced on one side with rocks rising out of the water, and there are several large rocks jutting out of the water near the opposite shore. On the cave side these are arranged to allow the planting of shrubs, vines, and plants among them, thus forming a kind of rock-garden. While in some places of the rocky knoll, the stones over-hang the water as seen in the plan, further on towards the bridge, the rockwork runs back somewhat from the water's edge, affording walking room between. Opposite the arbor across the lake is a carriage stand. There is a small wooded isle, towards the other end of the lake, with a boat shelter near. At several places about the lake are opportunities for making wild-gardens. A hedge of spruce, and some clumps of shrubs and trees, cut off the vegetable and fruit garden, carriage house, and laborer's cottage from the garden, as shown in the plan.

One objection to the making of more drives in small grounds than are needed to reach the stable is, that they are apt to lack dignity through being too tortuous. While such is not the case in the present instance, still had it not been for the unusual attractiveness of the rear grounds—proving a great delight to visitors in carriages, the back drive through the grounds would not have been planned here.

Much could be said in favor of home plats and pleasure grounds, being managed on a joint plan for making them

Fig. 103.—A FIVE AND ONE-HALF ACRE GARDEN.

The location of some of the leading features are shown by the letters as follows:—*A*, House, with Conservatory attached; *B*, Drives; *C*, Walks; *D*, Grapery, located on Floral Lawn; *E*, Barn; *F*, Laborers' Cottage; *G*, Arbors; *H*, Lake, with Rockery and Wild Garden adjacent; *I*, Vegetables and Fruit.

more attractive, through working with the extent of area
that comes from throwing a number of them together
into one.   The common trouble with the average garden
is, that owing to limited area, and then the detraction
that comes from positive lines of boundaries, buildings,
and walks, it is not easy to produce free garden effects.
The larger the garden, the less difficulty we meet here,
therefore it will often be advisable to throw a number of
these together to be managed and enjoyed jointly, all
with a view to having finer effects, and more gratifying
results generally.

Figure 104 shows a row of town houses, fifty feet back
from the line of the street, with the ground at the front
treated on such a plan.   It is easily seen how much more
satisfactory such a garden may be, in almost every way,

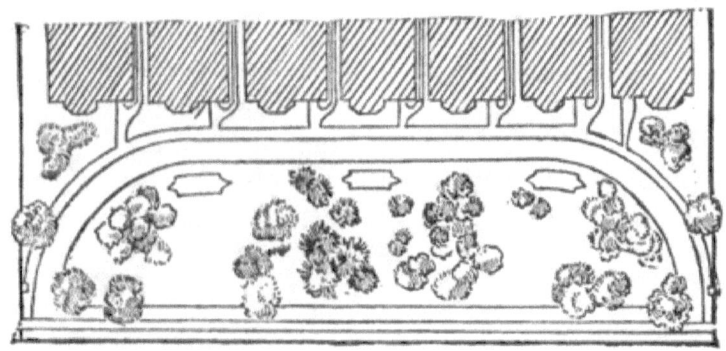

Fig. 104.—GARDEN FRONT TO A ROW OF HOUSES, USED AND KEPT UP
JOINTLY.

than several narrow ones instead, each arranged on a
plan of its own.   From any house of this row, the eye
may meet a beautiful garden scene, possessing breadth,
character, and a good variety of embellishments and
bringing pleasure and rest, such as no narrow twenty by
fifty-foot garden or any number of them could afford.

There comes a gain also, in the items of expense for

making and keeping, by such an arrangement. Let there be one garden to lay out, improve and keep up, and it could be done for one-half the money required for planting and keeping the same piece, if cut into seven gardens with seven plans, and calling for seven bargains for construction and keeping.

If real estate owners, who in so many cases put up rows of dwellings, would plan for having gardens of this kind, the increased attractions would at once allow of such an advance in rents, as could easily make up, and more too, for the land and the expense of making a really fine garden and caring for it. In such a case, the landlord might be the one to see the garden cared for. If owned by the people who occupy them, the management could devolve upon a trustee chosen by the owners, or they could themselves take yearly turns at keeping.

Figure 105 shows how three long lots of several acres each, side by side, may be thrown into one, and treated as a good sized joint garden, possessing many delightful features. All the parts are kept up and used jointly, excepting in the immediate vicinity of each house. There are three arbors, one near each house, which are designed for private use, as are also ample clothes-drying lawns. Each proprietor has a carriage house, two of them under one roof; each a share in a vegetable garden, shown in the upper right-hand corner.

This arrangement has much to recommend it in many respects. The grounds are immeasurably finer in garden effect than could be secured in working with divided areas. There is a grove of wood at the left; a fair lakelet with drive crossing it by a bridge, broad areas of lawn, and an extended carriage drive; not one of which features could be well carried out on a third portion of the whole, while by this plan such a general amplitude prevails, that all the families can have abundant room.

The conservatory is three in one, each family having a wing with a central bed for show plants, contributed by all, and is large enough and well designed for creat-

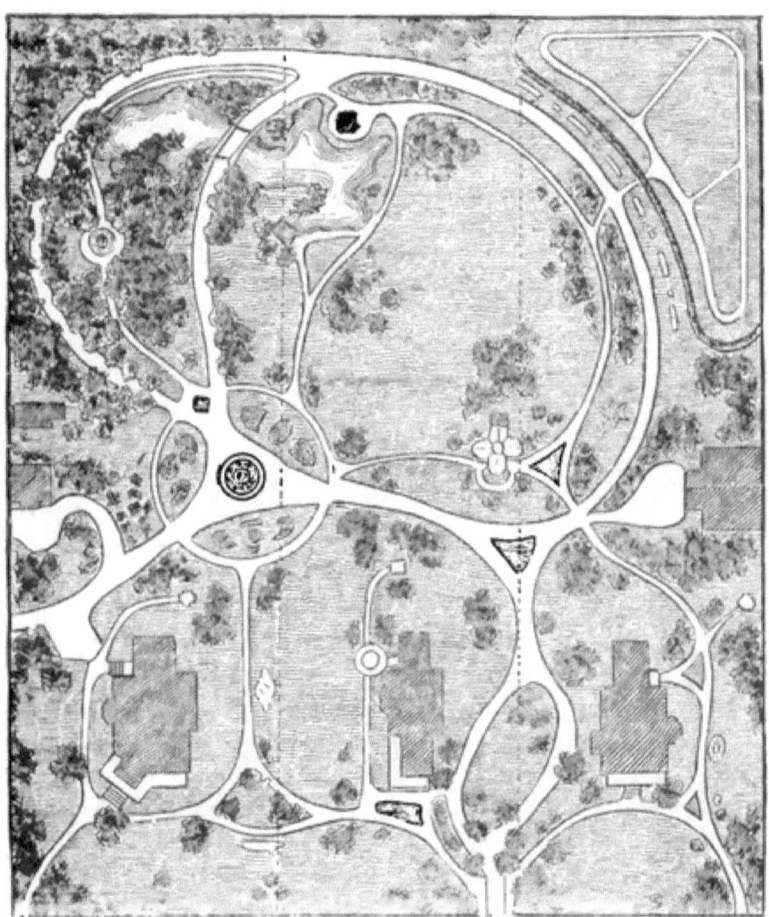

Fig. 105.—THREE TOWN RESIDENCES.

The rear grounds of which are thrown into a Park and Pleasure Ground, with Conservatory, Vegetable Garden, etc., used and supported conjointly. Three Houses, two Stables. Laborer's Cottage, Boat Houses, five Arbors, three of which are private, etc.

ing a fine effect as seen from all parts of the grounds. The floral circle in the left half of the grounds, is another beautiful feature, owing much of its effect to the largeness of the combined gardens.   It is readily reached by both walks and drives.

There are two carriage and four foot entrances, all of which lead conveniently to the houses and the rear pleasure gardens.

Of course, there is no limit to the variations allowable in carrying out this system.   Any number of houses and gardens, and of any size, might be embraced where suitably situated.   The idea of both a front and rear garden, as shown in figure 104, and the other in figure 105, might sometimes be combined, giving place for a close row of houses, or a number of double houses, or instead of having

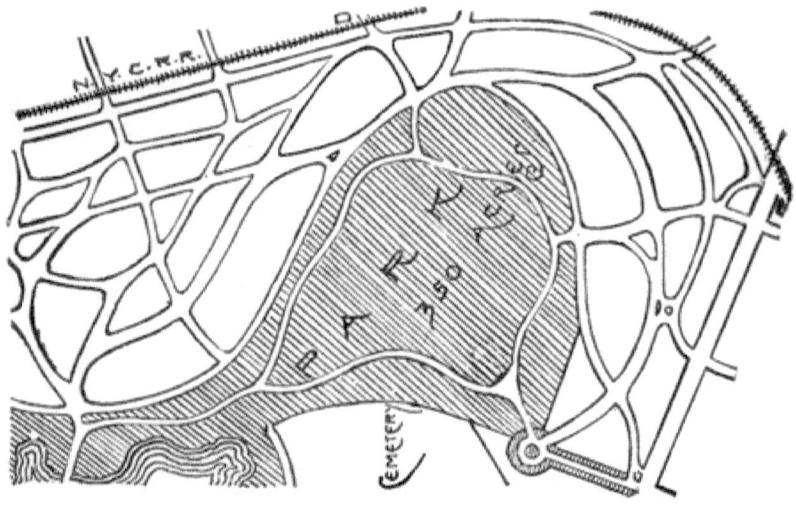

Fig. 106.—GROUNDS NEAR BUFFALO PARK.

the houses a uniform distance from the street, they might be scattered over the grounds, fronting on the gracefully curved drives.

A style of arranging town suburbs and summer resorts, has been developed in connection with some large public parks, both in America and England, which is worth noticing here.

The idea is well illustrated by the engraving, figure

106, which shows a section of Buffalo Park with adjacent lands called "Parkside," planned for laying out with curved drives and avenues, and irregularly shaped building lots, the former connecting with the park drives and circles at convenient distances.

This principle is applicable to suburbs independent of parks, and particularly to summer resort villages, such as are now springing up throughout the country, where-ever there are spots possessing natural attractions, out-lying large towns and cities. The success of these de-pends as much upon the joint action of property owners from year to year, as upon laying out the grounds origi-nally, to have graceful, winding highways, instead of the usual straight streets and sharp angles. In the plan illustrated, the sections formed average about twelve acres in extent, and these divide up into from three to twelve building lots each—large enough to admit of carrying out a joint system of laying out and keeping up each one with fine effect.

As wealth and a love for ornamental gardening increase in our land, there are more persons owning farms who enjoy improving them in matters beautiful, as well as useful. A good deal of landscape garden beauty may be combined with most farms, without impairing their value for raising crops or live stock. Figure 107 is a plan for laying out a small farm ornamentally. As shown there are six fields, besides orchards, groves, kitchen garden, and grass plats, adorned with trees, shrubs, flowers, etc. The driveways from the street lead gracefully to the main buildings, and throughout the farm. The grass plats in front of the house and the barn, as well as any others, may be kept closely clipped with the lawn mower, or else — especially the larger ones—they may be mown three or four times during the season for feeding to live stock. In such a plan the fields may be surrounded by hedges, or sometimes advantageously by wire fences. By

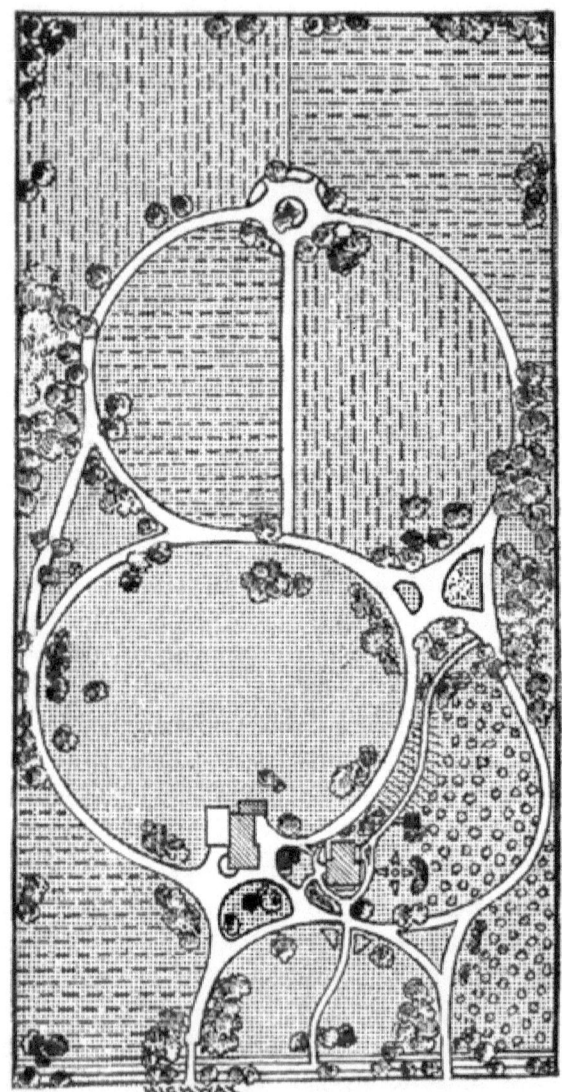

Fig. 107.—FARM PLANNED WITH PARK-LIKE DRIVES AND OTHER OR-
NAMENTAL FEATURES.

The House is located nearest to the street, a trifle to the right of the center, and
the Barn a little further back to the left.

running a wire fence around the plat, immediately back of the barn, and using it as a permanent pasture, it will present from the street and house the appearance of an extension of the ornamental grounds, because the grass being kept closely pastured, will look as well as if shorn with the lawn mower, while the fence may be so incon-spicuous as hardly to be seen a short distance off.

By running a lane from the pasture down through the center of the next section beyond, to the farm circle, lo-cated in the most distant point of the drive, live stock can easily be driven to any lot of the farm if desired.

In the plan, a walk leads from the house to the right, past a flower bed in the lawn, to the kitchen garden, thence near the drive, with shrubs and hardy flowers in places at the side, to the grove on the right. Here is a comfortable arbor to afford shelter, both from sun and rain. An arbor somewhat different in style from this one, occupies a grass plat in the center of the rear circle. Between the drive and fence of this circle, there are five spaces of grass that may have beds cut in them to be filled with shrubs and plants.

A farm of any size, or a fruit and vegetable garden, laid out on some such plan, may prove on this account in itself a great source of pleasure to the residents of the place, as well as to visitors.

CHAPTER XXV.

PORTICO, WINDOW, AND ROOF GARDENS.

Many persons live in houses that have no garden plats attached to them, but there is no need of their being altogether deprived of the pleasure of growing plants. Some of these houses have porticoes, all have windows, and every building has a roof, and these having access to

12

the needed air and light, may allow a great deal of gardening above terra firma.

Of such gardening, that done in outside window boxes and portico boxes is the most common, because the little gardens are easily prepared, are adapted to every place, and generally prove very successful. Figure 108, showing one of the former, will give an idea of the man-

Fig. 108.—WINDOW BOX WITH CLIMBERS.

ner in which these are made and arranged. For windows, a box is made, measuring for inside dimensions five inches and upwards deep, and the same in width, and of a length corresponding to the width of the window, the sill of which it is to set upon. Portico boxes may be the same as regards width and hight, but the

length is usually greater.   These are placed on the railing of the veranda, or on the floor at the front of the
railing, sometimes at the end of the veranda only, but
most frequently along the entire front.   When placed on
the rail, they are made in sections to fit between the
posts, but if on the floor at the front, they may be continuous.

I desire to impress the importance of ample size for
such boxes.   If made six inches high, and six, eight, or
even ten wide, the plants will be the better for it.   Beauty
here depends largely on their being well filled with good
sized, vigorous plants, and such require a fair bulk of
earth in which to grow.   Window boxes may be made
with a bottom outline shaped as in figure 109, and project beyond the window sill (indicated by the dotted

Fig. 109.—PLAN OF WINDOW BOX.

line), both in front and at the ends.   In this shape they
can be plenty large enough, and will look well.   The projecting weight may be in part sustained by a wire at each
end, running to a hook or strong screw at the top of the
window frame, and on these wires climbing plants may
be trained.

A pleasing arrangement of boxes for houses built with
the square, regular fronts, so common in towns, is to
have a box run the whole width of two or more windows,
and the space between, or along the entire front, resting
on the sill projections.   In a three story building—the
first floor being stores, and the others living apartments,
if a box is thus run the entire length at the second story
windows, and then for the third story a single box is
provided for each window, with none between, the effect
as seen from the street, is very fine.

The plants most suitable for such boxes, are those of drooping habit for along the edges, and climbers may be used if desired, for the sides of windows, or posts of the veranda, and then bright, free-flowering plants, such as Geraniums, Heliotropes, Cuphea, Fuchsias, and showy-leaved Dracænas, Begonias, Aspidistra, Coleus, Achyranthes, Dusty Miller, Caladiums, Cannas, etc. In fact, where space and sufficiency of soil admit, there need be no particular limit in the selection.

The Hanging Basket is a well known ornament, particularly suitable for suspending from the roof of the portico, or from a projecting hook in front, or at the side of a window. The most common material of which these are made is wire, the basket to be lined with moss, and rustic earthenware or fancy crockery ware. Here it should be observed that quite a number of plants are brought closely together, and the best results will not follow with a receptacle for earth too small to properly hold them. Whatever their kind, those measuring ten inches and upwards across, unless very deep, are best. If less than ten inches, they may look well when started, but with hot weather, and increased growth, they will not keep thus, but die out quickly. The plants named for window boxes, are also suitable for hanging baskets.

PLANT VASES, BOXES, AND LARGE PAINTED FLOWER POTS.

These are often used for decorating railings, posts, roofs, and the lawn. They do not differ materially as to their planting, from the hanging baskets and window boxes. In all attempts at growing plants in these receptacles, above all else the soil should be in fertile condition, for be it remembered, that much growth and beauty are expected from a small bulk of earth, consequently it should be the best attainable. Any good soil of loamy texture, well enriched with fine, old manure, will answer.

ROOF GARDENS.

A garden upon the roof affords a means of plant-growing, either in the open air or in a green-house, that we hope to see made much of in the near future. We talk about not having gardens in the cities, because there is no room. Is there less superficial area exposed directly to the light of the heavens after building than before ? The area is the same, but only so much nearer the light and pure air. In most cases, where there are flat roofs, and there could readily be more of them, there would be found ample opportunity for cultivating a fine collection of hardy and tender plants, even in the hearts of cities.

One of the finest public gardens in Europe is the Waverly Garden of Edinburgh, being really a roof garden over a market building. It embraces an area of about seventy-five by four hundred feet, all of which, except where there are some sky-lights, is devoted to flowers, grass, vases, walks, and seats. There are sixteen borders, averaging some seventy-five by four feet, besides a number of smaller square beds, and altogether using thousands of fine plants. There is also a large bed of grass kept neatly mown.

The beds and borders contain about a foot in depth of soil, and this is retained by a neat stone coping throughout. The edge of the roof, and the sky-lights, are guarded by ornamental railings, with posts, and these support many well filled vases of plants, fully one hundred in all. Taken altogether, this roof garden, with no advantages beyond those common to thousands of roofs throughout our cities, is a most charming place, affording delight to all who visit it.

The engraving (fig. 110), with the quoted matter which follows, appeared in the " American Agriculturist " some time ago from the pen of Samuel B. Parsons, Esq., of Flushing, N. Y. They bear so forcibly upon this subject, that I present them here:

"It is within the means of every man who builds a house to rent for eight hundred dollars per year, to have a garden on the roof, which, during the summer, can be filled with the most luscious fruits, and in the winter with plants, the beauty of which will afford a charm far beyond the trifling cost of maintenance.

"A glass roof costs but little more than a slate or tin one. Let the roof, therefore, be covered with glass, and let the garret floor be covered with concrete, sloping

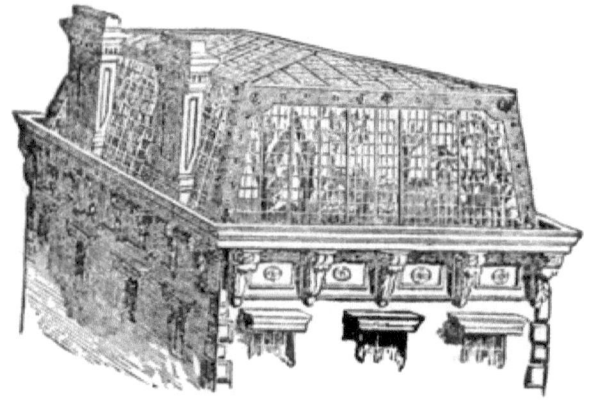

Fig. 110.—A ROOF CONSERVATORY.

gently from the center to the sides, around which a slight depression in the floor can carry the moisture or drip into the leaders, which pass from the roof of every house to the ground, and with slight expense a perfect green-house may be had. Now for heating. Every one knows that the upper rooms of his house are so warm from the ascending heat of his furnace, that registers are scarcely needed. Let the doors be kept open, and the waste heat of the house will keep the green-house at the highest desirable temperature without any extra trouble or expenditure.

"Its care would be a pleasant recreation for any of the

family.   A lady fresh from such occupations, would lend
new charms to the evening hours, and the memory of
her children in the upper air, would always have power
to bring a sparkle to her eye, or a glad expression to her
lip.   There are numerous florists in every city who would
be glad to keep such a place in perfect order for a very
moderate compensation.

"If a little extra strength is given to the beams which
sustain the upper floor, suf-
ficient earth could be placed
there to lay out the whole
space as a perfect garden,
with winding walks, de-
lightful carpets of green,
and roses, camellias, etc.,
planted in the soil.

"If the capabilities of
this plan, and its economy
were thoroughly understood
by architects and proprie-
tors, the time would soon
come, when a roof garden
would be considered just as
essential an appendage to
a house as a bath-room."

AN ATTACHED CONSER-VATORY.

Figure 111 represents a
small conservatory, built
over a bay window, and
reached from the second
floor. Where it would be undesirable to have a conser-

Fig. 111.—CONSERVATORY OVER
BAY-WINDOW.

vatory or garden on the top of the house, such a one from
being smaller, as well as more convenient, might be prefer-

red, and it would be practicable to combine it with almost
any house in one shape or another. The heating could
be done by extending the warming system from the house
into the plant apartment. With the beautiful, irregular
styles of houses that are now so much in demand, it
would be no trouble to plan excellent small conservatories
to be parts of them, not only serving to make the home
more interesting to the inmates, but adding additional
grace and brightness to the building as seen from the
street. If there were gardens adjacent to the house
needing bedding plants in the spring, some of these for
the summer flower beds and vases could be propagated
towards each spring, in addition to growing flowers
throughout the year, and the space thus turned to a
profitable, as well as a pleasure yielding account.

CHAPTER XXVI.

CHURCH, SCHOOL, ASYLUM, HOTEL, AND RAILROAD GARDENS.

It is gratifying to see the disposition manifested in
some places to improve with garden embellishments the
surroundings of schools and other institutions, such as
are named in the heading. There is room for good work,
for I can think of nothing that can go farther towards
educating the people to appreciate and desire fine gardens, than to establish them in places where they are
sure to be seen by many observers.

It is painful to admit that perhaps not one in ten country school houses is shaded by a single tree, or shows any
other garden embellishment whatever. In fact, a school-
house may usually be recognized by its bleak appearance,
and the entire absence of trees, shrubs, climbers, and

flowers. There is no excuse for this, because the stock necessary to improve the grounds, need not cost much, if bought, while in most cases no outlay would be required, as native plants and trees could be had for the digging. School trustees should see to it, that the work is done in every district, not by planting only, but also by properly protecting the trees, etc.

That there is little danger that trees will be damaged in school yards if somewhat protected, and with proper rules respecting their safety, is shown by the many cases of city school yards that abound in shade trees. Here, in fact, may sometimes be found the other extreme, and almost as objectionable as the one alluded to above—namely, too many trees.

In carrying out such improvements, the best way is to plant the trees in clusters, so that plenty of air and sunlight, as well as shade, may be present.

Figure 112 shows a school yard designed to present a great deal of natural beauty and variety, as well as to afford comfort to the children. It is intended that the general surface be finished with gravel, or other hard material, instead of grass. In the figure A, A, represent shrubbery and flower borders about eight feet wide, well guarded against intrusion from the children, by a stone or brick coping one foot high, with or without an additional light iron guard on the top. B is an ornamental raised bed or terrace, about a foot high at the lowest part, with the soil retained by a coping similar to that around A, A. From this terrace, which is grass-covered, a second one, smaller in diameter, rises above the surface about a foot, and is also retained by a coping of stone or brick. This one is surmounted by low-growing, bright flowers. C, C are grass-covered slopes of about two and a half feet rise, and surmounted by low-growing, attractive shrubs. By the novel means of such slopes, some grass for beauty may be had in perfect order, without danger

of its being trampled out of existence. *D* is a strip of
grass, on which is planted a heavy line of shrubbery, to
form a dividing line. There are also four shrubbery and
flower-borders against the school-house in the plan as
shown, also protected by copings. Strong-growing shade
trees are scattered about, and climbers adorn the buildings,
with some vigorous-growing shrubs or evergreens set to

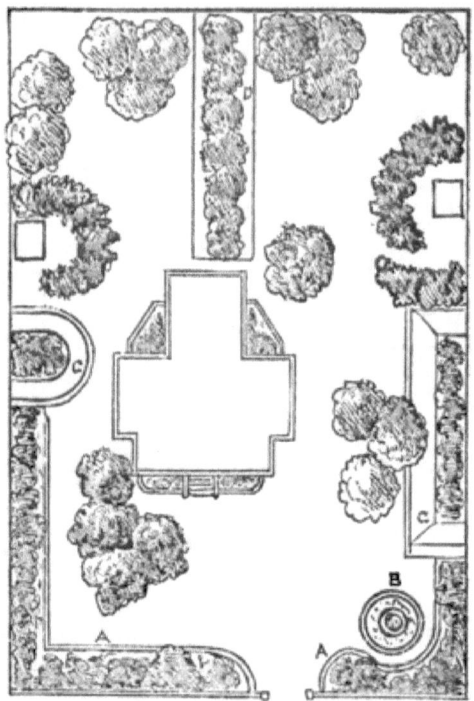

Fig. 112.—SCHOOL YARD IMPROVED WITH TREES, ETC.

hide the outhouses. A school yard like this, with little
attention, proves very attractive, and when it is tried it
is surprising how soon the children learn to respect and
love the adornments. With a good selection of trees,
shrubs, and flowers, there may be an abundance of bloom
all through the warm season, besides grass and shade.
Such arrangements in the school yard might also be of

great service in furnishing materials for the study of botany.

In the larger grounds, common about high schools and colleges, usually a style of gardening more natural in its features may be employed, owing to the more favorable circumstances. Sometimes very fine displays of ornamental gardening, as well as more useful botanical gardens are established, as at Harvard and elsewhere. Such improvements find appreciation from the patrons of the schools, and may readily be made to add much to their completeness as educational institutions.

TREATMENT OF CHURCH YARDS.

In adorning church yards, the aim should be towards introducing quiet and graceful beauty, consequently such trees as the Camperdown Weeping Elm, Kilmarnock Willow, Yellow Wood, Ginkgo, and the evergreens and flowering shrubs are to be preferred. There should be a great deal of clear lawn in proportion to other embellishments. Whatever trees are introduced should not be crowded, but receive a free setting well supported by grass, while the shubbery and evergreens may be arranged in well defined clumps. The climbers should be freely used for mantling the outside walls in places, and especially in those numerous cases where there are no garden surroundings.

GARDENS FOR HOSPITALS AND ASYLUMS.

Some of the most successful ornamental gardens in the country are those associated with hospitals, insane and other asylums. It is found that money may be as profitably spent in providing fine lawns, trees, shrubs, flowers, green-houses, etc., for aiding in the relief of unfortunates, as in any other direction for rendering these institutions as useful as possible.

Mr. Peter Henderson, in writing to the "American Agriculturist" of the fine gardens connected with the State hospitals for the insane, Mendota, Wis., says : " But the most important feature of the garden operations at this asylum is the employment of the patients as workmen. An average of fifteen are employed in the summer months during the growing season, who work on an average six hours each day, and Mr. Schatzka, who is evidently a careful and intelligent observer, assures me that the effect on the health of the patients is marked. The result is that a greater number of the garden hands have been discharged as cured in proportion to numbers than of others. Mr. Schatzka manages, by the aid of hot-beds, to fill numerous beds that are laid out in the lawn in front of the hospital with flowering plants. These he quaintly terms an 'eye pasture' for the patients. These beds give enough flowers to form bouquets for the sick wards during the summer months, and thus are a source of great pleasure to scores of the unfortunates within. Believing in the soothing effects of flowers on some species of insanity, a gentleman recently left a fund of ten thousand dollars for erecting a winter garden or conservatory, to be used as a promenade ground for the patients at an insane asylum in Ohio.

" Such a garden might be attached with profit to various other kinds of public institutions, for in nearly all cases the labor could be mainly done by the inmates, not only without cost, but to their physical, mental, and moral advantage. The grounds surrounding the various public buildings on Blackwell's Island, New York, and at Flatbush, Long Island, are, and have been so for many years, models of excellent cultivation, and reflect credit on the management ; but there are many others in the suburbs, and hundreds in all sections of the country, where no attempt whatever has been made, and in others it is so feeble that it has amounted to nothing.

There is no excuse for this. There are always men fitted to take charge of such work to be had for moderate salaries, who, with the free labor of the inmates of the institutions, many of whom would like the work, could produce results that would add vastly to the comfort and health of the inmates, to say nothing of the saving to the county or State."

Institutions of this character usually embrace a considerable extent of farm lands. In some cases these may, with good effect, be laid out something as shown in figure 107, which, while allowing the land to be utilized for garden and farm purposes may be laid out with reference to landscape garden effects. I recently made plans for laying out the grounds of a County Poor and Insane Asylum, the large buildings of which stand elevated some six hundred feet from the highway. The land between the buildings and the street was the best on the farm for gardening purposes, and had for many years been devoted to vegetable growing. In the new plan, while drives and walks were provided for through the front portion, these were so arranged as to leave several large areas in this front part for garden crops. Between the drives and these plats, liberal breadths about thirty-five feet wide are to be in grass, and kept nicely mowed as well as embellished with trees, shrubs, etc. On the whole it is planned for having about as much of the front devoted to vegetables as to ornamental gardening, and the former, so long as the garden is well kept up, detracts very little from the ornamental effect of the place, while practical minded tax-payers enjoy the combination and say it looks better thus.

In the great hotel building enterprises of the day, there is often a good opportunity to devote a part of the vast outlay to rendering them attractive by introducing some garden features. Where it is possible to embrace a small garden area on the ground, this would be the best

form of ornament.   Otherwise provision could be made
for some roof and veranda gardens.   What can go farther
towards making a hotel attractive to the guests, than to
have the dining-room and other windows opening upon
a garden filled with neatly kept grass, bright flowers,
and beautiful shrubs, together with walks, and perhaps
vine-covered seats or arbors.   The refreshing beauty and
comfort of such a spot would be appreciated by the trav-
elling public, and no doubt in many instances would
serve to make a hotel a favorite over rivals not having
these attractions.

The enterprise manifested by some of the great railroads in the way of improved stations and station gardens, may be considered as a beginning in the right direction in what may be called " Railroad Gardening,"
and an example that must sooner or later be followed
by all our railroad companies.   The manner of keeping
up lands along railroad lines and about stations in England, and elsewhere in Europe, is in marked contrast
with this country.   There nearly all railroad lands at
the side of the tracks are made even, and whether level
or sloping are well finished, put into grass and mown
like a park.   Masses and lines of trees are introduced in
some places.   What abundant chances for improvement
in this direction are afforded by the American railroads
generally.   One may travel thousands of miles in the
United States and see little besides weeds, thistles, and
brambles scattered over a rough surface, and through
unshapely ditches, with boulders and stumps along the
tracks.   It would cost something to bring the lands into
proper shape for grass, but in the long run, improvements
of this kind would pay, aside from the increased attractiveness of the road to travellers, for it would require
less expense to keep the surface mowed occasionally (the
grass yielded ought to pay for this) than is now required
in the occasional hacking away of weeds and brush, be-

sides there would be less danger from fire should the
sparks fall on the grass than might result from their
dropping in the dry rubbish so common by the sides of
the track.

CHAPTER XXVII.

PUBLIC PARKS AND PLEASURE GROUNDS.

The subject of public parks and pleasure grounds for
recreation, is one that is destined to grow in interest in
this country. The making of these is now only in its infancy, yet in view of their healthfulness and their importance to the public, there is little doubt that they will receive increased attention. The limits of the present work
do not allow much space to be devoted to these, yet an
attempt will be made to give such hints and suggestions
as may be useful to those who consider the subject.

BOTH PRESENT AND FUTURE WANTS TO BE CONSIDERED.

In all cases where public gardens are contemplated,
the scheme should be comprehensively conceived and ex-
cuted. Even in initiatory discussions of the subject, it
would be unwise to have in view merely the present
needs, but a broad view of the probable future growth
and wants of a town should enter into the calculations.
The important fact that results which follow on such
improvements reach far into the future must not be
lost sight of. It is safe to assume that most of the public parks and gardens, laid out and planted now, will
figure as important town gardens when our population
will, in most places, have increased many fold. How
quickly that time may arrive, who can tell ? Sixty years
ago our entire population was about nine millions, with

but nine cities in the Union of more the ten thousand inhabitants. Now we number above fifty million of people, and we have two hundred and fifty towns of more than ten thousand inhabitants. The child who lives sixty years from now may then be one of a population of one hundred and fifty millions or upwards, in the whole country, and will witness a proportionate increase in the average towns as great or greater. Yet sixty years is a comparatively short period in the life of an ornamental garden. In Europe there are many gardens that are more than four times as old. Some of the woody resorts in Rome have been woody resorts from the time of the Cæsars. Oaks, Chestnuts, and other trees that enter into gardens and parks as conspicuous embellishments are known to have lived from five hundred to two thousand years, and many of these are only in full prime, after they have been planted for a generation or longer. All these points suggest that the work of public garden making should be fixed on the broad basis of adaptability to the wants of ages—so far as these may be conjectured—rather than solely to immediate needs. The beauty of hundreds of American cities, of the next and future generations, will depend in a large measure on the manner in which the present generation shall meet the trust of initiating town embellishments. The subject is one that ought to be handled as wisely as its importance deserves, so that in time, the average of our towns may be. what they are not yet, the most beautiful on the face of the globe, so far as public gardening may serve to make them so.

AN IDEAL SYSTEM OF PUBLIC TOWN GARDENING.

What may be considered an ideal system of public town gardens? Briefly it is one that for the least outlay secures the greatest benefits in the way of wholesome rec-

reation, comfort, beauty, and healthfulness, to the greatest
number for the longest time. There should be such a
distribution of garden effects as to ensure accessibility
from all parts of the town, those inhabited by the poor
as well as the rich, and should contribute in the best
possible way to the attractiveness of the whole place.
Convenience and beauty should be considered as important in helping to build up a town as trade and manufac-
tures are. So much of attractiveness should be aimed at
by means of gardens, that few would prefer to live permanently out of the town that gives them their business.
And then only that system, which will provide for future
growth, ought to be acceptable with our many growing
towns.

"BEAUTIFUL PARIS" AS A MODEL.

Among all the cities of the globe, Paris, France, perhaps, comes nearest to possessing such an ideal as has
been outlined. What has given to her the proud position
of being the most beautiful city in the world, has been,
as much as anything, the admirable arrangement of her
streets, gardens, and boulevards, and the effective location
of public structures throughout the city in relation to
these. And this city, beautiful, convenient, healthful, and
economically governed, should prove an interesting one
for our people to look to as an example in the present
age of city making for lessons in rendering our own cities
similarly attractive.

In figure 113 is shown a plan of the boulevard and
public garden system of Paris (inside the walls—more
than one thousand ordinary streets being omitted), which
gives an idea of the manner in which these open up
all parts of a vast city of two million of people, bringing
air, sunshine, grass, and trees—the latter in numbers
reaching into hundreds of thousands—so as to leave no
part of the town far from some of them. Go where one

will in this metropolis, and the lengths of but a few
blocks can be passed over without coming upon a delightful, airy avenue, usually from one hundred to two hundred feet wide, partly shaded with from two to six rows
of trees, with inviting settees at close intervals. Small
parks, varying from three to forty acres each, are well distributed, and mostly excellent models for town gardens.

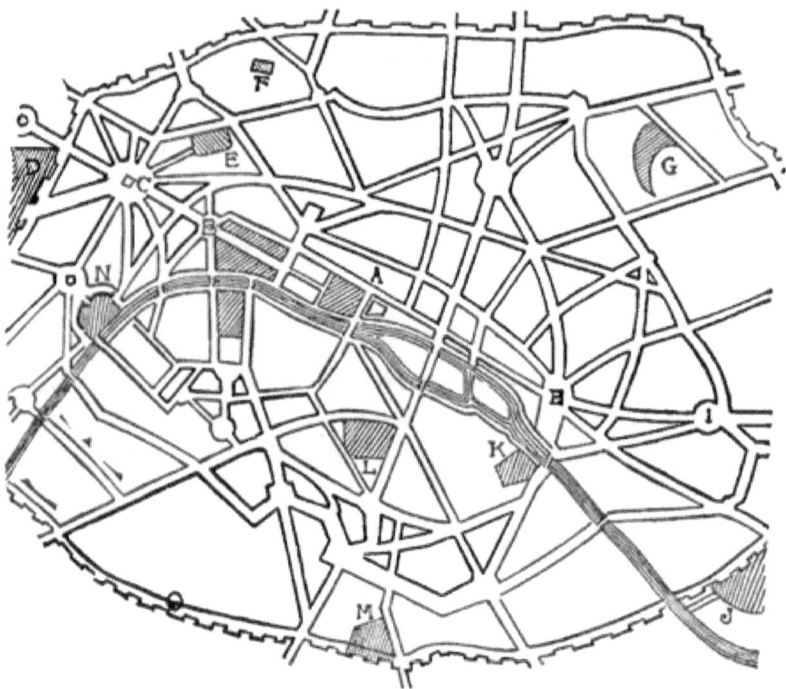

Fig. 113.—BOULEVARDS AND PUBLIC GARDENS OF PARIS.

A, the Louvre and Gardens of the Tuileries; *B*, Champs Elysées; *C*, Arc of
Triomphe; *D*, The Bois (Park) de Boulogne; *E*, Parc Monceau; *F*, Square des
Batignolles; *G*, Parc des Butts Chaumont; *H*, Place de la Bastile; *I*, Place de
la Nation; *J*, Bois (Park) de Vincennes; *K*, Garden of Plants; *L*, Luxem-
bourg Garden; *M*, Parc Montsouris; *N*, Froendero Garden; *O*, Wall skirted
by a Boulevard.

As may be seen, the general arrangement of boulevards
was made with a view to convenience, as well as beauty.
The Louvre at *A* being the central point, in general their
courses are in diverging lines from this part—opening

direct communications between the center and extremities. Then the cross boulevards are of a generally circular arrangement, an outer one running along the wall, around the entire city, and thus every part within the wall is in direct communication with every other part.

The plan of our national capital, a city which is gaining a wide reputation for town beauty, in many respects resembles that of Paris, and singularly enough the plan originated with a Frenchman, Major L'Enfant, of the French army, who assisted in Revolutionary times. General Washington approved of his plan and it was adopted, the wisdom of which course has since been fully confirmed, notwithstanding that for many years the plan of wide avenues, circles and squares was unappreciated. Because the City of Washington, thus in infancy, secured a plan of arrangement adapted to future growth, and then in time grew to fit it, she is destined to surpass many other cities in general attractiveness, because others, in time past, were never led into similar steps. In such facts as these may be found lessons well to be heeded by aspiring American towns at the present time.

PARIS, PAST, PRESENT, AND FUTURE.

So far as details are concerned, no doubt the plan of Paris would be susceptible of many improvements. It must be remembered, however, that this city, unlike our own cities, is one of great age, and that no farther back than the time of Napoleon III had but few attractions in the way of town gardens. The present admirable system of boulevards was secured only by piercing broad and clear through the solidly built and meanest parts of the old city, bringing in air, light, and trees, and working general improvement.

"It is not many years," says M. Robert Mitchell, of Paris, in speaking of these improvements, "since the boundaries of Paris inclosed an old city that was a disgrace to our civilization ; streets or rather fissures, without ventilation, and unhealthy districts where an entire population of poor people were languishing and dying. Now, however, thanks to the useful and important works that have lately been carried out, the sun shines everywhere, streets have been enlarged, and every one has sufficient air to breathe.

"Before the establishment of the Paris squares, the existence of a great number of children was passed in confined and unwholesome districts. The fresh air for them was only the threshold of a vitiated atmosphere. They were obliged to walk far before they could find a patch of verdure, or a bit of country. The children went out but little, it was thought useless to dress them or make them clean. How many times have we not noticed with painful emotions these little, ragged, pale creatures who never apparently thought of the filth in which they were obliged to live.

"Now, thank God, this dark picture has become bright, within a couple of steps of even the poor man's house, there are trees, flowers, and gravel walks where the children can run about, and seats where their parents may sit together and talk."

Great as has been the work of cutting the Paris boulevards, the making of scores, perhaps hundreds of miles of others is yet contemplated. Possessed of such a spirit of improvement, the present beauty of this famous capital, by the help of the gardening and other arts, is easily accounted for. But Paris will go on increasing in attractiveness, and must continue for time indefinite to stand as a marked example of what may be done to make beautiful and healthful cities, even under circumstances that would appear on their face most adverse, and far more so than anything known in America.

There is another aspect of the matter that ought to

interest us. Strange as it may appear, it is a fact that these improvements in Paris, have not only been made without cost to the town, but even with a balance on the right side, the vastly increased value of the splendid new sites for business purposes in the improved parts, having thus far, more than repaid all the cost of the work.

THE LESSON FOR AMERICAN ENTERPRISE.

Why, with our wealth, intelligence, and foresight, we should not in hundreds of instances, acquire the Parisian spirit of town improvement is hard to see. If the means at command to do with, should measure attainable results, it would not always be said that Paris is the most beautiful city on the face of the globe. Her example is now being followed in other French cities, such as Lyons and Rouen, and also elsewhere in Europe, but where can we expect so much in this direction as in our own land, preëminently favored in innumerable respects ?

With the majority of our towns, if a comprehensive, well devised plan, admitting of extension to any required degree would be adopted early, taking an example from Washington City in this respect, gains approximating in character to those acquired by Paris might soon be reached with a small corresponding outlay. True, the Paris boulevards, as stated, were made without direct pecuniary loss on account of the buildings that were destroyed, but where any town can, by judicious action, achieve equal results without making such a sacrifice of property, the gain must be greater yet.

It is on precisely these grounds that growing American towns should meet the case. Much of the land needed for complete systems of boulevards, squares, and parks, could, in many towns, be secured at a low cost now, to be laid out and improved in final details as the place grows, so that in time advantages, proportionally equal if not superior to those of Paris would result. There are few places that could not undertake such improvements, in some effective degree, and carry them out successfully, without any one greatly feeling the burden. To take a practical view of the matter, it may be seen that a town of one, ten, or a hundred thousand people, paying a special tax of but one dollar, for instance, per capita on an average, for initiating the work, and then afterwards say twenty to fifty cents annually for improving and keeping, would raise a sum of money, that with the help of good plans and prudent management, would accomplish results that would soon be priceless, and of which all could reap the benefit. It will be no credit to American civilization if the opportunities of hundreds of towns now needing these improvements are allowed to pass unimproved, in this latter third of the ninteenth century, with all our wealth and established prosperity, and with such examples as we have in Paris and other cities before us—equivalent lessons of which Paris herself in her pioneer efforts had not the benefit.

The radiating and cross principle of town boulevards, such as the French capital decided upon, should in some form and degree be considered most desirable for adoption by our growing cities. With some main avenues radiating from the center outwards, the system is adapted to a growth of any extent, allowing all parts to be readily reached from all others at any stage of growth. Besides the merit of convenience, a town which thus possesses the degree of irregularity that comes from such a system is beautiful in general appearance, for in cities as in architecture, the prevalence of too much regularity in the plan and general lines, is not conducive to the finest effects. Where it might be found necessary for carrying out such a system, to open highways through any old thickly settled parts, it could often be done as advantageously as similar work in Paris has been done.

THE LARGE PARK SYSTEM.

If there is one lesson more valuable than any other to be learned from the park system of Paris—and confirmed by the experience of other cities also—it is that cities should depend upon boulevards, squares, circles. and moderate-sized parks for town gardens, rather than exclusively upon large, and, as they often prove to be, enormously expensive parks.   The inborn American love for doing great things, may easily lead to the error of laying out large parks, when smaller ones would better serve the purpose.   In many cases a small park of five, ten, or forty acres, well arranged and cared for, is capable of more fully serving every true want which calls for a town garden, than a large one of hundreds of acres.

The desire for large parks for large cities need not be an unworthy one, but discrimination should be made between such as are largely made up of artificial decorative garden work, and very costly in construction and maintenance, and those of such a nature that a large degree of a natural kind of park attractions and benefits are secured for a comparatively small outlay.

In the vicinity of almost every town there are sites not far distant, possessing natural beauty in landscape, wood, and water, well suited for a park, and which may be bought at a moderate cost.   One or more new tracts of such land, of almost any extent, may be secured and converted into a park or system of parks, on some simple, well considered plan, having in view the presenting of nature in her most attractive moods.   Such a park, if so managed as to leave it mainly in a wild state, both now and in the future, may be made most delightful as a ground for public recreation, either alone, or as a part of a system embracing some more highly improved gardens in the town.   The wet places must be drained, some graceful driveways with a natural appear-

ance constructed, making them either of substantial material or depending in a measure on earth roads for summer
driving, as is done in the Richmond Park in the outskirts
of London. Trees, shrubs, and plants, for desirable new
groves, masses, and wilds, may be planted, shelters erected, and other improvements introduced. Then under certain mild regulations, allowing and providing for forest rov-
ing, boating, carriage driving, horse-back riding over meadow and hill, and other privileges of great freedom, such a
semi-natural park might be rendered immeasurably valuable as public recreation grounds. By introducing herds
of cattle, sheep, or deer, restrained by hurdles to keep
down the grass of meadows, a desirable attraction would
be gained, and at the same time the expense of mowing
such portions of the park be obviated.

A park or parks of such character, not so far off but
that they might be reached by carriages, street cars, or
the railroad, and then several small, well kept parks and
boulevards, in and near the town, to provide garden
beauty, fresh air, and comfort, near the center of population, to benefit every body every day, it is believed may
together afford the elements of a complete public garden
system, more fully for a certain expenditure than in any
other way.

GARDEN BOULEVARDS.

The idea of the Paris boulevards one hundred to two
hundred feet wide, has been for sometime adopted on a
small scale by a number of our cities. A common
width of these is one hundred and seventy-five feet,
and arranged with a wide center space, supporting
four rows of trees, or irregular arrangements of trees,
shrubs, and plants, with walks, settees, fountains, etc.,
and on each side a driveway and a side walk, next to the
private property. Narrower boulevards are planted with
two rows of trees in the middle, and a row at each side,

while still wider ones sometimes have a middle and two
side driveways, with trees on the plats between. Such
boulevards, or park-ways as they are also called, deserve to
be far more widely introduced, as means of augmenting
town beauty, and creating air spaces, where pure breezes
may have some vantage ground in cities.

But there is an enlarged form of boulevard that is entitled to consideration in American town gardening, where-
ever something more stately and complete is desired.   I
refer to the Grand Garden Boulevard, about four hundred feet wide, and of which in Paris there are several
illustrations.   One of these might even be introduced as
a substitute for a city park ; possessing all of its advantages, and a number in addition, with but few of its
disadvantages.

In such a grand boulevard, three hundred and fifty feet
or more wide, a breadth and length of base is secured,
that affords a chance for various garden effects impossible in a narrower area.   Long, ample, and, if desired,
winding drives, approximating closely to those of a large
park, are attainable, while the liberal width allows of a
free arrangement of walks, bridle paths, groups of trees,
shrubs, and flowers, and open areas of lawn. Even lakelets, rockwork, arbors, etc., in varied extent, may be introduced with little loss of fine effects, as compared with
large parks.

Figure 114 illustrates a garden boulevard, four hundred
and thirty feet wide, with great and small circles, and
narrow boulevards and streets, that open into it of two
hundred, one hundred and fifty, and one hundred feet in
width.   The plan shows two styles of laying out : the
lower part in the park, and the upper in the avenue style.
But in both, the natural style of arrangement mostly
prevails.   In addition to the main garden drives, there
are walk-bordered roadways for traffic along each side,
and into which private walks and drives open.

13

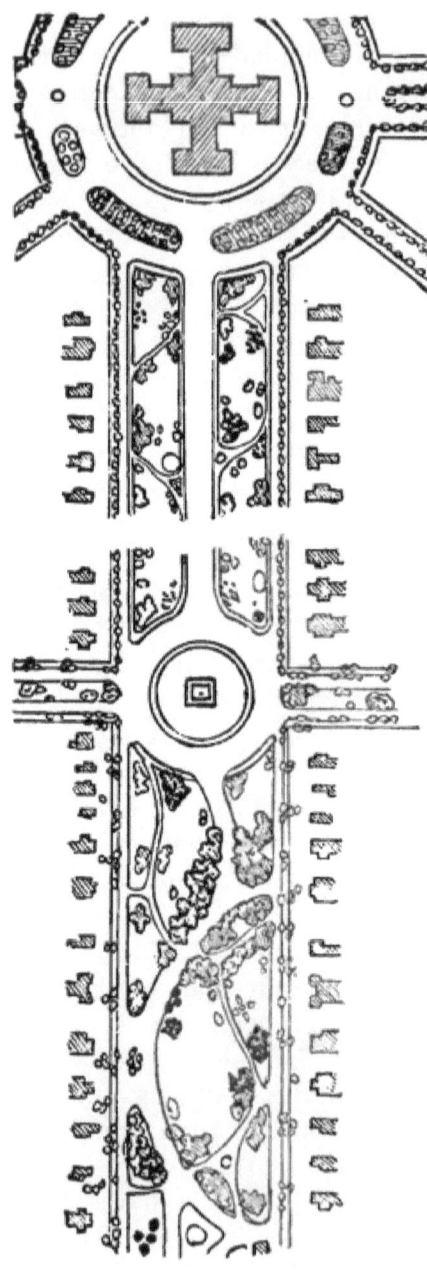

Fig. 114.—GARDEN BOULEVARD.

Such an avenue garden, in good shape, extending either as a main feature of a system of boulevards and parks or not, for one or any number of miles through a town, with wide circles at central points, supporting town halls, art galleries, museums, conservatories, or other edifices, and small circles at junctions with streets, containing monuments, statuary, or fountains, present an array of fine qualities difficult to equal. Add to this the area that on each side throughout the length, is embraced by private grounds, with residences setting back, let us suppose, at an average distance of about thirty feet, and altogether a garden is presented in effect, about five hundred feet wide, from house to house, and stretching far away, which for grandeur, richness, variety, and healthfulness, stands unequalled by any other kind of town garden.

The roomy circles shown in the plan are features of this system that must not be underrated.   Any structures of pleasing proportions built on these, will show to the best possible architectural advantage, and the value of any such in contributing to the effective appearance of a town, is virtually multiplied by the number of streets centering here—opening up vistas through which they are seen from a distance.   Let us imagine the effect on a town of having its imposing edifices located on great circles, like the one shown at the top of figure 114, into which, in this case, twelve streets and avenues open from different directions.   The beauty of a structure placed here would benefit a large part of the town, because in effect, belonging as an objective point to each street diverging from it.   Yet we constantly build towns in such a way that much of our attractive architecture is buried between masses of buildings and is only to be seen when it is reached.   The secret of the magnificence of cities like Paris, Edinburgh, and Washington, is largely found in such an arrangement of streets, edifices, and gardens, that they all contribute their full worth towards producing a grand, harmonious effect, with many of the avenues leading towards imposing structures, which then are seen through vistas of tree and garden beauty, that afford refreshing relief to the architecture.

It is for growing towns to note, that the city which succeeds by proper plans to so dispose of leading streets, public edifices, town gardens and parks, that each is used to the best advantage, is the one that secures the greatest amount of town attractiveness, and with the least expenditure of material and money.

Not least among the advantages of garden boulevards, is economy in the area employed, in proportion to the effects gained.   A smaller number of acres is required for a given length of these than might be supposed.   One four hundred and thirty feet wide, would require to the mile, about forty acres of land, not counting the two side roads, which are required as highways in any case. How could a better use for say one hundred and twenty acres be imagined as a large town garden, than in one such a broad garden boulevard, with all its varied beauty and numerous circles, supporting attractive architecture, stretching away for three continuous miles?

A GLANCE AT CENTRAL PARK, NEW YORK.

It may be interesting to note here that out of seven hundred and fifty acres—the area embraced by the well known Central Park of New York, there could have been made boulevards of the great length of six miles, and four hundred and thirty feet wide (not counting side drives), and fourteen miles of boulevards, from one hundred and twenty-five to two hundred feet wide, besides six parks of from fifteen to forty acres each, and still have fifty acres for large circles, and leaving sixty acres for the purpose of securing a large, natural park at some distance away.

If the equivalent of Central Park area had been managed on a plan something as shown by figure 115, affording superior sites for museums, fountains, statuary, etc., and also for other town buildings, that are mostly now hidden away, can it be doubted that far better effects would have been secured for the beauty of the city, and adding in many ways to its desirability as a place of residence, than has been wrought by the present system?

In considering the subject of Public Gardens generally, one may be pardoned for questioning, as they see the state of neglect and decay so conspicuous in late years in this noted garden, what its future is to be, and what its influence upon the development of upper New York.

If the blame for this is laid to corruption in the management, more than to the circumstances of its make up, size and location, it may be said that as the complete boulevard and small park system afford in great measure a reme-

dy against the defects of the latter nature, so the same system affords certain safeguards against extreme mismanagement not possessed by large parks. The garden avenues extending a great length through a town, are in all their details brought face to face with a large body of taxpayers, and mismanagement is exposed and becomes intolerable. At best but a small portion of all the people of a town can visit the large parks often, hence wholesale mismanagement frequently goes on without detection or check for a long time. And it is significant that if parks once happen to fall into a state of neglect and decay, they are liable to be shunned even by many of the otherwise regular visitors.

A lesson may be taken also from the unpleasant reputation which to some extent is associated with Central Park as a resort of the vicious classes, against constructing any large parks,

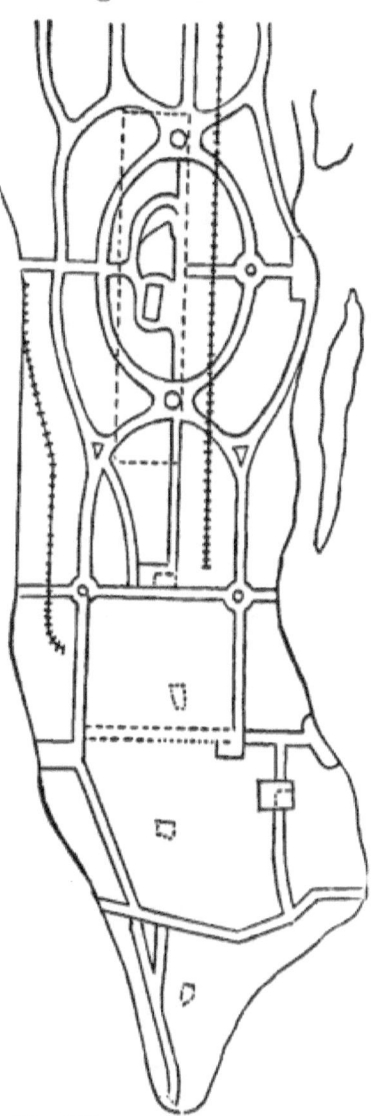

Fig. 115.—CENTRAL PARK AS IT MIGHT HAVE BEEN.

abounding in much close wood near the present or future

centers of large towns. It is a question whether this is not a state of things hard to disassociate from such a combination of circumstances in any place. In proportion as any system of centrally located town gardens can dispense with all woody solitudes (for such the clumps of woods become after nightfall), and instead have much openness, with small clumps of trees and shrubs, this serious fault is lessened. One great recommendation for boulevards and small parks, in the midst of cities, is, that from their comparative narrowness and openness, they offer few special attractions to the viciously inclined.

Turning from all that has been done in Paris in improving the city, by opening up the boulevard and small park system, there would be nothing wild in the idea of adopting in New York now, a system of parks and boulevards, something as shown in figure 115, and just suggested, dispensing entirely with Central Park as it now is. Such a move in New York would no doubt be attended, as something similar in Paris has been, by many important advantages, not excepting that of profit from a financial point of view. The present marvellously attractive Parc Monceau, of Paris, was formerly much larger than it now is, but the improvers of the city saw the policy of cutting it down, and along with other improvements, reduced it to less than half its former size, selling the cut off portions for residences at enormous rates. By a similar course with the larger New York Park, the city would gain directly in two ways, first by getting rid of a park that in more than one respect is too large, considering its location, and instead, drawing it out, so to speak, in order that it may contribute beauty, healthfulness, and convenience to many parts now deprived of them.

SMALL TOWN PARKS.

These, if well arranged, may be made to afford a good and varied show of park-like features, in a compass so

limited, that in large towns the land may be secured at
points that are readily accessible by the masses, while

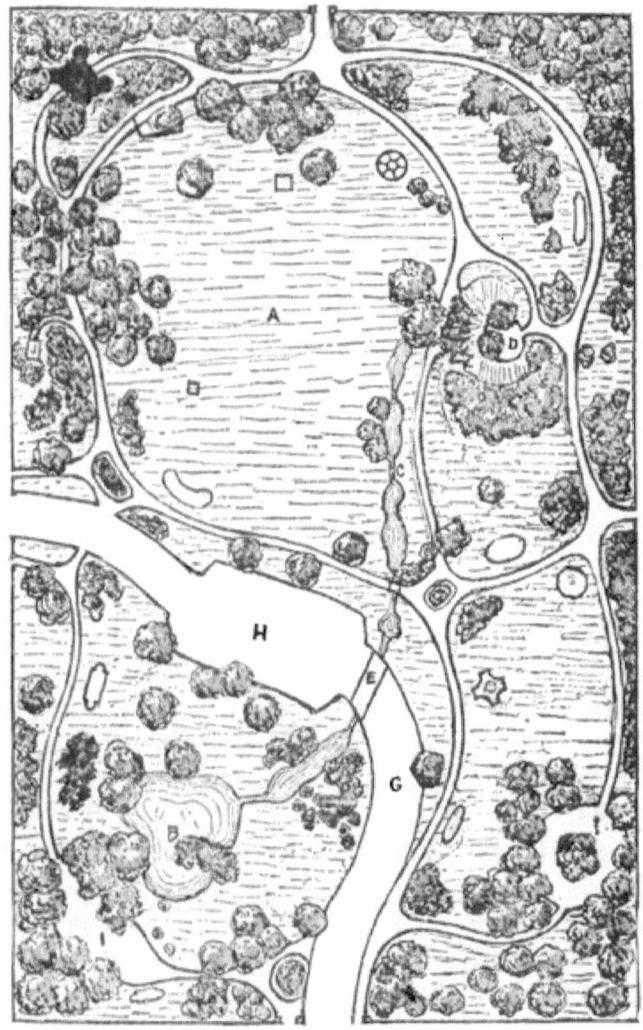

Fig. 116.—PLAN OF A TEN-ACRE PARK.

A, Main Grass Plat ; *B,* Lakelet; *C,* Rill, fed by Spring from Rockwork at *D* ; *E,* Bridge;
F, Arbor ; *G,* Drive ; *H,* Concourse; *i,* Walks enlarged in Shady Places ; *J,* Urinal.

small towns and villages that could not afford extended
garden systems, may have one or more parks of this kind.

Undoubtedly many small cities and towns are to-day debarred from having a park, from the false notion that one such, to be worthy of the name, must be large, or at any rate very expensive. Such is not, however, the case. Figure 116 is a plan of a ten-acre park, showing how much of garden and landscape attractiveness even a small area like this may be made to yield. Here are some hundreds of trees and flowering shrubs; open areas of lawn, the largest one about two acres in size, lakelet, rill, spring (natural or artificial), mound, rockery, bridges, arbors, flowers, ample walks, play grounds, etc., all disposed in a simple and largely natural style, and for showing boldness of character throughout. A short drive is also introduced. In parks of fifteen, twenty-five, or more acres, these may be brought in more freely, and there is greater latitude for creating fine garden effects.

A glance at the map of Paris, figure 113, shows a wise distribution of small parks through a large city. In that city about two hundred acres, divided into a dozen parks of from three to forty acres each, are thus employ-ed. These exquisite gardens are productive of an im-mense amount of comfort, pleasure, and healthfulness to the Parisians, and undoubtedly far more so, than if all were instead included in a single large town park.

It is a great recommendation for small town parks, that in our hot, dry summers, they could in many places be kept watered, with the effect of constantly having fresh, green lawns and foliage, a thing proportionally more difficult as a park is larger. In fact it is just at this season, when of all others we most enjoy cool, green lawns, that the large parks are so parched up as to be quite disagreeable.

Where Botanical, Zoölogical, or other collections are to be secured, small sized parks, if not too small, are well adapted to accommodating them.

TOWN SQUARES.

No parts of a town have greater need of garden spots, than those that are thickly settled. Often there is a square of one or several acres, or one could be made in places not admitting a larger square. But such plats are susceptible of being rendered much more attractive than they usually are. They should neither be exclusively devoted to trees for shade, nor be barren of them. A mean between the two, providing for an abundance of air, breeze, and sunshine, by keeping them well open in parts, and then grass, masses of trees and shrubs, flowers and walks tastefully arranged here and there should be secured.

Figures 117 and 118 represent two small squares, laid out on simple geometrical plans. The first has a grassy

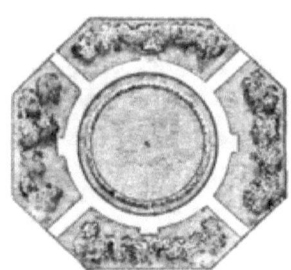

Fig. 117.

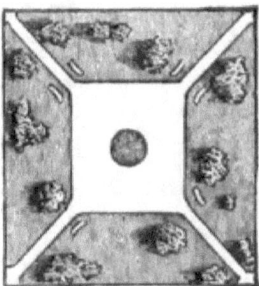

Fig. 118.

DESIGNS FOR SMALL TOWN SQUARES.

center, with a continuous flower-bed next to the walk, save a narrow strip of grass between. Seats may be placed in the depressions shown in the walks on four sides. The woody growths may be both shrubs and trees, arranged in masses as shown in the plan. Figure 118 has a square gravelled surface in the center, upon which is located a drinking fountain, piece of statuary, or candelabrum.

As a rule, the more simple a plan of this kind is, the

better. Sometimes, owing to strong architectural influences, the introduction of terraces, elaborate flower-beds, and other similar features is proper in squares. But even then the plan should be essentially simple as a whole.

To have a small square, or park of any size, in fine condition in thickly settled parts, and abounding in refreshing natural attractions, it must above all else be properly protected by a fence with gates, after the universal European fashion. This is absolutely necessary for keeping out that greatest of all enemies to low flowers, shrubs, and evergreens, dogs. These enjoy running and playing in such places, and by their lawless, and worst of all, filthy habits, in time kill every fine shrub or plant. But fences may be made inconspicuous, and not more than three or four feet high, if built of pointed pickets. A single width of coarse wire netting, with meshes two or three inches wide, fixed against the fence next to the ground, will keep out all small animals, and besides protect the place from paper and litter that are swept along the streets by the wind. Then the admission of dogs at the gates should be strictly prohibited, unless they are led by a cord or chain.

PLANTING PUBLIC HIGHWAYS.

All over this land, both in city and country, there is an inexcusable lack of shade and ornamental trees at the road sides. Foreigners wonder at this, as they find here a land rich in fine native trees, and an apparent lack of appreciation of their value. Throughout Europe the country roads are very commonly, and often for many miles in a stretch, made beautiful and comfortable by the use of trees.

If a persistent effort were made at once to plant trees along the highways, and to care for them, the next fifty, or even ten years, would mark a greater change for the better in the general appearance of our rural districts, then has taken place since the lands were cleared. Such an improvement would tend to greatly increase the values of lands, and besides, who can measure the increase of comfort to be gained for every living thing; in summer by abundant shade ; in winter by breaking the force of piercing winds, not to speak of advantages as effecting rainfalls and drouths.

In some of the States of late, laws have been made to encourage tree planting, by paying a bounty from the State treasury, to those who plant and protect trees. In Connecticut an act provides, that any person planting and protecting forest trees for one-quarter of a mile or more along any public highway, may receive, for ten years, one dollar per annum for each quarter of a mile so planted. In some instances, public spirited individuals have offered prizes of forty, twenty-five, twenty, and fifteen dollars for the best and largest rows of trees along any public road of a town, the award to be made by three non-resident experts. It is shown that bounties and prizes thus offered stimulate a great interest in the work of planting trees on public roads.

In planting street trees, the common arrangement in rows with the trees at equal distances apart, is not the only one, or perhaps not always the best. Too much of such planting tends to monotony. The rows should be broken now and then, by setting the trees more irregularly, placing some close together on both sides of the walk to form clumps, and then leaving open spaces elsewhere. In figure 107, and also in the lower half of figure 114, this idea is illustrated. Monotony may be further broken by introducing different kinds of trees, keeping each somewhat by itself.

A common fault in this work is, to plant so close that the trees have no chance to develop their beauty. This often comes from a desire to have a plenty of shade at once. The better way is to plant some trees to be permanent, say at thirty-five or forty feet apart for Elms, and twenty-five for other kinds of forest trees, and then to set rapid-growing kinds, like the Poplars, Silver Maple, Ailanthus, Catalpa, and European Alder, between these, to be removed when the better kinds need the space. If but two trees are needed in front of any premises, plant three, the middle one a fast grower, to be removed before many years.

RURAL IMPROVEMENT ASSOCIATIONS.

The movements on foot in some places for establishing these associations, and having in view as a chief object the beautifying of towns and villages, by planting trees, improving roadsides, and town gardens, is a most worthy one, and their universal introduction would soon work great changes in the appearance of towns and villages. Through the kindness of the Hon. B. F. Northrop, of Clinton, Conn., who has been prominent in establishing these associations, I am able to present the following plan, which was adopted by the village in which he lives.

CLINTON RURAL IMPROVEMENT ASSOCIATION.

1. This Association shall be called " The Rural Improvement Association of Clinton."

2. The object of this Association shall be to cultivate public spirit, quicken the social and intellectual life of the people, promote good fellowship, and secure public health by better hygienic conditions in our homes and surroundings, improve our streets, roads, public grounds, side-walks, and in general to build up and beautify the whole town, and thus enhance the value of its real estate and render Clinton a still more inviting place of residence.

3. The officers of this Association shall consist of a President, a Vice-President, a Treasurer, a Secretary, and an Executive Committee of fifteen, six of whom shall be ladies.

4. It shall be the duty of the Executive Committee to make

all contracts, employ all laborers, expend all moneys, and superintend all improvements made by the Association. They shall hold meetings monthly from April to October in each year, and as much oftener as they may deem expedient.

5. Every person, who shall plant three trees by the road side, under the direction of the Executive Committee, or pay three dollars in one year, or one dollar annually, and obligate himself or herself to pay the same annually for three years, shall be a member of this Association.

6. The payment of ten dollars annually for three years, or of twenty-five dollars in one sum, shall constitute one a life member of this Association.

7. Five members of the Executive Committee present at any meeting shall constitute a quorum.

8. No debt shall be contracted by the Executive Committee beyond the amount of available means within their control, and no member of the Association shall be liable for any debt of the Association, beyond the amount of his or her subscription.

9. The Executive Committee shall call an annual meeting, giving due notice of the same, for the election of officers of this Association, and at said meeting, shall make a detailed report of all moneys received and expended during the year, the number of trees planted under their direction, and the number planted by individuals, length of side-walks made or repaired, and the doings of the Committee in general.

10. This constitution may be amended at any annual meeting by a two-thirds vote of the members present and voting.

CHAPTER XXVIII.

GARDEN CEMETERIES.

So excellent in almost every respect are many of the large garden cemeteries of our country, that all that may be said in praise of them—and much praise is thus bestowed both at home and by foreigners—is usually well merited. But what on the other hand can be said of the strongly contrasted condition of thousands of small, old-fashioned grave-yards, which we all have met throughout the land, in a terribly neglected condition, overgrown with weeds, rank grass, and tangled brush. The only way in which the condition of these can be reconciled, is to look upon them as relics of a pioneer period. They are like the "log-huts" of past generations, old and faulty, but endeared to us by the ties that bind the departed dead to the living. Everywhere in the older sections of the country, log-houses and barns have given place to tasteful and often costly buildings, representatives of the increased prosperity of the community, but many times in the same community the burial place is still in the "log-hut" style.

If the people were satisfied to have them thus, no words of condemnation of such grounds—suggestive of cold and selfish forgetfulness—would be too strong. But believing that the dissatisfaction with these is widespread, and that the present condition is due more to not knowing what to do, than to a disposition against doing, we may feel hopeful of better things in time to come.

Indeed, we think there is enough love for the beautiful, enough wealth and enterprise, and enough respect for the dead in every section of country, to make and keep the burial places nearly or quite as well as those of the large cities to-day are kept. These grounds are usually of a few acres, but the joint property of hundreds of able persons, and actually representatives in every community of large sums of money. The arguments that force themselves upon every one's good sense, in favor of having these small areas in good and even beautiful shape, out of respect for their hallowed use, ought to be overpowering in aid of any movement in the direction of their improvement, and in every neighborhood there ought to be the persons ready to lead in and encourage the work.

That which contributes most largely to the beauty of the improved city cemeteries, are the garden features introduced. How appropriate in this country of cheap land is the idea to have all burial places, fair-sized, roomy, landscape gardens, varied with wood, groves, and single trees, lawns and flowers, arranged in good taste, with simple memorials to indicate the places of interment.

The key to the superior appearance of our leading cemeteries, is the fact that the prices at which all lots are sold, are fixed with a view to the expense of perpetually keeping the cemetery in order. This must be looked upon as one of the most important points connected with improved cemetery management. To the observance, or non-observance of this is due the vast difference between the best and the poorest of our rural cemeteries.

As the incidental expenses of keeping up any cemetery lot by sodding, mowing, etc., are very light, when many are taken care of together, only a small increase in the prices of lots is required to form a general fund, the interest of which provides perpetually for their care. In the beautiful Forest Lawn Cemetery, of Buffalo, containing two hundred and thirty acres, the price of lots is fixed at fifty cents per square foot, while in the new Buffalo City Cemetery, a few miles further from the city, the price is but twenty-five cents per square foot. These prices apply to all parts of the cemeteries, but then some sections accommodate lots of only one size, and others allow of lots of other sizes. Of course where land is cheap, the price can be kept at even lower figures than either of those named.

How is the work of cemetery improvement in any case to be inaugurated and carried out? First, let persons of public spirit carefully look over the matter, determining what improvements are desirable, as to size of grounds, and whether it is better to change the old or to start an entirely new cemetery. If an old association

exists, that can be strengthened for carrying out the new
purpose, let it be done and put to work, if not, then a
new organization should be formed.

As to cemetery officers, there should be a Board of
Trustees, composed of from five to twelve men, to be
chosen by the lot holders. The election should be yearly,
and the term of office not less than three years, with an
arrangement by which one or two trustees go out each

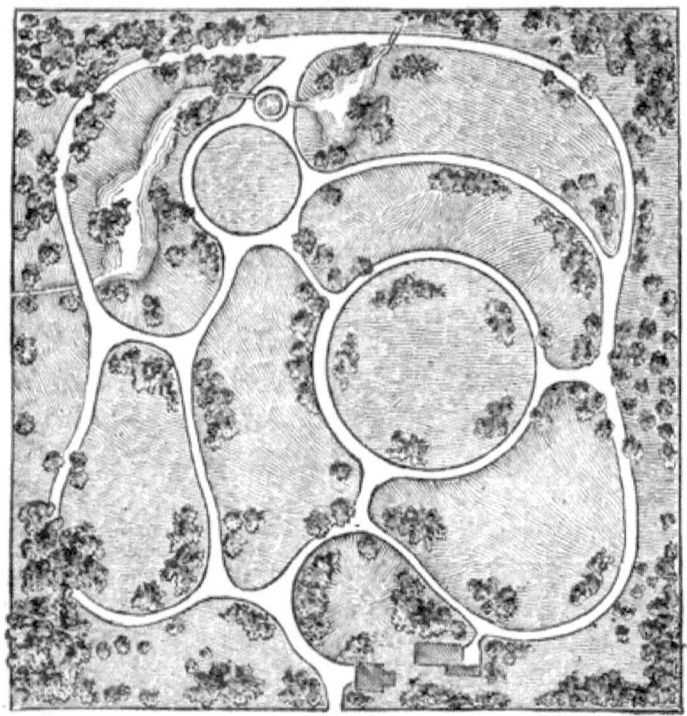

Fig. 119.—A GARDEN CEMETERY OF FIFTEEN ACRES.

year, and the same number of new or re-elected ones
come in. All affairs of the Association and the property,
should be managed by this Board, the members acting
without compensation. In addition to the trustees, a
secretary and treasurer should be appointed by the Board.
Reports should be required annually from the officers by
the lot-holders. There are laws in the different States

bearing upon cemeteries, and these should be procured to aid, where necessary, in perfecting the organization.

As regards the location of the improved cemetery, if lands can be procured for enlargement of the old grave-yard, lying directly adjacent, there are obvious reasons why this should be done, making such alterations as to adapt it to the new plan. If this cannot be done, some advantages might be found in starting a new cemetery, but this would in part, at least, be offset by the trouble incident to keeping up the old one and making removals.

The size and plan of the cemetery, are matters so intimately associated with the needs of respective communities, and with the style of arrangement, that anything said

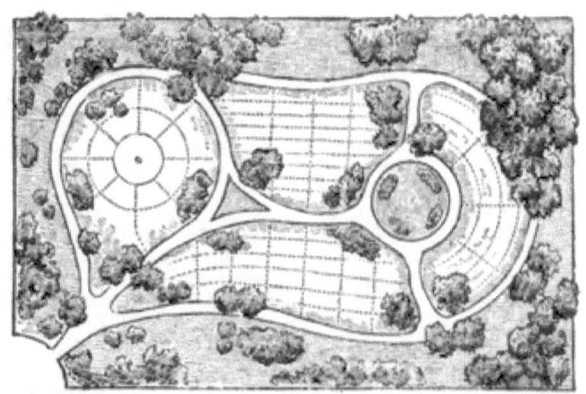

Fig. 120.—A GARDEN CEMETERY OF THREE ACRES.

on this point must be general. There are several things that should have weight in deciding as to size of the grounds, such as the probable wants of the future, taking growth of population into consideration. A scant area limits the possibilities of the gardener in producing broad, pleasing effects. On the other hand, the larger the area, the more expensive will it be to keep up. It would in every instance be the best and cheapest—considering the permanent nature of such work, and the desirability of doing well what is done at all, for the Board to secure the services of a skillful landscape architect to help decide these points, as well as to prepare a plan of the grounds, select and mark out the arrangement of the trees and shrubs, and other matters. Under any circumstances there should be a definite plan devised for guiding operations, and the arrangement from the start should be so complete as not to require, in a great many years, any important changes.

The grounds of the cemetery should be divided and sub-divided into sections and plats, with such avenues and walks as may be deemed necessary. A map should be kept where it can be readily inspected.

The lots should be of various sizes, generally with those of the same size together. They may vary from the size

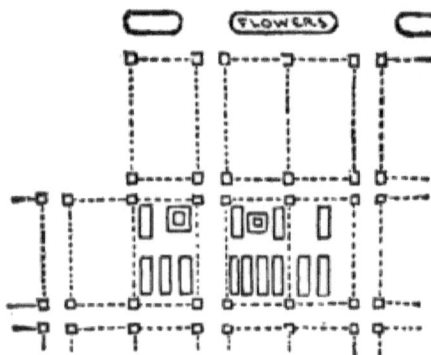

Fig. 121.—PLAN FOR DIVIDING CEMETERY GROUNDS.

of single graves to several thousand square feet each, the more desirable sections usually being laid out in largest lots. Dispensing with gravel or other walks throughout the cemetery, having in their stead, grass walks only, excepting some main walks and drives, is much preferable to cutting up the ground with the former. By this means there is a saving of expense in first construction ; the after care of the place is easier, and such a plan tends to increase the garden effect. Figure 121 shows one of the best plans for dividing cemetery lawns into lots and grass walks. The boundaries are marked by small stone, metal, or oaken slabs, so sunk down with the tops even with the ground, that the mower can pass over them. This plan is drawn to a scale of four feet to one-fourth of an inch.

No fences, rails, or walls, are now allowed around individual lots in the best cemeteries. In case anything of this kind is needed, it should be a low, stone coping or a low evergreen hedge.

The planting of trees, shrubs and flowers in cemeteries should only be allowed under the direction of an intelligent superintendent ; the injudicious bringing in of what were intended as adornments, has spoiled the beauty of many a cemetery. Flowers, as a rule, should be arranged either in beds along the drives and walks, or else on plats not used for burials.

The plan of regulating somewhat the size and form of tombstones, by keeping them within certain limits, is a good one, for the wide variations that often prevail in these, is not conducive to good effects.

Rules and regulations to be observed by lot-holders and visitors, should be posted up in one or more conspicuous places. These may apply to the admission of non-lot-holders ; prohibition of fast driving, driving on the grass, leaving horses unattended or unfastened, the picking or injuring of flowers. shrubs, and trees, the feeding or disturbing of water fowls or birds, forbidding children to come in unattended, or persons with refreshments, fire-arms, or dogs, or omnibuses, equestrians, etc.

PART IV.

CONSTRUCTING GARDENS.

CHAPTER XXIX.

PLANNING GARDEN IMPROVEMENTS.

No one who plants ornamental trees and shrubs, or otherwise permanently improves his land, can forsee how far the results of his work will live into the future. This thought suggests the importance of doing well whatever is done, as it is done but once for an indefinite time. In building our houses, the appearance of the finished structure is thoroughly studied from plans before construction ; we should act as wisely with the garden improvements, which endure quite as long. Trees and shrubs look small at the start ; they will not be so always, and after developing into conspicuous objects, we can scarcely count on replacing or moving them, if badly located at first. Obviously the proper time to avoid bad garden effects is before the work is begun.

This can be done by the help of good plans, prepared beforehand, in ample time to guide every operation in garden making. It is better to have such plans, even if procured at some cost of time and money, and if they show nothing more than the locating of the principal objects, than to start work with no plan, or a poor one, and to regret the results for years long to come.

Where one prefers to make his own plans for garden improvements, the way to proceed is, to prepare a map of the place as it now is, drawing it to some scale, such as sixteen or thirty-two feet to the inch. Upon this all the existing objects, such as buildings, entrances, trees, etc., should be located, giving each its exact position. Then with a pencil, the planning of improvements may be done, making and erasing as necessary, until something satisfactory is reached. Every object intended to be brought in should be given its proper size according to the scale. As the work progresses, the plan should often be viewed from various directions, by holding the upper surface of the paper nearly in line with the eye. This will better show how it will appear on the grounds when finished, than if looked at obliquely from above, because naturally we view our gardens not as if we were in a balloon, but with the eye, nearly on their own level. Sufficient time ought to be given to this work, so that all features may be deliberately studied in their relation to the whole. Remember, it is always a serious matter to make blunders in planning a garden, for when the work is once executed, and the trees are growing, they will stand as monuments—who can tell how long—pointing either to wise or unwise decisions on the part of the one who made the plan.

To secure the best results, with the fewest chances of failure, the services of a skilled landscape architect should by all means be employed. A matter of such far reaching importance should be entrusted only to a thoroughly competent person. There is no better field for ignoramuses and outright imposters, than that of gardening, because results are often years in developing, giving the imposters time enough to depart before their incompetency is discovered. As a rule, if a person cannot draw a plan that is graceful and pleasing to the eye, he is not to be trusted to plan the garden itself. This test, while generally reliable, is not always so, for a grand plan, in addition to appearing smooth and graceful on paper, must fit the place upon which it is to be employed. A knowledge of materials is quite indispensable on the part of the architect. He should be familiar with the natures and merits of all the plants he sets out ; the proper selections to make, and the soils and exposures most suitable for each ; the effects of sunshine, shade, moisture, dryness, upon them, the sizes and forms they attain at maturity, the shades of foliage, colors of flowers, and a multitude of other things in order to produce lasting good effects.

CHAPTER XXX.

LAYING OUT THE GROUNDS.

From the time the first spade is struck, until the garden is completed, there will be frequent need of consulting the plan for guidance. It must be early determined where excavations for walks, foundations, etc., are to come, that the material from these can be utilized in rough shaping. The soil of borders for trees and shrubs, as well as of flower beds, ferneries, etc., will probably need special preparation, and that is often best made while the rough work is in progress. Any rockeries, terraces, lakes, etc., to be introduced, must be located early.

All improvements and objects being in place on the map, their exact location on the grounds should be determined with the measuring tape and marked with stakes. Usually, in laying out, a place must be gone over a number of times in parts, because stakes get disturbed or covered up, and the surface keeps varying more or less during construction.

While most points are readily located by measurement, this is more difficult in the case of walks and other curves,

except as regards their starting places and general
position. In getting the curves, the practised gardener
trusts much to his eye, but a person of no experience
finds this is not easy. A rope can be used for such purposes to good advantage, by fastening one end at some

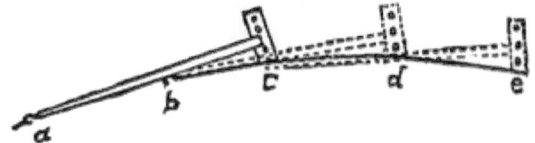

Fig. 122.—THE CURVE ROD.

definite point along the line, and then drawing on it, in
a way to produce the desired sweep, defining it afterwards with stakes.

The curve-rod shown in figure 122 is a useful implement
in this work. It consists of a six-foot rod with a wire hook
on one end, *a*, and a cross piece with holes in it at the
other, *c*, with a notch at the center, *b*. To use it, we
start with a stake at the hook at *a*, and one in the notch
at *b*, a third one is then put through one of the holes of
the cross piece, say the outer one for instance. Then
the rod is lifted leaving the
stakes to stand, and is moved
forward into position, *b*, *d*, setting a fourth stake at *d*. After
this we bring into position, *c*, *e*,
with a stake at *e*, and so on.
Such a course then leaves the
stakes on a good curve. By
using the one or the other end
of the cross-piece the curve

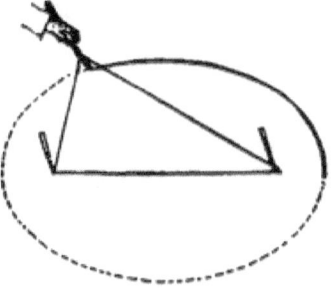

Fig. 123.—FORMING AN OVAL.

may be turned to the right or the left, or it may be
lengthened by inserting stakes in nearer the center.

A simple method of laying out an oval on the ground
is shown in figure 123. Two stakes are set, say at six,
ten, or any number of feet apart—this being governed

by the required size—around these a stout cord is placed
of such a length, that when the ends are tied, a loop will
be formed about one-fourth longer than the distance between the stakes.   By placing a marking stake in the
end of the loop drawn taut, it will, with moving it around
—being guided by the loop, as shown in the engraving—
form a perfect ellipse on the ground.   A little experi-
menting will enable one to construct a wider or narrower,
larger or smaller oval.

All small circles, squares, triangles, and so forth, are
readily laid out with the use of line, tape measure, or
ten-foot pole and stakes.

CHAPTER XXXI.

THE WORK ON THE GROUNDS.

After a first laying out of the grounds, operations may
commence, by passing over and roughly shaping them,
excavating, filling in, etc., as alluded to in the last chapter.

Whatever alterations are made in the surface, it should
be laid down, as a rule never to be disregarded, that as finished, at least six inches of good loamy soil—and as much
more as possible—should overlay every part of the place
that is to be planted or made into lawn.   Wherever considerable cutting down is necessary, the good surface soil
should first be stripped from such parts, and placed at one
side, and after moving enough subsoil to effect the needed
reduction, return the top soil again.   In mound-making,
instead of heaping up earth on the natural top soil, this
should first be stripped, and then the body of the mound
be made of subsoil, afterwards replacing the surface soil
on the top.

Another way of doing such work, is to do it along with the operation of trenching (described in connection with figure 124). As each section of surface soil is thrown over, laying bare the subsoil, add to or take from the latter enough material to effect the desired grade, afterwards replacing the top layer.

Where the walks, drives, foundation walls, fountains, etc., come, some earth will need excavating, and this may be used in general shaping. The good surface soil from such places should be kept separate and prized for use. By opening up for walks and drives at this stage, a convenient place is found for depositing any stones that turn up. If there are many of these, often the best and cheapest way to get rid of them, is by excavating deeply for walks and drives, and filling them in there; they will thus serve both as foundation and for drainage.

The best season for rough levelling, draining, and other coarse operations, is late summer or fall. The earth is then likely to be dry—a great point in economical moving—and no injury can possibly arise from the trampling of teams and packing of the soil by wheeling. Then, also, the earth has a chance to settle well by spring, so that the work of planting and lawn making may be commenced early, which is a great advantage. In filling in, ample allowance must be made for settling, by leaving the ground in its loose state, somewhat higher in deep places than in others. In case filling in must be done in the spring, to be followed soon by finishing the improvements, the materials need to be firmly compacted by beating or rolling to prevent settling out of shape.

DRAINAGE.

The thorough drainage of the soil is important in the pleasure ground. Few plants will succeed in cold, damp, undrained soil, and little comfort or satisfaction can be had from a garden in this condition. Warmth and air at the roots are essential for their growth, and these can never be well secured in undrained, wet soil.

In the work of draining, usually common drain tiles, or pipes, are laid in lines twenty to forty feet apart, and three or four feet deep for loamy soils, and fifteen feet and upwards apart, and about three feet deep for heavy soils. Land naturally open and dry may not require draining. The best style and size of tile is the round, with collars, and these may be from one and one half to two inches inside diameter for common tiles, with the cross mains two to four inches. The smaller the tiles, if they answer their purpose, the less liable are they to become obstructed, because the flow is more concentrated. The tiles should be so hard burned that they will give a clear ring when struck, but not over burned. It will pay to carefully examine the tiles and accept only such as come up to this standard, for soft tiles are not durable, while those that are hard burned, warped, or melted, make defective drains. Like a chain, the effectiveness of a drain is only measured by its poorest parts.

Drains may also be may of rubble stone or broken rocks, two or three inches in diameter, placed to a depth of fifteen inches in the bottom of a trench. Wooden drains, made of ordinary rough boards, cut into strips four inches wide and nailed together, by using three pieces, into a triangular box or pipe, breaking the joints. These drains, which answer very well for small jobs, should be laid with a point downward like the letter V.

The bottoms of drains must be even, and have sufficent fall throughout their length to make a ready flow towards the outlet. Generally the sewers from the buildings may be made a part of the sewage system of the garden, in which to lead the water.

PREPARING THE SOIL.

To secure a satisfactory growth of all trees, shrubs, flowers, and grass in the garden, the soil must be rich and deeply worked. That attempts at gardening may prove failures from other causes is possible, but lack of attention to these points is the most common reason why many places never look well—all the trees and plants having an unthrifty, half-starved appearance.

Few soils are so stubborn that draining and a thorough breaking up and manuring will not properly prepare them for planting. Such soils must be prepared by trenching or subsoiling to fifteen or more inches deep, at the same time working in from thirty to fifty loads of good stable manure to the acre. Top-dressing in alternate years will be required afterwards; this treatment will produce grand results with whatever is planted. If the soil should happen to be a heavy clay, or just opposite, a light sand or gravel, by mixing in some material of an opposite nature, for instance, with the clay using sand, loam, or lime, and with the sand or gravel, using marl, clay, peat, leaf-mould or loam in addition to the above treatment, the effect would be greatly beneficial.

Deep culture promotes growth, by giving the roots ample room for extension, and the soil, if properly broken up, retains moisture the entire depth to which it is loosened, preventing to an astonishing degree, injury from severe drouths. In the most ordinary method of culture, the surface soil only is overturned, leaving the subsoil below—usually of a compact sterile nature—unbroken. But when the best results are desired, the subsoil should be broken up, keeping both the surface soil and the subsoil separate.

For places large enough to admit the plow, a subsoil plow, following in the furrow of the common one, and run down deep, is used to secure deep culture. In

smaller places trenching with the spade takes its place.
Figure 124 shows how this operation is done.   First, the
surface soil occupying the space *A*, to the width of about
six feet across the plot is thrown out entirely, and the
subsoil underneath, *a*, is turned with the spade at the
same time, working some manure into the subsoil.   Then
the section of soil of space *B* is thrown over into space *A*,
and the soil of space *b* now brought to light, is treated as

Fig. 124.—TRENCHING.

that of *a* was.   This way of procedure is followed with
successive strips across the entire ground.   The opening
remaining at the end after the other side is reached, is
filled up with the soil first thrown out.

FINAL SHAPING OF THE SURFACE.

Shapeliness of the surface is one of the distinguishing
marks of a good garden, be it even, crowning, or undulating as to the top.   In going over the grounds to apply
the final touches, a careful eye to observe the work of
evening-up, is in many cases all that will be needed.   But
where the eye cannot be trusted, or if great precision is
desirable in the final contour, then a line and stakes for
small grounds, and regular levelling instruments for
large ones will be needed.

In using the line and stakes for this purpose, in common sized lots, first drive a stake at each corner of the
lot, *a, b, c, d*, in figure 125, and corresponding ones at the

corners of the house, *a, b, c, d,* of the same figure, all to
project say two feet above the ground. Then determine
where the final grade line is to be, at the point where each
stake stands, marking the same on the stake. Now
measure up on each stake one foot from the grade mark,
and cut a notch. By next stretching a line—or sighting

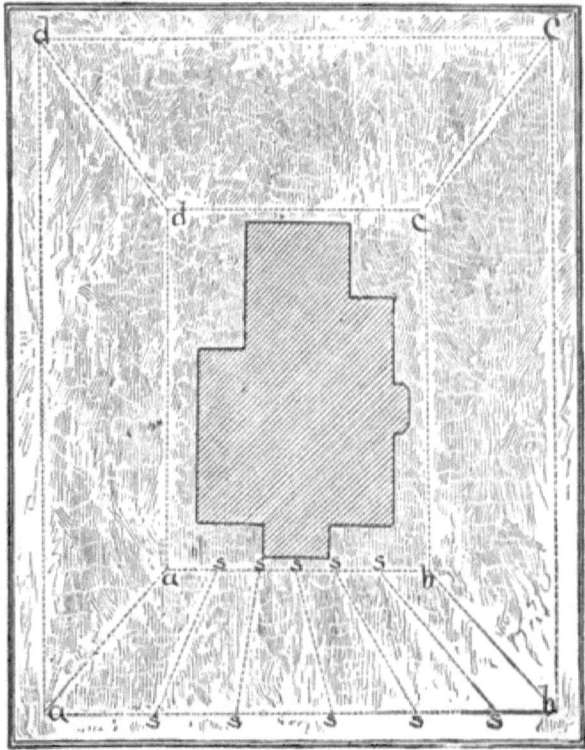

Fig. 125.—FINAL SHAPING OF THE SURFACE.

for long distances—from notch to notch thus made on
any two stakes, such a line—called the datum line—it is
plain, will be one foot above the desired grade as marked
on the corner stakes. By setting a row of stakes at intervals of say twenty feet between the corner stakes, along
the border, and a corresponding number which will come

closer together along the house as shown by the letter *s*
in the cut, we may indicate the desired grade throughout
on these, by simply measuring down one foot from the
datum line at any point, provided it is intended to keep
the desired grade straight. But most likely it ought to
be a departure from a straight line to some extent, with
probably a crowning point midway between corners. In
such case, the measure should be something less than a
foot, say ten or eight inches downwards on the stake at
the most crowning point, and then gradually increasing
the length of the measure in proceeding towards the corners, in order to make a generally curving contour, even
if slight.

With a row of an equal number of stakes between corner and corner all around the lot, as well as around the
house, marked with the desired grade in the manner described, we may now proceed to run lines, shown by dots

Fig. 126.—GUAGE FOR SLOPES.

in the figure, across the plot between the stakes of the
boundary row and corresponding ones at the house.
Along these cross lines the desired grade may also be
marked on the stakes, which should also be twenty feet
apart. By passing over the entire grounds in this way,
the new grade will be shown on stakes about twenty feet
apart all over the area, and the finishing of the grading
may be guided by these.

It remains for those having the work in charge to decide on how much, if at all, the general contour shall
vary from the straight line in all parts. The presence
of any desired undulations here and there about the
grounds, need not, with due allowance, interfere with this

work. Terraces and slopes may be shaped very perfectly as regards their surface on this principle. If these are to be straight in each part, and the angles and outlines all straight, it will not be difficult to indicate the desired grade on rows of stakes at the top and bottom of any slopes, and at the margins of terraces. Where the outlines of terraces are curving, a little more difficulty attends the laying out and shaping. For such work, and in fact for all cutting of slopes, the slope guage shown in figure 126 is a great help. By laying out the upper curve of the slope, marking it clearly on the ground of the upper level, and then using this guage the work of cutting down the slants is easily done. Slopes should seldom be made of a greater angle than forty-five degrees.

In thus shaping up the grounds, as directed, it is calculated that at this time the soil is distributed precisely as it shall appear when finished and clothed with grass. But if in any case the surface has become hardened by trampling or driving, it may be best now to carefully go over all with a spade, or in large pieces the plow, and work it over very evenly, preparatory to receiving the trees, shrubs, plants, and grass. This I repeat should be carefully done, with a view to changing the lay of the land as slightly as possible. No attention need be paid to the stakes now, as these are no more needed. In plowing this time, the soil from the first furrow is thrown above the common level, after the piece is overturned it should be drawn into the open furrow that is left by the plow in finishing, that all may become even again. A heavy harrow, along with a roller, should then be applied until the surface is thoroughly fined down. The roller serves to settle the soil, and reveal small mounds and deficiencies which may need correcting with the shovel and rake. In small plats that have been spaded, the rake and hand-roller will be used in place of the harrow, etc.

An earth float, made of a piece of common 3 by 4 or 2 by 6-inch rough scantling, with one handle, for a float nine feet long, is shown in figure 127.   Two handles are needed for one sixteen feet long.   This will be found to be a useful implement for the final shaping of the ground, by drawing it back and forth over the surface a number of times in different directions.   The walks being not yet

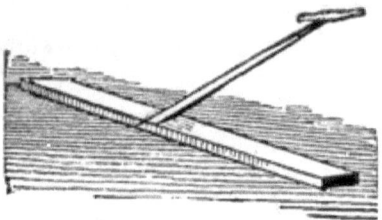

Fig. 127.—A FLOAT.

made, all stones and surface gravel can still be deposited in the openings for these.   After this last plowing, all driving, and wheeling should be, if possible, confined to the drives and walks.

CHAPTER XXXII.

PLANTING.

All things considered, spring is the best time to plant trees and shrubs, and the earlier it can be done, after the soil is dry enough to work, the better.   Still with great care being observed in not letting the roots be exposed to the air for a moment more than is absolutely necessary, there is no reason why success should not follow, even when the trees are considerably started.   I have planted Horse Chestnuts, Maples, Japan Quince, Althæas, and many others, that were in full leaf, and scarcely lost one. But when any are so far advanced as this. it is necessary to remove most of the leaves and to do the work with great painstaking. The Larch, Birch, Beech, and some others cannot be transplanted thus late with any prospect of success. All the evergreens may be set several weeks later than deciduous trees. Fall planting of deciduous trees is generally successful if done in October—there being more risk with delicate kinds than with others. This is the preferable season for setting all of the robust, hardy flowering plants, and especially Pæonies. But fall planting of every kind should be done, if possible, as early as the month of October, in order to give the roots a chance to "get hold of the ground," as gardeners say, and store up some strength against the winter.

Let us suppose that the stock for planting that was ordered from the nursery, has just arrived, and we find the garden not quite ready for setting them immediately. The trees should be taken from the shipping boxes and carefully heeled-in for a twofold purpose. First, to preserve the roots from drying; second, to so arrange them that the labels can be examined, and any requisite tree be readily taken out for planting. The heeling-in should be done by digging a trench about a foot deep, and two feet wide, in a convenient spot. The roots should be set into this trench, and fine earth sprinkled upon them, to come in contact with all parts, finishing by filling the trench with the earth first thrown out. The soil should then be firmed with the feet, so that it will be in close contact with all the roots.

Success in planting depends upon not letting the roots dry. More trees are killed from this cause than most people are aware. From the time that trees are lifted in the nursery, until they are finally planted, every means should be employed to guard against drying of the roots. They often suffer when heeled-in, by having the soil too loose about the roots. Evaporation goes on from the tops, the juices dry out, and under such circumstances they cannot draw in the moisture needed to make up for the loss. Evergreens, particularly, often suffer much from this cause.

When ready to plant, first go over the ground with the working plan in hand, and set a stake wherever a tree or shrub is to be planted. The work may be simplified by writing the name of the kind on each stake. Holes should be dug of ample size to accommodate the roots when spread out naturally, and the soil should be carefully kept in piles at the side of the holes and not needlessly scattered.

As the trees are being set, or preferably before, they should be pruned. This operation should be governed somewhat by the loss of roots in digging, but as all trees and shrubs lose some roots during that process, and as we do not know just how many, a safe rule for most kinds will be, to cut away about one third to one half of the last season's growth. Any long roots may be also shortened a little, and the ends of all roots that were bruised in digging, should be cut off smooth. Evergreens should also be pruned somewhat when planting them.

Set the trees so that when the earth is filled in, they will be as deep as they stood in the nursery. The principal feeding roots of the trees are near the surface, and to plant it deep is not to do the tree justice. An exception to this rule is to be made, however, with such things as budded roses, and dwarf pears, which should be planted with the union of stock and cion two inches below the surface.

The tree or shrub being in place, fine soil should be quickly sprinkled over the roots, and the plant so worked or shaken, that the earth will get well around and underneath all of the roots. The good planter gets down and works the soil in between the roots with his fingers or with a small pointed stick, and on account of this care he seldom loses a plant. Before much soil is filled in upon the roots, it should be pressed firmly with the feet, or even a rammer. Such firming is a most important part of the work, and probably has more to do with the success of the planting than any other one thing. If at planting, the soil happens to be dry, or the tree is considerably started, do not fill the hole quite full at once, but run water into the opening to thoroughly soak the soil, finally filling in the earth the next morning.

When trees are set singly, a space several feet across should be kept clear of grass for a few years. This space should be a little lower than the surrounding surface, in order that the tree may be perfectly watered in dry weather, and the soil worked. Where they are planted in masses or borders, the whole area they cover may be kept in cultivation, and the soil being in a thoroughly pulverized condition on the surface, admitting air and moisture, they will do better than they otherwise possibly could.

In some grounds, especially such as have been cut down by grading, sometimes nothing but the poorest, gravelly, sandy or clayey earth is available, although a facing loam from six inches upwards may be provided for making a lawn. It would be worse than useless to attempt to grow trees, shrubs, etc., in such a place without special preparation for whatever may be planted. Wherever a tree is to be set, one half to a cubic yard of the earth should be dug out, and the opening filled in with the same quantity of good soil from elsewhere, in which the tree should be planted. Where groups of trees and shrubs are to be planted, the entire area may be thus treated to a depth of one and a half or two feet.

CHAPTER XXXIII.

LAWN MAKING.

There are two ways of making a lawn, the one by sodding or turfing, the other by sowing grass seeds. For small gardens, the former is undoubtedly the best, while for larger areas, seeding is necessarily done, as it generally makes a good lawn, and is much cheaper, although more time is needed to bring it to perfection.

If it can be done, the ground to be put into grass ought to be allowed to settle during one or two good rains after the last grading spoken of in Chapter XXXI, and then be sodded or seeded. Otherwise some slight unevenness may appear after thorough settling. If the rain cannot be waited for, the earth may be settled with the roller. An earth rammer may also be brought into use, and if it is

Fig. 128.—AN EARTH-RAMMER AND SOD-BEETLE.

found that any spots are softer than others, they should be firmed by this tool, afterwards evening-up the surface as may be needed, by the use of the rake. Figure 128 shows an easily made earth-rammer and sod-beetle combined, that will be found useful in a garden. For firming earth it is used mostly in a perpendicular position, striking the soil with the heaviest end; but in setting sods evenly, these are struck mostly with one of the flat sides. It is worked out of a solid piece of five by five scantling, and about four and a half feet long.

In laying sod, the surface of the ground should first be slightly loosened with a rake to make a bed for the grass roots, and if dry, sprinkled as fast as the turf is brought. The best turf is that taken from a pasture lot or roadside, that has been kept low by grazing. That where sheep have been pastured is preferred, as these animals, by their habit of biting close to the ground, destroy the coarse weeds. The better way of taking up the turf is to have the sods in long pieces, and to roll them up. In cutting the sod some gardeners use the line, and others a board with a straight edge, in order that the cutting may be accurate. The board has this advantage, that it may be a foot wide, and then it can serve as a guage for width without any further measuring, by cutting closely along the sides. First, the cut should be made lengthwise with a sharp spade or turfing iron. Then starting at one end, one man with a sharp spade should cut the roots, so that the sod will be about an inch and a half thick, the assistant grasping the end and rolling it up, the grass side inwards, keeping on as the cutting proceeds, until a roll as large as it is convenient to handle is gathered. Where one man works alone, he may separate the sod by thrusting the spade in from the side, afterwards rolling it up. These rolls are readily transported, and quickly unrolled and laid, leaving the lawn surface with few seams, as compared with cutting the turf in square pieces. Sodding may also be as well done by using square sods that are cut about a foot or fifteen inches square.

In laying the sod, join all edges carefully, using a large knife in cutting. As the laying proceeds, if some portions of the turf happen to be a little thinner than others, soil should be worked underneath such parts. The different pieces should all be snugly pushed together as the work goes on. After being properly laid, all parts should be beaten with a wooden beetle, and afterwards well rolled. All of these operations are to be followed by a heavy sprinkling of water to encourage a new growth. Along the line of walks, drives, and borders, the turfing should be carried a little beyond the line, as it will be when finished, so that in dressing down the edges afterwards, the cutting will be through good, strong sod.

Where lawns are made by seeding, the work is commenced by turfing. All along walks, drives, borders, and wherever there is a termination in the grass plat, not otherwise bounded, a strip of turf about a foot wide should be laid down, as suggested in the preceding paragraph, for making a firm edge. But the ground where this edging strip of turf comes, should be cut down the thickness and width of the sod that its surface may be even with the part to be sown. Do not remove the soil quite as deep as the sod is thick, as some allowance should be made for compression in beating. All terrace slopes must be sodded also over their entire surface.

When ready to sow the seed, the surface should be passed over with the rake and mellowed up a little on the top to receive the seed. It is a common error to use grass seed too sparingly. It is better to use four or more bushels to the acre, than less than four.

As to kinds, where it is known that any one sort does well, it is best to sow only that one kind, as a rule Red Top or Bent grass, or Blue grass, are generally preferred. Where it is thought best not to depend on one alone, then several kinds should be mixed. Some always sow a little White Clover with the grass seed, for the greenness it maintains in drouths, but wherever lawns are kept watered this should not be added. The different grasses and their adaptability, are described in Chapter IV, of Part II.

In sowing, the seed should be divided into two portions, half to be sown by passing over the land in one direction, and then, after lightly raking over the surface, pass over the piece again, sowing the remaining half cross-wise. After the seed is sown, the rake should be again applied lightly, or else the surface should be gone over with a brush harrow, and after this let a thorough rolling be given.

The earlier the lawn can be seeded in the spring, provided the ground is dry enough to work well, the better. By sowing in March, or early in April, a respectable lawn may usually be established by mid-summer. The great advantage of early sowing is, that the seeds and young plants have the benefit of spring rains and cool, growing weather. I have made fair lawns by sowing in the middle of June, in hot, dry weather, with the use of plenty of water and a sprinkler, but at best it is up-hill work at such a time. Early fall sowing is generally successful. Some advise the sowing of a thin sprinkling of oats, along with the grass seed to shade the young grass. This sometimes has a very favorable effect.

As the grass starts up, and weeds with it, the mower must be kept at work on the new lawn. The weed seed lying in the ground usually comes up quickly, and will prove annoying for a while, but if the grass was sown thickly enough, and the mowing, together with going over the lawn and cutting out coarse growing weeds, is attended to for the first season or two, the lawn will come out all right in the end.

On the general care of lawns see Part V.

CHAPTER XXXIV.

WALKS AND DRIVES.

Good dry walks and roads are a great comfort about the home. As soon as the lawn is sown or sodded, with an edging of firm turf along the roads and walks, the work of construction may commence. The first thing to do in the way of putting down walks or drives is to cut the turf edge to the exact width desired. In principle of construction there is little difference between the two; but the walk being narrower and not subject to so severe usage as the driveway, there may be a little difference in details.

Stone flagging, asphaltum, and other composition walks are generally put down by those who follow making them as a business, hence there is no need of directions concerning their construction.

For ordinary walks and drives in pleasure grounds, those made of gravel are most common in all but small lots, and are perhaps the best. They are comparatively inexpensive, pleasant in use and easy to make. They should be constructed with a view to firmness, and with such a shape of surface, that water from rains and melting snows will be absorbed or promptly pass off.

The depth of excavation in making a walk, will depend somewhat on the nature of the sub-soil. If this be dry and absorbent, such as gravel or on high-lying rock with seams, then an excavation of a foot deep, or even less

Fig. 129.—DRAINS TO ROADS.

will be sufficient for walks, and no attention need be paid to under-draining them. But if the subsoil be retentive, such as clay, and requiring drainage, then the depth in the lowest parts where the drains come (see fig. 129), should be about fifteen inches deep, and one foot deep in the highest parts of the bottom. Underdrainage to walks may be provided as shown in figure 129, either in the center or at the sides. In this figure, two styles of drains are shown, one of tile and the other formed of stones. Often such surface drainage as is described a little further on in speaking of drives, is all that is provided for walks, and with satisfactory results, making a saving in the labor of construction.

Before laying any underdrains for walks, the surface of the opening should be so shaped as to descend towards the drains. The drains for walks may be made to communicate with a general system of drains. After being laid, the excavations are to be filled up with stones, large gravel and similar materials, to within four or six inches of the top. The lower layer of stones may be set regularly on their ends, as shown in figure 129, and if this is well done, the finer stones and gravel working into the chinks will cause them to bind.

The space above the coarse material should be filled in with good gravel of a size ranging from that of peas up to that of marbles. This may be obtained by screening, if gravel of the right size is not at hand. Any coarse gravel that comes from screening, may go at the bottom. In putting down the gravel, a little still firmer material, such as sand or a sprinkling of loam, or even fine clay, should be incorporated with it—all excepting a finishing coat to be laid on last—to cause it to pack. The gravel as it is wheeled in should be leveled with shovel and rake, and then thoroughly rolled with a heavy roller, wetting it freely as the rolling goes on, to aid in the packing. By such a course a walk can be made that will feel almost as firm to the foot as stone and be easier to walk on.

The walk as finished should come up to within half an inch or an inch of the grass at the edges, and it should be rounded up to be some higher in the middle, just how much higher may be a matter of taste, as well as one governed by the width of the walk. Straight walks are not generally made as rounding as curved ones. If we take an inch and a half as the average increase of hight in the center for a six-foot walk—going above this for serpentine walks, but a little less for straight ones, the hight will not be far out of the way. On width of walks and drives see Part III.

In road making, while the general material may be the same as that used in walks, the proportions throughout are on a heavier scale. As a rule, provision for draining

cf roadways is made by surface drainage—that is, gutters
are constructed along the sides, and sufficient roundness
cf surface of the road is maintained to easily incline the
water into these.

Fig. 130.—STONE PAVEMENT
ON SAND.

Figure 130 shows the con-
struction of a common stone
pavement bedded in sand. In
Europe one often meets with
paved walks, made of narrow
stone chips, with the surface
that comes to the top, dressed straight. These pave-
ments are comfortable to walk on, neat looking, and
there is no wear out to them.

Figure 131 represents a cross section of the favorite
roadway for pleasure grounds, parks, and cemeteries,
known as the Telford Road.
An excavation is made from
eighteen inches to two feet
deep, to receive the material
of the road. The body consists
of large stones set regularly
over the bottom, then broken
stone, averaging the size of a

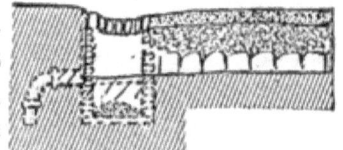

Fig. 131.—SECTION OF TEL-
FORD ROAD.

hen's egg, makes a middle course, and on top of this
is placed a finishing coat of about four inches of gravel.
The whole is made firm by hammering and rolling as
the work proceeds. The gutters consist of small sized
paving stones at the surface, set in a water-settled body
of sand.

In all roads or walks with gutters at the sides, as well
as at any low places, provision should be made for carrying away the accumulation of surface water. For this
purpose silt basins or lodges constructed of brick and
connecting with drains in the ground, are placed at
required points. In figure 131, the cross sectional outline of such a reservoir is shown. It should have a mova-

ble silt grate on the top, placed on a level with or a little lower than the bottom of the gutter. The basin may be eighteen inches or more across and three to five feet deep. The pipe connecting this with the drain below, should

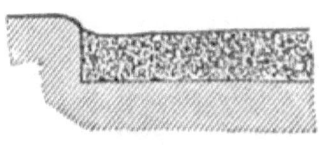

start from the basin at a foot and a half or more above the bottom, and in this space, any gravel or other washings can sink, to be removed occasionally by lifting the grate away.

Fig. 132.—SECTION OF
MCADAM ROAD.

Figure 132 shows a cross section of the true McAdam road, a road built up solid with small broken stones firmly rolled.

CHAPTER XXXV.

PREPARATION FOR SPECIAL PURPOSES.

As the shelter of masses of wood in breaking the gales of winter, admits of our growing a much larger variety of ornamental trees and plants, than would be possible without it, so too we may further enlarge the list of suitable garden materials by attention to some of the special wants of plants as to soil and other conditions.

ORDINARY BORDERS AND FLOWER BEDS.

The soil best suited to the large majority of all flowering plants, shrubs and trees, is one that is not too heavy, is friable, deeply dug, and well enriched with decomposed manure. Many failures in plant-growing come from not having the beds rich enough. In making new borders or preparing flower beds, the wild garden, etc., if the soil was not well manured at the first, then a coat of two or three inches of old and fine manure should be applied and well worked in. Some fine leaf mould from the woods could not fail to be greatly beneficial.

FERNS, RHODODENDRONS, ETC.

The plants brought under the head of "Ferns and other Shade-loving Plants" in Part II, as well as Rhododendrons, Kalmias, Andromedas, and some others, to do well, require a soil largely composed of vegetable matter, such as leaf mould or peat. These plants mostly have fine, delicate roots, that like coolness and moisture, hence the soil should be rather light in texture, and if not naturally so, should be improved by the addition of sand, together with other materials. A composition of equal parts of light, sandy loam, and leaf mould taken up in hollow places in dry woods, or else good peat, and all thoroughly mixed, would suit them. Good drainage is also needed for this class of plants, and yet they must never be allowed to suffer from excessive dryness in seasons of drouth, but should receive an occasional thorough watering at such times.

Many of this class of plants prove to be so delightful, and do so well in a prepared soil, that it is worth while to be at some expense and pains to meet their wants by special preparation. Even if land is naturally heavy, money spent on making excavations two or more feet deep, and filling them with the soil they need, will be well spent. Most of these plants like partial shade, but some do not. Different beds may therefore be made in both the shade and sun, and then all can be accommodated. The soil described is well suited to the Japan and other Lilies, but these require sun.

THE ROCKERY, ALPINES, ETC.

There is a considerable list of Alpine and other beautiful plants, natives mostly of high elevations, that do better and are more effective if planted on rocky or other mounds than elsewhere.

The important points to be observed in preparing rockeries for plants, is to have the right kind of soil, and to so place the rocks that the roots of the plants can penetrate the soil to any desired depth. Usually the roots of this class of plants are fibrous and of great length. The soil, therefore, should be light and easily penetrable, as well as moderately rich. Some fibrous peat, leaf mould, gritty sand, and fine, sharp stones may be used in it to good advantage.

Figure 133 will show the manner of arranging the stones in such places. Even if but little space is left in any places between the stones, so long as a layer of soil

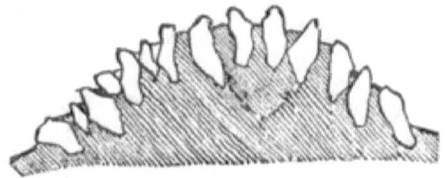

Fig. 133.—LAYING UP A ROCKWORK.

extends fully through to and connects with the body of soil below, it will answer. This is the important point in making rockwork of any kind. A pocket between rocks, with but a few handfuls of earth will dry out quickly, while one of similar appearance, but with the soil opening downwards, to give the roots access to moisture below, will keep the plants in good order in the dryest season.

Archways of rocks should be so constructed as to have some soil overlaying these, and some crevices filled with earth, however small in quantity, extending back to the body of soil; this will allow sedums, trailing tradescantias, and such plants to grow beautifully if started in the crevices.

Most of the Alpines delight in the sun and the lack

of much moisture, liable to occur in mounds.   But
where a rockery is made in the shade, many of the ferns
and wood plants are well adapted to the place.

In building rockwork, the stones should be arranged
with a view to suffering as little displacement from freezing in winter as possible.   Those buried in the soil should
have a large portion of their bulk underneath the surface.
The ground being generally elevated in such works, and
therefore dry, there is less danger of displacements than
if it were wet.

AQUATICS AND BOG PLANTS.

Provided the necessary water or moisture can be supplied, these plants in some or all of their kinds, prove interesting in the garden.   Where there are ponds, rills,
etc., in the grounds, very little preparation will be needed
to accommodate them.   The aquatics may be planted in
the water where it is about two feet deep, by anchoring
their roots to a stone and allowing them to settle to the
bottom together.   Bog plants may be set at the borders
of the water.   If the ground is heavy along the shore,
some sand and peat, muck or sphagnum, should be worked
into it wherever plants are to be set.   Sarracenias and
many orchids especially, are benefited by having these materials, if not present naturally, incorporated with the
soil in goodly quantity.

But it is easy to grow any of the aquatics, even the
much-admired fragrant Water Lily, without having a
natural body of water on the grounds.   Any contrivance
that will hold sufficient water, from a tank of masonry
work to a wooden tub or second-hand barrel—a molasses
cask sawed in two would be excellent—will answer to
grow them.   In the famous Kew Gardens, near London,
there is a very successful aquarium, growing a large collection of hardy species, and it consists of a simple brick

wall laid up with cement, to make a water tank about two feet deep, with the walls strengthened by buttresses, at short distances apart along the sides.

In artificial constructions of this kind, six or eight inches of loam, leaf mould, or swamp muck, should be placed in the bottom in which to set the plants. They may be held in place by placing a few stones over the roots.

A soil that is not naturally disposed to hold a great amount of moisture, may be prepared by adding to it such materials as sphagnum, leaf mould or peat. If such a soil is kept constantly charged with moisture by watering, bog plants may be made to thrive in any part of the grounds. Certain plants of this kind are so attractive that any attention paid to securing them and supplying their wants will be well rewarded.

CHAPTER XXXVI.

GARDEN ARCHITECTURE.

Not having space in this book to treat on Garden Architecture at any length, I pass over the subject with only noting some brief points.

Whatever is introduced, we should aim at having it of good quality and workmanship. Nothing is more annoying to cultivated taste than a cheap effort at having something elaborate. Better have but little garden architecture, even if there is room for it, and let it be well made, than to have more structures of a cheap, flimsy character. Work simple in design, but substantial in quality, harmonizes best with garden scenery.

All structures, from a stone coping to an elaborate conservatory, should have a deep, well laid foundation. Even the garden vase or piece of statuary should not be used without a substantial foundation or base. The depth of foundations of buildings will depend somewhat upon the nature of the soil, but six feet is safe in any place, and four feet may do for light, open soils. In setting copings, the pieces of which are of considerable length, foundations need only be made at the places where the joints or ends of the stones come, instead of along the whole length.

Foundations for plant houses, arbors, or other wooden structures should be carried well above the surface, to ensure dryness to the sills. A base board may be allowed to project down over the stone work if it be desired, to hide it, and this can be replaced whenever it begins to show signs of decay, where it comes in contact with the earth.

All planed wood-work should be thoroughly painted or, if finished with the natural surface, oiled. Oil finish is very pleasing about the garden, but in time it turns to a dull, dark color, and then it may be painted. The best colors for garden work are plain, unobtrusive ones. The grays and browns of stones, rocks, and tree trunks, show what colors are most in harmony with natural garden beauty. Such faint colors may be aimed at, and if lightened or otherwise varied to please the taste, are usually satisfactory. The bright green often met with in urns and trellises is in poor taste. It is a color for wire baskets that are to be hid in a protruding lining of moss, or may be tolerated in light wire screens, to be covered with verdure, but not elsewhere. Bronze is unobjectionable for garden iron work.

In employing rustic work in the garden, whether it is constructed on the grounds or bought ready made, let it be firmly put together, and braced with all the nails clinched. In its manufacture, the material is irregular and hard to nail or fasten, especially in hard-wood, and so far as appearances go, that which is poorly put together may look as well as the best, while in point of durability it is really very inferior.

PART IV.

MAINTENANCE.

GARDEN OPERATIONS ARRANGED BY MONTHS.

Half the secret of keeping a pleasure garden in proper condition, consists in duly regarding the little things that ought to be done, and of doing all work at the right time. In the pages which follow, the matters that relate to keeping up a garden are classified by months for the entire year, as a convenient guide to the work. It may not always be found, with our variable seasons and climate in different parts of the country, that the work under each month will be appropriate to that month for every place, but the arrangement at the least is valuable as showing about what needs doing at any time. The great merit of such a calendar is, that it enables the manager of the garden to anticipate the work, so that when the time arrives for doing, be it a little earlier or later than indicated, there may be preparations for it.

CHAPTER XXXVII.

JANUARY.

AN OUTLOOK.

At this season we stand on middle ground, between the past summer and the one to come, and it is an excellent time to consider any improvements it would be desirable to make during the new year. Flower beds to be filled with bedding plants may be studied for new ar-

15   (337)

rangements of their contents, as it is desirable to make changes here at times. Plans to guide such work are given elsewhere, and these may be the means of suggesting still other forms. Some of the most attractive beds are those planned by their owners. And yet original or untried plans should always be entered upon guardedly, as sometimes plants which look well on paper, fail to be satisfactory on the grounds. Look over the lists of garden materials with a view to new introductions. Much pleasure comes from extending ones acquaintance among trees, shrubs, and plants, and the true lover of a garden hardly feels satisfied unless making some additions to the collection every year.

PRELIMINARY PROVISIONS FOR STOCK.

The arrangement of the garden for the coming year being decided upon, then guage all purchasing of stock accordingly. Where many bedding plants are to be bought, usually by going to a florist now with the lists, contracts can be made for stock to be delivered at planting time, at lower rates than if bargained for at that time, besides the advantage of being able to get just what is wanted, a thing not so sure in the spring. Any hardy nursery stock that may be needed, had better be ordered soon, as early comers receive attention first at the nurseries, and it is a great advantage to have such stock at hand early in the spring. The same principle will apply to ordering seeds, and most other supplies for the garden.

OUTSIDE WORK.

Little can be done outside in the garden this month in the North. Whenever mild weather allows, pruning may be done, directions for which appear under February. It is a good time to lay in a stock of manure, and calculations should be made for such a supply, so that some which is old and rotten may always be on hand.

PESTS.

If rabbits trouble trees, some blood sprinkled about, or liver or bloody meat rubbed on the trunks, will keep them off. Mice sometimes girdle trees and shrubs under the snow, which may be prevented by trampling down the snow close to the tree. Now is a good time to trap these pests, as their food is scarce and they are easily tempted by bait. Destroy the eggs of the destructive caterpillar if any are seen around the twigs of trees, near the ends.

CHAPTER XXXVIII.

FEBRUARY.

PRUNING DECIDUOUS TREES AND SHRUBS.

In the South, pruning of all kinds of deciduous growths may take place at any time in the winter, while at the North mild weather in February and March is the preferred time with most gardeners. Pruning is an operation not invested with mystery, as is too much supposed. The cutting is based upon this principle: as trees and shrubs develop buds along the branches, so the cutting away of any part of a branch necessarily confines future growth to the remaining buds, and with the effect usually of improving both the shape and vigor of the growth. It is necessary, to be sure, to exercise judgment as to where the cuts should be made, and the operation must also be adapted to different kinds of plants and for different purposes, but beyond this there is no secret about this matter.

Trees, which it is desirable to make bushy, should have the ends of their branches cut back occasionally. Almost the entire list of moderate sized trees may be kept of compact and beautiful proportions—adapting such as would otherwise increase to be too large for small spaces —by this means. The Alders, Globe Acacias, Flowering Peaches, Camperdown Elm, Fountain Willow, and some others have need of a frequent or annual going over, to keep them symmetrical and shapely where such a form is desired. Rapid, slender growing trees, like the Silver and Cut-leaved Maples, Scarlet Oaks, Weeping Linden, etc., should, while young and growing fast, be headed-in several times to cause them to grow bushy. By such a course, there will be less danger of their limbs breaking from the ice and snow which sometimes gathers on them.

Trees near the house, or in streets, should usually have high heads, to allow of good views from the house and a free circulation of air. These should rarely be cut back, but a thinning out of lower branches before they become large, should be resorted to to effect openness underneath.

In any case where large branches need pruning away, the cut should invariably be made close to the trunk. To prevent splitting of the stump and possible injury to the tree by the weight of the branch at falling, first cut or saw half through the branch from below, about nine inches out; after this saw in from the top near to the tree until the limb falls, and then make a new clean cut close to the trunk, afterwards thoroughly coating the surface with thick paint, melted grafted wax, or shellac varnish, to keep out air and moisture. By such means the formation of new growth over the scar is encouraged, and in time this wound may have the appearance of any other part of the trunk—a vast improvement over the horrid stubs of branches, which are often seen projecting out a foot or two from the tree. Should the coating referred to be neglected, permanent injury may easily come to the tree from rain soaking in through the scar, causing it to rot at the heart. These instructions may in general apply also to the cutting away of small branches.

In simply heading-in small shoots of either trees or shrubs, it is well to make the cut just above and rather close to a bud, so that no wood will project beyond after the buds starts into growth.

Almost all kinds of trees, with close-growing heads, may by pruning low at the start, be kept shrub-like in general form, with the head starting at the ground. In any large garden some Maples, Oaks, Beeches, Planes, Horse-chestnuts, etc., are very pleasing in this shape, when growing on knolls or at one side of ample areas of grass.

In shrubs, while the careful training of some to partake of tree-like forms, with low, clean trunks, is desir-

Fig. 134.—NEGLECTED SHRUBS.   Fig. 135.—SHRUBS PROPERLY PRUNED.

able for the sake of variety—and almost any kind can be thus grown if pains are taken—still the bush form is ordinarily the preferable one.

Figure 134 shows forms of shrubs often met with, which have been allowed to grow at random and straggling by inattention. Lilacs, Snowballs, Purple Fringes, etc., of this shape abound; by pruning, they might exactly as well be kept in such pleasing forms as are indicated in figure 135. While generally, rounded outlines like these must be regarded as the finest for the flowering shrubs, each kind has peculiarities of habit, which should be preserved in a measure when the knife is used among them.

Those not familiar with the pruning of shrubs, often err from not cutting enough at each time the job is done. So long as a small number of buds are allowed to remain towards the base on any young branch of one or several season's growth, there is little danger of pruning too severely for the good of the plant. In the engravings, figures 136 and 137, two single stem shrubs are shown by the entire lines—or they may serve to represent branches at pruning time, and two places of cutting such stems, are indicated by cross lines. The first of these, figure 136, is badly cut as a timid pruner might do the work. The

Fig. 136.—
BADLY PRUNED.

Fig. 137.—
PROPERLY PRUNED.

second shows the right principle of cutting, where a fine bushy growth is desired. By cutting away only at the top, an ill-shaped, top-heavy new growth, as indicated by the dotted lines of figure 136 results, because upper branches have a tendency to grow strongest. But if we make the cut away down, vigorous branches, and fewer start out, and near the base, causing a low and vigorous growth as figure 137 shows.

This principle applies to the pruning of about every ordinary kind of vegetable growth, and amateurs should heed it as they are about handling the knife and shears.

But at the outset, in pruning shrubs, a certain difference of habit in the various kinds as to the manner of flowering should be observed, if we would gain the best results. One class of shrubs produce their flowers from buds that were formed in the previous season. Another class flower from buds that appear on the new wood of the current season. Of the first class, those of which

the flower-buds are prepared beforehand, some of the
principal are :

Lilacs.	Dwarf Almond.
Weigelas.	Snowy Mespilus.
Mock Oranges.	Leatherwood.
Calycanthus.	Privets.
Cornelian Cherry.	Viburnums.
Golden Bell.	Rhododendrons.
Honeysuckles.	Kalmias.
Flowering Currant.	Andromedas.
Flowering Peach.	Azaleas.
Deutzias.	Daphnes.
Dogwoods.	Dwarf Horse-chestnut.
Japan Quince.	Flowering Crab.

If these shrubs are pruned at this season, the flowers
will all be cut away. If the last year's growth of wood
was strong, some pruning of the branches by shortening-
in may be done, and yet enough buds remain for a fair
show of flowers. But the best way to prune these, is to
give them, once in every three or four years, such a severe
heading-in, in whole or part, as may be needful to
establish a good general form, and then regulate the
growth year by year, with summer pruning. (See notes
for June).

Of shrubs that flower upon the current season's growth,
the following are leading kinds :

Rose of Sharon, or Althæas.	Coronillas.
Burning Bush.	Amorpha.
Hypericums.	Bladder Senna.
Fall-flowering Spiræas.	Genistas.
Hydrangeas.	Roses.

Flowering Locusts.

The pruning of these may be as close as you choose
at this season, without detriment to the flower crop. Indeed, most of the kinds will flower all the more freely

during the coming season, if closely cut back. Some, like the Altheas and the Panicled Hydrangea, need this every year to prevent them from growing unshapely.

By discriminating between these two classes of shrubs, and adapting the pruning to the peculiar habits of each, then heeding the instructions on Summer Pruning given in June, no one ought to find any difficulty in pruning his shrubs satisfactorily.

Climbers on buildings, arbors, etc., need but little, and in fact as a rule no regular pruning. If they get thin and straggling, then the free use of the knife will work good results in the way of closer growth. Those on trellises and other places of limited extent, can be controlled to any desired degree by the use of the knife.

Deciduous Hedges may be trimmed at this time. The notes under April on trimming evergreen hedges are appliable in a large measure to these also. Honey Locust and Osage Orange hedges may be formed of a good size soonest by allowing the plants to grow untrimmed, until they are an inch through at the ground, and then cutting them down almost to the ground, somewhat as is shown in figure 137. Such treatment causes a vigorous new growth to start up, which will develop into a well formed hedge very quickly. Such hedges in after years must be trimmed annually the same as any other kinds of hedges.

MANURE.

Whether gardening for pleasure or profit, the ground must not be cropped year after year, not even of grass on the lawn, without returning some equivalent in the shape of manure. Hauling in a year's supply of manure may be done at any time during the winter. Every garden, unless a very small one, should have its manure-heap in some out-of-the-way, yet convenient, place. As to kinds, well decomposed stable manure, if it can be procured, even at a good deal of trouble, should be preferred to all others. Guano and superphosphates in moderate quantity are well enough, but if used alone—especially in heavy land—they do not provide that openness of the soil that tends to the retention of moisture, and the admission of air, so essential to perfect vegetation. Cow droppings, a year or upwards old, that have been turned occasionally to aid in decay, form the best of all manures. In time it will become as fine as the soil, and provision should be made to have a supply of this on hand for top-dressing the lawn, mixing with potting soils and other uses. Of the artificial manures, those composed largely of bone and other animal matter should be preferred. True and so-called Guanos of different kinds are in the markets, and these are mostly very good. Sometimes good street scrapings or similar matters are easy to procure; these, if allowed to lay a while, with an occasional working over, prove valuable for mixing with the soil or sub-soil. Refuse hops from breweries, after laying awhile and being forked over a number of times, become as fine and useful a manure as can well be found; it possesses high fertilizing properties. The same is true of decayed leaves from the woods, excepting that it takes a much longer time for these to become reduced to a fine friable mould.

RUSTIC WORK, TRELLISES, ETC.

Repairing and improving of these should be done before the press of other spring work comes on. Root rustic work, having shaved surfaces, ought to receive a coat or two of linseed oil yearly. Vases, trellises, or other painted garden work may now be put in order, by cleaning and painting. Prepare new trellises in good season. Plant-boxes, stakes, labels, and such things as will be needed during spring and summer, should now be made ready.

CHAPTER XXXIX.

MARCH.

THE LAWN.

As soon as the snow and frost leave the ground, and a few dry days have taken off the excess of moisture, all grass plats should be cleaned of any remaining fall-applied manure or other litter, by the use of the rake, and rolled to remove the roughness they usually present after winter. In many places fall manuring of the lawn is very reasonably objected too on account of the presence of the unsightly coat for so many months. Where this is the case, manure may be applied as soon as the snow leaves in the spring, and by leaving it on through the spring rains the benefits derived will nearly equal those of fall manuring, and the lawn be disfigured for a few weeks only.

GRAVEL WALKS.

Go over with a heavy roller, after the frost is gone, to settle them. Once in every three to five years the surface of the gravel ought to be turned over and rolled down again to give it new shape.

SHRUBS AND TREES.

There need be no hurry to uncover tender or newly planted shrubs and trees that have been protected. The alternate freezing and thawing they are subjected to in severe, late springs, is very injurious. When uncovered, they should at once receive any pruning they may need. If the general pruning of the hardy shrubs and trees has not yet been done, it should receive early attention.

ROSES.

After hard freezing weather is over, roses should be pruned. In the South this may be done earlier than March, in the North April may not be too late. When the winter covering is removed, pruning should follow; this should be governed by the kinds and the objects in view. Most of the monthly roses, such as the China, Bengal, and Noisettes, that may have wintered safely, should be cut back to mere stumps, leaving one to three eyes on each stem. The strength of the plant will then go into these, making strong shoots, loaded with an abundance of flowers. With the Bourbons and Hybrid Chinas, the shoots should be left with six or eight eyes, and by bending down the lower shoots they will form fine heads.

The Hybrid Perpetual and June Roses should have all decayed and weak wood cut out. Any crowded branches that will prevent the light and air from freely penetrating to the center, should be cut out. The remaining shoots, which are to produce flowers, should then be cut back to about six eyes from the base, or if the shoots are very strong, a few more may be allowed to remain. The pegging down system of managing these and the Bourbon Roses is usually very satisfactory. All shoots older than those of last year, should be cut away, and these that remain should be bent down, with the ends pegged to the ground or tied to stakes. By this treatment no other cutting back is needed, except to trim away weak and unshapely shoots.

Moss Roses will bear about the same treatment as the last named class, whether grown as bushes or pegged down, and they may be yet closer pruned. But this will not apply to the Princess Adelaide variety, which must not be severely pruned.

The Yellow Roses scarcely require any pruning, further than to remove dead and weak shoots. If the plants assume an unshapely form, they should be so pruned as to make a better head, even if it be at the expense of some flowers for the following season.

The Climbing Roses need only to have the poor wood cut away, and the strongest shoots shortened in. Nail and re-nail as needed, before the young growth starts.

BORDERS.

Early in the spring, any covering that was put on these in the fall, should be removed. Do not dig the soil until it is dry enough to work up loosely. Each spring, at the first working of the soil, a little rich manure—the older and finer the better, should be dug in.

IMPROVEMENTS.

Any contemplated garden improvements should be completed as soon as the ground will work well. Avoid working the soil when it is wet, as bad effects will be manifest for the entire season. Sodding may be done very early in the spring.

ANNUALS AND BULBS.

As soon in the spring as the soil will work up finely, whether now or later, bulbs of the Gladiolus for an early crop of flowers, may be planted, and seeds of most of the hardy annuals be sown in the open border. For this purpose drills from one to two inches deep should be opened, in which the seeds should be scattered along quite thickly, afterwards covering them with earth. If the soil where the drills are made is inclined to be lumpy, cover the seeds with some light mould that has been run through a fine sieve, and to which some sand has been added. After covering, press the soil quite firmly with the back of a hoe, or by patting it with the garden trowel. If the soil in which the seeds are sown is quite damp, watering it afterwards is not necessary, but otherwise this should be done, afterwards scattering a slight covering of clean straw, hay, or moss, over the watered parts, to retain moisture and prevent baking by the sun. But this covering must be taken off as soon as the young plants appear. Sometimes I have watered the bottom of the drill before dropping the seeds ; after covering with fine soil no further watering is necessary ; this method has always resulted well.

INSECTS, ETC.

Canker worms begin to ascend the trees as soon as the ground thaws. Any protector that is so contrived that they cannot get over it, placed around the tree, is the only sure preventive against their ravages. Mosses and Lichens on the bark of trees may be washed off with ley or soap suds.

CHAPTER XL.

APRIL.

PLANTING.

Early April, whenever the season is open, is the best time for planting trees, shrubs, and hardy plants, and the work should go on as soon as the soil is in good condition and the stock is at hand. If trees, etc., are set now, while the vegetation is yet inactive, there is a chance for the roots to become established in a more natural way, than if the setting is deferred considerably later, and the chances against loss are greatly lessened. Evergreens may be set several weeks later than deciduous trees, but the sooner even these are planted the better. For directions on planting see Part IV.

LAWNS.

New lawns may be started by seeding or sodding. Old lawns should be well rolled and thoroughly raked to remove the dead grass or manure, and to liven up the surface. The grass will start rapidly with warm weather, and the mower should be put in action as soon as needed.

PRUNING EVERGREENS.

Now is a good time for this work. If Spruces, Hemlocks, Firs, Arbor Vitæs, Junipers, and Japan Cypress, are in places too contracted to allow of their full development, they may be clipped every year and kept at almost any desired size. By thus cutting them they grow dense and handsome, which is very desirable, especially with that general favorite, the Norway Spruce, for this tree, without pruning, in time assumes an open style of growth not pleasing for small grounds. In gardens and cemeteries it is best to treat this tree by heading it back, at about twelve feet in hight, to form dense rounded specimens. The Pines are rarely better for pruning, although some kinds, like the White Pine, are very tractable under the shears. Whatever kinds are being pruned, their natural form of growth should usually indicate the shape, such as trimming the conical growers to a cone, and so on.

As a rule, no cutting should be done further back than the last year's growth, although no harm is likely to come from so doing, if for any reason it seems best. Always cut a branch back to some strong bud, so that the new growth may start apparently from the end of the remaining part. If the growth ought to be stopped in any direction, with a view to securing symmetry or to have the tree thicken, this may be effected without the blemish of a cut, by simply removing the center bud.

If any kind of evergreen is becoming bare at the base,

it may be improved by severely cutting the leader and side branches. The beauty of an evergreen depends much upon being furnished with branches to the ground, and it is a very ungardener-like practice, intolerable to every correct notion of evergreen beauty, to prune away the lower branches and expose a naked trunk.

Sometimes Pines are inclined to turn up a side shoot as a new leader. Such should be cut away, and in time the leader will come in the right place. If a leader in any conifer is lost by accident, another one may be had in its place, by tying a side shoot in an erect position. The American Arbor Vitæ, some of the Firs, as well as others, are inclined to form several leaders, and if allowed to do this they will assume a bad shape. By trimming all the branches, excepting the main one, that will be strengthened and better able to retain its position as leader.

EVERGREEN HEDGES AND CLIPPED TREES.

The most perfect form of a hedge for pyramidal growing kinds, is one that slopes more or less on the sides, as in figure 78, *A*, p. 232, thus admitting sun and light to the bottom, as well as the top. This should generally be the form for long hedges. The same engraving gives several forms suitable for shorter hedges of various kinds. In trimming, shears should be used, and the operation may be guided by the help of a stretched line, where precision is desirable, pains being taken to give it an even, unhaggled appearance. To allow a hedge to go untrimmed for a number of years, is certain to soon injure it beyond all remedy. Most hedge plants naturally grow to forty or more feet in hight, and to allow a row of these standing close in the hedge, to shoot up without check, is to bring disaster to the row in time.

The trimming of trees that are kept to definite forms, is not materially different in principle from that of hedges.

It should be done with care with a view to good form and evenness, going over the work several times if need be.

Box Edging may be reset in April or earlier. The ground where the line is to come should be rendered firm by treading or beating. Then a narrow trench is cut with great precision, the unbroken part on the line of the desired edging. The box plants pulled apart may have the ends of roots and tops clipped off a little, and then should be set along in the trench close together, and projecting an inch above the surface of the soil. Loose soil is then filled in by layers, and firmly trodden against the plants, until the trench is full. The edging should have the gravel of the walk brought up against it, so that no soil will show on the walk side of the line. If box edging is kept small by clipping—say to four or six inches in hight, it may last ten years without resetting. The edgings should be clipped annually at this season.

HARDY PLANTS.

These are benefited by being lifted, and divided if large, and set in new positions every three years for strong growers, and every five years for others. Clumps of such kinds as make many fibrous roots and numerous buds, may be divided with a sharp spade, leaving half a dozen or more eyes on each piece. Those that have large or coarser roots need more care. A knife should be used on these, taking care that each piece of root to be reset has at least one eye.

FLOWER BEDS.

Those to be planted with tender bedding plants may be worked over and made friable as a preparation towards receiving the plants later. By doing this now, the ground will be in a fine condition at planting time, besides the beds will look better if thus treated. See Annuals under **March.**

WEEDS.

The fight against weeds should commence with their first appearance. Some kinds, like the Chickweed, and Shepherd's Purse, start up early, and soon develop flowers and seeds, to make trouble afterwards if not kept down by cultivation. See Weeds under May.

ROCKWORK.

If the rocks have become disturbed by the action of the frost during winter, they should at once be put in order.

HARDY AQUARIUMS.

The ground in these should be kept covered with water in increasing quantity as the plants start into growth.

CHAPTER XLI.

M A Y .

THE LAWN.

The care of the lawn will be about the same for every month, from now until the end of the season, and will consist chiefly in keeping it properly mown, watered, and free from weeds. When the grass grows rapidly it will be necessary to mow about every week. It is always better and more economical of labor, to cut the grass when only two inches high, than to wait until it is four or six. The present hand lawn mowers are greatly preferable to the scythe for mowing even quite small places. On large grounds the horse mowers may be used with economy. Still, in mowing some parts, as about thickets and trees, the scythe and sickle are indispensable helps.

In running a lawn mower, the operator should be particular to always set both sides at the same hight, so that the surface of the grass may be even when the work is done. That no lines of uncut grass should be left, ought to occur to every mower, yet lawns may sometimes be seen that show defects of this kind.

WEEDS.

A large share of the annoyance in gardening comes from weeds. It is really surprising how soon slight neglect will show multitudes of weeds in lawn, walks, and elsewhere. A little labor judiciously applied, will easily keep a place clear of these. A great secret is to attack weeds when they are small, so small that they will not require removal when cut off. If this is done at the right time, it will be less work to keep a garden thoroughly clean than to keep it half clean. Now weeds are gross feeders, and rob the garden plants of food and moisture. The best way to remove spreading weeds, like plantain, dandelion, docks, etc., from the lawn, is to cut them off just below the crown, disturbing the soil as little as possible. Any holes that appear should be filled with earth, and the grass will soon spread over these spots. By cutting out every two weeks all that appear, every noxious weed may soon be exterminated, for no plant can live if its leafy or above ground portion is persistently destroyed every time it appears. Coarse grasses, unfit for lawns, sometimes start up from seeds carried in by the wind, and these must be treated as any other weeds. Allowing any kinds of weeds to go to seed in the ornamental garden is the hight of mismanagement.

For ridding walks of weeds, salting is the best plan, except near the edges, where salt will kill the roots of grass or plants that come near, here they must be handpicked.

PLANTING OUT.

Every year there are those who, in their haste to see the tender flowers in bloom, subject them to the exposure of chilly, windy days or frosts, only to enfeeble them and injure their future usefulness. As a rule, in the North, few tender green-house plants or half-hardy annuals should be set earlier than May 25th, while long experience shows that nine times out of ten, all tender things, like Coleus, planted as late as the first of June, will go ahead and excel in size and beauty, those that were set two weeks earlier. Verbenas, Roses, Carnations, Pinks, Stocks, and other plants that are not affected by a slight frost, may be planted out several weeks earlier. Gladiolus, Tigridias, and Dahlias, may be planted any time in the month. Tuberoses should not go out before the 20th of the month.

SUB-TROPICAL GARDENS AND ROCKERIES.

The former may be arranged for the season, and the latter brightened with tender flowering kinds, and those with showy foliage, as soon as warm weather is established.

SEED SOWING.

Seeds of all the hardy and half-hardy annuals may be sown any time during the month, and those of tender annuals after the 10th of the month, and earlier in the South.

ROSES, INSECTS, ETC.

Towards the end of May, and later, insects will begin to trouble rose bushes. The Rose Saw-fly, especially in its caterpillar state, known as the Rose Slug, is one of the most annoying pests, but with attention to keeping them down, the plants may be saved from serious depredations. In the fly state they are of a shiny black color, about one-fifth of an inch in length, and found mostly on the under side of the leaves, or flying from bush to bush. The first young slugs hatch out usually about June 1st, and increase in number during the month. These are of a pale green color, almost transparent, and feed upon the leaves, which soon look as if they had been burned. Dry slaked lime scattered over the leaves while wet with dew is a most convenient remedy that often proves effectual ; but a more sure one may be had in frequently syringing the plant with whale oil soap dissolved in water in the proportion of one pound to eight gallons of water; many of the flies can also be destroyed with this solution if applied when they first appear. The Rose Chafer, or Rose-bug, is a troublesome insect, a small beetle, with a slender body, tapering before and behind, measuring near three-eighths of an inch in length, and covered with ashen-yellow down. They usually appear towards the middle of June, and remain from four to six weeks. About the only way of destroying these is to pass over the plants daily, shake or brush them into tin vessels containing water upon which a little kerosene is floating, or they may be gathered on sheets and burned.

Mildew is a fungoid growth which shows itself upon the leaves and small twigs. It has a gray mould-like appearance, and seems to be invited by anything that causes the growth of the plant to be suddenly checked. The ordinary agent for destroying mildew is flowers of sulphur dusted upon the leaves after wetting them, every few days, until no more is seen. Rust frequently troubles Roses in the garden, appearing on the leaves. Cut off and burn the infected branches.

SUMMER MULCHING.

Borders containing Rhododendrons, Lilies, and other plants that love coolness and moisture at the roots, should early in the season receive a heavy mulch of leaves, cut straw, bog-hay, or tanbark.

CHAPTER XLII.

J U N E.

PLANTING OUT.

Early June should see all the beds planted, as now everything may be trusted outside. Those who wait until the present month for setting out their tender plants, have the satisfaction of seeing them start off with a vigorous growth from the first.

ROSES.

This is the great Rose month. After the Remontants or Hybrid Perpetuals have bloomed, by shortening in the branches somewhat, the plants will be inclined to flower better in the autumn. Monthly Roses flower more freely as a rule, for having the branches pegged to the ground. Observe last month's notes on insects.

SPROUTS, SUCKERS, AND "SPORTS."

All through the growing season a look-out should be kept for sprouts that may start up from the roots of shrubs like Lilacs, Oleasters, etc., or from strong-growing kinds of stocks, such as are used for grafting or budding. The stocks of Kilmarnock and other Willows, Weeping Poplar, Roses, and many others, often throw up such shoots. These should be removed as they appear, for if allowed to get a start they draw vitality from the tree, at the expense of the budded or grafted part. Many persons are deceived by such shoots, and permit them to grow, which of course in the end can only result in damage or outright death to the improved and always somewhat feebler part. We may sometimes meet a coarse, wild Willow or Rose in pleasure grounds, that made its start in this way, the improved part of which died long ago. Some handsome shrubs like the Waxberry, bend down the tips of the branches, which take root; the plants thus formed should be treated as weeds, unless it is desired to multiply them, when they should be removed and cultivated elsewhere for later planting.

Most of the shrubs, trees, and plants, with variegated, cut, or curled leaves, are what are called "sports"—that is, they are departures from the ordinary forms of the plants, and which have been propagated for these peculiarities which are more or less distinctly fixed. There is sometimes an inclination in such growths to revert to the normal form, and this should be prevented by cutting out any parts that fail to show the peculiarity. The beautiful variegated-leaved Kerria and Waxberry, need rather close watching on this account.

CONTROLLING THE HABITS OF TREES AND SHRUBS.

The Junipers of erect habit are striking garden ornaments if of good forms. But sometimes they are disposed to spread out and receive damage by the lodging of snow in the centers. A few wires placed closely around them will obviate this trouble, and lead to good forms. Weeping trees, like the American Willow, Poplar, Ash, etc., may be improved in symmetry by extending a large hoop around the tree, to which the branches are brought and secured. When a tree is crooked or is disposed to lean from the perpendicular, it should be straightened while young, by tying it to a stake driven in at its side, or if it merely leans over, by the less conspicuous means of setting a short stake a little ways off, drawing the tree towards it by means of a wire, one end of which is attached to the tree by means of a leather strap, and the other end wound around the stake. It may be noted that crooks in young tree trunks naturally decrease as

the tree grows. Honeysuckles and other climbers, grown
as standards, by stopping the leading shoots at five or six
feet, should be furnished with stakes or supports as
needed.

SUMMER PRUNING.

Those shrubs which flower on last season's growth (see
Pruning under February), and which if pruned severely
in winter, are robbed of flower buds, may have their
growth controlled by summer pruning. This is best
done by shortening back the old wood just after flowering,
cutting out entirely any branches that seem to be useless
and in the way. By these means a free growth of young
wood for flowering the next year will be promoted. Then
later, throughout the growing season, any shoots that
grow too rank may be pinched back to control the form
of the shrub. The tendency of Fir trees to run up
tall and lose their lower branches, may be overcome by
cutting back the leading shoots occasionally. Early
summer pruning of the Norway Spruce, cutting away
one half of the young growth now, will lead to the starting
of many side buds on each, causing the tree to become
very compact.

HEDGES AND CLIPPED TREES.

Any treatment that tends to check the growth of these,
without impairing healthfulness, is desirable. Shearing
either evergreens or deciduous kinds, just as the present
season's growth begins to harden, has some such an effect.

THE LAWN.

Pains should be taken to have it well and evenly mowed.
Keep all verges properly clipped along the walks, borders,
and buildings. To leave this undone, is to give a place
a slovenly appearance. See under May and July.

WALKS AND DRIVES.

Keep them clear of weeds and litter. Roll those of gravel occasionally, and keep the edges tidy. Sprinkling the walks tends to agreeable coolness.

BORDERS AND FLOWER BEDS.

Tender bedding plants of every description should now be out. Hyacinths and Tulips produce better flowers if the bulbs are lifted after the foliage begins to wither, keeping them in a dry, cool place during summer, and resetting them again in October. Annuals that were sown in the border, should be thinned where they are crowded. Work the soil frequently to keep down weeds, and promote the growth of the plants. Small borders kept open around trees, need careful attention as regards this. See Flower Beds under July.

MISCELLANEOUS.

Save seeds from Pansies and other plants, and for fall flowers of Pansies, sow towards the end of the month. In the Wild Garden remove, or keep in check, coarse weeds. Keep Hardy Plant Aquariums supplied with water. Peg down Verbenas and Monthly Roses. Any young trees of a delicate nature are benefited by having their trunks protected from the hot sun for a few years, by matting bound around them, and a mulch over the roots. Provide Sweet Peas with trellises, and all other climbers with the needed support.

INSECTS.

Sometimes the white grub works much damage to the roots of plants. · If plants in the beds or border that were healthy, are seen to turn yellowish and cease growing, suspect the presence of the white grub and dig down, find, and kill it. Angle, and other worms, sometimes trouble lawns, and may be killed by slaking a half peck of lime in a barrel of water, and after it is well settled applying the clear liquid freely with a watering can. This lime water will also destroy the aphides that attack the roots of trees or plants, and in fact all soft bodied worms and insects, and do the most delicate plants no harm. If Plant Lice or Wooly Aphides appear on the stems and leaves, bend these down into a pail of tobacco or quassia water; if on the trunks and branches, use a brush, and vigorously apply the liquid. Ants are often troublesome, and may be destroyed by putting some fresh bones or a sponge saturated with sugar water in places where they resort, and after they collect upon and cover these, which they soon will do, drop them into boiling water or burn them. This should be repeated until all the ants are gone.

CHAPTER XLIII.

JULY AND AUGUST.

SUMMER WATERING.

Nothing can go farther towards making our gardens pleasant in summer, than to have the grass, plants, and trees in green, vigorous condition during the hot, dry spells, so common at this season. Where water is plenty this is easily accomplished. In watering lawns, means must be provided to conduct the water to all points where it is needed, and a contrivance must be provided for distributing it properly. Stands and distributing nozzles for this purpose are for sale by dealers. Late in the day is the best time to have the sprinkler in operation. Ter-

16

race slopes require some extra care, to have them properly watered at this season.

Trees and shrubs if thoroughly watered at times during dry weather, will repay the trouble, in greatly increased growth and beauty. Thorough watering is the means of getting large trees in a few years. The best time to water trees is during or immediately after a rain, because the atmosphere being then charged with moisture, water at the root does more good. Water thoroughly by giving each tree a half dozen or more bucketfuls. If there is no depression around the tree to hold water, puncture the soil with the tines of a spading fork, for a space as far across on the ground as the top of the tree is wide. In cultivated borders, the soil can be drawn back from each plant or tree to be watered, forming a basin about it, and filling it again and again with water, until there is enough. The next day the basin may be covered, and the surface of the soil mellowed with a rake.

In watering Flower Beds, where plants stand close together, the digging fork may be used for puncturing the soil to admit the water. Rockwork and the out-door fernery will require occasional waterings during dry weather. Supply hanging baskets, plant boxes, and vases with plenty of water at all times. Enough water should be used on these to thoroughly moisten every portion of the soil each time it is applied. Do not be satisfied when the surface looks wet, but be sure the earth is soaked to the very center.

Where there are no public water-works and connections for summer watering, every garden should have a handy water-barrow. For large grounds, the best form to choose is one with a removable tub, so that while one tub is being emptied another may be filling. The pumping of water by wind or other power into tanks sufficiently elevated to give a head for forcing the water through pipes and hose, all around a place, is easily arranged, affording a complete, economical, and independent water-works in every garden.

FLOWER BEDS.

These ought now be nearly or quite at their best, and the keeping of them in presentable shape will be one of the chief cares at this time. Carpet beds should be gone over every week, and the plants carefully clipped with a view to keeping them low and solid, and maintaining clearly defined lines between the different kinds in the design. This is work upon which a great deal of skill may be expended. Common shears, or sheep shears, having a spring to open them, are used. All clippings should be removed, as well as any weeds that may start up. To reach all parts of beds that are closely covered, a bridge consisting of a large plank supported at the ends must be used.

Cut away the fading flowers of all plants; if allowed to ripen seed, the flowering will be impaired—besides, faded flowers mar the beauty of collections. Double Balsams are more attractive if they have some pruning. Leave one, three, or five branches, as best suits the fancy, and cut away the others. If the first spikes of strong Gladiolus are cut when fairly in flower, they will usually throw up a number of new spikes.

SEED SOWING AND PLANTING.

There are a number of hardy plants that ripen their seeds by mid-summer, and if it is desired to propagate these, the seeds should be sown soon after they are ripe, or any time before the middle of September. Then the seedling plants will be strong enough to winter over in safety and flower the next season. Sow in a seed-bed of fine soil; keep watered and shaded until the plants are up. The Common or White Lily (*Lilium candidum*), should be transplanted now, as this is its natural season of rest.

MISCELLANEOUS.

Read instructions on care of lawn, walks, weeds, etc., of previous months. Dahlias, Gladiolus, Hollyhocks, and all tall-growing plants, should be provided with stakes as needed. Let them be simple, neat, and painted of some inconspicuous color. Remove the seed-pods of Rhododendrons early after flowering. Borers in Acacia and fruit trees should be dug out, whenever there are signs of their presence near the root. Aquariums must be kept filled with water to make up for evaporation. On Summer Pruning read the notes under June.

CHAPTER XLIV.

SEPTEMBER.

EARLY FROSTS.

In this month, in many parts of the country, we may look for the first touches of frost. As there is usually a good deal of fine, warm weather after the first frosts, flower-beds, plants, vases, etc , should be covered on nights when frost is threatened, with a view to keeping up the beauty for such later delightful spells of weather.

PLANTING DUTCH BULBS.

Planting at the approach of the fall and winter season seems so contrary to the general order of things to many, that this, the only course for securing fine collections of Tulips, Hyacinths, etc., is often neglected. The planting of such bulbs may be done at any time during the

months of September, October, and November, or even
later, provided the ground remains unfrozen. It is best,
however, to not defer the work much after the first of
October. Set Tulips five or six inches apart, and about
five inches deep. Hyacinths may be planted six or eight
inches, and Crown Imperials at a foot or more apart, and
at the same depth as for Tulips. Crocuses and Snow-
drops need not be more than two or three inches apart,
and about the same depth. Planting these in clumps is
the most effective way to arrange them. Crocuses and
other low-growing kinds may be planted about the lawn
in the grass, and will thus produce a pleasing effect early
in the season.

HARDY PLANTS.

Such kinds as have finished flowering and are past
active growth, may be taken up, divided, and reset during this month and the next. See notes on these under
April. By doing this early, the replanted portions have
a chance to become established before winter, and flower
better the next year than if divided in spring. This is
particularly true of Pæonies, which should be divided in
October.

CHAPTER XLV.

OCTOBER.

THE LAWN.

Grass usually grows with vigor during this month, and
the mowing must be kept up as needed. Because the
end of the season is near, do not allow weeds to start up
and disfigure the grass plat; keep late weeds from the
walks, drives, and borders.

BORDERS AND FLOWER BEDS.

Read the directions on Bulb Planting and Hardy Plants
for last month.   Take up Tuberoses, Dahlias, Gladiolus,
Cannas, Caladiums, Tigridias, Madeira Vines, Erythrinas,
a few days after the frosts have blackened the plants.
All of these, excepting Erythrinas, should be dried off in
the shade, and when perfectly dry, stored until spring.
The best place for them is one that is cool and dry, and
there is nothing better to pack them in than dry sand.
Gladiolus and Tigridias may go into paper bags.

As soon as the flower-beds become disfigured by frosts,
clear them, coat the surface with manure, and dig them
over for the winter, leaving the clods of earth from the
spade or digging fork unbroken during this operation,
so that the air and frost may have full effect on the soil
during winter.   The freezing of the water, held by the
earth in this shape, causes its small particles to be
rent asunder, just as the freezing of sap in plants lacer-
ates the vessels, and makes the texture of the soil more
friable the next year.   In borders, where shrubs and
hardy plants are growing, the digging should not be
done near to them so deeply as to injure the roots.

AUTUMN SEED SOWING.

Early in October, seeds of Sweet Alyssum, Callirrhoë,
Candytuft, Centaurea, Clarkia, Larkspur, Lupines, Mig-
nonette, Nemophila, Portulaca, and lawn grasses, may
be sown wherever the soil is well drained and not heavy.
Then they will start up early in the spring, and in the
case of the annuals, will flower freely, much earlier than
will spring sown ones.   In the South and on the Pacific
Coast, all hardy and half-hardy annuals may be sown in
the fall, and Gladiolus be planted.

SEEDLINGS.

Pansies and other plants from seeds sown in the summer, will be showing up well by this time. Early in the month they may be pricked out into beds of fine soil, at a distance of several inches apart each way, to allow them to develop into strong plants by winter. These, in the spring, may be set where wanted for flowering. Pricking out or dibbling small plants is frequently done in the garden. The dibble may be merely a smooth-pointed stick for small plants, as large as a finger. In using the dibble a hole is made, and in this the seedling is held, while the dibble is thrust into the soil a second time, in a way to crowd the earth firmly against the roots, afterwards pricking a little soil into hole number two, to even the ground. If a tip of a leaf will break when pulled, without bringing up the plant, it is considered firmly enough planted. After being thus set, the plants should be well watered.

IMPROVEMENTS.

Usually, now is the season of the year to make improvements and alterations, in the line of grading, draining, trenching, etc. The soil is often dry at this time, and the air cool and bracing, a state of things under which men and teams will do almost double the work they would if land is loaded with water, and the weather disagreeable.

Trees, shrubs, and hardy plants may be planted in October, where everything is ready for it. The earlier it is done after the tenth, the better, in order that they may gather up strength before winter. If the leaves remain at planting time, they should be stripped off before taking up the trees, etc. Evergreens seldom do well planted in the fall.

CHAPTER XLVI.

NOVEMBER AND DECEMBER.

FALL MANURING.

Every other year, or every three years, the lawn should receive a top-dressing of manure, and provided the right article of this is at hand, the fall months is the best time to apply it. The best top-dressing is an inch deep of thoroughly decayed manure, and if so old and fine that there will be nothing left to rake off in the spring, all the better. Objections to fresh manure are its offensiveness, and that it is liable to contain weed seeds, which will make trouble. If such manure is at hand, the applying of it may be deferred until February or March, for the sake of not having it on so long, while some prefer that time for applying any kinds of fertilizers. Bone manures are excellent for the lawn and free from weeds. Manure should also be applied occasionally as a surface dressing under plantations of all evergreen and deciduous trees and shrubs. Put on several inches here, and it will tell in increased vigor very perceptibly. Where it is desirable to do an extra job on specimen trees, the sod may have four or more cuts made into it in diverging lines from the tree, as far out as the limbs extend, and then each section of sod between the cuts be lifted and rolled up outwards all around, so as to expose the soil below. Then remove three or four inches of the soil, throw in some fine old manure at the bottom of the opening, and afterwards fill in the earth again and roll the sods in their place, to firm them down.

FALL PROTECTION.

The best time to apply any fall protection is in the last days before winter sets in, which is usually about the latter part of November. There are many trees, shrubs, and plants, that are hardy after they become well established, and the roots have had a chance to push below the frost line, that should be protected for a few years. Partial protection, by covering the surface over the roots with a mulch of straw, hay, or leaves, will be all that is needed by many kinds. Such a covering, four inches thick, is enough, and more might cause mildew. Shrubs that are tender. should also be protected with straw or matting above the ground. Bring the branches together, lash a cord around them, and place the straw about them for their entire length, completing by winding strong twine around the whole with the turns at short distances apart. If a tree with branches too large to be brought together into one bundle, is to be protected, then a number of different bundles may be made, afterwards drawing these together somewhat and binding them. Roses and other plants that can be bent to the ground, by taking away a spadeful of earth at the root on one side, may be protected by completely covering them with six inches of soil.

Many evergreen trees cannot well be brought together to bind with straw ; these may have boughs of any kind of evergreens placed over and against them to keep off sun and wind, which more than anything else injure evergreens in winter. A hood, made of seven-eighth inch matched stuff, as shown in figure 138, may also be used for such purposes. The lower growing evergreens may be covered by strewing straw over them. Globe-headed evergreens, like the dwarf Arbor Vitæs, and some others, are at times liable to suffer from snow lodging in the tops, causing the branches to spread out of shape. This may be prevented by nailing two boards of a suitable length into the form of a letter V, and then inverting this over them, lashing a cord around both, to bring

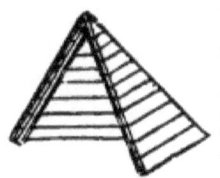

Fig. 138.—
A PLANT HOOD.

in the side branches somewhat. In protecting with ever-green boughs, thrust the ends into the earth, so that they will freeze fast and keep their positions.

Hardy Plants in the borders are benefited by a slight covering over the roots during the winter. In nature they are usually protected by leaves. Cover the surface with a light coat of straw, coarse manure, or leaves, and the plants will flower all the stronger for it. Fall-planted bulbs, like Hyacinths, should receive special attention in this respect. Such rather tender plants as Pampas Grass, the tender kinds of Liatris, Erythrina, Tritomas, etc., may be lifted and stored for the winter in dryish earth in the cellar, or any cool place where it does not freeze hard.

Artificial plant aquariums and fountains, that are in danger of being damaged by the water in them freezing, should have it emptied, and a shed of boards placed over the basins to keep out wet and snow. Before putting on this cover, fill up beneath with some straw or leaves, to keep the frost from injuring the masonry.

Heavy snows may injure shrubs and trees, if allowed to remain on them. Shake out accumulations of it, that are liable to freeze fast or turn into ice. If sleet gathers on the trees and there is danger of injury to them, prop up the branches in good time to obviate this. Young trees in places subject to sweeping winds, should be se-cured to stakes in the winter; to prevent injury by their being whipped and wrenched about.

INDEX.

GENERAL INDEX.

Alpine Plants....................332
Annuals, hardy, sowing 348
   Selections...... 156
April, Operations in............349
Aquatic Plants... 334
Architecture, American...........14
Arrangement.....................161
Associations, Rural Improvement 300
August, Operations in..... 361
" Beautiful Paris," a model......281
Beds. Raised Geometric... 214
Beetle, Sod.....................324
Bird Houses.....................243
Boat Houses... 244
Border, Arabesque....... 216
   Ribbon 215
   Scroll 215
Borders.........................331
Borders and Flower Beds.........360
Boulevards, Garden..............288
Boulevards of Paris... 282
Boundaries, Planting of.........196
Boundary Wall, Hidden...........177
Box Edging......................352
Bridge of Rocks............ 226
Bridges........................242
Carpet Bedding..................207
Carpet Beds. Plants for.. 213
Cemeteries, Garden..............301
Church Yards....................275
Cities, Shade Trees in...........20
Climbers as Festoons............205
   as Screens and Arches.....204
   on Arbors.................203
   on Fences and Gate-posts..200
   on Houses.................201
   on Verandas.... 203
   Pruning of................344
   Uses of...................169
Clipped Trees...............223-351
Clover, White 24
Conservatories..................245
Conservatory, Detached, Gothic..245
Conservatory over Bay Window....271
Coping, Stone...................238
Corners, Designs for 215
Curve Rod.......................311
Curves, to Lay Out..............311
December, Operations in.........368
Draining........................313
Drives.........................327
Dutch Bulbs, Planting of... 364
Evergreens, Pruning of..........350
Farms, Tree Planting on..........18
February, Operations in 339
Fence, Tight Board 239
Fences.. 236
   Hurdle....................237
   Sunken 177

Ferns, Hardy....................218
Ferns, Soil for.................332
Fertilizers 345
Float for Leveling..............320
Flower Beds............331-363
   and Borders............. ..366
   Designs for...............211
   Location of...............216
Flowers, Misuse of.... 209
Flowering and Ornamental Plants.206
Fountains.......................230
Front Lots, Adorning Small......249
Frosts, Early...................364
Garden Architecture.............335
Gardening, Ornamental, American
   Progress in........... 12
   Literature of..............11
   Materials of...............23
   Past, Present, and Future......9
   Profits of.................16
   Requirements of American...10
   Time Required for Effects....21
Gardens, Constructing...........308
   Hospital and Asylum... ...275
   Hotel.....................277
   Public Town.... 280
   Railroad Station..........278
   School....................273
Grass, Creeping Bent.............24
   Dog's Tail.................24
   Green or June.......... 24
   Kentucky Blue..............24
   Perennial Rye..............24
   Red Fescue.................24
   Red Top....................24
   Reed Canary................24
   Rhode Island Bent..........24
   Sweet Vernal...............24
   Tall Fescue................24
   Yellow Oat.................24
Grasses.........................24
   Agrostis alba. var. *stolonifera*..24
   Agrostis vulgaris.........24
   Anthroxanthum odoratum... ..24
   Avena flavescens.........24
   Cynosurus cristatus.......24
   Festuca elatior..........24
   Festuca ovina, var *rubra*.......24
   Lolium perenne 24
   Phalaris arundinacea 24
   Poa pratensis............24
Gravel Walks, Care of...........346
Green-house, Lean-to............246
Grotto, Artificial..............224
Ground, The, and the Grass........23
Grounds, A Corner Lot 253
   A Deep Front Lot..........251
   Adornment of Small........247
   and Street Level...........170

Grounds, Buffalo Park, Grounds near.262
     Final Shaping............ 316
     Farm made Park-like............263
     Five and one-half Acre Garden..255
     Four Acres on Hillside.......255
     Garden Front to Row of Houses.259
     Laying Out.....................310
     Three-fourths of an Acre......254
     Three long Lots form a Joint
       Garden......................260
     Work on......................312
Hanging Baskets.................268
Hardy Plants.................351–365
Hedges...........................231
     Evergreen...................351
     Pruning.....................344
     Stiles for...................233
Highways, Planting..............298
Home Buildings..................166
Hood for Protecting Plants.......369
Improvements, Planning.........308
Insects..........................361
     Canker Worms...............349
January, Operations in 337
July, Operations in.............361
June, Operations in.............357
Lakelet, Improved...............228
Lawn, Care of...............346–353
     Grouping on.................191
     Seeding.....................326
Lawns, French Method with.....217
Major and Minor Embellishments..162
Manure..........................344
Manuring, Fall..................368
March, Operations in............346
May, Operations in..............353
Miscellaneous Natural Materials..160
Mulching, Summer................356
Nature as a Teacher.............161
November, Operations in... ..368
October, Operations in..........365
Ovals, to Form..................311
Park, Central...................292
Parks, Small Town...............294
Pests...........................339
Plant Houses....................245
Plant Vases, Boxes, etc.........268
Planting, Manner of.............322
Planting, Time for..............320
Plants, Aquatic and Bog.........334
Plants, Planting out Tender.....355
Paris, Past, Present, and Future..283
Parks, Public...................279
Protection, Fall................368
Pruning Deciduous Shrubs........341
     Deciduous Trees.............339
     Summer......................359
Rabbits and Mice................339
Rhododendrons...................332
Rill, Improved..................229
Road-making.....................329
     McAdam......................330
     Stone in Sand...............330
     Telford.....................330
Rock Archway....................224
     Border......................221
     Bridge......................226
     Garden......................221

Rock Grotto 224
     work.......................220
     work. Making...............333
Rocks, Substitutes for..........227
Roof Gardens....................269
Roses...........................347
     Insects on..................355
Rural Improvement Association...300
Rustic-work.................336–345
Seat, Folding...................240
     Garden, Shaded..............229
     Stone or Marble.............240
Seedlings.......................367
Seed Sowing.....................363
     Autumn......................366
September, Operations in.......364
Shrubs, Comparative size of.... 25
     Deciduous................... 27
     Rate of Growth of....... 21–22
     Scatterings of..............195
     Use in Small Places.........252
     Utility of..................185
Slopes, Gauge for...............319
Snows, Danger from..............370
Soil, Preparing The.........315–331
Sports..........................357
Stiles..........................233
Structures, Foundations for.....336
Subtropical Gardens.............218
Suckers and Sprouts.............357
Summerhouse, Rustic.............241
Surface, The....................167
Tender Perennials...............159
Terraces, Shaping...............319
Town Squares, Small.............297
Towns, Park System for..........287
Trees and Shrubs, Controlling Hab-
     its of......................358
Trees, Clipped..................223
     Comparative Size of......... 25
     Deciduous................... 27
     Future Size of..............197
     Grouping of.................186
     Heeling-in..................321
     Planting in Cities.......... 20
     Planting on Farms........... 18
     Rate of Growth of....... 21–22
Trees, Shrubs, and Flowers, Group-
     ing of......................189
Trellises.......................345
Trenching.......................315
Turf, Cutting, and Laying.......324
Undulating Borders..............168
Walks...........................327
     and Drives..................177
     as Embellishment............181
     Curved and Straight.........178
     Objective points in.........182
Wall of Brick...................238
Water Fowl......................231
Water in Gardening..............227
     Trees near..................230
Watering in Summer..............361
Weeds...........................354
Wild Garden.....................218
Window Boxes for Plants.........297
Window Gardens..................255
Woodwork, Care of...............336

INDEX OF TREES AND SHRUBS.

Acacia, Japanese.... 59
Ailanthus 53
Alder, Black.... 83
   Common Cut-leaved.......... 55
   European.. 54
   Hawthorn-leaved.... 55
   Hoary......... 55
   Imperial Cut-leaved.......... 54
   Linden-leaved.... 55
   Oak-leaved.... 55
   Red-leaved.... 55
   Speckled. 55
Almond, Double White.......... 64
   Dwarf.......... 64
   Flowering.......... 64
Andromeda, Cateshy's.... 97
   Free Blooming.......... .. 97
   Marsh. 97
Angelica Tree.......... 73
Apple, Flowering 60
Aralia, Manschurian 72
Arbor Vitæ, American 107
   Buist's 108
   Burrow's.......... 108
   Chinese.......... 110
     Golden.......... 110
     Rollinson's.. 110
     Weeping Chinese.......... 110
   Dwarf Dense 108
   Geo. Peabody 108
   Globe-headed.......... 108
   Hacker's.......... 109
   Heath-leaved.......... 108
   Hoopes' Dwarf.......... 109
   Hovey's.. 108
   Nee's Plicate.......... 108
   Oriental.... 110
   Parsons'.. 108
   Queen Victoria's.......... 108
   Round-headed.......... 109
   Siberian. 108
   Tom Thumb.......... 109
   Upright . ... 108.
   Vervæne's.......... 108
   Weeping.......... 108
Ash, American White 44
   Aucuba leaved. 44
   Bosc's. 44
   Cloth-like leaved.......... 44
   European 45
     Dwarf Crisp-leaved 45
     Dwarf Globe-headed.......... 45
     Golden-barked.......... 45
     Hooded-leaved.......... 45
     Single-leaved 45
     Variegated-leaved.......... 45
     Weeping.. 45
     Willow-leaved.. 45
   Flowering.......... 45
   Gold-spotted-leaved.......... 44
   Rufous-haired.. 44
   Showy.......... 45
   Walnut-leaved.. 44
   Weeping.......... 45

Aspen. American.......... 35
   Large American Weeping 35
Azalea, Clammy. 95
   Flame-colored.......... 95
   Hybrids.......... 95
   Oriental. 72
   Purple.......... 95
   Smooth.......... 95
Balsam Fir.......... 104
Barberry, American 86
   European.......... 86
   Evergreen.......... 117
   Purple-leaved.......... 86
   Violet-fruited.......... 86
Basswood.......... 46
Bayberry.......... 98
Beech.......... 40
   American.......... 41
   Broad-leaved.......... 41
   Copper.......... 41
   Crested-leaved.......... 42
   Cut-leaved.......... 42
   European.......... 41
   Fern-leaved.......... 42
   Golden Variegated.......... 41
   Large-leaved.... 41
   Purple-leaved.......... 41
   Purple, Rivers'.......... 41
   Weeping.... 41
Bilsted.......... 53
Birch, Canoe.... 57
   Cherry.......... 57
   Cut-leaved Weeping 57
   Downy-leaved.......... 57
   Elegant Weeping.......... 57
   European, White.......... 56
   Graceful Weeping.......... 57
   Indian Paper.......... 58
   Nettle-leaved.......... 57
   Paper.......... 57
   Purple-leaved.......... 57
   Pyramidal.......... 57
   Sweet 57
   Yellow.......... 58
   Young's Weeping.......... 57
Black Alder.......... 83
Blackberry, Cut-leaved.......... 94
   Double.......... 94
Bladder-nut, American.......... 81
   Asiatic.......... 81
   European.......... 81
Bladder Senna, Aleppo.......... 81
   Common.......... 81
   Oriental 81
Box.......... 117
Box Elder.......... 40
Bramble, Purple.......... 94
   White 94
Buckthorn.......... 68
Burning-bush.. 73
   Broad-leaved.. 73
   European.. 73
   Purple-leaved.......... 73
Butternut.......... 36

Button-bush...................... 88
Button-wood..................... 37
Buckeye........................ 32
    Dark Red.................. 33
    Dwarf Pendulous............ 34
    Flesh-colored.............. 33
    Long-racemed.............. 34
    Ohio.. 33
    Purple................... 34
    Small.................... 34
    Whitley's 24
    Yellow................... 33
Callicarpa.... 85
Calycanthus... 84
Caragana....................... 79
Carolina Allspice................ 84
Catalpa, Bunge's................ 41
    Common................. 42
    Dwarf, American........... 43
    Golden... 43
    Hardy... 43
    Kæmpferi 43
Cedar, California White.... 107
    Deodar..................107
    Indian...................107
    Japan...................107
    Mount Atlas..............107
    Lebanon.................107
    White 106
    Dwarf..................106
    Variegated...............106
Cercidiphyllum 50
Cherry, Aucuba-leaved........... 63
    Double-flowering 63
    European Bird 63
    Weeping 63
Cinquefoil, Shrubby.............. 98
Clethra 85
    Acuminate-leaved. 85
Clethra, Alder-leaved............ 85
Corchorus................... .. 97
Cornelian Cherry.... 67
    Variegated 67
Cotoneaster, Box-leaved.......... 88
    Downy.................. 88
    Frigid.... 88
    Loose-flowered 88
    Money-wort-leaved........ 88
    Round-leaved 88
Crab, Chinese Double, Rose-flower-
    ing........................ 60
    Garland, Flowering.......... 60
    Rivers' Semi-double........ 61
Currant, Crimson-flowered...... 87
    Gordon's................. 87
    Missouri.. 87
    Yellow-flowered........... 87
Cypress, Lawson's..............106
    Pyramidal 106
    Silver-leaved.............106
    Upright.................106
    Variegated...............106
    Weeping.... 106
    Nootka Sound............106
Deciduous Cypress... 52
    Chinese Weeping.......... 52
    Weeping 52
Deutzia, Crenate-leaved.......... 96

Deutzia, Graceful............... 95
    Rough-leaved 96
Dogwood, Alternate-leaved..... 66
    European 67
    Flowering 66
    Osier.. 67
    Red-branched 67
    Red Siberian 67
    Round-leaved... 66
    Weeping 66
Elder, American................ 71
    Cut-leaved 71
    European 71
    Golden-leaved 71
    Variegated-leaved........ 71
Elm.......................... 27
    American, White.......... 27
    Ash-colored.............. 29
    Belgian 28
    Blandford's 29
    Broad-leaved 29
    Cornish................. 28
    Dampier's Pyramidal 29
    Dove's.. 29
    English.... 27
      Berard's............. 27
      Clemmer's.. 27
      Cork-barked.......... 27
      Curled-leaved 28
      Golden-leaved 28
      Nettle-leaved......... 28
      Plume-like........... 28
      Purple-leaved........ 28
      Serrate-leaved........ 28
      Twiggy............. 28
      Variegated-leaved...... 28
      Webb's Curled-leaved. 27
      Weeping Cork-barked.. 27
      Weeping, Small-leaved... .. 27
    Monumental 28
    Red 29
    Superb................. 29
    Scotch 28
      Crisp-leaved Weeping.. 29
      Huntingdon's... 29
      Rough-leaved Weeping... .. 29
      White Margined... .. 29
    Slippery 29
      Weeping 29
    Weeping 27
    Weeping Camperdown........ 28
    Wych 28
Exochorda.................... 89
Fir, Hudson's Bay Dwarf.........105
    Pinsapo.................105
Flowering Apple................ 60
Forsythia, Fortune's... 84
    Very Green.............. 84
    Weeping.... 84
French Mulberry 85
Fringe-tree, Virginian.......... 66
Garland Flower................ 98
Golden Bell................... 84
Golden Chain.................. 64
Ginkgo....................... 48
    Broad-leaved 49
    Variegated-leaved......... 49
Hackberry.. 60

Hackmatack... 44
Hazelnut, American................. 84
   Constantinople. 85
   Cut-leaved.. 84
   Purple-leaved.................. 84
Hemlock Spruce.................. .104
   Dwarf........................104
   Dense........................104
   Sargent's Weeping 104
   Small-leaved. 104
Hercules' Club.................. 73
Hickories..... 36
Hickory, Common............. 36
   Shell Bark 36
High Bush Cranberry.......... 76
Hobble Bush. 77
Holly, American............113
Honey Locust.... 59
   Caspian..... 59
   Chinese 59
   Thornless. 59
   Weeping.... 59
Honeysuckles, Bush... 77
   English Fly.................. 78
   Fragrant.................... 77
   Ledebour's................. 77
   Mountain 78
   Standish's.................. 78
   Tartarian................... 77
Hop-Hornbeam................ 65
Hop-Tree................... 72
Hornbeam, American.......... 65
   English...................... 65
   Hop 65
Horse-chestnut................ 32
   Chinese... 33
   Cut-leaved.. 32
   European.. 32
      Double Red 32
      Double White............ 32
      Van Houtte's Dwarf......... 32
   Memminger's 32
   Red-flowering............. 32
      Golden................ 32
      Dwarf..... 32
Hydrangea, Changeable........... 86
   Large-flowered............. 86
   Panicled................... 86
Indian Bean................. 43
Indian Currant............... 96
Indigo, False, Common............. 83
Inkberry..................... 83
Ironwood. 65
Japan Globe Flower..... 97
Judas-tree, American 65
   Oriental...... 66
June-berry.................... 62
Juniper, American Pyramidal..... 111
   Canadian Trailing............ 110
   Chinese... 112
   Common................... 110
   Daurian. 112
   Globular. 112
   Irish...................... 111
   Japanese.................. 112
   Lee's..................... 112
   Lovely.................... 112
   Polish... 111

Juniper, Prostrate................ ..112
   Reeves'...................112
   Robust Irish....... .... .111
   Savin......................111
      Cypress-leaved.............111
      Tamarisk-leaved 111
      Variegated-leaved......... 111
   Scaled.....................112
   Swedish.. 111
Kentucky Coffee Tree.......... 53
Kœlreuteria................. 65
Laburnum, Alpine........... 65
   Alschinger's............... 64
   Common... 64
   Large-leaved.............. 65
   Oak-leaved................ 65
   Park's.................... 64
   Purple-flowered.... 65
   Scotch.................... 65
Larch, American.... 44
   European................. 43
   Glaucous................ 43
   Weeping................. 43
   Japan................... 44
Laurel, Broad-leaved............ .114
   Narrow-leaved............114
Lead plant.................. 83
Leather-leaf 97
Lilac, Chinese.............. 70
   Common.................. 69
   Emod's.................. 70
   French Red 70
   Golden-leaved............. 69
   Josika's.................. 70
   Persian................. 69
   Rouen................... 70
   Verschaffelt's............. 70
Lime................ 46
Linden, American............ 46
   Broad-leaved............. 46
   European 46
      Broad-leaved............ 46
      Fern-leaved............. 46
      Golden Broad-leaved... 47
      Grape-leaved............ 46
      Hairy-styled............. 47
      Pyramidal. 47
      Red Cut-leaved.......... 46
      Red-twigged.. 47
      Small-leaved.. 46
      White-leaved 46
      White-leaved Weeping....... 46
      Yellow-twigged.......... 47
   Japan................... 47
Liquidambar.... ..:........... 53
Locust, Besson's............... 58
   Black.................... 58
   Clammy................... 59
   Globe................... 58
   Golden.................. 58
   Honey................... 59
   Moss.................... 59
   Parasol................. 58
   Pyramidal............... 58
   Rose................... 59
   Yellow.................. 58
Madeira Nut 36
Magnolia....... 49

Magnolia, Chinese White	50	Mountain Ash, Hybrid	61
Cucumber	49	Oak-leaved	61
Ear-leaved	50	Weeping	61
Great Laurel	50	Mulberry, Black	55
Great-leaved	50	Downing's Ever-bearing	55
Hall's Japan	51	Japan	56
Heart-shaped	50	Paper	56
Lenne's	52	Red	55
Norbert's	52	White	55
Purple	50	Nettle Tree, American	60
Showy-flowering	52	European	60
Slender-growing	51	Nut-bearing Trees	36
Soulange's	52	Oak, Burr	30
Sweet Bay	50	Chestnut	30
Long-leaved	50	Cut-leaved	30
Thompson's	52	English Royal	30
Umbrella	50	Contorted-leaved	31
Very Dark Purple	51	Curled Pyramidal	31
Mahonia	117	Cut-leaved	31
Maiden Hair Tree	45	Dark-leaved	31
Maple	37	Golden-leaved	31
Ash-leaved	40	Large-leaved	31
Curled	40	Louett's	30
Variegated	40	Purple-leaved	31
Black Sugar	37	Pyramidal	31
Cork-barked	40	Silver-leaved	31
Curled-leaf	38	Weeping	31
Douglas' Sycamore	38	Japanese	31
Dwarf Scarlet	37	Mongolian	31
Eagle's Claw	38	Mossy-cup	30
English	40	Pin	30
European Sycamore	38	Red	30
Golden-leaved	38	Scarlet	30
Japanese	39	Shingle	30
Large-leaved	40	Southern Over-cup	30
Lorberg's	38	Swamp, White	30
Norway	37	Turkey	31
Cut-leaved	38	White	30
Palmate-leaved	40	Willow	30
Red	37	Oleaster, European	82
Red Colchicum	39	Garden	82
Schwerdler's	38	Silver-leaved	82
Silver-leaved	38	Osage Orange	61
Crisp-leaved	38	Paper Mulberry	56
New Cut-leaved	38	Paulownia	56
Wagner's Cut-leaved	38	Peach, Blood-leaved	64
Striped	40	Flowering	64
Sugar	37	Pea-tree, Arborescent	71
Swamp	37	Chinese	80
Sycamore	39	Siberian	70
Tartarian	40	Pepperidge	54
Velvety	39	Persimmon, American	59
Medlar	62	European	60
Mespilus	62	Japan	60
Mezereum	98	Pine, Austrian	99
Mist-Tree	68	Bentham's	100
Mock Orange	75	Black	99
Dwarf	75	California Mountain	101
Double	75	Cluster	100
Garland	75	Corsican	99
Golden-leaved	75	Dwarf, or Mountain	100
Gordon's Late	76	Heavy-wooded	101
Large-flowering	76	Highland	100
Red-twigged	76	Jeffrey's	101
Mountain Ash	60	Lofty Bhotan	101
American	61	Mugho	100
Elder-leaved	61	Lambert's	110
European	61	Pitch	101

Pine, Pyrenean 100
   Sabine's... ... .101
   Scotch 100
   Short-leaved, Yellow........100
   Swiss Stone.. 102
   Table Mountain.............100
   Taurian... 100
   Weymouth..................101
   White.................. ...101
     Compact White..........101
     Silver-white............ ...101
Plane, American............. 37
   Oriental.... 37
Plums, Dwarf Double-flowering.... 68
   Flowering.... 63
Poplar....................... 34
   Abele...... 35
   Athenian Weeping........... 35
   Balsam................... 35
   Carolina.................. 35
   " Eugenie "............... 35
   Cottonwood............... 35
   Gray..................... 35
   Lombardy................. 35
   Necklace................. 35
   Parasol de St. Julien 35
   Silver.................. ... 35
   Weeping.................. 35
   White... 35
See Aspen.
Privet, Box-leaved.... 82
   Common 82
   Laurel-leaved............. 82
   Oval-leaved. 82
   Weeping........ 82
   White-berried.. 82
Purple Fringe............. 68
Quince, Japan 87
Red-bud... 65
Red Cedar..... 111
   Bedford's................112
   Light Green..............112
   Silvery-leaved... 111
   Variegated, alba...........112
   aurea.... 112
   Weeping....... 111
Retinispora, obtuse-leaved... 109
   Pea-fruited....... ... .109
     Golden................109
     Heath-like 109
     Thready-branched 109
   Plume-like................109
     Silver-tipped............108
     Gold-tipped.............109
   Squarrose.................109
Rhododendron, American.......116
   Hybrids 116
   Pontic..................116
Rose, Bengal.............. 93
   Bourbon.................. 93
   China.................... 93
   Climbing................. 92
   Hybrid Noisette... 93
     Perpetual, or Remontants.... 92
     Tea................ 93
   June, or Summer..... 92
   Moss.................... 92
   Prairie. 93

Rose, Tea 93
   Yellow, or Austrian........... 92
   of Sharon................. 74
St. Johnswort 89
   Kalm's... 89
   Shrubby 89
Sassafras.... 61
Service-berry, ... 62
Shad-flower.................. 62
Shrubby Althæa... 74
Shrubby Trefoil.............. 72
Silver-bell Tree............ 71
Silver Fir Cephalonian............105
   Cilician.................105
   Great...................105
   Lovely..................105
   Noble...................105
   Nordmann's..............105
   Siberian................105
Smoke-tree................. 68
Snowball................... 76
   Japan.... 76
Snowberry.................. 96
Snowy Mespilus............. 62
Sophora, Japan .:........... 54
   Weeping................. 54
Sour Gum.................. 54
Spice Bush................. 72
Spindle Tree............... 73
Spiræa..................... 89
   Billard's................. 90
   Douglas's................. 90
   Fortune's................. 90
   Golden-leaved 90
   Mountain-Ash-leaved........ 91
   Plum-leaved.......... 90
   Reeves'.................. 90
   Thunberg's................ 90
Spruce, Black..............103
   Colorado Blue............103
   Douglas's.................104
   Doumets'.. 103
   Dwarf White 103
   Glaucous................103
   Hemlock.................104
   Himalayan 104
   Menzies'................103
   Norway..................102
     Barry's 102
     Clanbrasil's............103
     Conical...............103
     Ellwanger's Dwarf..........103
     Finedon Hall............102
     Gregory's Dwarf..........103
     Inverted-branched 102
     Maxwell's 103
     Pigmy Dwarf...........103
     Pyramidal 102
     Small-formed 103
   Obovate-coned...........104
   Oriental.................104
   Smith's 104
   White 103
Stagger-bush................ 97
Strawberry Bush............ 73
Stuartia................... 78
Styrax, Japan............... 89
Sumach, Cut-leaved..... 69

Sumach, Fragrant...... 68
    Osbeck's Chinese... 68
    Staghorn.................. 69
    Venetian................. 68
Sweet Gum.. 53
Sweet Pepper Bush 85
Sweet-scented Shrub............. 84
Syringa.,............... 47
Tamarack........... 44
Tamarisk.......... 72
Thorn, Common Hawthorn........ 67
    Evergreen. 67
Torreya, Californian... 113
    Florida.................113
    Japanese.. 113
Umbrella Pine............113
Viburnum, Lantana-leaved... 77
    Nepal................ 77
    Plum-leaved.... 77
    Rough-leaved...... 77
Virgilia................ 54
Walnut, Black 36
    European 36
    Cut-leaved 36
    Dwarf.. 36
Wax-berry................. 96
Wax Myrtle 98
Way-faring Tree...... 77
Weigela, Rose-colored..... 80
    Variegated-leaved............ 80
    White-flowered............. 80
White Alder................ 85
White Cedar.................106
" White Cedar "...............107
Wig-Tree................. 68

Wild Olive........ 82
Willow, American Weeping....... 48
    Babylonian. 47
    Fountain................. 48
    Goat................. 47
    Three-colored 48
    Weeping........... 47
    Golden 47
    Japan Weeping.......... 48
    Kilmarnock Weeping...... 47
    Laurel-leaved........... 48
    Palm-leaved............. 48
    Ring-leaved............. 48
    Rosemary-leaved......... 48
    Royal................ 48
    Salmon's Weeping.... 47
    Shiny-leaved............ 48
    Silky Weeping.......... 48
    Wisconsin Weeping.... 48
    Wolsey's Weeping........ 84
Winterberry, Common......... 83
    Smooth-leaved. 83
Witch Hazel. 68
Withe-rod 77
Yellow-wood........ 53
Yew, American... 114
    Beautiful..............114
    Dova-ton's..............114
    English................114
    Golden 114
    Irish 114
    Japanese 144
    Weeping................110
Yulan.............. 15

INDEX OF HARDY HERBACEOUS PLANTS.

Acanthus 134
Aconite...... 138
Acorus.................134
Adam's Needle , ...137
Adder's Tongue...... 127
Adonis, Spring............135
Aletris....................138
Alfredia Nodding... 125
Allium, Golden............133
Alstræmeria.... 138
Amianthium... 138
Amsonia.................139
Anemone.................125, 139
Anthericum 125
Artemisia................135
Arundo Donax............135
Asphodel.................139
Aster.... 139
Astilbe, Japan........... 125
Avens, Scarlet............142
Baneberry.............138
Baptisia..................139
Bee-Balm 144
Bell-Flower............ 126
Bellwort 145
Berlandiera...............140
Bitter Vetch 131
Blazing Star.............129

Bleeding Heart...... 127
Bocconia.. 135
Boltonia.................140
Bowman's Root.... 142
Brodæa 140
Brunella 140
Bugle, Blue-flowered.............138
    Red-leaved 135
Bupthalmum.............135
Buttercup................144
Butterfly Tulip... 140
    Weed...............139
Callirrhoë...............140
Campanula................126
Canada Tick-Trefoil............128
Candytuft, Perennial... 128
Cardinal Flower..............143
Catch-fly.............131, 133
Catnip, Mussin's........ 144
Centaurea 140
Chelone...................140
Cinquefoil, Pyrenian..........144
Clary, Silver.............137
Clematis, Erect..... 140
Clintonia 140
Colchicum 126
Colic Root................138
Columbine............... ...125

Comfrey, Variegated	137	Loosestrife	129, 143
Compass Plant	137	Lotus	143
Cone-Flower	141	Lungwort	132, 143
Coreopsis	140	Lupine	143
Coronilla	141	Lychnis	131
Costmary	145	Mallow, Moren's	143
Crosswort	141	May Apple, Oregon	138
Cranesbill	142	Meadow Rue	145
Crocus	126	Meadow Saffron	126
Crowfoot	144	Meadow-Sweet	133
Crown Imperial	127	Milfoil	138
Cupidone	140	Milkweed	139
Cup Plant	137	Mimulus	144
Daffodil	131	Mint, Variegated	136
Daisy	125	Monarda	144
Dame's Violet	128	Moneywort	143
Day Lily	128, 136	Monkey Flower	144
Desmodium	128	Monkshood	134, 138
Dog's Tooth Violet	127	Moss Pink	132
Doronicum	141	Mountain Everlasting	139
Dragon Head	144	Mountain Spurge	144
Dropwort	133	Nierembergia	144
Eringo	135	Pachysandra	144
Eupatorium	142	Pæony	131
Evening Primrose	144	Pansy	134
False Indigo	139	Pasque Flower, American	139
Feverfew	132	Pea, Perennial	129
Flag	129	Pentstemon	132
Flame-Flower	133	Pentstemon, Scarlet	144
Flax, Perennial	143	Periwinkle	134
Fleabane, Rose	142	Phlox, Perennial	132
Fleur de Lis	129	Pink	127
Flower of Jove	131	Pink Root	133
Forget-Me-Not	131	Plantain Lily	127, 136
Foxglove	127	Polyanthus	132
Fraxinella	127	Polygonum	144
Funkia	127	Poppy, Perennial	132
Gaura	142	Primrose	132
Gentian	142	Pulmonaria	132
Geranium	142	Purity	133
Gillenia	142	Pyrethrum	132
Globe Thistle	135	Queen of the Prairie	133
Golden Aster	141	Ragged Robin	131
Golden Rod	145	Ranunculus	144
Grass, Ribbon	134	Red-hot Poker Plant	133
Grasses, Ornamental	135	Reed	135
Greek Valerian	132	Rhubarb	136
Groundsel	144	Rocket Flower	128
Gypsophila	142	Rose Mallow	143
Harebell	126	Sage, Southern	132
Hawkweed	143	Variegated	137
Heart's-ease	134	St. Bernard's Lily	144
Hedge Nettle	145	St. Bruno's Lily	125
Hollyhock	126	Satin Flower	145
Horsemint	144	Sea Pink	145
Hyacinths	128	Senecio	144
Hyssop	143	Senna, American	140
Iris	129	Sisyrinchium	145
Jacob's Ladder	132	Skullcap	144
Jonquil	129	Solomon's Seal	145
Knotweed	141	Snake's Head	140
Larkspur	126	Sneezewort, Double	138
Lavender Cotton	137	Snowdrop	128
Liatris	129	Snowflake	130
Lilies	130	Speedwell	134
Lily of the Valley	126	Spigelia	133
Lobelia	143	Spiræas, Herbaceous	133
Leopard's Bane	141	Spurge	142

Squill........................133
Stachys.......................145
Star Flower, Spring...........145
Star Grass 138
Star of Bethlehem.............131
Stokesia, Blue................132
Stork's Bill..................142
Sunflower.....................142
    Graceful..................136
Sweet William.................127
Thalictrum....................145
Thrift........................145
Thyme, Variegated 137
Trefoil, Bird's-foot..........143
Triteleia.....................145
Tritoma.......................133
Tulips 133

Turfing Daisy.................144
Uvularia......................145
Valerian 145
    Red.......................140
Verbena, Hardy................145
Veronica......................134
Violet........................134
Virginia Cowslip..............143
White Cup.....................144
Whorl Flower..................136
Winter Aconite................142
Wood Hyacinth.................133
Woodruff......................125
Wormwood......................135
Yarrow........................138
Yucca.........................137

INDEX OF CLIMBERS.

Actinidia polygama............122
Akebia quinata................122
"American Ivy"................118
Ampelopsis....................118
Clematis......................121
Climbing Bittersweet..........122
Cocculus Carolina.............123
Dutchman's Pipe 122
Grape Vine....................123
Grecian Silk..................123

Honeysuckles..................120
Ivy, European.................123
Jessamine, White..............123
Moonseed, Canadian............123
Pepper Vine...................118
Staff Tree....................122
Trumpet Vine..................122
Virginia Creeper..............118
Wistaria......................119
Woodbine, Common..............120

INDEX OF ALPINE AND ROCK PLANTS.

Acantholimon 146
Alyssum.......................146
Arabis........................146
Arenaria......................146
Aubrietia.....................146
Barrenwort 147
Bluets........................147
Bulbocodium...................146
Camassia......................146
Catchfly, Alpine..............149
Catchfly, German 147
Cerastium.....................146
Claytonia 147
Clematis, Herbaceous..........147
Columbine, Wild...............146
Epimedium.....................147
Erinus, Alpine................147
Gentian, Stemless.............147
Geum, Mountain................147
Golden Tuft...................146
Ground Ivy....................147
Harebell......................146
Houseleek.....................149
Houstonia 147
Kidney Vetch..................146
Live-for-ever.................149
Lychnis, Rock.................147
Meadow Saffron, Spring........146

Milfoil, Woolly 146
Mitchella 147
Mouse-ear Chickweed...........146
Opuntia 147
Partridge Berry 147
Phlox 147
Pine-barren Beauty 148
Prickly Pear..................147
Pyxidanthera..................148
Quamash.......................146
Rock Cress....................146
Sandwort......................146
Saxifrage.....................148
Sedum 149
Sempervivum...................149
Soapwort, Rock................148
Speedwell, Alpine 149
Spring Beauty.................147
Strawberry, Barren............149
Stonecrop.....................149
Thrift, Common................146
    Prickly..................146
Toadflax, Alpine..............147
Tunica, Rock..................149
Waldsteinia 149
Wallflower, Alpine............147
Wood Sorrel 146

INDEX OF AQUATIC AND BOG PLANTS.

Arisæma............................ 153
Arrow Head.. 155
Calopogon........ 133
Caltha...... 153
Calypro. Northern..............153
Cardinal Flower..................154
Cat-Tail.... 155
Centaury.......................154
Cypripedium.... 153
Darlingtonia......... ... .154
Drosera 154
Fringed Orchis....................154
Globe Flower... 155
Sabbatia.........................154
Sarracenia.... 155
Sundew. 154
Sweet Flag..... 153

Golden Club. 154
Grass of Parnassus...............154
Green Dragon.................. 153
Habenaria 154
Ladies' Slipper........... 154
Marsh Calla.....................154
Marsh Marigold........... 153
Orontium 154
Pickerel Weed..................155
Pitcher Plant......................155
Pitcher Plant, California... 154
Pogonia.........................154
Pontederia......................155
Trollius........................155
Typha...........................155
Water Lily......................154
Water Shield.... 153

INDEX OF FERNS AND SHADE-LOVING PLANTS.

Adam and Eve.... 150
Anemone 150
Aplectrum. 150
Asarum 150
Bloodroot.........................152
Bunch-berry...... 150
Christmas Rose...................152
Club Moss.... 152
Cornus, Dwarf. 150
Cowslip, American...............150
Cypripedium......................150
Dodecatheon......................150
False Solomon's Seal 152
Ferns...........................151
Fritillaria .. ..'.....152
Helleborus....... 152
Helonias, Spiked..............152
Hepatica.........................152
Jack in the Pulpit................150
Lady's Slipper.... 150

Liverleaf.... 152
May Apple 153
Meadow Beauty....................152
Orchis, Showy... 152
Podophyllum... 153
Polygala, Fringed................152
Ramondia... 152
Rattlesnake Plantain... 152
Rhexia............................ 152
Selaginella....................152
Shooting Star 150
Smilacina........................152
Snakeroot, Canada..... 150
Snakeroot, Virginian 150
Solomon's Seal, False.............152
Trailing Arbutus..................:..150
Trillium........................152—153
Violet.... 153
Wake Robin........ ....152—153
Wood Lily......... 153

INDEX OF THE BOTANICAL NAMES OF TREES AND SHRUBS.

Abies alba........ , ...103
    var. carulea........ 103
    amabilis.. 105
    balsamea...... 104
    Canadensis.............104
        var. deusa.............104
        var. microphylla.............104
        var. nana.............104
        var. Sargentii.... 104
    Cephalonica... 105
    Cilicica.................... 105
    Douglasii.................104
    excelsa...............102
        var. Barryii.............102
        var. Clanbrasilana.............102
        var. inverta.... 102
        var. Finedonensis.... 102
        var. Gregoriana..... 103
        var. Maxwelliana.............103
        var. pyramidalis... 102
    Fraseri, var. Hudsonica...... ...105
    grandis................ 105
    Menziesii .... ,....103
    nigra.................. 103
        var. Doumeti.............103
    nobilis............... 105
    Nordmanniana............ 105
    obovata................104
    orientalis. 104
    pectinata................ 105
        var. compacta........... 105
        var. pendula.... 105
    Pichta....................105
    polita.................104
    Pinsapo 105
    Smithiana....................104
Acacia Nemu 59
Æsculus.................. 32
    carnea superba................. 34
    Chinensis. 33
    flava.... 33
    glabra.. 33
    Hippocastanum................. 32
        var. flore pleno............. 32
        var. rubra fl. pl............. 32
        var. laciniata 32
        var. nana Van Houttei. 32
    Memmingeri.... 32
    parviflora 34
    Pavia 33
        var. atrosanguinea.. 33
        var. carnea pubescens.... ... 33
        var. purpurea................ 34
        var. Whitleyi................ 34

Æsculus pumila pendula........... 34
    rubicunda 32
        var. foliis aureis..... 32
        var. nana.... 33
Acer campestris............ 40
    Colchicum rubrum.. 38
    dasycarpum.......... 38
        var. crispum novum... 38
        var. heterophyllum lacinia-
            tum 38
        var. Wagneri..... 38
    macrophyllum 40
    palmatum 40
    Pennsylvanicum............ 40
    platanoides........... 37
        var. cucullatum. 38
        var. dissectum 38
        var. laciniatum...... 38
        var. Lorbergii.......... 38
        var. Schwerdterii. 38
    polymorphum........... ... 39
    Pseudo-Platanus............ 38
        var. aureo-variegata......... 38
        var. Douglasi. 38
        var. purpurea............. 39
        var. velutinum.. 39
    rubrum............ 37
        var. fulgens............. 37
        var. tomentosum... 37
    saccharinum............ .. 37
        var. nigrum............ 37
    Tartaricum................ 40
Ailanthus glandulosus...... ... 53
Alnus glutinosa 54
    var. laciniata imperialis..... 54
    var. quercifolia........ 55
    var. rubro-nervis......... 55
    incana................ 55
        var. laciniata............. 55
    tillacea 55
Amelanchier Canadensis........... 62
    var. Botryapium............. 62
    vulgaris 62
Amorpha canescens 83
    fruticosa.............. 83
    var. angustifolia............. 83
Andromeda floribunda........... 97
    Mariana.. 97
    polifolia 97
Aralia Chinensis........... . 72
    var. elata............ 72
    spinosa................ 73
Azalea arborea... 95
    calendulacea.................. 95

Azalea mollis...................... 95
    nudiflora...................... 95
    viscosa........................ 95
Berberis Aquifolium............117
    Canadensis.................... 86
    vulgaris var. purpurea........ 86
        var. fructu violacea...... 86
Betula alba...................... 56
    var. fastigiata............... 57
    var. foliis purpureis......... 57
    var. pendula elegans.......... 57
    var. pendula laciniata........ 57
    var. pendula Youngii.......... 57
    var. populifolia.............. 57
    var. pubescens................ 57
    var. tristis.................. 57
    var. urticifolia.............. 57
    Bhojpaltra.................... 58
    costata....................... 58
    lutea......................... 58
    lenta......................... 57
    papyracea..................... 57
    pumila........................ 58
Biota............................107
Broussonetia papyrifera.......... 56
Buxus sempervirens...............117
Cephalanthus occidentalis........ 83
Callicarpa Americana............. 85
    purpurea...................... 85
Calycanthus elongatus............ 84
    floridus...................... 84
    glaucus....................... 84
    lævigatus..................... 84
    macrocarpus................... 84
Caragana Altagana................ 70
    arborescens................... 71
    Chamlagu...................... 70
Carpinus Americana............... 65
    Betulus....................... 65
    var. pendula.................. 65
Carya alba....................... 36
Cassandra calyculata............. 97
Castanea vesca................... 34
    var. Americana................ 34
    Japonica...................... 34
    pumila........................ 34
Catalpa Bungei................... 43
    Kæmpferi...................... 43
    speciosa...................... 43
    syringæfolia.................. 43
    bignonioides.................. 43
    var. aurea.................... 43
    var. nana..................... 43
Ceanothus Americanus............. 85
Cephalotaxus drupacea............115
Cedrus Atlantica.................107
    Deodara.......................107
    Libani........................107
Celtis australis................. 60
    occidentalis.................. 60
Cercidiphyllum Japonicum......... 60
Cercis Canadensis................ 65
    Japonica...................... 66
    Chinensis..................... 66
Chionanthus Virginica............ 66
Cladrastis tinctoria............. 53
Clethra acuminata................ 85
    alnifolia..................... 85

Colutea arborescens.............. 81
    cruenta....................... 81
    Halepica...................... 81
Cornus alternifolia.............. 66
    circinata..................... 66
    florida....................... 66
    Mas........................... 67
        var. variegata............ 67
    sanguinea..................... 67
    Sibirica var. variegata....... 67
Corylus Americana................ 84
    Avellana, var. purpurea....... 84
        var. laciniata............ 84
    Colurna....................... 85
Cotoneaster affinis.............. 88
    buxifolia..................... 88
    frigida....................... 88
    laxiflora..................... 88
    microphylla................... 88
    nummularia.................... 88
    rotundifolia.................. 88
Cratægus Oxyacantha.............. 67
    Pyracantha.................... 67
Cupressus Lawsoniana.............106
    var. argentea.................106
    var. erecta...................106
    var. pendula..................106
    var. pyramidalis..............106
    var. variegata................106
    thyoides......................106
        var. nana.................106
        var. variegata............106
Cryptomeria Japonica.............107
Cytisus purpureus................ 64
Daphne Cneorum................... 98
    Mezereum...................... 98
Deutzia crenata.................. 96
    var. fl. pl................... 96
    var. fl. alb. pl.............. 96
    var. purp. pl................. 96
    gracilis...................... 96
    scabra........................ 96
Diervilla arborea-grandiflora.... 80
    candida....................... 80
    hortensis nivea............... 80
    rosea......................... 80
Dimorphanthus Mandshuricus...... 72
Diospyros Kaki................... 60
    Lotus......................... 60
    Virginiana.................... 59
Elæagnus argentea................ 82
    hortensis..................... 82
Euonymus alatus.................. 73
    Americanus.................... 73
    atropurpureus................. 73
    Europæus...................... 73
        var. atropurpureus........ 73
    latifolius.................... 73
Exochorda grandiflora............ 89
Fagus ferruginea................. 41
    sylvatica..................... 41
    var. aurea variegata.......... 41
    var. cristata................. 42
    var. cuprea................... 41
    var. laciniata................ 42
    var. macrophylla.............. 41
    var. pendula.................. 41
    var. aspleniifolia............ 42

Fagus sylvatica...... 41
   var. purpurea.................. 41
   var. purpurea major.... 41
   var. purpurea Riversii........ 41
Forsythia Fortunei................ 84
  suspensa 84
  viridissima 84
Fraxinus Americana................ 44
   var. ancubæfolia.... 44
   var. Boscli 44
   var. juglandifolia............. 44
   var. pannosa.... 44
   var. punctata 44
   var. rufa.... 44
   var. spectabilis.............. 45
  excelsior..................... 45
   var. atrovirens.... 45
   var. aurea................... 45
   var. aurea-pendula.......... 45
   var. cucullata 45
   var. globosa................. 45
   var. pendula................. 45
   var. salicifolia.............. 45
   var. concavæfolia variegata... 45
   var. monophylla........... ... 45
   var. scolopendrifolia......... 45
Ginkgo adiantifolia 45
Glyptostrobus pendulus............. 58
Gymnocladus Canadensis 52
Gleditschia Caspica... 53
  Sinensis 59
  triacanthos.. 59
   var. Bujotii.................. 59
   var. inermis... 59
Halesia diptera................... 79
  tetraptera................... 71
Hamamælis Virginica............. 68
Hibiscus Syriacus... 74
Hydrangea arborescens..... 87
  Hortensia.................... 86
  paniculata grandiflora........ 86
  quercifolia 87
  radiata 87
Hypericum Kalmianum............ 89
  prolificum.. 89
Ilex glabra....................... 83
  lævigata.................... 83
  opaca......................113
  verticillata.... 83
Juniperus Barbadensis............112
  Canadensis 110
  Communis 110
   var. alpina... 110
   var. alpina pyramidalis........110
   var. Cracovica..............111
   var. Hibernica.... 111
   var. Hibernica robusta.......111
   var. nana 111
   var. Suecica 110
  Chinensis....................111
   var. Japonica...............112
   var. Leeana.................112
   var. Reevesiana 112
  Daurica.....................112
  hemisphærica................ 112
  Occidentalis, var. venusta.....112
  prostrata. 112
  Sabina......................112

Juniperus Sabina.... 112
   var. alpina..................111
   var. cupressifolia...........111
  vars. tamariscifolia...........111
   var. variegata..............111
  squamata 112
  Virginiana 111
   var. Bedfordiana............111
   var. glauca.................111
   var. pendula................112
   var. Schottii...............112
   var. variegata alba..........112
   var. variegata aurea........ 112
Juglans cinerea... 36
  nigra.... 36
  regia........................ 36
   var. laciniata 36
   var. præparturiens.......... 36
Kalmia angustifolia..............113
  latifolia....................113
Kerria Japonica................. 97
Kœlreuteria paniculata 65
Laburnum alpinum............. 64
  Alschingeri.................. 64
  vulgare..................... 64
   var. macrophylla........... 64
   var. Parkii............. ... 64
   var. quercifolia 64
Larix Americana............... 44
  Europæa. 42
   var. glauca................. 43
   var. pendula... 43
  leptolepis 44
Leucothöe Catesbæi.............. 97
Libocedrus decurrens 107
Ligustrum laurifolium 82
  ovalifolium.................. 82
  vulgare..................... 82
   var. buxifolia 82
   var. leucocarpa............. 82
   var. pendula................ 82
Lindera Benzoin................. 72
Liquidambar styraciflua.......... 53
Liriodendron Tulipifera.......... 36
Lonicera cærulea................ 78
  fragrantissima 77
  Ledebourii................... 77
  Standishii.... 78
  Tartarica.................... 77
  Xylosteum 78
Machura aurantiaca............. 61
Magnolia acuminata.......... ... 49
  conspicua.................... 50
  cordata...................... 50
  Fraseri 50
  glauca 50
   var. longifolia.............. 50
  grandiflora 50
  hypoleuca 52
  Lennei 51
  macrophylla................. 52
  Norbertiana................. 50
  parviflora... 51
  purpurea.................... 50
  Soulangeana................. 52
   var. gracilis................ 51
  speciosa 52
  stellata..................... 51

Magnolia Thompsoniana............ 52
  Umbrella 50
Mespilus Germanica............. 62
Morus alba 55
  var. fastigiata................. 55
  nigra... 55
  rubra........ 55
  Tokwa.... 56
Myrica cerifera.... 98
Negundo aceroides........... 40
  var. crispum...... 40
  var. foliis argenteis 40
Nyssa multiflora.................. 54
Ostrya Virginica.................. 65
Paulownia imperialis...... 56
Pinus Austriaca.... 100
  Benthamiana 100
  Cembra....................102
    var. pygmaea..............102
  excelsa 101
  Jeffreyi 101
  Lambertiana................100
  Laricio.... 100
  mitis.......................100
  Mugho. 101
  Pallasiana..................100
  Pinaster....................100
  ponderosa...... 101
  pumilio.....................100
  pungens... 100
  Pyrenaica 100
  sylvestris 100
    var. horizontalis... 100
Podocarpus Japonica............114
Potentilla fruticosa.............. 98
Pyrus Japonica.... 88
Philadelphus coronarius............ 75
  var. nana................... 75
  dianthiflora................ 76
  Gordonianus................ 76
  grandiflorus................ 76
  nivalis...................... 76
  sanguineus............ 76
Populus alba................... 35
  var. nivea................. 35
  balsamifera................ 35
  dilatata................... 35
  Graeca pendula............ 35
  grandidentata pendula........... 35
  monilifera. 35
  tremuloides......... ...,........ 35
Prunus avium, fl. pl........... 63
  domestica, fl. pl.... 63
  nana. 64
  Padus...................... 63
  Sinensis.. 63
  spinosa, fl. pl....... 63
  tomentosa.... 63
  triloba.... 63
Ptelea trifoliata.................. 72
Pyrus Americana.............. 61
  aucuparia................. 61
  var. pendula.............. 61
  coronaria. 60
  hybrida.................... 61
  quercifolia................ 61
  sambucifolia............... . 61
  spectabilis................ 60

Quercus................. 29
  alba........................ 30
  bicolor.... 30
  Cerris 31
  coccinea................... 30
  Daimio..................... 31
  dentata.................... 31
  imbricaria................. 30
  lyrata..................... 30
  macrocarpa................. 30
  Mongolica.................. 31
  palustris................... 30
  Phellos.................... 30
  Prinus..................... 30
    var. laciniata............. 30
  Robur...................... 30
    var. argentea variegata.. 31
    var. atropurpurea........ 31
    var. concordia.. 31
    var. contorta............. 31
    var. cucullata............. 31
    var. fastigiata........... 31
    var. laciniata............. 31
    var. latifolia cucullata...... 31
    var. Louetti.............. 31
    var. macrophylla.......... 31
    var. nigricans.............. 31
    var. pendula.............. 31
  rubra...................... 30
Rosa Bourboniana..... 93
  centifolia muscosa.......... 92
  Damascaena.... 92
  Indica.......... 93
  Indica odorata. 93
  Indica odorata hybrida....... . 93
  lutea...................... 92
  Noisettiana hybrida... 93
Rubus fruticosus. 94
  var. laciniatus........... 94
  Nutkanus.................. 94
  odoratus.................. 94
Retinispora.—(See Thuja.)
Rhamnus catharticus..,...... .. 68
Rhus, aromatica... 68
  Cotinus,................... 68
  glabra, var. laciniata....... 69
  Osbeckii.................. 68
  typhina................... 69
Ribes aureum. 87
  Gordonianum................ 87
  sanguineum................ 87
Robinia hispida................ 59
  var. grandiflora.......... 59
  Pseudacacia................ 58
    var. aurea............... 58
    var. Bessoniana............ 58
    var. Bella-rosea.......... 58
    var. fastigiata.......... 58
    var. inermis............ 58
    var. inermis rubra monstrosa.. 58
    var. pyramidalis.......... 58
    var. spectabilis........... 58
  viscosa.................... 59
Salisburia 49
Salix, alba var. vitellina............ 47
  Babylonica................ 47
    var. Salmonii 47
    var. annularis. 48

Salix Caprea...... 47
    var. pendula... ... 47
    var. tricolor... 48
    Japonica pendula... 48
    laurifolia. ... 48
    lucida ... 48
    palmæfolia... 48
    purpurea pendula... 48
    regalis... 48
    rosmarinifolia... 48
    sericea pendula... 48
    Wolseyana pendula... 48
Sambucus Canadensis... 71
    nigra... 71
        var. aurea... 71
        var. laciniata... 71
Sassafras officinalis... 61
Sciadopitys verticillata... 113
Sophora Japonica... 54
    var. pendula ... 54
Spiræa callosa... 90
    Douglasii... 90
    Fortunei... 90
    opulifolia, var... 90
    prunifolia... 90
    Reevesiana... 90
    salicifolia, var. fl. pl... 90
    Billardi... 90
    sorbifolia... 91
    Thunbergii... 90
Staphylæa Colchica... 81
    pinnata... 81
    trifolia... 81
Stuartia pentagyna... 78
    Virginica... 79
Styrax Japonica... 89
Syringa Chinensis... 70
    dubia... 70
    Emodi... 70
    Josikæa... 70
    Persica ... 69
        var. alba... 70
    Rothomagensis... 70
    Verschaffeltii... 70
    vulgaris ... 69
    var. variegata... 69
Tamarix Gallica... 72
Thuiopsis dolabrata... 115
    Standishii... 115
Taxodium distichum... 52
    distichum pendulum ... 52
    Sinense pendulum... 52
Taxus adpressa... 114
    baccata... 114
        var. aurea... 114
        var. Canadensis... 114
        var. Dovastoni... 114
        var. fastigiata ... 114
Thuja... 107
    (Biota) orientalis... 110
        var. aurea... 110
        var. elegantissima... 110
        var. filiformis pendula... 110
        var. semper aurea... 110
    (Retinispora), plumosa... 109
    plumosa... 109
        var. argentea... 109
        var. aurea... 109

Thuja pisifera, var. aurea... 109
    var. ericoides... 109
    var. filifera... 109
    obtusa... 109
    squarrosa... 110
    occidentalis... 107
        var. alba... 108
        var. aurea... 108
        var. Burrowii... 108
        var. conica densa... 108
        var. compacta... 108
        var. cristata... 108
        var. ericoides... 108
        var. globosa... 107
        var. Hackerii... 109
        var. Hoveyi... 108
        var. nana... 109
        var. pendula... 108
        var. plicata... 108
        var. pyramidalis... 108
        var. rotundata... 109
        var. Sibirica... 108
        var. Vervaeneana... 108
        var. Warreana... 108
Tilia Americana... 46
    var. macrophylla ... 46
    cordata ... 47
    Europæa... 46
        var. alba... 46
        var. alba-pendula... 46
        var. dasystyla... 47
        var. laciniata... 46
        var. laciniata rubra... 46
        var. microphylla... 46
        var. platyphlla... 46
        var. platyphylla aurea... 47
        var. pyramidalis... 47
        var. rubra... 47
        var. sulphurea... 47
        var. vitifolia... 46
Torreya Californica... 113
    nucifera... 113
    taxifolia... 113
Ulmus campestris ... 28
    var. aurea... 28
    var. Belgica... 28
    var. Cornubiensis... 28
    var. cucullata... 28
    var. monumentalis... 28
    var. plumosa... 28
    var. purpurea... 28
    var. serratifolia... 28
    var. suberosa pendula... 28
    var. urticæfolia... 28
    var. variegata argentea... 28
    var. viminalis... 28
    fulva... 29
    var. pendula... 29
    Dovæi... 29
    montana... 28
        var. alba marginata... 29
        var. Camperdowni... 28
        var. cinerea... 27
        var. crispa... 29
        var. Huntingdoni ... 29
        var. latifolia ... 29
        vrr. pendula ... 29
        var. pendula rugosa... 29

Ulmus montana... 28
    var. pyramidalis Dampieri.... 29
    var. superba................ 29
Viburnum Opulus.... 76
    var. sterilis.......... 76
    Nepaleuse........................ 77

Viburnum nudum. **77**
    plicatum **76**
    prunifolium **77**
    rugosum... .. .. **73**
Virgilia......................... **54**

INDEX OF THE BOTANICAL NAMES OF HARDY HERBA-
CEOUS PLANTS.

Acanthus latifolius...... 134
    mollis........................124
Achillea filipendula..............138
    millefolium roseum............138
    Ptarmica fl. pl................138
Achlys triphylla..................138
Aconitum autumnale... 134
    Japonicum....................138
    Napellus.....................138
Acorus gramineus..............134
Actæa alba... ... .138
    spicata.......................138
      var. rubra...................138
Adonis vernalis................**125**
Ajuga pyramidalis..............**138**
    reptans.......................135
Aletris aurea...................**138**
    farinosa......................**138**
Alfredia cernua.................135
Allium Moly.....................138
Alstrœmeria aurantiaca... 138
Amianthium muscaetoxicum.......13\
Amsonia angustifolia 139
    Tabernæmontana...............139
Anemone appenina...............125
    cylindrica. 139
    Japonica.....................125
      var. alba...................125
    patens, var. Nuttalliana.......139
    nemorosa, fl. pl...............125
    Pennsylvanica.................**139**
    ranunculoides.................**139**
    sylvestris....................**139**
Antennaria dioica...............**139**
Anthericum Liliago............**144**
    Illiastrum....................125
    ramosum 125
Aquilegia cærulea 125
    chrysantha...................125
    glandulosa...................125
    Skinneri.....................**125**
    caryophylloides...............125
    vulgaris......... 125
Armeria vulgaris...............**145**
Artemesia Stelleriana............**135**
    vulgaris **135**
Arundo Donax..................**135**
Asclepias tuberosa... ....**139**
    verticillata..................**139**
Asperula odorata................125
Aster longifolius................139
    Novæ Angliæ..................139
    Novi Belgii. 139
    oblongifolius.................136
Astilbe Japonica................125

Baptisia alba....................139
    australis......................139
Bellis perennis..................125
Berlandiera tomentosa...........140
Betonica officinalis...... ..140
Bocconia cordata................135
Boltonia glastifolia 140
Brodiæa congesta...............140
    grandiflora 140
Brunella grandiflora.............140
Bupthalmum speciosum ... .135
Callirrhoë alcæoides 140
    involucrata 140
    triangulata...................140
Calochortus Gunnisoni...........140
Campanula persicæfolia...... ...126
    Trachelium 126
    sarmatica... 126
    grandiflora..................126
Cassia Marilandica **140**
Catananche cærulea............**140**
Centaurea macrocephala..........**140**
    montana......................140
Centranthus ruber.... 140
Chelone glaber..................140
Chrysopsis Mariana..............140
Clematis erecta.... 140
    integrifolia 140
Clintonia borealis... 140
Colchicum autumnale............126
Convallaria majalis..............126
Coronilla varia..................147
Crocus vernus... 126
Crucianella stylosa **141**
Dactylis glomerata.. 125
Delphinium azureum 126
    cœlestinum...................116
    formosum 126
    grandiflorum.................127
    pyramidalis..................127
Desmodium Canadense......... ..128
Dianthus barbatus..............127
    deltoides.....................127
    dentosus.....................127
    plumarius .... - ...127
    Querterii....................127
Dicentra eximia.................127
    spectabilis...................127
Dictamnus Fraxinella.............127
Digitalis purpurea...............127
Doronicum Caucasicum...........**141**
Echinacea purpurea.............141
Echinops Ritro. ... .135
Elymus arenarius... 135
Eranthis hyemalis. 142

Erianthus Ravennæ. 135
Erigeron macranthum.............142
E odinm Manescavi...............142
Eryngium amethystinum...........135
  yuccæfolium... 135
Erythronium albidum.............127
  Americanum........ 127
  Dens-canis....................127
Eulalia Japonica, variegata.......135
  var. zebrina.. 135
Eupatorium ageratoides...........142
Euphorbia corollata 142
  Myrsinites... 142
Festuca glauca...................135
Fritillaria imperialis... 127
Funkia alba. 128
  *cærulea.......................128
  Japonica......................128
  Sieboldii.....................128
  undulata medio-picta...... ...136
Galanthus nivalis.. 128
Gaura angustifolia...............142
Gentiana Andrewsii 142
  cruciata......................142
Geranium platypetalum...........142
  sanguineum....................142
Genm coccineum...................142
Gillenia trifoliata....... 142
Gynerium argenteum...............135
Gypsophila acutifolia 142
  paniculata....................142
Helianthus angustifolius 142
  mollis... ... .142
  orgyalis......................136
Hemerocallis flava...............128
  fulva.........................128
  Kwanso, var...... 136
Hesperis matronalis..............128
Hibiscus Californicus............143
  grandiflorus..................143
  Moscheutos....................143
Hieracium aurantiacum............143
Hyacinthus orientalis............128
Hyssopus officinalis.............143
Iberis cornæfolia... 128
  Gibraltarica..................128
  sempervirens..................128
Iris Florentina..................129
  Germanica.. 129
  Ibirica.......................129
  Kæmpferi.....................129
  lævigata......................129
  Pavonia.......................129
  pumila.... 129
  reticulata....................129
  xiphioides....................129
  Xiphium.......................129
Lathyrus grandiflorus............129
  latifolius....................129
Leucojum æstivum..... 130
  autumnalis....................130
  vernum 130
Liatris elegans,.................129
  pumila........................129
  spicata.. 129
Lilium auratum...................130
  Canadense.....................130
  candidum...... 130

Lilium Catesbæi....... 130
  excelsum.... 130
  Krameri.......................130
  longiflorum...................130
  Pomponium.....................130
  speciosum roseum..............130
  superbum......................130
  tenuifolium 130
  tigrinum......................130
  Thunbergianum.................130
Linum perenne....................143
Lobelia cardinalis...............143
  syphilitica...................143
Lopanthus anisatus...............143
Lotus corniculatus...............143
Lupinus polyphyllus..............143
Lychnis Chalcedonica.............131
  Flos-cueni....................131
  Flos-Jovis....................131
  Haageana......................131
  Viscaria, fl. pl.............131
Lysimachia cletaroides...........143
  nummularia... 143
  vulgaris......................143
Lythrum Salicaria................129
Malva Morenii....................143
Mentha rotundifolia, var.........136
Mertensia paniculata.............143
  Virginica.....................143
Mimulus cardinalis...............144
Monarda didyma...................144
Muscari botryoides...............128
  comosum.......................128
  moschatum.....................128
Myosotis dissitiflora............131
Narcissus Jouquilla..............129
Nepeta Masseni....... 144
Nierembergia rivularis..........144
Œnothera Missouriensis...........144
  speciosa......................144
Ornithogalum pyramidale... ..131
  umbellatum....................131
Orobus vernus....................131
Pæonia Moutan....................131
  officinalis...................131
  tenuifolia....................132
Pachysandra procumbens...........144
Panicum virgatum.................135
Pentstemon barbatus..............144
Phalaris arundinacea, var........134
Phlox divaricata.................132
  reptans.......................132
  subulata......................132
Physostegia Virginiana...........144
Platycodon grandiflorum..........126
Polemonium cæruleum... 132
  reptans.......................132
Polygonatum vulgare. 145
  var. macranthum.. 145
Polygonum cuspidatum.... 144
  vaccinifolium.................144
Potentilla pyreniaca.............144
Primula vulgaris.................132
Pulmonaria angustifolia..........132
  maculata......................132
Pyrethrum Tchihatchewä...........144
Ranunculus bulbosus..............144
  fascicularis..................144

Ranunculus rhomboideus..........144
Rheum Emodi................106
   palmatum..................136
Rudbeckia maxima 141
   nitida....................142
Salvia argentea.................137
   azurea....................137
   officinalis tricolor.........137
Santolina Chamæcyparissus 137
Sedum cruciatum...............137
   spectabilis.......... 137
Senecio aureus....   ...145
Silene maritima................133
   orientalis...   ...133
   Pennsylvanica.............133
   Schafta.... 133
Silphium laciniatum...........137
   perfoliatum.. 137
Sisyrinchium grandiflorum........145
Spigelia Marilandica...........133
Spiræa Aruncus...............133
   filipendula................133
   Japonica 125
   venusta.... 133
Stachys coccinea...............145
   lanata.... 145

Stokesia cyanea...... 133
Symphytum officinale, var.. 137
Tanacetum Balsamita.... 145
Thalictrum aquilegifolium........145
   speciosum.................145
Thymus citriodorus...........137
   Serpyllum, var.............137
Tradescantia Virginica.........133
Triteleia uniflora..............145
Tritoma Uvaria...............133
Valeriana officinalis...........145
Verbena bipinnatifida...........145
   montana,....   ...145
Veronica amethystina...........134
   gentianoides... 134
   longifolia..................134
Vinca major..................134
   minor......................134
Viola blanda 134
   cornuta.... 134
   pedata....................134
   tricolor...................134
Wahlenbergia grandiflora... 126
Yucca angustifolia............137
   baccata. 137
   filamentosa...............137.

INDEX OF THE BOTANICAL NAMES OF CLIMBERS.

Actinidia polygama... 122
Akebia quinata 122
Aristolochia Sipho.............122
Ampelopsis bipinnata...........118
   indivisa...................118
   quinquefolia.. 118
   Royli....................118
   tricuspidata...............118
   Veitchii 118
Celastrus scandens.............122
Clematis coccinea.............121
   Jackmanii.................121
   Virginiana.... 121
Cocculus Carolinus 123
Hedera Helix, var. Hibernica......124
Jasminum officinale...........123
Lonicera brachypoda...........120
   var. reticulata.............120
   Caprifolium, var. pallida......120
   flava.......................120
   var. Canadensis 120
   Halleana...............100
   Periclymenum...........120
   var. Belgica.............121

Lonicera Periclymenum.............120
   sempervirens... 120
   var. Brownii...............120
   var. minus... 120
   Standishii 121
Menispermum Canadense.... 122
Periploca Græca,..............123
Tecoma radicans 122
   grandiflora................122
Vitis æstivalis,...............123
   cordifolia.................123
   heterophylla 122
   indivisa 123
   vulpina..................123
Wistaria brachybotrys...........119
   frutescens 119
   var. alba. 119
   var. magnifica.. 119
   Japonica alba 119
   Sinensis........... 119
   var. alba... 119
   var. fl. pl............119
   multijuga................119
   var. alba..... 119

INDEX OF THE BOTANICAL NAMES OF ALPINE AND ROCK PLANTS.

Acantholimon glumaceum.........146
Achillea tomentosa.... 146
Alyssum saxatile..............146
   var. compactum............146
Anthyllis montana.............146
Aquilegia Canadensis..........146
Arabis, sp...... 146
Arenaria, sp..................146
Armeria plantaginea...........146
   vulgaris.. 146
Aubrietia, sp 146

Bulbocodium vernum........... ...146
Cerastium Boissieri.... 146
   tomentosum 146
Camassia, sp..... 146
Campanula Carpatica...........146
   isophylla................146
   rotundifolia 146
Cheiranthus alpinus...........147
Claytonia Virginica... 147
Clematis, sp.................147
Epimedium alpinum............147

Epimedium pinnatum.............147
Erinus alpinus...................147
Gentiana acaulis................147
Geum montanum...................147
Houstonia cærulea..... 147
serpyllifolia 147
Linaria alpina 147
Lychnis Lagascæ................147
Viscaria, var. splendens... ...147
Mitchella repens................147
Nepeta Glechoma.................147
Opuntia Rafinesquii.............147
Oxalis violacea.. ... .147
Pentstemon acuminatus..........147
Phlox amœna..................148
Douglasii 147
Pyxidanthera barbulata..........148
Saponaria ocymoides.. 148

Saxifraga cordifolia............148
crassifolia..................148
ligulata....................148
Virginiensis................148
Sedum acre.....................149
Kamtschaticum..............149
populifolium...............149
pulchellum.................149
Sieboldii..................149
spectabile.................149
Telephium..................149
var. hybridum..........149
Sempervivum, sp 149
Silene alpestris...............149
Tunica Saxifraga 149
Veronica alpina....... 149
Waldstenia fragarioides.........149

INDEX OF THE BOTANICAL NAMES OF AQUATIC AND BOG PLANTS.

Adiantum pedatum........... . ..151
Anemone Apennina 150
nemorosa 150
var. bracteata... 150
Aplectrum hyemale..............150
Arisæma triphyllum.............150
Aristolochia Serpentaria........150
Asarum Canadense...............150
caudatum...................150
Virginicum.................150
Aspidium fragrans 151
acrostichoides.............151
munitum....................151
Asplenium ebeneum.... 151
Camptosorus rhizophyllus... ...151
Cheilanthes tomentosa.... 151
vestita 151
Cornus Canadensis..............150
Cypripedium acaule.............150
Calceolus 150
Dodecatheon Meadia.... 150
var. lancifolium.......150
Epigæa repens..................150
Fritillaria atropurpurea........152
lanceolata 152

Goodyera, sp ... .152
Helleborus atrorubens....... ...152
niger.......................152
Helonias bullata,.... 152
Hepatica, sp...................152
Lomaria Spicant................151
Orchis spectabilis.............152
Pellæa atropurpurea 152
Pteris aquilina................152
Podophyllum peltatum....... ...153
Polygala paucifolia............152
Polypodium vulgare.............152
Ramondia Pyrenaica.............152
Rhexia Virginica...............152
Sanguinaria anadense..........152
Selaginella sp 152
Smilacina stellata.... 152
Trillium cernuum...............152
erythrocarpum..............153
grandiflorum...............153
nivale.....................153
Viola Canadensis...............153
pubescens. 153
sagittata..................153
Woodsia Ilvensis...............152

INDEX OF THE BOTANICAL NAMES OF FERNS AND SHADE-LOVING PLANTS.

Acorus Calamus... 153
Arisæma Dracontium....... 153
Brasenia peltata 153
Calla palustris.. 154
Calopogon pulchellus 153
Caltha palustris...............153
Calypso borealis...............153
Cypripedium arietinum..,.. 154
candidum...................153
parviflorum... 154
spectabile.................153
Darlingtonia Californica...... ..154
Drosera filiformis.............154
rotundifolia...............154
Habenaria blephariglottis......154
ciliaris....................154

Habenaria fimbriata............154
psycodes...................154
Lobelia cardinalis.............154
Nymphæa odorata...............154
Nuphar advena.................154
Orontium aquaticum...... ...154
Parnassia asurifolia...........154
Pontederia cordata.............155
Pogonia, sp...................154
Sabbatia chlorcides............154
lanceolata.................154
Sagittaria variabilis.. 155
Sarracenia purpurea...........155
Trollius laxus.................155
Typha angustifolia............155
latifolia..................155

Forest Planting.

By H. NICHOLAS JARCHOW, LL. D. A treatise on the care of woodlands and the restoration of the denuded timberlands on plains and mountains. The author has fully described those European methods which have proved to be most useful in maintaining the superb forests of the old world. This experience has been adapted to the different climates and trees of America, full instructions being given for forest planting of our various kinds of soil and subsoil, whether on mountain or valley. Illustrated. 250 pages. 5x7 inches. Cloth. $1.50

Soils and Crops of the Farm.

By GEORGE E. MORROW, M. A., and THOMAS F. HUNT. The methods of making available the plant food in the soil are described in popular language. A short history of each of the farm crops is accompanied by a discussion of its culture. The useful discoveries of science are explained as applied in the most approved methods of culture. Illustrated. 310 pages. 5x7 inches. Cloth. $1.00

Land Draining.

A handbook for farmers on the principles and practice of draining, by MANLY MILES, giving the results of his extended experience in laying tile drains. The directions for the laying out and the construction of tile drains will enable the farmer to avoid the errors of imperfect construction, and the disappointment that must necessarily follow. This manual for practical farmers will also be found convenient for reference in regard to many questions that may arise in crop growing, aside from the special subjects of drainage of which it treats. Illustrated. 200 pages. 5x7 inches. Cloth. . . $1.00

Barn Plans and Outbuildings.

The proper and economical erection of barns and outbuildings requires far more forethought and planning than is ordinarily given to their construction. To aid those who intend to build or remodel old farm buildings is the object of this book. It gives detailed information and illustrations on barns of every description and for all purposes, as well as plans and descriptions of every kind of farm buildings. All these are given in so plain and clear a manner as to be readily understood by any one. New revised and greatly enlarged edition, 375 illustrations, 5x7 inches, 404 pages, Cloth . . $1.00

Herbert's Hints to Horse Keepers.

By the late HENRY WILLIAM HERBERT (Frank Forester). This is one of the best and most popular works on the horse prepared in this country. A complete manual for horsemen, embracing: How to breed a horse; how to buy a horse; how to break a horse; how to use a horse; how to feed a horse; how to physic a horse (allopathy or homeopathy); how to groom a horse; how to drive a horse; how to ride a horse, etc. Beautifully illustrated. 425 pages. 5x7 inches. Cloth. $1.50

Diseases of Horses and Cattle.

By DR. D. McINTOSH, V. S., professor of veterinary science in the university of Illinois. Written expressly for the farmer, stockman and veterinary student. A new work on the treatment of animal diseases, according to the modern status of veterinary science, has become a necessity. Such an one is this volume of over 400 pages, written by one of the most eminent veterinarians of our country. Illustrated. 426 pages. 5x7 inches. Cloth. $1.75

The Ice Crop.

By THERON L. HILES. How to harvest, ship and use ice. A complete, practical treatise for farmers, dairymen, ice dealers, produce shippers, meat packers, cold storers, and all interested in icehouses, cold storage, and the handling or use of ice in any way. Including many recipes for iced dishes and beverages. The book is illustrated by cuts of the tools and machinery used in cutting and storing ice, and the different forms of icehouses and cold storage buildings. Illustrated. 122 pages. 5x7 inches. Cloth. $1.00

The Secrets of Health, or How Not to Be Sick, and How to Get Well from Sickness.

By S. H. PLATT, A. M., M. D., late member of the Connecticut Eclectic Medical Society, the National Eclectic Medical Association, and honorary member of the National Bacteriological Society of America; our medical editor and author of "Talks With Our Doctor" and "Our Health Adviser." Nearly 600 pages. An index of 20 pages, so that any topic may be instantly consulted. A new departure in medical knowledge for the people—the latest progress, secrets and practices of all schools of healing made available for the common people— health without medicine, nature without humbug, common sense without folly, science without fraud. 81 illustrations. 576 pages. 5x7 inches. Cloth. $1.50

STANDARD BOOKS.

Hunter and Trapper.

By HALSEY THRASHER, an old and experienced sportsman. The best modes of hunting and trapping are fully explained, and foxes, deer, bears, etc., fall into his traps readily by following his directions. Illustrated. 92 pages. 5x7 inches. Cloth. $0.50

Batty's Practical Taxidermy and Home Decoration.

By JOSEPH H. BATTY, taxidermist for the government surveys and many colleges and museums in the United States. An entirely new and complete as well as authentic work on taxidermy—giving in detail full directions for collecting and mounting animals, birds, reptiles, fish, insects, and general objects of natural history. 125 illustrations. 204 pages. 5x7 inches. Cloth. $1.00

Hemp.

By S. S. BOYCE. A practical treatise on the culture of hemp for seed and fiber, with a sketch of the history and nature of the hemp plant. The various chapters are devoted to the soil and climate adapted to the culture of hemp for seed and for fiber, irrigating, harvesting, retting and machinery for handling hemp. Illustrated. 112 pages. 5x7 inches. Cloth. $0.50

Alfalfa.

By F. D. COBURN. Its growth, uses and feeding value. The fact that alfalfa thrives in almost any soil; that without reseeding, it goes on yielding two, three, four and sometimes five cuttings annually for five, ten, or perhaps 100 years; and that either green or cured it is one of the most nutritious forage plants known, makes reliable information upon its production and uses of unusual interest. Such information is given in this volume for every part of America, by the highest authority. Illustrated. 164 pages. 5x7 inches. Cloth. $0.50

Talks on Manure.

By JOSEPH HARRIS, M. S. A series of familiar and practical talks between the author and the deacon, the doctor, and other neighbors, on the whole subject of manures and fertilizers; including a chapter especially written for it by Sir John Bennet Lawes of Rothamsted, England. 366 pages. 5x7 inches. Cloth. $1.50

Practical Forestry.

By ANDREW S. FULLER. A treatise on the propagation, planting and cultivation, with descriptions and the botanical and popular names of all the indigenous trees of the United States, and notes on a large number of the most valuable exotic species. Illustrated. 300 pages. 5x7 inches. Cloth. $1.50

Irrigation for the Farm, Garden and Orchard.

By HENRY STEWART. This work is offered to those American farmers and other cultivators of the soil who, from painful experience, can readily appreciate the losses which result from the scarcity of water at critical periods. Fully illustrated. 276 pages. 5x7 inches. Cloth. . . $1.00

Irrigation Farming.

By LUTE WILCOX. A handbook for the practical application of water in the production of crops. A complete treatise on water supply, canal construction, reservoirs and ponds, pipes for irrigation purposes, flumes and their structure, methods of applying water, irrigation of field crops, the garden, the orchard and vineyard, windmills and pumps, appliances and contrivances. New edition, revised, enlarged and rewritten. Profusely illustrated. Over 500 pages. 5x7 inches. Cloth. $2.00

Ginseng, Its Cultivation, Harvesting, Marketing and Market Value.

By MAURICE G. KAINS, with a short account of its history and botany. It discusses in a practical way how to begin with either seed or roots, soil, climate and location, preparation, planting and maintenance of the beds, artificial propagation, manures, enemies, selection for market and for improvement, preparation for sale, and the profits that may be expected. This booklet is concisely written, well and profusely illustrated, and should be in the hands of all who expect to grow this drug to supply the export trade, and to add a new and profitable industry to their farms and gardens, without interfering with the regular work. New edition. Revised and enlarged. Illustrated. 5x7 inches. Cloth. . . . $0.50

Truck Farming at the South.

By A. OEMLER. A work giving the experience of a successful grower of vegetables or "garden truck" for northern markets. Essential to anyone who contemplates entering this profitable field of agriculture. Illustrated. 274 pages. 5x7 inches. Cloth. $1.00

Henderson's Practical Floriculture.

By PETER HENDERSON. A guide to the successful propagation and cultivation of florists' plants. The work is not one
for florists and gardeners only, but the amateur's wants are
constantly kept in mind, and we have a very complete treatise
on the cultivation of flowers under glass, or in the open air,
suited to those who grow flowers for pleasure as well as those
who make them a matter of trade. New and enlarged edition.
Beautifully illustrated. 325 pages. 5x7 inches. Cloth. $1.50

Mushrooms. How to Grow Them.

By WILLIAM FALCONER. This is the most practical work
on the subject ever written, and the only book on growing
mushrooms published in America. The author describes how
he grows mushrooms, and how they are grown for profit by
the leading market gardeners, and for home use by the most
successful private growers. Engravings drawn from nature
expressly for this work. 170 pages. 5x7 inches. Cloth. $1.00

Play and Profit in My Garden.

By E. P. ROE. The author takes us to his garden on the
rocky hillsides in the vicinity of West Point, and shows us
how out of it, after four years' experience, he evoked a profit
of $1000, and this while carrying on pastoral and literary
labor. It is very rarely that so much literary taste and skill
are mated to so much agricultural experience and good sense.
Illustrated. 350 pages. 5x7 inches. Cloth. . . $1.00

Fumigation Methods.

By WILLIS G. JOHNSON. A timely up-to-date book on
the practical application of the new methods for destroying
insects with hydrocyanic acid gas and carbon bisulphid, the
most powerful insecticides ever discovered. It is an indispensable book for farmers, fruit growers, nurserymen, gardeners,
florists, millers, grain dealers, transportation companies, college and experiment station workers, etc. Illustrated. 313
pages. 5x7 inches. Cloth. $1.00

Fungi and Fungicides.

By PROF. CLARENCE M. WEED. A practical manual concerning the fungous diseases of cultivated plants and the
means of preventing their ravages. The author has endeav-
ored to give such a concise account of the most important
facts relating to these as will enable the cultivator to combat
them intelligently. 90 illustrations. 222 pages. 5x7 inches.
Paper, 50 cents; cloth $1.00

Insects and Insecticides.

By CLARENCE M. WEED, D. Sc., professor of entomology and zoology, New Hampshire college of agriculture. A practical manual concerning noxious insects, and methods of preventing their injuries. Many illustrations. 334 pages. 5x7 inches. Cloth. $1.50

How Crops Grow.

By PROF. SAMUEL W. JOHNSON of Yale college. New and revised edition. A treatise on the chemical composition, structure and life of the plant. This book is a guide to the knowledge of agricultural plants, their composition, their structure and modes of development and growth; of the complex organization of plants, and the use of the parts; the germination of seeds, and the food of plants obtained both from the air and the soil. The book is indispensable to all real students of agriculture. With numerous illustrations and tables of analysis. 416 pages. 5x7 inches. Cloth. $1.50

Tobacco Leaf.

By J. B. KILLEBREW and HERBERT MYRICK. Its Culture and Cure, Marketing and Manufacture. A practical handbook on the most approved methods in growing, harvesting, curing, packing and selling tobacco, with an account of the operations in every department of tobacco manufacture. The contents of this book are based on actual experiments in field, curing barn, packing house, factory and laboratory. It is the only work of the kind in existence, and is destined to be the standard practical and scientific authority on the whole subject of tobacco for many years. 506 pages and 150 original engravings. 5x7 inches. Cloth. $2.00

Coburn's Swine Husbandry.

By F. D. COBURN. New, revised and enlarged edition. The breeding, rearing and management of swine, and the prevention and treatment of their diseases. It is the fullest and freshest compendium relating to swine breeding yet offered. Illustrated. 312 pages. 5x7 inches. Cloth. $1.50

Home Pork Making.

The art of raising and curing pork on the farm. By A. W. FULTON. A complete guide for the farmer, the country butcher and the suburban dweller, in all that pertains to hog slaughtering, curing, preserving and storing pork product— from scalding vat to kitchen table and dining room. Illustrated. 125 pages. 5x7 inches. Cloth. . . . $0.50

Harris on the Pig.

By Joseph Harris. New edition. Revised and enlarged by the author. The points of the various English and American breeds are thoroughly discussed, and the great advantage of using thoroughbred males clearly shown. The work is equally valuable to the farmer who keeps but few pigs, and to the breeder on an extensive scale. Illustrated. 318 pages. 5x7 inches. Cloth. $1.00

The Dairyman's Manual.

By Henry Stewart, author of "The Shepherd's Manual," "Irrigation," etc. A useful and practical work, by a writer who is well known as thoroughly familiar with the subject of which he writes. Illustrated. 475 pages. 5x7 inches. Cloth. $1.50

Feeds and Feeding.

By W. A. Henry. This handbook for students and stockmen constitutes a compendium of practical and useful knowledge on plant growth and animal nutrition, feeding stuffs, feeding animals and every detail pertaining to this important subject. It is thorough, accurate and reliable, and is the most valuable contribution to live stock literature in many years. All the latest and best information is clearly and systematically presented, making the work indispensable to every owner of live stock. 658 pages. 6x9 inches. Cloth. . . $2.00

The Propagation of Plants.

By Andrew S. Fuller. An eminently practical and useful work describing the process of hybridizing and crossing species and varieties and also the many different modes by which cultivated plants may be propagated and multiplied. Illustrated. 350 pages. 5x7 inches. Cloth. . . $1.50

Gardening for Pleasure.

By Peter Henderson. A guide to the amateur in the fruit, vegetable and flower garden, with full descriptions for the greenhouse, conservatory and window garden. It meets the wants of all classes in country, city and village, who keep a garden for their own enjoyment rather than for the sale of products. Finely illustrated. 404 pages. 5x7 inches. Cloth. $1.50

Prize Gardening.

Compiled by G. BURNAP FISKE. This unique book shows how to derive profit, pleasure and health from the garden by giving the actual experiences of the successful prize winners in the American Agriculturist garden contest. Every line is from actual experience based on real work. The result is a mine and treasure house of garden practice, comprising the grand prize gardener's methods, gardening for profit, farm gardens, the home acre, town and city gardens, experimental gardening, methods under glass, success with specialties, prize flowers and fruits, gardening by women, boys and girls, irrigation, secrets, etc., etc. Illustrated from original photos. 320 pages. 5x7 inches. Cloth. $1.00

Gardening for Profit.

By PETER HENDERSON. The standard work on market and family gardening. The successful experience of the author for more than thirty years, and his willingness to tell, as he does in this work, the secret of his success for the benefit of others, enables him to give most valuable information. The book is profusely illustrated. 376 pages. 5x7 inches. Cloth. $1.50

The Window Flower Garden.

By JULIUS J. HEINRICH. The author is a practical florist, and this enterprising volume embodies his personal experience in window gardening during a long period. New and enlarged edition. Illustrated. 123 pages. 5x7 inches. Cloth. $0.50

Market Gardening and Farm Notes.

By BURNETT LANDRETH. Experiences and observation for both north and south, of interest to the amateur gardener, trucker and farmer. A novel feature of the book is the calendar of farm and garden operations for each month of the year; the chapters on fertilizers, transplanting, succession and rotation of crops, the packing, shipping and marketing of vegetables will be especially useful to market gardeners. 315 pages. 5x7 inches. Cloth. $1.00

The Study of Breeds.

By THOMAS SHAW. Origin, history, distribution, characteristics, adaptability, uses, and standards of excellence of all pedigreed breeds of cattle, sheep and swine in America. The accepted text book in colleges, and the authority for farmers and breeders. Illustrated. 371 pages. 5x7 inches. Cloth. $1.50

Animal Breeding.

By THOMAS SHAW. This book is the most complete and comprehensive work ever published on the subject of which it treats. It is the first book which has systematized the subject of animal breeding. The leading laws which govern this most intricate question the author has boldly defined and authoritatively arranged. The chapters which he has written on the more involved features of the subject, as sex and the relative influence of parents, should go far toward setting at rest the wildly speculative views cherished with reference to these questions. The striking originality in the treatment of the subject is no less conspicuous than the superb order and regular sequence of thought from the beginning to the end of the book. The book is intended to meet the needs of all persons interested in the breeding and rearing of live stock. Illustrated. 405 pages. 5x7 inches. Cloth. . . $1.50

Forage Crops Other Than Grasses.

By THOMAS SHAW. How to cultivate, harvest and use them. Indian corn, sorghum, clover, leguminous plants, crops of the brassica genus, the cereals, millet, field roots, etc. Intensely practical and reliable. Illustrated. 287 pages. 5x7 inches. Cloth. $1.00

Soiling Crops and the Silo.

By THOMAS SHAW. The growing and feeding of all kinds of soiling crops, conditions to which they are adapted, their plan in the rotation, etc. Not a line is repeated from the Forage Crops book. Best methods of building the silo, filling it and feeding ensilage. Illustrated. 364 pages. 5x7 inches. Cloth. $1.50

Stewart's Shepherd's Manual.

By HENRY STEWART. A valuable practical treatise on the sheep for American farmers and sheep growers. It is so plain that a farmer or a farmer's son who has never kept a sheep may learn from its pages how to manage a flock successfully, and yet so complete that even the experienced shepherd may gather many suggestions from it. The results of personal experience of some years, with the characters of the various modern breeds of sheep, and the sheep raising capabilities of many portions of our extensive territory and that of Canada—and the careful study of the diseases to which our sheep are chiefly subject, with those by which they may eventually be afflicted through unforeseen accidents—as well as the methods of management called for under our circumstances, are carefully described. Illustrated. 276 pages. 5x7 inches. Cloth. $1.00